W9-AVF-065

Committing to Results: Improving the Effectiveness of HIV/AIDS Assistance

An OED Evaluation of the World Bank's Assistance for HIV/AIDS Control

http://www.worldbank.org/oed
http://www.worldbank.org/oed/aids

2005
The World Bank
Washington, D.C.

Cover photos: Upper-left and lower-left, courtesy of Martha Ainswoth; upper-right, © Peter Parker/Panos Pictures; lower-right, Masaru Goto for the World Bank Photo Library.

ISBN 0-8213-6388-3
e-ISBN 0-8213-6389-1
DOI: 10. 1596/978-0-8213-6388-1

Library of Congress Cataloging-in-Publication Data
Ainsworth, Martha, 1955–
    Committing to results : improving the effectiveness of HIV/AIDS assistance: an OED evaluation of the World Bank's assistance for HIV/AIDS control / Martha Ainsworth, Denise A. Vaillancourt, Judith Hahn Gaubatz.
        p. cm. — (Operations evaluation studies)
    Includes bibliographical references.
    ISBN-13: 978-0-8213-6388-1
    ISBN-10: 0-8213-6388-3
    1. Economic assistance—Developing countries—Evaluation. 2. AIDS (Disease)—Economic aspects—Developing countries. 3. HIV infections—Economic aspects—Developing countries. 4. AIDS (Disease)—Developing countries—Prevention. 5. HIV infections—Developing countries—Prevention. 6. World Bank. I. Vaillancourt, Denise. II. Hahn Gaubatz, Judith. III. Title. IV. World Bank operations evaluation study.

HC60.A4575 2005
362.196'9792'0091726—dc22   2005052329

World Bank InfoShop   Operations Evaluation Department
E-mail: pic@worldbank.org   Knowledge Programs and Evaluation Capacity
Telephone: 202-458-5454   Development (OEDKE)
Facsimile: 202-522-1500   E-mail: eline@worldbank.org
                                                           Telephone: 202-458-4497
                                                           Facsimile: 202-522-3125

 Printed on Recycled Paper

Contents

Tables

Acknowledgments

This evaluation was prepared by the Health and Education Cluster of the Sector, Thematic, and Global Evaluations group of the Operations Evaluation Department (OED). The task leader of the evaluation was Martha Ainsworth, the main drafter of the report, under the overall direction of Gregory Ingram, Ajay Chhibber, and Alain Barbu. The evaluation report is based on inputs from many OED staff and consultants who conducted desk reviews, inventories, surveys, and field-based studies.

The seven Project Performance Assessment Reports (PPARs) were led and prepared by OED staff members Denise Vaillancourt (Brazil, Chad, and Uganda), Timothy Johnston (Kenya, India, and Zimbabwe), and Martha Ainsworth (Cambodia and India). Sheila Dutta was a member of the PPAR team for the India AIDS I Project. The four country case studies were authored by: Chris Beyrer, Varun Gauri, and Denise Vaillancourt (Brazil); A. Edward Elmendorf, Eric Jensen, and Elizabeth Pisani (Indonesia); Judyth Twigg and Richard Skolnik (Russia); and Denise Vaillancourt, Sarbani Chakraborty, and Taha Taha (Ethiopia). Ahila Subramanian conducted empirical analysis of the relation between project expenditures and AIDS awareness and behavior using Indian data, and Han Kang provided additional research on the Bank's response in India. The report team extends its gratitude to the hundreds of individuals in government, civil society, the donor community and the Bank who were interviewed for the PPARs and country case studies, and who are acknowledged individually in these respective reports.

Desk reviews of the HIV/AIDS portfolio were conducted by Hazel Denton, Judith Hahn, and Elaine Wee-Ling Ooi, and of AIDS components in non-health projects by Ahila Subramanian and Kavita Mathur. The team expresses appreciation to Donald Bundy and Seung-Hee Lee in the education sector and to Jocelyne Do Sacramento in transport for their kind assistance in assembling the AIDS portfolio in their sectors. The inventory of analytic work was launched with support from the Bank's HNP anchor and the Global AIDS Advisor's office, based on a survey of Bank staff and official recording systems conducted by Negda Jahanshahi and updated by Judith Hahn and Kavita Mathur. The team extends its thanks to the hundreds of participants at the 13th International AIDS Conference on Africa in Nairobi and the Bank's human development staff, who completed questionnaires on the reach, quality, and usefulness of the Bank's analytic work. The results were compiled and analyzed by Judith Hahn.

The evaluation team is grateful for insights on the overall Africa MAP program provided by Debrework Zewdie, Keith Hansen, and Jonathan Brown. The self-administered questionnaires and format of structured interviews of Africa

MAP task team leaders and Country Directors were developed by the evaluation team. Judith Hahn and Martha Ainsworth interviewed the task team leaders and A. Edward Elmendorf interviewed country directors in African countries with MAP projects. The evaluation team greatly appreciates the time contributed by the respondents: current or past country directors Pedro Alba, Yaw Ansu, Robert Calderisi, David Craig, Makhtar Diop, Hafez Ghanem, Mats Karlsson, Ali Khadr, John McIntire, Emmanuel Mbi, Oey Meesook, Judy O'Connor, Hartwig Schafer, Mark Tomlinson, Hasan Tuluy, and Antoinette Sayeh; and task team leaders Nicolas Ahouissousi, Michael Azefor, François Decaillet, Jean Delion, Jacomina de Regt, Timothy Johnston, Ibrahim Magazi, Miatudila Malonga, John May, Eileen Murray, Peter Okwero, Gylfi Palsson, Mohammed Pate, Nadine Poupart, Miriam Schneidman, Julia van Domelen, Albertus Voetberg, and Christopher Walker. The team expresses its gratitude to these and other task team leaders, who also provided country-specific data on the implementation of the Africa MAP projects as of the summer of 2004 through a survey questionnaire. Judith Hahn, Han Kang, and Martha Ainsworth compiled the results. Patrick Mullen reviewed the national strategies of 21 African countries with MAP projects and five countries with non-MAP World Bank AIDS assistance.

The timelines of the World Bank and international response, in Appendix B, were prepared by Martha Ainsworth and Judith Hahn based on World Bank documents, published literature, the evaluation case studies, and interviews with key individuals. The extensive and invaluable assistance of Deirdre Bryden of the World Bank's Archives department is gratefully acknowledged, as well as interviews with the following key informants: Jacques Baudouy, Eduard Bos, David de Ferranti, Joy de Beyer, Richard Feachem, Ishrat Husain, Paul Isenman, Edward Jaycox, Jean-Louis Lamboray, Callisto Madavo, Anthony Measham, Michael Merson, Jeannette Murphy, Mead Over, Ok Panenborg, David Peters, Peter Piot, Wendy Roseberry, Sven Sandstrom, Jean-Louis Sarbib, Grant Slade, and Debrework Zewdie. Thanks are extended to Rose Gachina for searching the speeches of World Bank officials for their AIDS content and to Carolyn Schiller for hunting down key correspondence.

The evaluation team is grateful for the substantial comments of two external reviewers of the work at every step, Joan Nelson and Heinz Vergin. Comments from the following individuals on the approach and design papers were also greatly appreciated: Olusoji Adeyi, Alain Barbu, Jonathan Brown, Soniya Carvalho, Laura Cooley, Clara Else, Christopher Gerrard, Peter Godwin, Patrick Grasso, Keith Hansen, Gregory Ingram, Nalini Kumar, Uma Lele, Ruth Levine, Michael Merson, Michael Porter, Ray Rist, Sandra Rosenhouse, Miriam Schneidman, J. Shivakumar, Susan Stout, Jagadish Upadhyay, Howard White, and Debrework Zewdie.

The External Advisory Panel for this evaluation consisted of Helene Gayle (Gates Foundation), Jeffrey O'Malley (Program for Applied Technology in Health [PATH], India), Mary Muduuli (Ministry of Finance, Uganda), and Mechai Viravaidya (Thailand Parliament and Population and Community Development Association). The evaluation team is enormously grateful for their sage advice and perspectives on the intermediate outputs and final report, offered in the course of three meetings in Washington. The responsibility for interpreting the results and using this advice rests with the evaluation team, however.

William Hurlbut and Caroline McEuen edited the report and Maria Pilar Barquero provided invaluable logistical and production assistance throughout the preparation process. Julius Gwyer set up the evaluation Web site (www.worldbank.org/OED/AIDS).

Finally, we wish to acknowledge the generous financial support of the Government of Norway, through the Ministry of Foreign Affairs and the Norwegian Agency for Development Cooperation.

Acting Director-General, Operations Evaluation: *Ajay Chhibber*
Acting Director, Operations Evaluation Department: *R. Kyle Peters*
Manger, Sector, Thematic, and Global Evaluation: *Alain Barbu*
Task Manager: *Martha Ainsworth*

Foreword

In 1981, only a year after the World Bank began direct lending for the health sector, the first cases of AIDS were detected, and by 1985 it was clear that HIV/AIDS had already spread widely in parts of Sub-Saharan Africa. In the two decades since, knowledge of HIV/AIDS has grown, but the epidemic continues to spread and erode development gains, not just in Africa, but in many parts of the world. Through the end of fiscal year 2004, the Bank had committed $2.5 billion in lending (of which about $1 billion had disbursed) and sponsored more than 200 pieces of analytic work to advance knowledge about the disease in developing countries. OED has reviewed the Bank's response to this major threat from the early days to the present and assessed the effectiveness of the Bank's country-level assistance.

Early Bank action on HIV/AIDS focused mainly on support for national programs based in Ministries of Health and launched economic analysis of the impact and policy options in fighting the disease. However, broader action was constrained by a lack of government interest in borrowing for the disease. Toward the end of the 1990s, the Bank made a firm commitment to raising demand for HIV/AIDS assistance among borrowers. The Bank has since developed formal or informal strategies for addressing the problem in all of the Regions and in many sectors, and the priority given to HIV/AIDS in country assistance strategies markedly increased. Demand for Bank assistance also grew rapidly.

The Portfolio and Its Performance

The Bank's HIV/AIDS portfolio through the end of fiscal year 2004 consists of 106 projects, 70 of which account for 96 percent of the total commitments. But this is still a "young" portfolio—only 18 of the 70 projects have closed and been evaluated. The outcome ratings of the completed AIDS projects are similar to those of other health projects. Ratings of institutional development impact for AIDS projects are substantially higher than for the sector as a whole, however.

The Bank's assistance has helped to strengthen commitment to fighting HIV/AIDS, improve the efficiency of national programs, and strengthen institutions, mainly those linked to

Ministries of Health. The Bank has also encouraged governments to enlist nongovernmental organizations in public HIV/AIDS programs, although the coverage and efficacy of those efforts have rarely been assessed. Prevention was an objective of more than 90 percent of the projects, but planned prevention activities targeting those most likely to spread HIV were often not implemented, which has likely reduced the overall effectiveness of the Bank's lending.

Knowledge and awareness of the disease and risk behaviors have improved in countries that receive Bank assistance. However, monitoring, evaluation, and research have been weak and have contributed little to assessing or improving the impact of Bank-supported projects. For instance, rates of HIV prevalence are too often used to measure impact, when they reveal nothing about the number of new infections, a more credible indicator of progress.

The Bank has added to the store of knowledge about HIV/AIDS, and in many instances it has helped to raise political commitment in countries receiving Bank assistance. Its research and analysis are generally perceived to be of high quality and usefulness among those who read them, study surveys found. However, the surveys also found that the research and analysis are not effectively reaching policy makers in Africa, particularly Francophone Africa.

An Early Look at the Africa Multi-Country AIDS Program

The Africa Multi-Country AIDS Program (MAP) committed $1 billion and enlisted more than two dozen countries to launch major AIDS activities, which have helped raise political commitment, increase the number of actors, and scale up activities. As of the end of fiscal 2004, none of the Africa MAP projects had closed, so it is too early to assess their effectiveness. However, some design features of the MAP raise concern about the ultimate effectiveness of the projects, and in some cases there is evidence that planned mitigation measures are not being implemented or may be inadequate.

The MAP relies on national AIDS strategies for setting priorities, but most of these strategies do not prioritize or cost activities. It was designed for

rapid approval of projects, and greater supervision and monitoring and evaluation were to make up for the less detailed preparation. In practice, however, this appears not to have been the case. Another feature of the design, the engagement of civil society, has been hindered by unclear objectives, activities that are often not prioritized, and lack of consideration for cost-effectiveness relative to alternatives. The mechanisms used for political mobilization may not be well suited for ensuring efficient and effective program implementation.

Conclusions
The fight against AIDS requires both rapid action and determined long-term building of capacity and sustainability. In recent years, international assistance for AIDS, especially for treatment, has dramatically increased, and the Bank's role has begun to shift again as it works in ever-widening partnerships. The Bank's comparative advantage continues to be helping to build institutions, assess alternatives, and improve the performance of national AIDS efforts. While it is important for the Bank to engage with partners, its most important partners remain the developing countries themselves.

Recommendations
In the next phase of its response, the Bank should help countries turn their commitment to HIV/AIDS into actions that will have a sustainable impact on the epidemic. Several recommendations apply to all Bank HIV/AIDS projects:

- Help governments to be more strategic and selective, and to prioritize activities that will have the greatest impact on the epidemic.
- Strengthen national institutions for managing and implementing the long-run response, particularly in the health sector.
- Improve the local evidence base for decision making through improved monitoring and evaluation.

For the Africa MAP in particular, the Bank should:

- Conduct a thorough assessment of national strategic plans and government AIDS policy and inventory the activities of other donors as a standard part of individual project preparation.

- Articulate the objectives of engaging different segments of civil society in specific activities and subject these activities to rigorous evaluation.

- Focus multisectoral support for implementation on the sectors whose activities have the greatest potential impact on the epidemic and ensure that the resources to supervise their activities are forthcoming.

Ajay Chhibber
Acting Director-General, Operations Evaluation

Main Evaluation Messages

- Bank assistance has induced governments to act earlier or in a more focused and cost-effective way.
- It has helped raise political commitment, create or strengthen AIDS institutions, enlist nongovernmental organizations, and prioritize activities.
- Political commitment and capacity have been overestimated and need to be continuously addressed, as appropriate, in the country context.
- Failure to reach people with the highest-risk behaviors likely has reduced the efficiency and impact of assistance.
- Lack of monitoring and evaluation and directed research are major impediments to improved effectiveness.
- The Bank needs to help governments prioritize and implement the activities that will have the greatest impact on the epidemic.
- It needs to continue to help strengthen national institutions for managing and implementing the long-run response.
- It needs to help improve the local evidence base for making decisions.

Executive Summary

The global AIDS epidemic has profoundly affected the quality of life and progress toward poverty alleviation in many of the poorest developing countries, especially in Sub-Saharan Africa. Since the late 1980s, but particularly over the past decade, the World Bank has launched efforts to prevent HIV/AIDS and to mitigate its impact through participation in global programs; financing analytic work; engaging in policy dialogue; and providing loans, credits, and grants for HIV/AIDS projects. As of June 2004, the World Bank had committed $2.46 billion in credits, grants, and loans to 62 low- and middle-income countries for 106 projects to prevent, treat, and mitigate the impact of HIV/AIDS, of which about $1 billion had been disbursed.

Objectives and Methodology

This evaluation assesses the development effectiveness of the Bank's country-level HIV/AIDS assistance against the counterfactual of no Bank assistance. It identifies lessons from this experience and makes recommendations to improve the relevance, efficiency, and efficacy of ongoing and future activities. For the purposes of the evaluation, *HIV/AIDS assistance* includes policy dialogue, analytic work, and lending with the explicit objective of reducing the scope or impact of the AIDS epidemic. Few HIV/AIDS projects have been completed and the vast majority of projects and commitments are ongoing. With this in mind, the three substantive chapters address:

• The evolution and phases of the Bank's institutional response and an overview of the portfolio of HIV/AIDS assistance since the start of the epidemic

• Findings on the efficacy of the "first generation" of completed World Bank country-level HIV/AIDS assistance and lessons from that experience

• An assessment of the assumptions, design, risks, and implementation to date of 24 ongoing country-level AIDS projects in the Africa Multi-Country AIDS Program (MAP).

The evaluative evidence comes from detailed timelines of the World Bank and international response; an inventory and desk review of the Bank's HIV/AIDS lending portfolio; in-depth field assessments of completed AIDS projects; field-based case studies of Bank HIV/AIDS assistance in Brazil, Ethiopia, Indonesia, and Russia; interviews and surveys of Bank task team leaders for the Africa MAP and country directors in those countries; a review of the national AIDS strategies of 26 countries receiving Bank assistance; commissioned background papers; an inventory of the Bank's analytic work on HIV/AIDS; and surveys of Bank staff and African AIDS workers on the reach, quality, and usefulness of that work. Most of this material is in the appendixes to this report and/or posted on the evaluation Web site (www.worldbank.org/oed/aids). The report also draws on completed OED evaluations of: the Bank's health, nutrition, and population (HNP) programs; nongovernmental organizations (NGOs) in World Bank projects; community development; and capacity building in Africa. It complements OED's recent evaluation of World Bank involvement in global programs, including global programs in health.

The Evolution of the Bank's HIV/AIDS Assistance

The first AIDS cases were reported in the United States in 1981. For several years thereafter, the international research community strived to understand the cause and modes of transmission of the new disease. By 1985, it became evident that a serious HIV/AIDS epidemic of unknown magnitude was taking place in parts of Sub-Saharan Africa. At that point, the Bank had been lending directly for health projects for only about five years; it had limited expertise on health or AIDS and followed the lead of the World Health Organization (WHO). Two factors framing the response of the Bank and the international community were, first, the great uncertainty and rapidly changing information about a totally new disease—its epidemiology, its spread, and how to fight it—and, second, the extraordinary stigma and denial of the disease.

There have been two distinct phases to the Bank's response to HIV/AIDS. During the first phase, from 1986 to 1997, the Bank's response was constrained externally by low demand for HIV/AIDS assistance by developing countries. Internally, the Bank's response was held back by the focus of the Bank's health sector leadership on vital health system reforms, eclipsing the urgency of investing in preventing the rapidly

spreading HIV epidemic. As late as 1997, the Bank's health, nutrition, and population (HNP) strategy contained no discussion of the AIDS epidemic, mentioning it only in a remote part of an annex in the context of emerging diseases.

Nevertheless, during this period about $500 million was committed in loans and credits to 8 free-standing projects and 17 significant components to support national AIDS programs on 4 continents in countries at all stages of the epidemic. The initiative for AIDS strategies and lending came primarily from individual health staff in the regional and technical operational groupings of the Bank, but not in any coherent way from the Bank's HNP leadership or top-level management. The Bank collaborated closely with the WHO Global Program on AIDS (GPA) in project design and in launching important analytic work on the cost-effectiveness of AIDS interventions.

The second phase of the Bank's response, from 1998 to the present, is one of high-level institutional mobilization and advocacy in which the Bank began to take a proactive role in raising awareness and demand for AIDS support among its staff and client countries. Several significant developments in 1996–97 may have contributed to this shift: the creation of the Joint United Nations Program on HIV/AIDS (UNAIDS), which took on a strong advocacy role and was capable of directly reaching high-level Bank management; the issuance by the Bank of a major research report that highlighted AIDS as a development issue; and the development of highly active anti-retroviral therapy (HAART) in 1996. There was also increasing international evidence of the scope and impact of the epidemic.

Since 1998, HIV/AIDS strategies or business plans have been completed in nearly all geographic groupings of the Bank, and an additional $2 billion has been committed to support national HIV/AIDS programs in 55 countries at all stages of the epidemic. Roughly half of the new commitments since 1998 have been through more than two dozen projects of the Africa MAP, and the balance to projects in South Asia, Eastern Europe, Latin America, and the Caribbean. The main objectives of these projects, as articulated in design documents, have been to prevent the spread of HIV, provide treatment and care, mitigate the impacts of AIDS, build national institutions, and provide public goods.

The Development Effectiveness of Completed HIV/AIDS Assistance

As a result of the recent dramatic increase in commitments, most of the Bank's HIV/AIDS lending assistance is ongoing: only 18 freestanding AIDS projects or projects with significant AIDS components, accounting for $636 million in disbursements, had closed as of June 2004. Case studies and project assessments for this evaluation concluded that, in addition to increasing the resources for AIDS in these countries, the Bank induced several governments to act earlier and/or in a more focused and potentially more cost-effective way than would have been the case otherwise. The principal contribution of the Bank's country-level HIV/AIDS assistance relative to the counterfactual of no assistance has been to: (a) help generate, deepen, and broaden political commitment to controlling the epidemic; (b) enhance the efficiency of national AIDS programs by helping governments focus on prevention, cost-effectiveness, and prioritization of activities in the face of scarce resources; (c) help create or strengthen robust national and sub-national AIDS institutions, usually linked to high-level units in the Ministry of Health (MOH), to enhance the long-run response; and (d) encourage governments to build the capacity of NGOs and create mechanisms to enlist them in the national response, often expanding access to prevention and care among the high-risk groups most likely to contract and spread the infection.

However, there were also shortcomings. The capacity of NGOs and community-based organizations (CBOs) to design, implement, and evaluate AIDS interventions was overestimated in virtually all countries, as was political commitment in many cases. Implementation was also delayed because of overly cumbersome procedures in processing subprojects and withdrawing funds. The projects underinvested in prevention programs for high-risk groups, which are key in stopping the spread of HIV. This was often because of a failure to implement planned activities, rather than overlooking them in design. Last, the projects as a group often failed to implement planned evaluation, monitoring, and research, which are public goods and should be among the highest priorities of government HIV/AIDS programs. The resulting dearth of information severely limits the ability to establish plausible attribution of changes in HIV/AIDS knowledge, risk behavior, and epidemiological outcomes to government programs supported by the Bank's assistance. It also implies that there was limited data for improving decision making and the effectiveness of programs over time.

A number of lessons were garnered from the first generation of AIDS assistance:

- Commitment to fighting AIDS from top leadership is necessary—but not sufficient—for results: efforts are needed to raise, broaden, and sustain political commitment.
- Strengthening the institutional capacity of the Ministry of Health to address HIV/AIDS is critical to the effectiveness of the national AIDS response.
- Even in countries with a strong civil society, implementation capacity for AIDS programs cannot be taken for granted. Bank projects need to invest in the capacity of civil society and develop more flexible project implementation procedures to engage it more effectively.
- Strong incentives and supervision are critical to ensure that interventions for high-risk groups are implemented by government and civil society to the extent necessary to reduce HIV transmission.

In addition to country-level assistance, the Bank has sponsored or managed analytic work on HIV/AIDS that informed that assistance. The evaluation identified more than 230 pieces of analytic work on HIV/AIDS—economic and sector studies, research, and journal articles—sponsored or managed by the Bank through the end of June 2004. This material is not systematically tracked in the Bank's internal record-keeping system, nor does any existing Web site assemble it in a comprehensive way. Surveys of two key audiences revealed that those who had read the most prominent studies gave them high marks for technical quality and usefulness. However, the surveys also revealed that the Bank's analytic work on AIDS is not reaching key audiences in the African policy community, particularly government policy makers. The nonavailability of reports in French and low access to the Internet are major barriers to greater access in Sub-Saharan Africa. Further, the level of familiarity of Bank staff who manage AIDS projects with HIV/AIDS analytic work and toolkits was much lower than anticipated.

The Ongoing Africa Multi-Country AIDS Program

The projects of the Africa MAP account for about two-thirds of the Bank's active HIV/AIDS projects globally, and about $1 billion, or half, of ongoing AIDS commitments. The goal of the first phase of the MAP is to "intensify action against the epidemic in as many countries as possible," with the explicit objectives of scaling up prevention, care, support, and treatment programs and to prepare countries to cope with those who develop AIDS. The program uses country eligibility criteria and a project design template to meet these goals and objectives. The emphasis of the program is to raise political commitment through engagement of all segments of government and civil society and to dramatically and rapidly expand the implementation of HIV/AIDS interventions.

The first two MAP projects were approved in 2000, and as of June 2004 about $255 million of the $1 billion of new commitments had been disbursed. Because none of the projects had closed, the OED evaluation focuses on assessing the key design features of the Africa MAP, the assumptions that underlie the approach, and the risks that were anticipated and those that were not, in light of the evidence from completed HIV/AIDS assistance and implementation of MAP projects to date (as of August 2004).

The Africa MAP has succeeded in enlisting at least two dozen countries to launch major HIV/AIDS initiatives with $1 billion of new resources, and it appears to have contributed to heightened political commitment. This alone is an enormous accomplishment, given the lack of demand for AIDS assistance by most of these countries in the 1990s. In this sense, it has ad-

dressed the major earlier impediment to broader impact. There is evidence of broad mobilization of civil society, on a greater scale than most (but perhaps not all) of the completed HIV/AIDS projects, and engagement of many more sectors of the economy. Mechanisms have been created to finance an AIDS response from civil society in many countries where they did not previously exist. MAP resources have disbursed, on average, somewhat faster than for those health projects in the first dozen countries. The objective of "scaling up" interventions is being pursued.

However, the overarching objective of the MAP is to prevent HIV infection and mitigate its impact; broader implementation and political commitment are a means to that end. The MAP approach relies heavily on the technical and strategic guidance of each country's national strategic plan (one of the eligibility criteria), coupled with strong monitoring and evaluation (M&E), heavier than standard project supervision, and the existence of proven, locally evaluated pilot projects to ensure the efficiency and efficacy of the activities that will be scaled up. The risks of the project design associated with these factors that ensure efficiency and effectiveness were not assessed in the design of the MAP. Because of the emphasis on rapid preparation of the projects, less up-front analytic work and fewer baseline assessments were conducted. The strategic input of the Bank at the design stage—which might have provided some insurance against these risks—was less than in previous HIV/AIDS projects.

Because all of the Africa MAP projects were still active as this report was being concluded, it is too early to know whether these risks have been mitigated by project-specific features or by technical assistance and other inputs from the MAP management unit, ACT*africa*. However, the evidence to date suggests that in many cases the national strategic plans are not sufficiently prioritized. Like the completed projects before them, there are signs that weak M&E in many Africa MAP projects have not produced the anticipated "learning by doing," and that many activities are being scaled up that have never been evaluated locally. Supervision appears to be no greater than for health lending, while the average complexity of the projects and the number of activities is far greater. As a result, there is a risk that many of the actors that have been mobilized politically behind the fight against HIV/AIDS are engaged in implementing activities for which they have little capacity, technical expertise, or comparative advantage, diverting scarce capacity from other poverty-reduction activities and resources from actors that can use them effectively. These potential risks have been created by weaknesses in the design of the MAP that impact the effectiveness and efficiency of resource use. The mid-term reviews of these projects and the next phase of lending provide an opportunity to develop mechanisms to minimize these risks and improve the effectiveness of the Bank's assistance.

Recommendations

In the next phase of its response, the Bank should help governments use human and financial resources more efficiently and effectively to have a sustainable impact on the HIV/AIDS epidemic. The Bank should focus on building capacity; developing strong national and sub-national institutions; investing strategically in public goods and the activities likely to have the largest impact; and creating incentives for monitoring, evaluation, and research based on local evidence that is used to improve program performance.

To promote this objective in *all Bank HIV/AIDS assistance*, the report makes the following recommendations:

- *Help governments to be more strategic and selective, to prioritize, using their limited capacity to implement activities that will have the greatest impact on the epidemic.* Greater prioritization and sequencing of activities will improve efficiency, reduce managerial complexity, and ensure that the most cost-effective activities are implemented first. In particular, the Bank should ensure that public goods and prevention among those most likely to spread HIV are adequately supported in all countries, and help high-prevalence countries to assess the costs, benefits, affordability, sustainability, and equity implications of different treatment and care options.

- *Strengthen national institutions for managing and implementing the long-run response, particularly in the health sector.* Expanded responses among other priority sectors are appropriate in specific settings, but should not come at the expense of investments in strengthening the capacity of the health sector to respond. In addition, Bank assistance should consider separate institutions, where appropriate, to satisfy the objectives of political mobilization and implementation of activities on the ground; develop explicit strategies for building, broadening, and sustaining political commitment; and make greater use of institutional and political analysis to improve the performance of local institutions.

- *Improve the local evidence base for decision making.* The Bank should create incentives to ensure that the design and management of country-level AIDS assistance are guided by relevant and timely locally produced evidence and rigorous analytic work. Specific actions include: an immediate systematic and in-depth inventory and assessment of ongoing M&E activities in all HIV/AIDS projects and components, as the basis for a time-bound action plan to improve the incentives for M&E, with explicit targets; pre-identification of a program of commissioned research and analytic work on priority issues to AIDS programs in each country; enhanced use of independent evaluation of pilot projects and of major ongoing program activities; and actions to make the Bank an "AIDS knowledge bank."

The *Africa MAP* is designed to mitigate risks concerning political commitment and implementation, but there are few structural mechanisms to assure efficiency or efficacy. These risks can be reduced through the following actions (in addition to the recommendations above, which apply to all projects):

- *A thorough technical and economic assessment of national strategic plans and government AIDS policy and an inventory of the activities of other donors should become a standard part of project preparation.* When national strategic plans are not adequate as a basis for prioritization and sequencing of activities, the Bank should engage clients in strategic discussions, informed by analytic work, to identify programmatic priorities that reflect the stage of the epidemic, capacity constraints, and the local context. Follow-on projects should be structured to ensure that those priority activities, including public goods and prevention among those with high-risk behavior, are pursued.

- *The objectives of the engagement of different segments of civil society in specific activities need to be clearly articulated, to distinguish between those engaged for political mobilization and those with the expertise and comparative advantage in implementing activities with a direct impact on the epidemic.* The results of ongoing community-driven development (CDD) AIDS activities should be rigorously evaluated with respect to their effectiveness in raising awareness, changing behavior, or mitigating impact, as should the cost-effectiveness of alternatives before they are renewed.

- *The Bank should focus multisectoral support for implementation on the sectors with activities that have the greatest potential impact on the epidemic—such as the Ministry of Health, the military, education, transport, and others, depending on the country—and ensure that the resources to supervise their activities are forthcoming.* The objectives of multisectoral action against AIDS and the key actors with respect to each of the objectives need to be more clearly defined. An assessment of the relation between MAP support for line ministries and the AIDS activities in non-health sector assistance and their relative effectiveness should be conducted to improve their complementarity and the efficiency of supervision.

ACRONYMS AND ABBREVIATIONS

AFR	Africa Region (Sub-Saharan Africa)
AIDS	Acquired immune deficiency syndrome
ANC	Ante-natal clinic
APL	Adaptable Program Loan
ARCAN	Africa Regional Capacity Building Network Project
BSS	Behavioral Surveillance Survey
CAS	Country Assistance Strategy
CBD/CDD	Community-based and community-driven development
CBO	Community-based organization
CD	Community development
CDC	U.S. Centers for Disease Control and Prevention
CDD	Community-driven development
CSW	Commercial sex worker
DCHDP	Disease Control and Health Development Project (Cambodia)
DHS	Demographic and Health Survey
EAP	East Asia and the Pacific region
ECA	Eastern Europe and Central Asia Region
ESW	Economic and sector work
FY	Fiscal year
GFATM	Global Fund to Fight AIDS, TB, and Malaria
GLIA	Great Lakes Initiative on HIV/AIDS
GPA	Global Programme on AIDS
HAART	Highly active antiretroviral therapy
HDN	Human Development Network of the World Bank
HIV	Human immunodeficiency virus
HNP	Health, nutrition, and population (previously PHN)
HRG	High-risk group
IAEN	International AIDS Economics Network
IAVI	International AIDS Vaccine Initiative
IBRD	International Bank for Reconstruction and Development
ICASA	International Conference on AIDS and STDs in Africa
ICR	Implementation Completion Report
IDA	International Development Association
IDI	Institutional development impact
IDU	Injecting drug user(s)
IEC	Information, education, and communication
IGAD	Inter-Governmental Authority on Development
LAC	Latin America and the Caribbean region
LACP	Pan-Caribbean Partnership Against AIDS
LQAS	Lot quality assurance sampling
LUSIDA	Argentina AIDS and STD Control Project

MAP	Multi-Country AIDS Program
M&E	Monitoring and evaluation
MDG	Millennium Development Goal
MICS	Multiple Indicator Cluster Survey
MOH	Ministry of Health
MSM	Men who have sex with men
MTCT	Mother-to-child transmission
MTR	Mid-term review
NAC	National AIDS Council
NACO	National AIDS Control Organisation (India)
NCHADS	National Center for HIV/AIDS, Dermatology and STDs (Cambodia)
NGO	Nongovernmental organization
OED	Operations Evaluation Department of the World Bank
PAPSCA	Program to Alleviate the Social Costs of Adjustment (Uganda)
PEPFAR	President's Emergency Program for HIV/AIDS Relief
PLWHA	People living with HIV/AIDS
PPAR	Project Performance Assessment Report
PRSC	Poverty Reduction Support Credit
PRSP	Poverty Reduction Strategy Paper
SACS	State AIDS Control Societies (India)
SIDALAC	Regional AIDS Initiative for Latin America and the Caribbean
SIP	Standard Investment Project
STD	Sexually transmitted disease
STI	Sexually transmitted infection
STIP	Sexually transmitted infection project
TA	Technical assistance
TAP	Regional HIV/AIDS Treatment Acceleration Project
TB	Tuberculosis
TTL	Task team leader
TWG	Technical Working Group
UNAIDS	Joint United Nations Programme on HIV/AIDS
VCT	Voluntary counseling and testing
WDR	World Development Report
WHO	World Health Organization

Note: All dollar figures are in U.S. dollars unless otherwise noted.

Chapter 1: Evaluation Highlights

- HIV/AIDS is turning back the clock on development.
- The impact can be prevented, but governments are reluctant to act.
- The Bank has committed $2.5 billion to HIV/AIDS lending and sponsored more than 200 pieces of analytic work.
- The evaluation reviews the Bank's response and assesses country-level HIV/AIDS assistance.

Introduction

The global AIDS epidemic has profoundly affected both the quality of life and progress toward poverty alleviation in many of the poorest developing countries, especially in Sub-Saharan Africa. In countries that have been less severely affected, it threatens to do so in the absence of effective and timely prevention efforts.

Since the late 1980s, but particularly over the past decade, the World Bank has launched efforts to prevent HIV/AIDS and mitigate its impact through participation in global programs; financing analytic work; engaging in policy dialogue; and providing loans, credits, and grants for HIV/AIDS projects. As of June 2004, the World Bank had committed $2.46 billion in credits, grants, and loans to 62 low- and middle-income countries for 106 projects to prevent, treat, and mitigate the impact of HIV/AIDS (see figure 1.1), of which about $1 billion had been disbursed.[1]

The Rationale for World Bank Involvement

The World Bank has assisted governments in improving health outcomes since the early 1980s.[2] Good health is an asset in its own right and an objective of public policy. It is also central to the World Bank's mandate of poverty reduction: better health contributes to higher productivity and incomes, while poor health both results from and exacerbates poverty (see, for example, CMH 2001; Jamison and others 1993; World Bank 1993). This would be sufficient rationale for the Bank to be concerned about AIDS, as one of many other health problems facing developing countries. Yet the Bank has put forward additional arguments for a role in preventing the spread of HIV and mitigating its impact—and for the urgency of doing so.

First, the economic and poverty impact of HIV/AIDS is exceptional (World Bank 1993, 2000a). In Sub-Saharan Africa, AIDS is the major killer of adults at the peak of their reproductive and economic lives (box 1.1). It has wiped out the hard-won gains in life expectancy over the past half-century in the hardest-hit countries.[3] AIDS-related illness is dramatically raising the demand for expensive medical care and fueling a resurgence of tuberculosis (TB), its most common opportunistic infection. AIDS deaths are robbing the workforce of some of its most skilled members, leaving families without breadwinners and children without parents. While the impact of AIDS on economic growth is varied (see, for example, Arndt and Lewis 2000; Bell and others 2003, 2004; Cuddington

Figure 1.1: World Bank–Supported HIV/AIDS Projects, 1988–2004

Completed   Ongoing   Both

1993; Kambou and others 1992; and discussion in World Bank 1997a), the distributional impact in terms of worsening poverty is unambiguous.

Second, in some developing regions, HIV/AIDS is only beginning to make inroads and has not spread widely. By encouraging governments in those areas to intervene early to prevent the spread of HIV, the Bank can help to avert the worst impacts on health and poverty.

Third, governments are reluctant to act. Because there is a lag of a decade or more between HIV infection and AIDS, the early and explosive spread of HIV is invisible to policy makers. During this period, only a few people are sick. Indeed, even when HIV prevention is launched, its impact is observable mainly in the long run. In the short run, other endemic diseases may be debilitating or killing many more people. Moreover, the social stigma and denial attached to some of the behaviors that spread HIV—sexual

The AIDS epidemic's impact is exceptional, it is just emerging in some countries, and governments are reluctant to act.

intercourse and intravenous drug use—make policy makers extremely reluctant to intervene in a timely manner.[4] Both early and late in an epidemic, the constituency for prevention is small and politically marginalized; demand for prevention among the general population is diffuse and weakened by denial. Yet in the absence of a cure, prevention is the only way to reduce the ultimate size of an AIDS epidemic. The World Bank is in a strong position to encourage governments to act, given its mandate for poverty reduction, its experience of over two decades of support for health systems, its convening power at high levels of government, and its multisectoral reach.

Objectives of the Evaluation

This evaluation assesses the development effectiveness of the Bank's country-level HIV/AIDS assistance and identifies lessons to improve the relevance, efficiency, and efficacy of ongoing and future activities. It focuses on evaluating *country-level* assistance because this is the most direct way that the Bank can influence outcomes and because of the enormous recent efforts by the

Box 1.1: The Global HIV/AIDS Epidemic

As of the end of 2004, 39 million people worldwide were living with asymptomatic human immunodeficiency virus (HIV) infection or acquired immune deficiency syndrome (AIDS), and more than 20 million had died of AIDS[a] since the beginning of the epidemic. More than 95 percent of people living with HIV/AIDS (PLWHA) live in low- and middle-income countries; nearly two-thirds are in Sub-Saharan Africa and nearly one in five live in South or Southeast Asia (see table). In 2004, 4.9 million people were newly infected and 3.1 million died of AIDS.

Globally, HIV is spread most frequently through unprotected sex with an infected partner and by sharing infected injecting equipment. It is also spread from HIV-infected mothers to their children through childbirth and breastfeeding; through transfusion of contaminated blood and blood products; and in health facilities that do not take precautions to protect patients and staff. Thus, most of the infected are prime-aged adults; about 5 percent are children under 15. AIDS is now the leading cause of death in the world for people aged 15–59.[a]

Estimates of HIV Infections and AIDS Mortality by Region as of December 2004

Region	Persons living with HIV/AIDS	Number of new infections in 2004	Number of AIDS deaths in 2004
Sub-Saharan Africa	25.4 million	3.1 million	2.3 million
South and Southeast Asia	7.1 million	890,000	490,000
Latin America and Caribbean	2.1 million	293,000	131,000
Eastern Europe and Central Asia	1.4 million	210,000	60,000
East Asia	1.1 million	290,000	51,000
Middle East and North Africa	0.5 million	92,000	28,000
North America, Western Europe, and Oceania	1.6 million	70,000	23,200
Total	39.4 million	4.9 million	3.1 million

Source: UNAIDS 2004a.

a. Kaiser Foundation Web site (www.kff,org/hivaids/timeline), accessed November 28, 2004.

Bank and the international community to scale up implementation on the ground. This evaluation complements OED's recent evaluation of World Bank involvement in global programs, including a case study of 14 global programs in health, one of which was UNAIDS.[5]

The World Bank can act to reduce HIV/AIDS at the country level directly, through helping governments to implement HIV/AIDS prevention, care, and mitigation, and indirectly, by supporting activities that reduce social vulnerability to infection. Examples of the latter are policies and programs to raise literacy, reduce poverty, and improve the status of women, all of which the World Bank also finances. For the purpose of this evaluation, *HIV/AIDS assistance* includes policy dialogue, analytic work, and lending with the explicit objective of reducing the scope or impact of the AIDS epidemic. This

is not to deny the importance of indirect channels; rather, it is recognition that OED has recently completed or has ongoing evaluations of many Bank activities that affect social vulnerability,[6] while the Bank's direct HIV/AIDS assistance has never been evaluated by OED.[7]

This evaluation is forward-looking. The Bank's HIV/AIDS project portfolio is young: only 9 free-standing AIDS projects and 22 with AIDS components of at least $1 million have closed (see table 1.1). Among the completed components, only half comprise at least 10 percent of the total World Bank commitment. In contrast, nearly two-thirds of projects and commitments have been launched since 2000. Further, as will be discussed in the next chapter, a change in Bank strategy in Africa precipitated fundamental changes in the preparation and design of AIDS projects beginning in 2000, compared with the "first

This report evaluates direct country-level assistance for HIV/AIDS control—policy dialogue, analytic work, and lending.

generation" of completed projects.

The Bank has never adopted an institution-wide strategy for HIV/AIDS, but its policy objectives can be inferred from Regional strategies and the objectives of country lending: to assist governments in preventing the spread of HIV, strengthening health systems to treat and care for AIDS patients, mitigating other impacts, and developing national institutional capacity to manage and sustain the long-run response. This evaluation assesses the effectiveness of country-level HIV/AIDS assistance against these policy objectives and brings to bear the lessons from past assistance for improving the relevance, efficiency, and efficacy of the Bank's ongoing and future HIV/AIDS activities. It also offers insights on the efficacy and lessons from four approaches that are central to the Bank's current country-level AIDS assistance:

- Building government commitment to fight HIV/AIDS
- Adopting multisectoral approaches in the national AIDS response
- Engaging nongovernmental organizations (NGOs) and communities in Bank-supported HIV/AIDS assistance

- Strengthening information, monitoring, and evaluation in national AIDS programs to enhance "learning by doing" and improve decision making.

The evaluation assesses the development effectiveness and lessons from countries with past assistance and examines the quality of a subset of the ongoing portfolio—the Africa Multi-Country AIDS Program (MAP)—including the extent to which these lessons have been incorporated. The rationale for a closer look at the Africa MAP is that, first, these projects account for about two-thirds of active projects and about half of ongoing AIDS commitments and, second, the design of the Africa MAP is somewhat of a departure from the standard investment projects that make up the completed AIDS project portfolio and the active project portfolio in other Regions. Further, the Africa MAP addresses the most severely affected continent and signals the start of a long-term, 10-to-15-year commitment by the Bank. Both Africa and other Regional groupings within the Bank are in the process of assessing which aspects of this approach to keep, which to modify in the next round of lending, and which might be applicable to other Regions.

Analytic Framework and Methodology

The challenge of this evaluation is to assess the difference that the Bank's country-level

---

Table 1.1: Distribution of World Bank HIV/AIDS Lending[a] by Project Status

| | Type of project | | | | | |
| | Free-standing AIDS | | AIDS component | | Total | |
Project status	Projects (number)	Commitments ($ millions)	Projects (number)	Commitments ($ millions)	Projects (number)	Commitments[c] ($ millions)
Closed	9	577.7	22	96.4	31	674.1
Active	44	1,535.8	31	254.7	75	1,790.5
Total	53	2,113.5	53[b]	351.1	106	2,464.6

Source: Appendix C.

a. Projects with components of more than $1 million allocated for HIV/AIDS.

b. In only 20 projects (9 closed and 11 active) does the AIDS component exceed 10 percent of the total Bank commitment.

c. The amount committed for closed projects in this table reflects what was actually disbursed.

Box 1.2: The Distribution of HIV across Risk Groups and the Stages of an Epidemic

HIV and other sexually transmitted diseases (STDs) tend to spread most rapidly among people who practice high-risk behaviors—those who have unprotected sex with many partners or who share unsterilized injecting equipment, for example. These individuals are not only more likely to become infected but, by virtue of their behavior, to unknowingly transmit HIV to others, including spouses and children who do not practice high-risk behavior. The extent of spread from populations with high-risk to those with lower-risk behavior depends on the level of interaction between them; it is not easily predicted and varies across cultures and geographic areas. High-risk groups (HRGs) are groups of people with identifiable characteristics—such as occupation, workplace, or location—that practice higher-risk behavior, on average, compared with the general population. Examples include sex workers, injecting drug users (IDUs), and occupational groups that separate people from their families (such as long-distance truckers, sailors, members of the military, migrant workers, or miners). HIV spreads at different rates within countries; regional differences are common.

Epidemiologists have classified countries according to the extent of infection of different population groups. In countries with a *nascent* epidemic, HIV has yet to spread, even among people who practice high-risk behavior. An epidemic is *concentrated* when infection levels have risen substantially among those who practice high-risk behavior but have yet to rise in the general and much larger low-risk population. A *generalized* epidemic is one in which HIV has moved out of populations with high-risk behavior and substantially infected the low-risk population.

In reality, there is a continuum in infection rates in different groups; these "stages" are intended to highlight where an epidemic is in relation to that continuum. For the purposes of this report, a nascent epidemic is defined as one in which HIV prevalence is less than 5 percent in high-risk populations. A concentrated epidemic is defined by HIV prevalence of more than 5 percent in high-risk populations but less than 5 percent in the general population, and a generalized epidemic is defined by HIV prevalence of 5 percent or more in the general population.[a]

a. There are different conventions for a "cutoff" point in HIV prevalence for defining these stages. For a generalized epidemic, World Bank (2000a) used a 7 percent threshold in the general population; at the other extreme, UNAIDS has used a rate of only 1 percent. This report uses an intermediate value, 5 percent, the same used in World Bank (1997a), which classified all developing countries by "stage" of the epidemic in 1997 and in 1999, in an updated edition.

HIV/AIDS assistance has made relative to what might have happened in the absence of that assistance (the counterfactual). The evaluation's conceptual framework is based on documenting the results chain that links the Bank's assistance (inputs) to government actions (outputs) to individual and household behavioral outcomes and epidemiological impacts (Appendix A). By assessing the counterfactual at different points in this results chain—documenting the activities of the Bank, the government, internal actors, and other international donors, and establishing a timeline of events—the evaluation assesses the plausibility of attribution of outputs and outcomes to the Bank's assistance. One of the important characteristics of countries that will be useful in understanding both the relevance and efficiency of the Bank's assistance is the internal distribution of HIV within countries, or "stage" of the epidemic (box 1.2).

The evidence for this evaluation was distilled from background papers, country case studies, OED project assessments, and in-depth interviews (box 1.3), in addition to published and unpublished research and evaluation literature referenced at the end of this report. It also draws on findings and lessons from other OED evaluations that are relevant to the Bank's HIV/AIDS assistance—in particular, those on the Bank's lending in health, population, and nutrition (Johnston and Stout 1999); social funds (Carvalho and others 2001); nongovernmental organizations (NGOs) in World Bank projects (Gibbs, Fumo, and Kuby 1999); community development (OED 2005a); and capacity building in Africa (OED 2005b).

The next chapter reviews the evolution of the Bank's HIV/AIDS assistance in relation to its inferred policy objectives and to interna-

The analytic framework is based on the results chain linking Bank assistance to government actions, outcomes, and impacts.

tional developments. Chapter 3 assesses the development effectiveness and lessons from the "first generation" of completed HIV/AIDS projects. Chapter 4 reviews the assumptions and design of the ongoing Africa MAP in light of these findings. Chapter 5 offers conclusions and points to the changing relevance of Bank HIV/AIDS assistance in the light of the dramatic increase in international resources. The final chapter presents recommendations.

Box 1.3: Evaluation Building Blocks

- Timelines of World Bank assistance and international HIV/AIDS events (Appendix B).
- An inventory of the Bank's HIV/AIDS lending portfolio in the health, nutrition, and population; education; transport; and social protection sectors (Appendix C).
- Review of project appraisal, supervision, and completion documents; Country Assistance Strategies; Poverty Reduction Strategy Papers (Appendix D); and Regional HIV/AIDS strategic documents.
- An inventory of Bank-sponsored analytic work on HIV/AIDS (Appendix E) and surveys of the Bank's human development staff and participants in the 2003 Nairobi AIDS Conference on the reach, quality, and usefulness of the Bank's analytic work (Appendix F).
- Detailed evaluations (OED Project Performance Assessment Reports, PPARs) of completed HIV/AIDS projects in Brazil, Cambodia, Chad, India, Kenya, Uganda, and Zimbabwe.
- Field-based country case studies to evaluate the entirety of World Bank lending and nonlending HIV/AIDS assistance in Brazil, Ethiopia, Indonesia, and Russia (Appendix G).
- A review of national HIV/AIDS strategies in 26 countries receiving World Bank assistance (Mullen 2003a, b); and analysis of the statistical association between state-level HIV/AIDS spending and AIDS awareness in India (Subramanian 2003).
- Self-administered questionnaires completed by current and former Bank task team leaders on the design and implementation of 24 country-level Africa MAP projects effective for at least a year, as of August 2004 (Appendix H).
- Interviews with the task team leaders for 19 Africa MAP projects (Appendix I) and the country directors for 26 of the 28 approved country-level MAP projects as of June 30, 2004 (Appendix J).

Chapter 2: Evaluation Highlights

- When AIDS appeared, the Bank had just started lending for health.
- The Bank worked with WHO, conducted economic analysis, and financed national programs where there was local interest or initiative from Regional staff.
- Broader action was constrained by lack of borrower interest and the Bank's internal preoccupation with health reform.
- Since 1998 the Bank has helped increase demand through advocacy and by accelerating approvals.
- AIDS projects do as well as other health projects on OED outcome ratings, and better than average on institutional development ratings.

The Evolution of the World Bank's Response to HIV/AIDS

B y the end of June 2004, the Bank had committed nearly $2.5 billion for 106 free-standing AIDS projects or projects in the health, education, transport, or social protection sectors with AIDS components of more than $1 million (figure 2.1).[1] Over that same period, the Bank financed or managed at least 230 completed pieces of analytic work on HIV/AIDS, including research and operational economic and sector work (figure 2.2).[2]

Two Phases of the World Bank Response

The evolution in World Bank strategies and assistance can be divided into two phases distinguished by the strategies adopted, the size and content of the HIV/AIDS lending portfolio, international partnerships, and the degree of institutional commitment. These phases are discussed below, based on timelines of the World Bank's HIV/AIDS lending, strategies, analytic work, and institutional response (in Appendices B-1 and B-2) and interviews conducted for this evaluation.

In assessing the Bank's response, it is important to keep in mind, first, that HIV/AIDS was a totally new disease. Little was initially known about it. The history of the past two decades has been one of an extended learning process about the characteristics of HIV, its modes of transmission, and its treatment. For example, even after the major modes of transmission were established, it was not clear how easily (or not) HIV spread sexually or how long the incubation period was.[3] Some research produced seemingly conflicting policy conclusions.[4] Programmatic decisions, particularly in developing countries, were often based on intuition, notional "best practice," or hypothetical effectiveness, with incomplete information on the true extent of infection or risk behavior. This sometimes contributed to contentious views on how the epidemic should be addressed. The learning process about the disease, both scientifically and in terms of its impacts, is ongoing. Appendix B-3 provides a timeline of some key international events, scientific developments, policy prescriptions, and spread of HIV/AIDS since the first cases were reported in 1981.

A second factor framing the Bank's response is that HIV/AIDS was—and remains—incredibly sensitive to discuss, and those infected are often stigmatized. This is both because HIV is spread sexually and through injecting drug use and because it is nearly always fatal. The intense denial of the problem in virtually all countries has been facilitated by the lack of information on the prevalence of HIV and risk

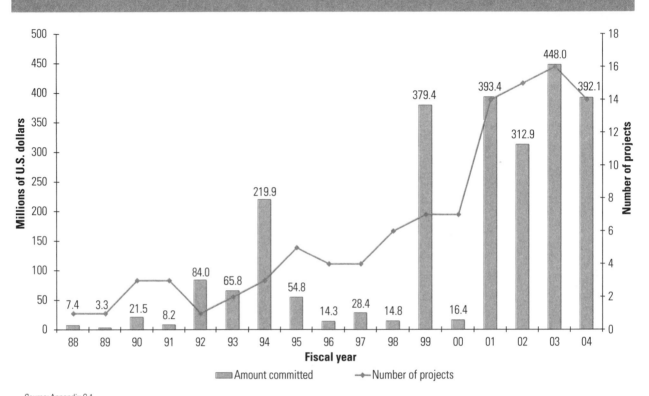

Figure 2.1: New AIDS Commitments and Projects, by Fiscal Year of Approval

Source: Appendix C.1.

Note: AIDS projects are defined as AIDS projects and components greater than US$1 million, including projects in health, education, and social protection sectors. The full amount of the commitment is attributed to the year of approval.

behaviors and the general atmosphere of uncertainty about the epidemic.

1986–97: The Tension Between AIDS and Health Priorities

In its initial response, the Bank collaborated closely with the newly formed World Health Organization (WHO) Global Program on AIDS (WHO/GPA). The first AIDS cases were reported in the United States in 1981. During the first several years, the international research community strived to understand the cause and modes of transmission.[5] As of 1985, when it became clear that a serious HIV/AIDS epidemic of unknown magnitude was taking place in parts of Sub-Saharan Africa, the Bank had been lending for health projects for only about five years, mainly for expansion of primary health care infrastructure to rural areas.[6] It had very limited expertise on health or AIDS and followed the lead of the WHO. In 1986, Bank management decided to support AIDS prevention and control through the lending program[7] and to offer technical assistance in economic analysis to the GPA, formed in 1987.[8] A Bank staff economist was assigned to work with GPA to document the economic impact of the epidemic. Out of this collaboration came the Bank's first analytic work on the direct and indirect costs of HIV/AIDS in Africa (Over and others 1988, 1989) and the jointly sponsored *Tanzania AIDS Assessment and Planning Study* (1992), which assessed the demographic impact of AIDS, the cost-effectiveness of interventions (information, STD treatment, blood screening, condoms), treatment and care options, and the need for survivor assistance for orphans and house-

HIV/AIDS was a totally new disease . . . and it remains a very sensitive issue.

Figure 2.2: Trends in Analytic Work by Fiscal Year of Completion

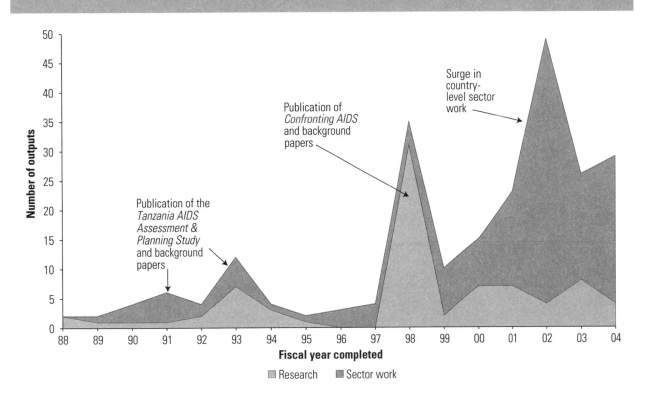

holds. GPA also played a key technical role in development of the first free-standing Bank-supported AIDS projects in Zaïre (1988), India (1992), and Brazil (1993).

The initiative for AIDS strategies and lending came primarily from health staff in the Regional operational groupings of the Bank. The Africa Region developed four AIDS strategies (box 2.1).[9] In 1991, an HIV/AIDS specialist was recruited to the Africa Technical Department to provide support for HIV/AIDS lending and to coordinate an informal working group of staff working on AIDS.[10] While other regions did not develop formal strategies, an "AIDS in Asia" technical support unit was set up in 1993 in the East Asia and Pacific (EAP) Region and in 1995 the Latin America and Caribbean (LAC) Region sponsored multi-year Regional technical and analytic support through the Regional AIDS Initiative for Latin America and the Caribbean (SIDALAC), based in the Mexican Health Foundation in Mexico City. The Regional vice president for Africa repeatedly raised the issue of AIDS with African leaders, ministers of health and finance from the mid-1980s and chaired a symposium on the development impact of AIDS at the annual meeting of the African Development Bank in 1993. However, AIDS was rarely raised as an issue in Country Assistance Strategies (CASs):[11] in fiscal 1994-95, only 28 percent of the 96 CASs mentioned HIV/AIDS, and this was often only to set the context (Appendix D). OED could find no evidence that other top Bank management raised the issue with borrowers or pushed the issue to a higher level internally during this first phase.

Bank HIV/AIDS lending supported national programs on four continents in countries at all stages of the epidemic, but broader action was constrained by lack of client interest.[12] Between 1988 and 1997, the Bank committed $500.5 million in credits and loans to 8 free-

As the AIDS epidemic broke, the Bank was just starting to lend for health.

13

Box 2.1: The Bank's AIDS Strategies in Africa during the First Decade of the Response

Acquired Immunodeficiency Syndrome (AIDS): The Bank's Agenda for Action in Africa (1988) calls for country-level assistance: policy dialogue on AIDS prevention and control; reviews of the current and potential spread of AIDS and other STDs; financing priority activities through free-standing AIDS projects and AIDS components, or restructuring active health projects and structural adjustment loans; mobilizing donor resources; training Bank staff; launching Regional studies and programs; and assisting governments to establish sub-regional AIDS research and training centers.

Combating AIDS and Other Sexually Transmitted Diseases in Africa: A Review of the World Bank's Agenda for Action (1992). This strategy updates the country-level action plan to include developing multisectoral policies for coping with the impact of the epidemic; allocating prevention resources to groups with low HIV but high STD infections and to "core transmitter" groups, such as sex workers and truck drivers, who are not only most likely to become infected, but also to transmit HIV to their partners in the general population; setting priorities for prevention; integrating HIV and STD responses; and strengthening the health infrastructure. It further calls for strengthening and broadening the Bank's analytical and operational agenda by assessing the impact of AIDS on development in countries where HIV has or is likely to spread and on non-health sectors; including STD/HIV overviews in non-health sector studies; conducting analytical work on the effectiveness of STD/HIV interventions; raising the priority of lending for parts of the health system critical to STD/HIV prevention and control; increasing involvement of nongovernmental organizations (NGOs) and community-based organizations (CBOs); improving information of Bank staff inside and outside of the health sector; and continued collaboration with WHO/GPA. However, AIDS should not dominate the Bank's health agenda in Africa.

Regional AIDS Strategy for the Sahel (1995). HIV prevalence was low in the Sahel, which fed denial. Leaders were reluctant to address the epidemic early, and grants from other sources were viewed as adequate to finance the immediate response. The two-pronged strategy includes: (1) country-level support through lending and sector work that focuses on medium- to longer-term strategies to develop sustainable policies and programs, such as strengthening communications; accelerating condom social marketing programs; expanding clinical management of STDs; increasing assistance for NGO and private sector initiatives; broad-based policy analysis and program coordination; and (2) Regional advocacy and capacity-building programs with grant financing from the donor community to bring urgency to the issue by mobilizing political and opinion leaders; supporting pilot projects; conducting studies and research; and providing technical support and training.

AIDS Prevention and Mitigation in Sub-Saharan Africa: An Updated World Bank Strategy (1996) highlights prevention and mitigation of the household and sectoral impacts of the epidemic and the slow progress in developing multisectoral policies. Interventions need to be targeted early in the epidemic to the highest risk groups, at which time they are most cost-effective, and the care of AIDS patients needs to be integrated with primary health care services. Research and pilot efforts had succeeded in changing risky behavior and lowering HIV infections rates but needed to be expanded in depth and breadth to slow the epidemic. Five new areas for Bank attention are: generating political commitment; changing risk behaviors; mobilizing resources to intensify the breadth and depth of programs; increasing the analysis of AIDS and its impacts; and improving the design and implementation of cost-effective measures to mitigate the epidemic.

standing AIDS projects and 17 AIDS components of more than $1 million (box 2.2). Most of the projects were in countries that had requested assistance (Brazil, India) or that already had some degree of government commitment to addressing AIDS (Cambodia, Uganda, Zimbabwe). In Burkina Faso, Chad, and Kenya,[13] AIDS projects were launched in parallel with health projects. Two projects launched in countries where government commitment was weak—Indonesia and Zaïre—were eventually cancelled.[14] Countries where the epidemic was the most devastating—such as Haiti and Zaïre—not only had weak health systems but major unrest and governance problems. The availability of grant monies from GPA and other sources to address AIDS may have contributed to low demand for World Bank assistance, but denial of the problem (including within ministries of health) was also still common and there were many competing priorities for funding, both within and outside the health sector, for which there was strong demand. In addition to free-standing projects and components, many ongoing health projects were "retrofitted" with AIDS activities to accelerate the response.[15]

Internally, mobilizing resources to fight any single disease, including HIV/AIDS, was seen by the Bank's health sector leadership as a lower priority than reforming weak health systems in poor countries, which would lead to improvements in all health outcomes over the longer run. During the 1990s, the health sector's strategy shifted from an emphasis on extending primary health care to an emphasis on reform of health systems, launched by the 1987 policy paper, *Financing Health Services in Developing Countries: An Agenda for Reform* (Johnston and Stout 1999). The importance of these reforms in Sub-Saharan Africa was widely recognized and there was concern that the urgent need to address the AIDS epidemic might somehow compete with this agenda, given scarce capacity. The 1992 AIDS strategy for Africa, for example, cautioned that an expanded role of the Bank in AIDS should not be allowed to overtake the critical agenda for strengthening health systems. The Africa Region's major analytic paper for improving health outcomes—*Better Health in Africa* (1994)—acknowledged that AIDS is "the most dramatic new threat to Africa" (p. 19) and a major reason for the urgency of health system reform. But AIDS is grossly neglected in the document, which focuses on making health systems work better. The analysis relies on burden of disease data that show AIDS as the fifth-ranking disease among women and seventh-ranking among men;[16] AIDS does not figure in the main conclusions and recommendations of the report,[17] and HIV is absent from the country-level health indicators in the annexes.

Within this broader health reform agenda, AIDS did gain some ground in the early 1990s.

- The *World Development Report 1993: Investing in Health* (WDR) advocated that governments provide a cost-effective package of basic health services that included low-cost HIV prevention. It justified early and effective prevention because HIV was widespread and spreading rapidly; the cost-effectiveness of preventive interventions is lower when infections move out of high-risk groups into the general population; the consequences of AIDS are severe and costly; and prevention is politically charged. The WDR made specific programmatic recommendations[18] and highlighted AIDS as a development issue that required national leadership, along with the involvement of many agencies both inside and outside government, including NGOs.

- *Disease Control Priorities in Developing Countries* (1993) highlighted the need for communicable disease control. The chapter on HIV/AIDS and STDs provided a comprehensive review of the disease burden, the epidemiology of HIV/AIDS and STDs, and evidence of the effectiveness and cost-effectiveness of key interventions for prevention and care, particularly approaches that target services to people most likely to transmit HIV and other STDs (Over and Piot 1993).

But the systemic approach did not favor singling out individual diseases, and by the end of the period AIDS was even less strategically prominent in the Bank's health sector strategy. The 1997 *Health, Nutrition, and Population (HNP) Sector Strategy* was the first major product of the Bank's newly configured HNP family. It defined the sector's objectives as improving HNP outcomes of the poor, enhancing the performance of health care systems, and securing sustainable health care financing. The annex tables to the *Strategy* reveal that 2 percent or more of adults in 30 African countries and more than 5 percent in 15 countries were infected with HIV/AIDS

The Bank supported many national AIDS programs, but broader action was limited by lack of borrower interest and denial.

Within the Bank's health sector, action on any single disease was a lower priority than health system reform.

15

Box 2.2: The "First Generation" of World Bank HIV/AIDS Projects

The first free-standing AIDS project was the Zaïre National AIDS Control Project ($8.1 million credit, 1988).[a] It was the first World Bank health project in that country and appears to be the first free-standing Bank health project for a single disease.[b] It built on a 1987 health sector study and a strong research base established by *Projet SIDA*, the first international AIDS research project in Africa, based in Kinshasa.[c] Other AIDS projects in Africa followed two models: the AIDS/sexually transmitted infection projects (STIPs) in Zimbabwe (1993), Uganda (1994), and Kenya (1995),[d] all countries with generalized epidemics, and projects that linked substantial HIV/AIDS activities with population or reproductive health, in Burkina Faso (1994), Chad (1995), and Guinea (1998), countries with concentrated epidemics.[e]

Substantial projects also were launched in other Regions. The India National AIDS Control Project ($84 million credit, 1992) emphasized awareness, prevention, blood safety, and setting up the institutions for directing the national AIDS response. At that time, HIV had taken off in several Indian states but not in others, and with fewer than 100 reported AIDS cases, the epidemic was largely in-

visible to policy makers. The Brazilian AIDS and STD Control Project ($160 million loan, 1993) financed prevention for both the general population and high-risk groups; better services for HIV and STD patients; institutional development, including training of service providers and upgrading laboratory services; and surveillance, research, and evaluation. A free-standing AIDS and STD Control Project ($30 million loan) was approved for Argentina in 1997. Both Brazil and Argentina had concentrated epidemics. The Indonesian HIV/AIDS and STD Management Project ($24 million loan) was approved in 1996, in anticipation that Indonesia, with a nascent epidemic, might follow the route of the explosive AIDS epidemic in Thailand. The other significant East Asian project was the Cambodia Disease Control and Health Development Project (DCHDP, $30.4 million credit, 1996), the first health project in that low-income, war-torn country. In addition to vital health infrastructure, the project had major components for AIDS, TB, and malaria. Formal AIDS components or activities were financed as part of new health projects in six additional countries[f] and in a social protection project in Uganda.[g]

a. The total project cost of $21.9 million included an International Development Association (IDA) credit and parallel financing from other donors. Zaïre is now known as the Democratic Republic of Congo.

b. OED was unable to identify any previous free-standing projects for single diseases in the Bank's portfolio before 1988.

c. *Projet SIDA* was funded primarily by the U.S. Centers for Disease Control and Prevention (CDC), with the collaboration of the U.S. National Institutes of Health, the Institute of Tropical Medicine (Antwerp), and the Ministry of Health of Zaïre.

d. A $19.2 million STD Prevention Project for Nigeria was fully prepared and appraised over the period 1993-95, to be financed by a $13.7 million credit and with the strong support of the minister of health. However, negotiations were not pursued for reasons unrelated to the project that had to do with overall relations between the Bank and Nigeria.

e. The integration of HIV/AIDS, STD, and reproductive health services was a theme promoted by the 1994 International Conference on Population and Development (ICPD), in Cairo.

f. Brazil (1988), Haiti (1990), Madagascar (1991), Mali (1991), Morocco (1990), and Rwanda (1991).

g. The Program to Alleviate Poverty and the Social Costs of Adjustment (PAPSCA, 1990).

as of 1994. Yet there is no discussion of HIV/AIDS, the impact of the epidemic on health systems, or on priorities anywhere in the main body of the report.[19]

Yet there were other pressures in 1996–97 from outside and inside the Bank stressing the exceptionality of HIV/AIDS as a health and development problem to the Bank's management. In 1996 the Bank became one of six cosponsors of the newly formed Joint United Nations Program on HIV/AIDS (UNAIDS), with the mission to "lead, strengthen, and support an expanded response" to the global AIDS epidemic and to

improve coordination of the HIV/AIDS activities of U.N. agencies.[20] That partnership required an institution-level dialogue with the cosponsors. UNAIDS became a force for global advocacy, capable of getting the attention of top Bank management through the media and other channels (Poate and others 2002). The year 1996 also marked the advent of highly active antiretroviral therapy (HAART), which dramatically reduced AIDS mortality rates in high-income countries and in Brazil, but at the time was unaffordable (more than $10,000 per patient yearly) and difficult to administer in the most severely affected low-income countries.

Pressure also came from the Bank's research department, which released *Confronting AIDS: Public Priorities in a Global Epidemic*[21] in November 1997. The Policy Research Report assembled evidence on the economic impact of the AIDS epidemic, its economic and societal determinants, and the effectiveness of AIDS interventions in developing countries. It made the economic case for government involvement in fighting AIDS and proposed principles for setting government priorities in resource-constrained settings. Two key priorities for countries at all stages of the epidemic, based on principles of epidemiology and public economics, were to provide public goods and to ensure that the people most likely to contract HIV and transmit it to others engage in safer behavior. The report also advocated improving access of AIDS patients to cost-effective health care and integrating AIDS mitigation programs and policies with poverty reduction programs. It called for early action to prevent HIV in countries where the epidemic was not yet widespread.[22]

1998 to Present: Institutional Mobilization and Advocacy

The winter of 1997 and spring of 1998 were a turning point with respect to high-level commitment within the Bank and advocacy to raise demand among borrowers. This new climate was signaled by speeches of high-level Bank management to policy makers: President Wolfensohn emphasized AIDS at his February 1998 speech to the Economic Commission for Africa,[23] and the Regional vice president for Africa delivered a speech at the 12th International AIDS Conference in Geneva in June.[24] In 1999, the Regional vice presidents for Africa and South Asia both addressed Regional AIDS conferences. Following the Asian AIDS Conference in December 1999, President Wolfensohn wrote to South and East Asian heads of state, emphasizing the economic impact of the epidemic and the need to act as soon as possible. In 2000, he called for a "War on AIDS" in an address to the U.N. Security Council in January and AIDS was the first item before the Development Committee at the Spring Meetings of the World Bank and the IMF.

The most recent period has seen completion of Bank HIV/AIDS strategies in nearly all Regions and in many sectors. The Africa Region launched a new strategy in 1999 to accelerate action (box 2.3) and an AIDS

In 1998, high-level Bank management became proactive in raising demand for HIV/AIDS assistance among borrowers.

Box 2.3: Intensifying Action against HIV/AIDS in Africa

In 1999 the Africa Region of the Bank unveiled a new AIDS strategy. It finds the HIV/AIDS epidemic to be a major threat to development in Sub-Saharan Africa and identifies the lack of political commitment, competing priorities, insufficient resources, inadequate capacity, and cultural norms as the major impediments to action. Noting that many interventions have been shown to be cost-effective in changing behavior and reducing HIV transmission, the strategy focuses on advocacy and mobilizing resources to increase coverage of national programs. Its four "pillars" are: advocacy to strengthen political commitment; mobilizing additional resources; support for HIV/AIDS prevention, care, and treatment; and expanding the knowledge base. The strategy advocates a "decentralized participatory approach."

It also proposes programmatic priorities in relation to the stage of the epidemic:[a]

- In countries with relatively lower HIV prevalence, "priority should be given to changing the behavior of those at highest risk of contracting and spreading HIV," and "quickly followed by broader approaches to reach other vulnerable groups, such as women and youth."

- In countries with high HIV prevalence, strategies should be adopted to "strengthen interventions targeted to groups at highest risk" and extend rapidly the coverage of programs to "all vulnerable groups in all urban areas and rural districts. These countries must also move rapidly to provide care and mitigate the impact of the epidemic."

a. World Bank 2000a, p. 19.

Campaign Team for Africa (ACT*africa*) unit was created to provide resources and technical support to country teams to mainstream HIV/AIDS activities in all sectors. AIDS strategies or business plans have been developed for Central America (2003), Eastern Europe and Central Asia (2003), South Asia (2004), and East Asia and the Pacific (2004). The Middle East and North Africa Region commissioned analytic work showing the consequences of inaction (Robalino and others 2003) and will release a formal strategy in 2005. Major strategic papers and analytic work have informed Bank efforts in Latin America (2003) and the Caribbean (2000). Both the education and transport sectors of the Bank have developed AIDS strategies and are fostering AIDS components and activities in sectoral projects. Country and Regional economic and sector studies, including toolkits, have overtaken research in the Bank portfolio of analytic work (figure 2.2). The priority given AIDS in CASs between fiscal years 1994–95 and 2000–02 increased dramatically (box 2.4).

Box 2.4: AIDS Increased as a Priority in Country Assistance Strategies

Although the recognition of AIDS as a priority rose quickly among Regional health staff, especially in Africa, it was much slower to develop as a priority in the Bank's overall development agenda, represented by the Country Assistance Strategies (CASs). In fiscal years 1994–95, AIDS was mentioned as a priority by the Bank or both the Bank and government in fewer than half of the CASs for countries with generalized AIDS epidemics, and rarely in countries with concentrated or nascent epidemics (see figure, left panel). The CASs for Côte d'Ivoire, Ethiopia, Mozambique, Republic of Congo, Uganda, and Zimbabwe—all with generalized epidemics—either did not mention AIDS or did so only to set the context. This picture had changed radically by fiscal years 2000–02 (see figure, right panel). In both periods, the Bank was more likely to raise AIDS as a critical issue than was the government. However, over time the priority of AIDS rose among both the Bank and government, and more so, the more severe the epidemic.

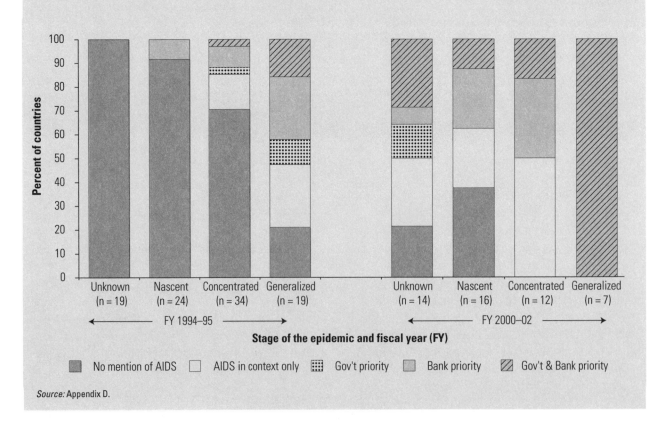

Source: Appendix D.

Two new instruments have helped to accelerate AIDS project approval and increase client demand. The MAP is organized around country eligibility criteria, a project template, a funding envelope sufficient for multiple projects, and appended appraisal documents for the first projects in the series. Following approval of this package by the Bank's Board, appraisal documents for each subsequent project are circulated to the executive directors for information. Any operation can be scheduled for Board discussion at the request of at least 3 executive directors within 10 days of its circulation, after which approval by the Regional vice president becomes effective.[25] The rationale for this approach is that the eligibility criteria and project design template can be quickly adapted to individual countries, greatly reducing preparation time and thereby accelerating implementation. The MAP also permits funding of Regional (non–country-specific) projects. The second innovation was approval of International Development Association (IDA) grants for AIDS projects, in September 2002. All AIDS projects or components approved in low-income countries since then have been eligible for IDA grants, as have 25 percent of AIDS projects or components in blend countries (those eligible for both IDA credits and International Bank for Reconstruction and Development [IBRD] loans).[26]

Project approvals have accelerated since 1998, particularly among low-income African countries. The Bank's Board to date has approved envelopes of $500 million each for two Africa MAPs, in 2000 and in 2001. As of the end of June 2004, a total of 29 country-level projects and 2 Regional projects had been approved through the first and second African MAPs. A $155 million Caribbean MAP was approved in 2001, with 8 free-standing country projects and one regional project approved by June 2004. Free-standing AIDS projects have been launched in most of the rest of South Asia—Bangladesh, Bhutan, India (a second project), Pakistan, and Sri Lanka—and major projects that link HIV/AIDS and TB control have been approved in Moldova, Russia, and Ukraine. A third AIDS project was approved for Brazil. Altogether, 45 free-standing AIDS projects and 32 substantial components totaling nearly $2 billion in AIDS commitments have been approved since 1998—roughly 4 times the commitments of the previous decade—with slightly more than half of the total destined for Sub-Saharan Africa. The vast majority of these projects are active (table 2.1). The share of AIDS projects in Sub-Saharan Africa has risen slightly, compared with the closed project portfolio, but Africa's share of commitments has doubled. The share of commitments in Latin America and the Caribbean has fallen to a quarter of what it was in the closed portfolio. However, AIDS commitments have increased in absolute terms in all Regions.

In parallel with these internal Bank developments, there has been a sharp increase in the international commitment to fight HIV/AIDS since 2000. The Millennium Development Goals (MDGs) were adopted in 2000, including the goal of reversing the spread of HIV; the U.N. General Assembly Special Session on HIV/AIDS (UNGASS) was held in 2001, leading to the formation of the Global Fund to Fight AIDS, TB, and Malaria (GFATM), and the "3 by 5" initiative was launched in 2003 to get 3 million people in developing countries on antiretroviral care by 2005. The global resources for fighting AIDS have dramatically increased. As of March 2005, the GFATM had committed $1.6 billion for AIDS in 128 countries. In 2003 the U.S. government announced the President's Emergency Plan for AIDS Relief (PEPFAR), a $15 billion fund to combat AIDS in Africa, the Caribbean, and Vietnam over five years.

The Portfolio of World Bank Project Assistance

Among the 106 closed and active AIDS projects in table 2.2, 70 projects in 56 countries account for $2.36 billion in AIDS commitments, or 96 percent of the total. These include all 50 free-standing country-level AIDS projects and 20 AIDS components that amount to at least 10 percent of World Bank commitments. Eighteen of the 70

Table 2.1: Distribution of AIDS Projects[a] and Commitments by Region, as of June 30, 2004 (US$ million)

Region	Closed projects		Active projects		Total commitments	
	Number (%)	Amount committed[b] (%)	Number (%)	Amount committed (%)	Number of projects (%)	Amount committed (%)
Sub-Saharan Africa	16	199.1	45	1,132.5	61	1,331.6
	(51.6)	(29.5)	(60.0)	(63.3)	(57.5)	(54.0)
Latin America and Caribbean	6	356.1	14	239.0	20	595.1
	(19.4)	(52.8)	(18.7)	(13.3)	(18.9)	(24.1)
South Asia	3	92.3	8	296.5	11	388.8
	(18.8)	(13.7)	(10.7)	(16.6)	(10.4)	(15.8)
East Asia and Pacific	4	15.9	3	25.9	7	41.8
	(12.9)	(2.4)	(4.0)	(1.4)	(6.6)	(1.7)
Eastern Europe and Central Asia	1	2.7	4	87.6	5	90.3
	(3.2)	(0.4)	(5.3)	(4.9)	(4.7)	(3.7)
Middle East and North Africa	1	8	1	9	2	17.0
	(3.2)	(1.2)	(1.3)	(0.5)	(1.9)	(0.7)
Total	31	674.1	75	1,790.5	106	2,464.6
	(100)	(100)	(100)	(100)	(100)	(100)

a. Includes operations in health, education, social protection, and transport with AIDS components exceeding US$1 million.

b. The amount committed for closed projects in this table reflects what was actually disbursed.

projects have closed and 52 are active. All but one of the AIDS components is embedded in a health or population project.[27]

Half of these projects have been in countries with concentrated epidemics, about a quarter in countries with generalized epidemics, and one-eighth each in countries with nascent epidemics or an epidemic of unknown distribution (table 2.2).[28] About half of the projects in the Africa MAP are in countries with concentrated epidemics and a third are in countries with generalized epidemics. A higher share of projects in the closed than in the active portfolio addressed countries with generalized epidemics.

The main objective of these projects, as articulated in design documents, has been to prevent the spread of HIV (see table 2.3). More recently approved projects (those that are

Half of Bank-supported AIDS projects are in countries with concentrated epidemics.

still active) are more likely to have explicit objectives related to treatment and care of AIDS patients and mitigating the impact of HIV/AIDS than are completed projects. Active projects are less likely to articulate objectives related to institutional strengthening and providing public goods. Table 2.3 understates the types of activities that were supported, however, because of the general way that objectives often are articulated: for example, three-quarters of projects actually undertook or planned treatment and care activities—56 percent of closed and 83 percent of active projects—although fewer than half had an explicit treatment and care objective.[29]

The outcomes of completed AIDS projects, as rated by OED against their objectives, are similar to those of other health projects. OED rates the outcome of every completed project against its stated objectives, in terms of its relevance, efficacy, and efficiency.[30] Figure 2.3 presents OED outcome ratings of the 9

Table 2.2: Distribution of Closed and Active Projects by Stage of the Epidemic (percent)

Stage of the epidemic	Closed	Active Non-MAP	Active Africa MAP	Active Caribbean MAP	Total Active	All projects Percent	All projects N
Nascent	16.7	20.0	6.9	—	9.6	11.4	8
Concentrated	44.4	46.7	48.3	62.5	51.9	48.5	34
Generalized	38.9	13.3	34.5	—	23.1	27.1	19
Unknown	—	20.0	10.3	37.5	15.4	12.8	9
Total	100.0	100.0	100.0	100.0	100.0	100.0	
N	18	15	29	8	52		70

Note: "N" is the number of projects. The 70 projects are in 56 countries. Three countries (Brazil, Kenya, Uganda) had three projects each and 8 (Burkina Faso, Chad, Congo DR, Guinea, Guinea-Bissau, India, Rwanda, and Sri Lanka) had two projects each. See Appendix C.1.

Table 2.3: Stated Objectives of the World Bank's HIV/AIDS Projects (percent)

Objective	All projects	Closed	Active
Prevention-related[a]	93	79	96
Treatment and care[b]	43	28	48
Institutional[c]	37	50	33
Mitigate impact	36	22	40
Public goods[d]	16	39	8
Other[e]	29	22	31
Number of projects	70	18	52

Note: These objectives are as articulated in the appraisal documents. Column totals exceed 100% because most projects had more than one objective. The fact that a project didn't have an explicit prevention-related objective does not mean that preventive interventions were not undertaken.

a. Includes: prevent the spread of HIV or lower the incidence; increase access to prevention interventions; change behavior; raise awareness; reduce morbidity and mortality from a preventable condition.

b. Includes: increase access to/strengthen capacity for care and support; reduce morbidity and mortality, improve the quality of life of people with AIDS, increase life expectancy; increase access to treatment/strengthen capacity to treat; reduce incidence of and treat opportunistic infections and TB.

c. Includes: build implementation capacity; build or strengthen institutions; strengthen activities in non-health sectors.

d. The two types of public goods cited were blood safety and research/surveillance/data collection.

e. Includes encouraging NGOs and the community response; promoting a multisectoral response; supporting the national AIDS program; reducing stigma and discrimination; "scaling up" the response.

completed free-standing HIV/AIDS projects and ratings of 3 project components that were the subject of an OED field assessment.[31] Half of the projects were rated (fully) satisfactory, meaning that the project "achieved, or is expected to achieve, most of its major relevant objectives efficiently with only minor shortcomings." A quarter of the projects were rated moderately satisfactory, which applies when the project "achieved or is expected to achieve its major relevant objectives efficiently but with either significant shortcomings or modest overall relevance." Finally, a quarter of the projects were rated moderately unsatisfactory or unsatisfactory. An unsatisfactory rating is assigned when the project "has failed to achieve and is not expected to achieve most of its major relevant

The outcome ratings of AIDS projects are comparable to those of the health portfolio.

Figure 2.3: OED Ratings for Completed Projects

A. Outcome in Relation to Objectives

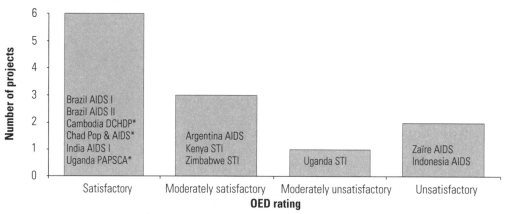

Note: None of the projects or components were rated highly satisfactory or highly unsatisfactory.
* Rating for the AIDS component, based on OED Project Performance Assessment Report.

B. Institutional Development Impact

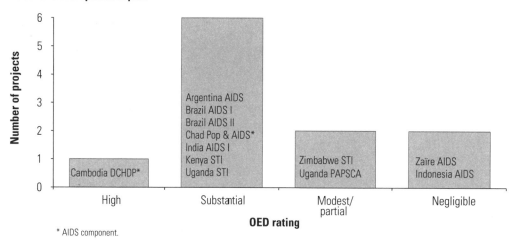

* AIDS component.

C. Sustainability

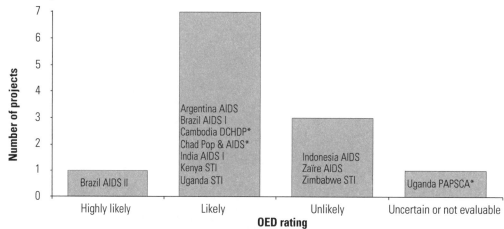

* AIDS component.

objectives, with only minor development benefits" or, in the case of moderately unsatisfactory, "when it achieves only some of its major relevant objectives but with positive efficiency." The number of projects is small, but the AIDS project outcome ratings—75 percent moderately satisfactory or better—are similar to the outcome ratings for the 159 HNP projects completed from fiscal year 1994 to fiscal year 2003 (67 percent moderately satisfactory or better) (OED 2004c, Appendix table A-1).

Both of the projects with unsatisfactory outcomes were cancelled after partial implementation. The Indonesia AIDS and STD project was the Bank's first attempt to preemptively launch an AIDS response through a free-standing operation in a country with a nascent epidemic. At that time, Indonesia was a middle-income country with long, active, and largely successful experience with the Bank in both health and population assistance. HIV was rare, even among those at high risk of infection, but officials were mindful of the explosive takeoff of the epidemic in Thailand, and projections suggested that the same could happen in Indonesia. The project was prepared in an "emergency" mode, as a three-year operation that was to develop an institutional response and would finance NGOs to pilot interventions to high-risk groups, prior to their widespread replication in later operations. But the project got off to a slow start, government was not as committed to enlisting NGOs or working with high-risk groups as had been thought during project preparation, and the new AIDS office in the Ministry of Health competed with other units with overlapping responsibilities. Political commitment was weakened when the predicted explosion of HIV did not occur. Following the East Asian economic crisis, only about 18 months after the project's launch (but already at its midpoint), the project was cancelled with only $4.8 million of the $24.8 million loan disbursed. The Zaïre project was well prepared, but failed because of low commitment, low capacity, and political and economic chaos. The credit was cancelled with only $3.3 million of the $8.1 million credit spent. The performance of both the Bank and the borrower in these two projects was rated unsatisfactory by OED (see Appendix C-2).

AIDS projects rate better than health projects on institutional development.

OED ratings of the institutional development impact (IDI) for these AIDS projects are substantially higher than for the HNP sector as a whole. Two-thirds of the 12 AIDS projects received IDI ratings of substantial or high,[32] compared with only 36.5 percent for the HNP sector as a whole (OED 2004c, Appendix table A-1). However, their sustainability ratings (67 percent "likely" or higher) are similar to the rest of the HNP portfolio (62 percent). Lack of sustainability in 4 of the 12 projects was linked to low political commitment, economic turmoil, or doubts about the long-run ability to finance drugs and support NGOs.

Chapter 3: Evaluation Highlights

- Bank assistance has helped strengthen commitment to fighting HIV/AIDS.
- It has helped improve the efficiency of national programs and strengthen institutions, mainly linked to ministries of health.
- It has encouraged the use of NGOs, but the efficacy of those efforts is rarely measured.
- Prevention targeting those most likely to spread HIV, though planned, was often not implemented.
- Monitoring, evaluation, and research have been weak and contributed little to improving impact.
- Knowledge, awareness, and risk behaviors have improved in countries receiving Bank assistance.
- Bank research and analysis are not reaching policy makers in Africa.
- The research and analysis are generally perceived to be of high quality and usefulness.

Findings from the First Generation of Bank HIV/AIDS Assistance

The Bank's overall policy objectives, inferred from Regional strategies and the objectives of country lending, have been to assist governments to prevent the spread of HIV, strengthen health systems to provide cost-effective treatment and care for AIDS patients, mitigate other impacts, and develop national institutional capacity to manage and sustain the long-run response. The severe lack of good information on which to base decisions is a theme that runs through most—if not all—strategy and project documents.

The technical recommendations of the Bank in Regional strategies and country-level assistance have followed evolving international knowledge, but with an emphasis on the need to prioritize in light of scarce capacity, limited resources for health, and other demands for assistance from within and outside the health sector. The revealed priorities in lending, strategic documents, and Bank analytic work put foremost on the agenda the production of public goods,[1] prevention (for efficiency, because AIDS is fatal and incurable, and because of the positive externalities), and affordable and cost-effective care and mitigation services for AIDS patients and their families. These prioritization principles, coupled with an understanding of the way that HIV and other STDs spread, resulted in a typology of programmatic priorities at different stages of the HIV/AIDS epidemic that has guided both the Bank and the international community since the mid-1990s (see box 3.1).

This chapter presents the findings and lessons—in terms of policies, institutions, services, and outcomes—of the Bank's country-level HIV/AIDS assistance to date, based on a review of the portfolio; assessments of completed AIDS projects; and case studies in Brazil, Indonesia, and Russia. It also presents an assessment of the reach, technical quality, and utility of the Bank's analytic work on AIDS, based on surveys of Bank human development staff and delegates at an African AIDS conference.

Findings and Lessons from the Bank's Country-Level HIV/AIDS Assistance

Political Commitment and AIDS Policy

The Bank's assistance has helped to generate, deepen, and broaden political commitment. OED's assessment found that the first India AIDS Control Project, including the policy dialogue around it, likely advanced the government response to HIV/AIDS by several years relative to

Box 3.1: Government Priorities and Stage of the Epidemic

When financial or human resources are scarce, policy makers need to decide what to finance first with public funds to have the greatest impact with available resources—ensuring efficiency—while also promoting equity.

Providing public goods that are essential to stop the HIV/AIDS epidemic—such as improving access to information, monitoring HIV and risk behavior, and evaluating pilot projects—is a priority for governments to finance at all stages of an AIDS epidemic. This is because everyone can enjoy or benefit from these activities, even if some beneficiaries do not pay. The private sector is unlikely to provide them in sufficient quantity. A public good may not be provided at all unless financed by the government.

A second government priority is preventing HIV and its transmission among those most likely to pass it to others. Prevention among individuals who practice high-risk behavior directly protects their partners and indirectly prevents many more secondary infections in the low-risk, general population (the partners' spouses, children, and other sexual or injecting partners).[a] In other words, when people with the highest risk of HIV transmission adopt safer behavior, it reduces everyone's chance of getting HIV. The cost-effectiveness of preventing HIV among those most likely to contract and spread it, relative to alternative interventions, is highest in nascent and concentrated epidemics, because the potential benefits in terms of stopping transmission to the entire population are greatest.

In generalized epidemics, this strategy will still prevent a greater number of secondary infections than would one of untargeted prevention. Unless the interventions are very expensive to deliver, they are still likely to be cost-effective relative to alternatives, and necessary to bring the epidemic to a halt. However, they will not be sufficient.[b] The cost-effectiveness of preventive interventions for relatively lower-risk populations improves in a generalized epidemic, but their benefits accrue mainly to the person who uses them, and the cost of providing these services to the entire population can be expensive. The demand for treatment and social assistance also is dramatically higher in generalized epidemics, when HIV is widespread. To ensure both efficiency and equity in a generalized epidemic, the priority for public resources should be on ensuring that the highest-risk behavior is addressed and providing these other services as efficiently as possible, while ensuring equity in access to them by the poor.[c] While these are general principles, the specific types of activities and cost-effectiveness of alternatives in a given setting will vary, depending on a host of epidemiological, social, political, and economic factors.

a. Hethcote and Yorke 1984; Over and Piot 1993.

b. Nagelkerke and others (2002), for example, found that in India (a concentrated epidemic) a sex worker intervention would eventually extinguish the epidemic; in Botswana (a generalized epidemic), no single intervention would have this effect, but a sex worker intervention would reduce HIV prevalence by half.

c. The importance of ensuring HIV prevention among those with the highest-risk behavior in a generalized epidemic is well established in epidemiological research (see Over and Piot 1993; World Bank 1997a) and advocated by UNAIDS (2004b, p. 17) and the Bank's own Regional strategies (for example, World Bank 2000a, p. 19).

the counterfactual of no project. Further, the government contributed nearly twice the counterpart funds agreed to in the credit agreement, a sign of increased commitment.[2] In Brazil, federal programmatic AIDS expenditures rose from an average of $9.3 million annually in 1990–92 to $53 million annually in 1993–2002, during the first and second AIDS projects. During the financial crisis of 1998, AIDS spending *increased*, an indication of strong commitment.[3] The Sexually Transmitted Infection Project (STIP) in Kenya supported the Ministry of Health (MOH) and AIDS control program in the development of a Parliamentary Sessional Paper on HIV/AIDS that defined the policy and legal framework, but there was no political backing for its recommendations. In 1998–99, the project and other donors sponsored meetings with leaders and a parliamentary session at which the president declared AIDS a national disaster, raising commitment and improving implementation. The Argentine AIDS and STD Control Project funded virtually the entire AIDS prevention program, which previously did not exist. The Bank's policy dialogue that highlighted the consequences of inaction was in large part responsible for that country's agreement to borrow and the opening of a national dialogue on AIDS. A number of strategies have been used to raise government commitment in Bank projects (see box 3.2).

Box 3.2: What Has Worked in Building Political Commitment?

- **Epidemiological and Behavioral Surveillance,** especially in nascent and concentrated epidemics when denial is high and the epidemic is "invisible." When the first round of national HIV surveillance in India found that 2 percent of pregnant women in Andhra Pradesh were HIV-positive, the chief minister spoke out publicly and allocated the state's own funds to supplement funding from the national program. The 1989 announcement that 44 percent of brothel-based sex workers in the northern town of Chiang Mai were infected spurred government action in Thailand.[a]

- **Analytic Work,** when done in a way to engender ownership and address the concerns of a relevant audience. The analysis of the economic impact of AIDS in Russia by Ruehl and Pokrovsky (2002) was widely disseminated and raised the commitment of senior officials. In Chad, research, data collection and analysis, and strengthening of the sentinel surveillance system have provided concrete, region-specific information to sensitize officials.

- **Pilot Projects,** which can demonstrate the political and technical feasibility of controversial interventions. The pilot testing of the Cambodian 100 percent condom program among sex workers in Sihanoukville helped to mediate strong discomfort among policy makers about interventions in commercial sex. Channeling resources to areas with effective programs and higher commitment can have a similar effect of demonstrating the political and technical

feasibility of new programs, as in the first India AIDS Control Project.

- **High-Level Policy Dialogue with Public Officials and Key Leaders,** supplemented by study tours to hard-hit countries, public forums, and south-south interactions. Policy dialogue has been important in most cases, including in Ethiopia and other African countries in the MAP (see Chapter 4). Visits by Cambodian officials of the AIDS program, the Ministry of Health, the Ministry of Economy and Finance, and provincial health authorities to India, Kenya, South Africa, and Thailand were reported to have solidified commitment to attacking AIDS, to decentralizing the national program, and to strengthening the health system to care for the rising number of AIDS patients.

- **Leveraging** through project conditionality or design. Conditions in the first India AIDS project created the National AIDS Control Organization (NACO); the Cambodia DCHDP elevated the National AIDS Office within the Ministry of Health to the National Center for HIV/AIDS, Dermatology, and STDS. In Brazil, the project design kept the focus of the program on prevention among the most marginalized groups.

- **Engaging** NGOs to broaden the political constituency for HIV/AIDS control in the long run, as was the case in Argentina, Cambodia, Chad, India, and Uganda. In Brazil, NGOs were already strong advocates following the democratization movement of the 1980s, but the Bank project helped them become implementers as well.

a. World Bank 2000e.

Experience in building political commitment in the first generation of AIDS assistance has highlighted two lessons.

First, commitment to fighting AIDS from top leadership is necessary but not sufficient for results; efforts are needed to raise, broaden, and sustain commitment to fight HIV/AIDS at all levels of government and society. For example, in Brazil, the needle-exchange programs launched by the municipality of Santos and the state of São Paulo in 1989–90 were halted by the Federal Narcotics Council and the political leadership in the State Secretariat of Health, respectively. In the Indian state of Andhra Pradesh, NGOs were hampered in their attempts to work with sex workers because local law enforcement was not fully behind the objectives of the AIDS program. At the time of OED's mission to Cambodia, brothels in Battambang province had been closed for several months, even while government was trying to expand the 100 percent condom use program in commercial sex. When commitment rests with an individual or political regime, it is fragile. The strong commitment of the minister of health to the 1988 National AIDS

An important lesson is that commitment to fighting AIDS must be raised, broadened, and sustained at all levels of government.

Control Project in Zaïre was not enough to overcome the lack of interest in the rest of government. During the Kenya STIP, the National AIDS and STD Control Program was demoted from a department to a division in the Ministry of Health, undercutting its ability to lead the national response. Over the period 1990–92, Brazil's national AIDS control program was disarticulated by a change in government, and Brazil was isolated from the international AIDS community. Thus, commitment to fighting AIDS needs to be more widely entrenched across the political and institutional spectrum than in a head of state or minister of health. It also needs to be sustained: in Uganda and Thailand, a sense of complacency has taken hold with respect to safe sexual behavior because of the perception that prevention has succeeded and that antiretroviral treatment is available. In places such as San Francisco, Sydney, and Amsterdam, as complacency has taken hold, risk behaviors have returned and HIV incidence has risen.

Second, generating political commitment early in an epidemic requires a deliberate strategy. The Indonesia case study found that declaring HIV (an invisible problem at the time) a national "emergency" is not persuasive in the absence of credible data to show it, based on local conditions. Political leaders may be willing to take reasonable measures in a quiet way that does not grab attention, if they are convinced that the potential for spread exists. In a nascent epidemic, public goods are the priority and may not be controversial. Experience shows that analytic work can contribute to generating political commitment when it is based on local data, relevant to key decision makers, and there is ownership of the results—although it is no guarantee of success (see box 3.3).

With respect to AIDS policy, Bank assistance has enhanced the efficiency of national AIDS programs by helping governments to focus on prevention, cost-effectiveness, and prioritization of activities in the face of scarce resources. In the early 1990s, the Government of India approached the Bank with a proposal for an AIDS project that would finance blood safety, even though most

infections could be attributed to heterosexual transmission. Following an intensive dialogue with the Bank and the WHO, the government prepared a National Strategic Plan for 1992–97 that broadened the scope of the project to embrace involvement of states and to focus on awareness-raising among the general population and on behavior change among high-risk groups. The OED case study on Brazil concluded that the national response has been more focused on HIV prevention among groups with high-risk behavior, including marginalized groups such as injecting drug users (IDUs) and sex workers, than might have been the case in the absence of the Bank's involvement.[4]

The Bank also supported key laboratory and treatment monitoring infrastructure—a public good—to improve the efficiency of the government's treatment program. The OED case study on Russia concluded that in the absence of World Bank engagement on HIV/AIDS, the government's approach would have been less targeted to the main drivers of the epidemic and less in tune with international best practice in key areas. The Bank's persistence in policy dialogue promoted and achieved acceptance of harm reduction, the involvement of IDUs and sex workers, emphasis on HIV prevention, and replacement of mass HIV testing of the population with sentinel behavioral and serological surveillance. In Cambodia, the Disease Control and Health Development Project (DCHDP) financed the AIDS response of the Ministry of Health, which embraced prioritization and sequencing of activities to reflect capacity constraints and improve cost-effectiveness. Scarce capacity was focused on the areas where policy and programs can make the biggest difference.

Institutions for the Long-Run AIDS Response
The Bank has helped to create or strengthen robust national and subnational HIV/AIDS institutions. The first India National AIDS Control Project created the National AIDS Control Organization (NACO), a semi-autonomous entity under the Ministry of Health and Family Welfare, and State AIDS Control

Box 3.3: Analytic Work Can Build Commitment, But It Is Not a Panacea

During extended project negotiations over the Russia TB and HIV/AIDS project, the economic impact of AIDS was identified as a potentially effective lever for increasing government commitment. With Department for International Development (DFID) funding, Bank staff teamed with researchers from the Russian Federal AIDS Center to develop a computer model of the economic consequences of the AIDS epidemic.[a] In the most pessimistic scenario, the model forecast a 4 percent decline in GDP by 2010. The results were disseminated in the Russian broadcast and print media, through op-ed articles, letters to the editor, press conferences, and presentations to government. Respondents to the OED case study believe it had a major impact on government commitment at the highest levels. Within a year, President Putin mentioned AIDS for the first time in a speech to a domestic audience.

Epidemiological modeling can be precarious in a nascent epidemic when very little reliable information is available on risk behaviors in the population. In the mid-1990s, HIV prevalence in Indonesia was low, even in high-risk groups, but stakeholders feared that HIV would take off among sex workers there in much the same way that it had in Thailand. Using 1993 as the start date

for the epidemic, a researcher from the U.S. Centers for Disease Control and Prevention (CDC) projected an explosive increase in HIV that got the attention of policy makers. The AIDS and STD Prevention and Management Project was launched in early 1996 in an "emergency" mode to pilot—in two provinces over three years—interventions among sex workers that could be replicated nationally. However, by early 1997 the predicted explosion in HIV had not occurred. The project was not performing well and its rationale and urgency, based on the projections, were undermined. Recently the dialogue has resumed, sparked by rising HIV among IDUs and its spread to sex workers.

In Ethiopia, a 1996 social sector analysis carried out jointly with Ethiopian experts estimated that HIV/AIDS accounted for 7.7 percent of all life years lost nationwide and 17.7 percent in Addis Ababa. It also projected HIV prevalence, AIDS cases, and mortality through 2020 and assessed the impact of the epidemic on health expenditure. However, the analysis left the Ministry of Health unconvinced of the urgency to address the HIV/AIDS epidemic. The validity of the AIDS data was also questioned. Addressing issues in the health system and health conditions that were affecting rural areas following a period of famine and war was felt to be more urgent.

a. Ruehl and others 2002.

Societies (SACS) in all 25 states and 7 union territories.[5] The Argentine LUSIDA project institutionalized HIV prevention within the Ministry of Health, where previously the response had focused almost entirely on treatment and blood safety. While LUSIDA was launched as a separate unit, by the end of the project the functions had been embedded in the Ministry of Health. The Cambodia DCHDP elevated the AIDS control program within the Ministry of Health and roughly doubled the public budget for the National Center for HIV/AIDS, Dermatology, and STDs (NCHADS) over the project's life, financing the program's basic functions (activities, training, supervision) and extending operations to all provinces.[6] The Brazil AIDS projects created HIV/AIDS and STD Control Coordination Units within all 27 states and in 150 municipalities to design and implement AIDS action plans. The Kenya and Uganda STIPs changed the "rules" for project implementation and budgetary transfers to districts, strengthening the institutional response at the district level and raising political commitment.

The Bank has helped build or strengthen national and subnational institutions for the fight against AIDS.

Bank assistance often financed collaborative responses in a small number of other key sectors, usually through its support to the Ministry of Health, to improve the effectiveness of the response on the ground. In Brazil, for example, support to prevention programs among high-risk groups involved inputs from the police and security forces, to move them from punitive policies to become partners in prevention. Condom programs in the prison system required inputs and cooperation from the Ministry of Health, Ministry of Justice, and Ministry of Interior. In India, during the first AIDS project, activities were launched to varying degrees in the ministries of education, information and broadcasting, tourism, mines, labor, social justice and employment, and women's affairs. The Kenya STIP provided information and condoms for security forces, but met resistance from religious groups on sex education in the schools. At the time, Kenyan government commitment was still relatively weak. The Uganda STIP funded condoms and sexually transmitted infection (STI) treatment in the military, among police, and in prisons.[7] The ministries that became engaged tended to be those most severely affected by AIDS and with a comparative advantage in addressing it.[8]

An important lesson arising from this experience is the need to strengthen the institutions and capacity of Ministries of Health, the lead technical and implementation agencies in the national AIDS response. The first phase of the Bank's HIV/AIDS assistance strengthened institutions highly placed within the Ministry of Health (as in Brazil and Cambodia) or high-level autonomous units linked to the Ministry of Health (as in India). Assistance to low-level units of the Ministry (as in Kenya and Zaïre) was relatively less successful, primarily because low organizational prominence often signals low political commitment within or outside the Ministry of Health.[9] Elevating the institutional home of the national response within the Ministry has been a condition for several of the projects (Cambodia, India). In contrast, placing the responsibility for coordination of AIDS projects in the Ministry of Planning in Chad was associated with low ownership by the Ministry of Health, which was charged with implementation.

Strengthening the capacity of Ministries of Health has been central to success.

Enlisting the Nongovernmental Sector[10]

World Bank assistance has encouraged governments to create the mechanisms to enlist NGOs in implementing a national response and has financed capacity building in the nongovernmental sector. Among the 18 completed HIV/AIDS projects, 17 had planned

NGO or community-based organization (CBO) involvement, and at least 15 succeeded (see table 3.1).[11] The stated objective of their involvement was generally to deliver preventive services, in many cases to marginalized, high-risk populations not easily reached by government, and mitigation and care services to hard-hit communities. Mechanisms for government financing of NGOs were set up in Argentina, Brazil, Burkina Faso, Cambodia, Chad, India, Uganda, and even Indonesia, where the legal framework was finalized just before the project was cancelled, but remains for the potential benefit of future activities. The recruitment models of the projects ranged from contracting NGOs for delivery of well-specified interventions in specific locales (as in India and Uganda PAPSCA) to providing funds that could be tapped by NGOs with a proposal that satisfied eligibility criteria in terms of the type of intervention (as in Argentina, Brazil, Chad, and the Uganda STIP), or a combination of these. The Cambodia DCHDP contracted with the Khmer HIV/AIDS Alliance (Khana), with support and guidance from the International HIV/AIDS Alliance, to build the capacity of 40 national NGOs to prepare and implement AIDS interventions. Prior to the project, international NGOs were working throughout the country, . but there were few indigenous NGOs. The Chad Population and AIDS Project created a social fund and a social marketing agency that have engaged local NGOs, decentralized the response, and reformed the way population and HIV/AIDS activities are carried out.

NGOs have played an important role in expanding access to prevention and care among groups at greatest risk of contracting and spreading HIV (high-risk groups) and in empowering them to become key stakeholders. Projects in Brazil particularly, but also in Argentina, Burkina Faso, Cambodia, Chad, and India engaged NGOs to become involved in service delivery to high-risk groups (see figure 3.1). Implementation was most successful and coverage easiest to track when NGOs were enlisted strategically and systematically and when there were parallel efforts to create an enabling environment through legal reform

Table 3.1: Number of NGOs and CBOs Supported by Completed AIDS Projects

Projects[a]	Fiscal year of operation	NGOs	CBOs
Uganda *PAPSCA* (AIDS component only)	1990–1995	4	
Haiti *First Health and AIDS*	1990–2001	7–9	
Rwanda *Health and Population*	1991–2002	13	
India *AIDS I* (6 states[b] only)	1992–1999	149	
Brazil *AIDS I*	1993–1998	181	
Uganda *STIP*	1994–2002		935[c]
Burkina Faso *Population and AIDS Control*	1994–2001		650[c]
Chad *Population and AIDS Control*	1995–2001	18	50–60[d]
Cambodia *DCHDP*	1996–2002	40	
Brazil *AIDS II*	1998–2003	795	

Source: PPARs, ICRs.

a. Projects in Zimbabwe, Bulgaria, and Sri Lanka did not finance any NGOs. The project in Kenya was supposed to, but the NGO contracts were not executed. Figures were unavailable for the projects in Zaïre, Indonesia, and Guinea.

b. Andhra Pradesh, Delhi, Maharashtra, Tamil Nadu, Uttar Pradesh, West Bengal. Of the total, 109 were in Tamil Nadu. These states were visited by OED; NGOs were supported in other states but the number is not known.

c. Includes NGOs and CBOs. A 9-month extension of the Burkina Faso project financed 600 subprojects (included in this figure) through a community-driven development (CDD) pilot in one region (Poni).

d. Includes local associations and local NGOs.

and sensitization of law enforcement. However, NGOs may not always be better placed than government to work with them. In Indonesia, the departments responsible for health, social affairs, and tourism, for example, all have regular contact with female and transvestite sex workers.

The lack of political will, the low capacity of NGOs and CBOs, and the Bank's cumbersome procedures were often major impediments to enlisting civil society. Despite the project's plans, the Kenya STIP provided only limited direct financial support for local NGOs and none for national NGOs, because the Ministry of Health never awarded three "umbrella" contracts to provide support and capacity. Notwithstanding planned capacity-building activities, *the existing capacity of NGOs to design, implement, and evaluate AIDS interventions was overestimated in virtually all countries receiving Bank HIV/AIDS assistance.*[12] Implementation was also delayed because of lack of familiarity with Bank procedures and overly cumbersome procedures in withdrawing funds. The efforts of NGOs in India

and elsewhere were hindered by funding gaps between cycles and sporadic availability of funds brought about by the government's budgetary processes. These issues were found to be common in Bank projects involving NGOs, according to an earlier OED evaluation (Gibbs and others 1999).

Bank assistance has encouraged governments to enlist NGOs in their response to AIDS.

While these activities expanded access to information and services, very little is known about the quality, efficacy, or coverage of the NGO/CBO AIDS activities financed through Bank projects or the degree to which they complement or com-pete with decentralized government pro- grams. NGOs and CBOs can make a major contribution to the national response through their reach, their local expertise, their flexibility, and the potential cost-effectiveness of their activities. However, the efficacy of their efforts is rarely measured; to the extent that Bank project-sponsored NGO AIDS activities have been monitored, results are generally measured in terms of outputs.[13] As a

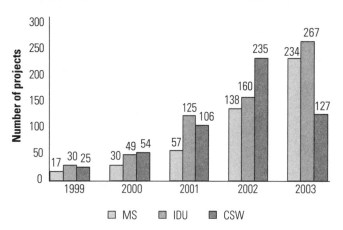

Figure 3.1: Growth in Targeted Interventions for High-Risk Groups in Brazil, 1999–2003

Source: Beyrer and others 2004.

Note: MSM = men who have sex with men; IDU = injecting drug user; CSW = commercial sex worker.

But, the capacity of NGOs was consistently overestimated and the efficacy of NGO and CBO activities supported by Bank assistance has rarely been calculated.

result of the lack of evaluation, there is little evidence about the conditions under which NGO service delivery is more cost-effective than government services in any of the countries. The extent to which NGOs are economizing on scarce public sector capacity or increasing the administrative burden is not known. There is little systematic information on the coverage of NGO- or CBO-delivered AIDS services, their effectiveness in targeting the highest-risk populations, or the extent to which they are complementing decentralized government activities. OED's 1999 evaluation of NGOs in World Bank–supported projects more generally was unable to link NGO or CBO involvement to higher outcomes, institutional development, or sustainability (Gibbs and others 1999).

Prevention targeted to those most likely to spread HIV was planned, but often not implemented.

Three important lessons arise from this experience. *First, even in countries with a strong civil society, the*

Bank and other donors should not take for granted the existence of implementation capacity when it comes to AIDS programs. Second, Bank projects need to develop more flexible project implementation procedures.[14] Third, much remains to be learned about the conditions under which government-NGO partnerships in AIDS programs are effective, efficient, sustainable, and complementary to local government activities.

Service Delivery

The first generation of HIV/AIDS projects primarily supported awareness and prevention in the general population, in high-risk groups, and, in hard-hit countries, medical training and drugs for treatment and care. Two-thirds or more of closed free-standing AIDS projects provided information, education and communication (IEC), STD treatment, condoms, counseling and testing to the general population, IEC and condoms targeted to high-risk groups, and training to medical staff in treatment and care (see figure 3.2).[15] The extent of investment in other treatment, care, and mitigation services depends on the stage of the epidemic and was less consistent. However, public goods, including HIV and behavioral surveillance, operational research, evaluation, and prevention for high-risk groups should be a high priority for government at all stages of the epidemic; the expectation is that these activities should have been universally supported.

The shortfall in prevention targeted to high-risk groups is often the result of a failure to implement planned activities. Almost all of the projects planned some interventions targeted to those most likely to spread HIV through risky behavior,[16] but priority was often given to lower-risk populations in implementation. An objective of the Indonesia project was to pilot interventions to sex workers in two provinces; to the extent that the project was executed before it was cancelled, the emphasis on high-risk groups was diluted. Both the Kenya and Uganda STIPs were to include activities targeted to high-risk populations, but the implementers pitched the program to the wider population.[17] In Argentina, where the main modes of transmission are

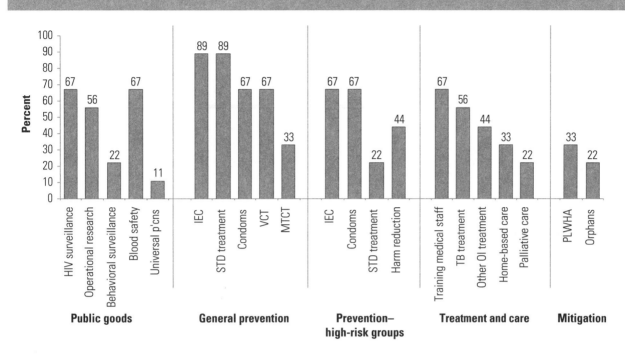

Figure 3.2: Activities and Interventions Supported by Closed Free-Standing AIDS Projects (n = 9)

Source: PPARs and ICRs.

Note: IEC = information, education, and communication; VCT = voluntary counseling and testing; MTCT = prevention of mother-to-child transmission; OI = opportunistic infections; TB = tuberculosis; PLWHA = people living with HIV/AIDS. *Harm reduction programs* (such as needle exchange, bleach for sterilization of injecting equipment, drug rehabilitation) reduce the likelihood of transmission among injecting drug users (IDUs). *Universal precautions* (such as sterilization of medical equipment, use of rubber gloves and other protective gear) prevent transmission in medical settings.

among men who have sex with men (MSM) and IDUs, LUSIDA initially financed NGO interventions for women and children. Only late in the project, with strong encouragement from the Bank and after a new government took office in 2002, were these efforts focused on IDUs and MSM. The failure to implement interventions to those at higher risk is often a product of political and social stigma and lack of the expertise on the part of government and NGOs needed to work with them.

There is often resistance to implementing interventions for high-risk groups, both in government and civil society. *An important lesson is that including these interventions in implementation plans or on a list of interventions to be supported does not ensure that they will be implemented to the extent necessary to reduce HIV transmission.* Strong incentives and supervision by the Bank are critical to ensure that they are implemented.

Evaluation, Monitoring, and Research

Evaluation, monitoring, and research, which are public goods and should be among the highest priorities of government HIV/AIDS programs at all stages of the epidemic, have been under-implemented (see figure 3.2). They can improve the relevance, efficacy, and efficiency of program design and management, are important for accountability and transparency, and can raise political commitment. They take on particular significance in HIV/AIDS programs because of the dearth of information at the country and local levels on the epidemic and on program efficacy.

Evaluation, monitoring, and research have been under-implemented.

Evaluation and research have been grossly neglected in the Bank's HIV/AIDS projects.[18] The interventions supported often have been shown effective in controlled research settings in other countries[19] or promoted on the basis of international notions of what constitutes a good program, without the benefit of locally evaluated pilot interventions. The STIPs in Kenya, Uganda, and Zimbabwe, for example, did not conduct or evaluate any local pilot activity of syndromic STD management or training before going to a national scale. When pilot interventions have been undertaken, they have often expanded without evaluation of their efficacy or cost-effectiveness. The feasibility and efficacy of Cambodia's 100 percent condom use program was demonstrated in Sihanoukville, for example, but it was never fully evaluated and the cost-effectiveness relative to alternatives was not assessed before it was expanded nationwide.[20] The cost-effectiveness of pilot interventions was not evaluated in the first Brazil AIDS project, despite an explicit project component for monitoring and evaluation (M&E). The second Brazil AIDS project, which also featured evaluation as a prominent objective, was equally unsuccessful in getting evaluation done—in a country with lots of capacity to do it. The efficacy and cost-effectiveness of the main programmatic activities of national AIDS control programs supported by the Bank—such as IEC, capacity building, syndromic STD management, and condom programs—by and large have rarely been independently evaluated.

Project budgets for research and analytic work generally have not been used to inform programs, often allocating resources based on demand by researchers rather than for evaluation of high-priority programmatic areas. OED's assessment of the first and second AIDS projects in Brazil found, for example, that the research program was "ad hoc and uncoordinated in its conception," generating a large amount of information that was of limited use for improving program performance and impact.

Project research budgets have not been used to inform the programs.

Bank assistance has helped governments expand coverage of epidemiological and behavioral surveillance, but implementation often has been delayed, and the systems have not been brought to focus on the highest-risk behavior. The Indian HIV surveillance system did not achieve national coverage until 1998, the last year of the first AIDS project; almost all surveillance was of pregnant women, among the last populations in which HIV rises.[21] There was no national behavioral survey until 2002, well into the second AIDS project. National HIV surveillance in Brazil was not achieved until the second AIDS project, in 2000.[22] Only pregnant women are systematically followed, in an epidemic that remains concentrated in IDUs, MSM, sex workers, and other high-risk groups. Brazil's first national behavioral survey did not take place until 1998.[23] National programs in Ethiopia and Uganda, which once systematically monitored HIV in sex workers and truck drivers, no longer do so, despite the Bank's support. In contrast, the Cambodia DCHDP financed government implementation of HIV and behavioral surveillance of high-risk groups, with technical inputs from other donors. Yet at the time of OED's assessment, there was still no nationally representative survey of risk behavior of men and women in Cambodia.

The overwhelming M&E emphasis of Bank-supported AIDS projects has been on monitoring, but it has often been poorly designed, under-implemented, and under-supervised. Key issues that have arisen include:

- There are often too many indicators, but with *no plan* to ensure that the information is collected, *no incentives* to collect it, and *little use of the data* in decision making (Wilson 2004).
- Projects are often launched without *baseline data* that should be critical to their design. The lack of behavioral baseline data in Indonesia led the project to believe that the epidemic was about to take off among sex workers, while it eventually spread through injecting drug use. In almost every country where population-based HIV prevalence surveys have been conducted, levels were lower than those predicted by surveys of pregnant women—with enormous implications for the design of treatment and mitigation programs.[24]

- The indicators are not always *appropriate to the objective* being assessed. For example, lack of understanding of the basic epidemiology of HIV has led many projects to select HIV prevalence as an indicator of program impact (see box 3.4). There have been few attempts to monitor HIV incidence,[25] proxies for incidence, or AIDS mortality. Treatment indicators tend to be in terms of the number of people receiving treatment, not the extent to which they are actually healthier or live longer.

- Repeated national surveys conducted by government and donors *have failed to ensure the comparability of questions across surveys*, making it impossible to track changes in behavior over time—in Cambodia,[26] Chad,[27] India, and Uganda,[28] for example—even when both surveys are sponsored by the same agency. This is evidence of a lack of collaboration among the Bank, sponsoring agencies, and government.[29]

- Project *output data* is too often not monitored; without it, the attribution of changes in outcome to public programs is impossible.[30]

This experience points to multiple needs: (1) to identify fewer monitoring indicators and ensure that they are relevant to objectives; (2) to ensure a viable implementation plan for collecting monitoring data; (3) to commission independent evaluation of key program components; (4) to provide incentives to borrowers and Bank staff to ensure that monitoring and evaluation take place and are used for decisions—such as by linking the availability of M&E results to key programmatic decisions and to continued funding; (5) to improve the coordination among government, donors, and technical assistance to ensure the comparability of large population-based surveys over time; and (6) to structure research and analytic work in such a way that it will inform key programmatic decisions.

Monitoring has suffered from too many or inappropriate indicators, lack of baseline data, and failure to ensure comparability over time.

Outcomes and Impacts

This section reviews evidence of trends in knowledge and behavior in a few of the countries that have received World Bank assistance. In many of the countries, the Bank was not the only donor supporting HIV/AIDS control and was part of a broader collaboration.[31] It is not possible in

---

Box 3.4: The Limited Usefulness of HIV Prevalence as an Indicator of Program Impact

The goal of HIV/AIDS prevention programs is to reduce the number of new HIV infections, or *incidence*. However, measuring incidence is complicated and expensive; it involves monitoring a cohort of HIV-negative people over time to count how many become HIV positive. Trends in knowledge and risk behaviors are predictors of HIV incidence and easier to monitor—for example, changes in the onset of sexual activity among youth, the frequency of sex with casual or commercial sex partners, condom use in casual and commercial sex, and injecting drug use behaviors.

Most national AIDS programs monitor the percentage of the population infected with HIV, or HIV *prevalence*. The number of HIV-positive people can rise or fall, depending on whether more people become infected than die over a given period. When HIV prevalence "stabilizes," it means that new infections and deaths are in balance: both could be high or both could be low.[a] HIV prevalence declines when deaths exceed new infections. Thus, neither "maintaining stable HIV prevalence" nor "reducing HIV prevalence" (both of which are often the objectives of HIV/AIDS projects and national plans) indicate success in prevention programs, since they reveal nothing about the number of new infections.

Changes in HIV prevalence are a useful proxy for HIV incidence only when AIDS mortality is expected to be low—for example, early in an epidemic or among young adults who have only recently initiated sexual activity or drug-injecting behavior. A third instance would be if all HIV-positive people could be kept alive. Then HIV prevalence would *rise* at a rate exactly equal to the number of new infections. While not generally useful in measuring the success of prevention programs, in mature epidemics HIV prevalence is useful in predicting the demand for treatment and related services. Among pregnant women, it measures the need for services to prevent HIV transmission to children.

a. Wawer and others 1997.

most cases to attribute these trends to public policy in general —as supported by the Bank or implemented by government or donors— because monitoring of the outputs has been poor, making it difficult to link outputs to outcomes, and establishing a counterfactual is also difficult. Knowledge and behavior can change based on the personal experience of individuals whose friends or family members contract HIV or die of AIDS. Nevertheless, it is useful to know whether trends in these countries that the Bank has supported have moved in the correct direction, even without clean attribution to government. Even then, poor monitoring and lack of coordination among donors and government in data collection have resulted in limited availability of trend data.

It is difficult to isolate the impact of the Bank on outcomes, partly because of poor monitoring and evaluation.

Knowledge and awareness of HIV/AIDS. Knowledge of modes of preventing HIV has increased in Burkina Faso, Kenya, and Uganda, countries that received early support from the Bank and many other donors (figure 3.3a). The percentage of respondents who spontaneously report condom use as a way to avoid AIDS has increased modestly in Burkina Faso and Kenya, but has more than doubled in Uganda. The percentage of women in Chad responding correctly to a prompted question on condom use to avoid AIDS[32] has tripled in three years. The share of 15–19-year-olds who have never had sex has been creeping upward (figure 3.3b), among both men and women, reducing their exposure to the risk of HIV/AIDS (as well as to pregnancy and other STDs).[33] Unfortunately, the results on other measures of knowledge, sexual behavior, and condom use in risky sex — the variables of key interest to AIDS programs— are difficult to compare between the 1998 and 2003 surveys. Even in these countries where changes have occurred, the counterfactual is elusive. Would these parameters have changed even in the absence of the Bank's support?

In Tamil Nadu state of India the percentage of ever-married women of reproductive age

who had heard of AIDS rose from 23 to 87 percent between 1992/93 and 1998/99; the percentage who spontaneously reported that condoms prevent HIV transmission rose from 3 to 10 percent.[34] In the state of Maharashtra (with the second-highest project expenditures), AIDS awareness rose from 19 to 61 percent and spontaneous reports of condoms for prevention rose from 6 to 12 percent over that period. Per capita state spending on HIV/AIDS in India over the 1990s is associated with higher levels of knowledge of HIV/AIDS transmission in as well as higher receipt of interpersonal information on HIV and condoms in 2001 (see box 3.5), although there was no relationship between spending and risk behavior.[35]

Risk behavior. In Kenya, the share of men who ever used a condom rose from 34 to 49 percent between 1993 and 2000;[36] the share with more than one sexual partner declined from 27 to 19 percent between 1998 and 2000, while the percent who used a condom in their last episode of sex with a non-regular partner rose from 43 to 63 percent. In Uganda, condom use with non-regular sexual partners rose modestly from 1995–2000 in association with STIP support for condom social marketing—from 20 to 38 percent among women and from 36 to 59 percent among men.

The Indian state of Tamil Nadu received the largest share of funds during the first National AIDS Control Project (1992–99). Between 1996 and 1999, the percentage of truck drivers in urban Tamil Nadu reporting commercial sex dropped by half, from 40 to 20 percent, and condom use among truck drivers who bought sex rose from 55 to 80 percent by 1999, and 94 percent by 2001.[37]

Consistent condom use among sex workers in urban areas of Cambodia more than doubled, from less than 40 percent to more than 90 percent between 1997 and 2001 (see figure 3.4). Over the same period, the percent of high-risk men who used brothel-based sex workers in the past 12 months declined by 55–65 percent (NCHADS behavioral surveillance data, cited in OED 2004a). The $4.9

Figure 3.3a: Among Respondents Who Had Heard of AIDS, Percentage Spontaneously Reporting Condom Use as a Way to Avoid AIDS

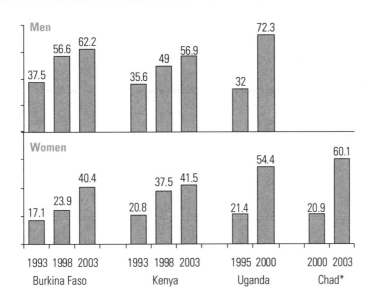

*For Chad, answers are from a prompted question on condom use (not spontaneous).

Figure 3.3b: Percentage of 15–19-Year-Olds Who Have Never Had Sex

Source: Demographic and Health Survey data (Burkina Faso, Kenya, Uganda) and OED 2005c (Chad).

Box 3.5: The Relationship Between Public Spending, AIDS Knowledge, and Receipt of Information in India

During the first National AIDS Control Project (1992–99), state and union territory governments spent a mean of Rs.13.1 (US$0.29) per capita on all HIV/AIDS programs and Rs.3.2 (US$0.07) per capita on HIV/AIDS public awareness. Has there been any impact on awareness and knowledge?

A study of the relationship between awareness and knowledge from the 2001 India National Behavioral Surveillance Survey (BSS) and levels of state per capita spending on AIDS and AIDS awareness from 1992–2001 found that higher state spending on HIV/AIDS programs in the 1990s is associated with higher HIV prevention knowledge and access in 2001:

➡ A 3-rupee (US$0.07) increase in public HIV/AIDS spending per capita (1992–99) is associated with a 1 percentage point increase in HIV/AIDS prevention knowledge and in reported receipt of general information and condom-specific information.

➡ A 3-rupee increase in public spending on AIDS awareness is associated with a 3 percentage point increase in re-

ported receipt of general and condom-specific HIV/AIDS information.

The study controlled for other factors that also might have affected AIDS awareness over that period: state-level marital status and literacy levels from the 1991 and 2001 Indian census; state income (gross national product, GNP) per capita; the extent of the AIDS epidemic (proxied by the percentage of respondents who knew someone with AIDS); and the gender and area of residence of the respondents. These results are suggestive of an impact of public information, but would need to be confirmed by more formal evaluation linking the project's IEC inputs to changes in knowledge.

Questions on *misinformation* about AIDS were also asked in the BSS, but the results were not reported in the final report. Release of the data to researchers would allow further analysis of the possible impact of public information spending on reducing misinformation.

Source: Subramanian 2003.

million AIDS component of the Cambodia DCHDP credit funded roughly half of the costs of the government's national AIDS program over the life of the project (1996–2002), which emphasized raising condom use among high-risk groups. Roughly two-thirds of all HIV/AIDS spending in Cambodia over the same period was from U.N. agencies, bilateral and multilateral donors, and international NGOs, most of it implemented outside of the Ministry of Health.

Epidemiological outcomes. In several countries supported by the Bank, HIV prevalence in specific population groups has declined. However, in the absence of information about HIV incidence or AIDS mortality, it is impossible to interpret these results in terms of reducing the spread of HIV. Indeed, in countries like Brazil where ever larger numbers of AIDS patients are receiving antiretroviral therapy, HIV prevalence would be expected to remain at

Trends in HIV prevalence are not indicative of prevention success.

current levels or even climb if treatment efforts succeed in reducing mortality.

STIs in Kenya and Zimbabwe appear to have declined during the course of the STIPs. In Nairobi, syphilis prevalence among women attending antenatal clinics declined from 7 percent in 1995 to 5 percent in 2000. From 1996 to 2000, the share of reported cases of vaginal and urethral discharge declined compared with other STI syndromes, a decline that corresponds to strengthened training and syndromic management of STIs sponsored by the project. Moreover, the share of these infections increased in 2001 when drug availability fell following the end of the project (OED 2002, Annex B, p. 27, citing, for share of discharge, NASCOP 2002). In Zimbabwe, STI drug availability (supported by the project) and training of health practitioners (supported by other donors) rose dramatically while reported cases of bacterial STIs declined during the life of the project. It cannot be discerned whether these changes in STI incidence had any effect on HIV incidence in the two countries.[38]

AIDS morbidity, mortality, and other welfare outcomes. Although a high percentage of projects have invested in strengthening treatment and care of AIDS patients and, in hard-hit countries, assistance to people living with HIV/AIDS (PLWHA) and orphans, there has been very little evidence collected on the outcomes of these activities. One of the few exceptions is the Brazil AIDS program's monitoring of AIDS patients. The Bank provided major support for setting up and improving the quality of laboratories and testing facilities, including services to evaluate and monitor the viral and immune status of HIV/AIDS patients, in order to improve the efficiency and efficacy of the national treatment program. The death rate of AIDS patients has declined dramatically, particularly since the broad introduction of triple antiretroviral therapy (see figure 3.5).

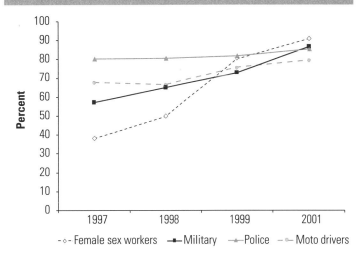

Figure 3.4: Increase in Consistent Condom Use among High-Risk Groups in Urban Cambodia, 1997–2001

- ◇ - Female sex workers — ■ — Military — ▲ — Police — ● — Moto drivers

Source: NCHADS behavioral surveillance data, as cited in OED 2004a.

The Reach, Perceived Quality, and Relevance of the Bank's Analytic Work on HIV/AIDS

In 1996, President Wolfensohn called for the World Bank to become a "Knowledge Bank." As was seen in Chapter 2, there has been an extreme lack of information on most aspects of the AIDS epidemic and available information has changed rapidly. Further, in the area of AIDS, the Bank faced a problem of low client demand for assistance; some types of information can have a major impact on generating commitment. Knowledge was one of the four pillars of the Africa Region's most recent AIDS strategy, which included several actions to improve access to information.[39]

To measure the scope of the Bank's analytic work on AIDS, OED conducted an inventory. An important finding is that the Bank's analytic work on HIV/AIDS is not very accessible, even for those within the institution. It is not systematically recorded in the internal record-keeping system, nor does any existing Web site pull together all of the material in a comprehensive way.[40] The inventory of analytic work summarized in Appendix E is based on responses to a questionnaire sent to task managers of AIDS projects and to AIDS researchers, and from a search of publica-

tions and document databases maintained by the Bank (intranet, Business Warehouse, ImageBank), bibliographies of AIDS project appraisal documents, and official recording systems (SAP). Because of the irregular reporting conventions and recall biases that can be expected, this inventory is an indicative rather than a definitive list.

Little evidence has been collected on the effect of AIDS treatment and mitigation measures on welfare outcomes.

Using key products in this inventory, OED assessed the extent to which the Bank's analytic work on HIV/AIDS is reaching key internal and external audiences, the perceived technical quality of the work, and its usefulness through surveys conducted for two key audiences: (1) 212 Bank staff working in the human development sectors who were attending the Human Development Forum in November 2003;[41] and (2) 466 delegates at the 13th International Conference on AIDS and STDs in Africa (ICASA), held in Nairobi, Kenya, in September 2003.[42] Recognition of and access to the Bank's analytic work as well as its perceived quality are key dimensions of efficacy. The audiences reached and the perceived usefulness of specific reports to them is a measure of their relevance. In both

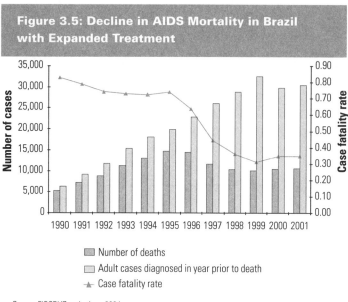

Figure 3.5: Decline in AIDS Mortality in Brazil with Expanded Treatment

- Number of deaths
- Adult cases diagnosed in year prior to death
- Case fatality rate

Source: FIOCRUZ and others 2004.

surveys, respondents were first asked if they had heard of a specific report and, if so, whether they had read it. All respondents who had read the report were asked to rate the technical quality and its usefulness to their work.[43] A list of the analytic work that was included and detailed results are in Appendix F. The main findings are as follows.

The Bank's analytic work on HIV/AIDS is not very accessible.

The Bank's analytic work on AIDS is not reaching key audiences in the African AIDS community. Government policy makers had low recognition and readership of most of the studies, including those for which they are the main intended audience. Their levels of recognition and readership were akin to the levels of national and local NGOs. The respondents with the highest recognition and readership were other donors; academia recognized many of the studies at the same rate but had read fewer. Surprisingly, the international NGOs had relatively low recognition and very low readership—only slightly higher than policy makers and national NGOs.

Lack of French translations and Internet access are barriers to African users of Bank research.

The non-availability of these reports in French and low access to the Internet are major barriers to greater access in Sub-Saharan Africa. Among the delegates who completed a French questionnaire, only 29 percent could read technical AIDS articles in English without difficulty; 59 percent could read them with difficulty, and 12 percent not at all. Among the studies that had been published in French, the Francophone respondents had equal or higher recognition compared with English-speaking respondents, but the readership for reports only available in English was substantially lower for French-speaking delegates. With respect to the Internet, while 90 percent of delegates had some access, only half of African respondents had regular Internet access (at home or at their offices), compared with 94 percent of non-Africans.

Bank staff who should be most familiar with cross-sectoral analytic work and toolkits—particularly the task team leaders for AIDS projects—often are not familiar enough. Although about 80 percent of the 29 task team leaders had read the Bank's Policy Research Report, *Confronting AIDS*, only 30 percent had read the World Bank/UNAIDS manual on M&E of AIDS programs, and only 55 percent had read the MAP support toolkit.[44] Task team leaders for AIDS projects are being asked to work across sectors, yet only 30 percent had read *AIDS and Education: A Window of Hope*, and 35 percent had read the paper on social protection of orphans and other vulnerable children in Africa.

Regional human development staff are most likely to read AIDS reports about their Regions (rather than reports on the global problem), and sector staff are most likely to read reports about AIDS in their sectors. Nevertheless, readership of some non-Regional reports was relatively high. Among the four Regions for which there were adequate staff responses (Africa, East Asia, South Asia, Eastern Europe and Central Asia), a higher percentage of South Asian human development staff had read the main (non-Regional) AIDS reports and were equally likely to have read about AIDS in Thailand as respondents from the East Asia Region.

Among respondents who had read the reports, both the international community

and Bank human development staff gave them high marks on technical quality and usefulness. Half or more Bank respondents rated the quality of 8 out of 10 reports as high or very high, and 4 reports received high or very high ratings by 70 percent or more of respondents. Among the ICASA respondents, technical quality ratings were even higher, from 60 to 79 percent high or very high. Bank staff rated the 10 studies as either useful or one of the most useful from 31 to 65 percent of the time, but only 3 surpassed 50 percent.[45] The ICASA respondents found the papers much more useful than Bank staff, rating them very to most useful from 57 to 75 percent of the time. Five of the 12 papers received 70 percent or higher very or most useful, and five others, 60 percent or higher.

Bank reports get high marks for technical quality and usefulness.

Chapter 4: Evaluation Highlights

- The Africa MAP has enlisted more than two dozen countries to launch major AIDS activities.
- Political commitment has risen, the number of actors has grown, and activities are being scaled up.
- The MAP relies on national AIDS strategies for setting priorities, but most do not prioritize or cost activities.
- The MAP design called for increased supervision and M&E over other projects, but this appears not to be the case.
- Civil society is engaged but objectives are unclear, activities are often not prioritized, and cost-effectiveness is not considered.
- The mechanisms for political mobilization may not be well suited for ensuring efficient and effective program implementation.
- It is too early to assess whether these risks have been mitigated and the projects are meeting their objectives.

An Assessment of Ongoing Assistance: The Africa MAP

From September 2000 through the end of June 2004, 29 country-level Africa MAP projects were approved, amounting to roughly $1 billion in commitments, of which about $255 million had been disbursed.[1] Since all of these projects are still active and some only recently launched, information on their effectiveness is not yet available. As these projects are completed, OED will evaluate them individually, in depth, through project assessments. This chapter reviews the objectives of the Africa MAP program, the assumptions underlying the rationale, and the validity of the assumptions, based on the evidence from previous chapters. This is followed by an assessment of the program's design and risks, based on available evidence from implementation to date.

The assessment of this chapter uses the findings and lessons from the first generation of completed projects (based on PPARs and case studies) of the previous chapters; a review of program and project documents (including self-evaluations sponsored by ACT*africa*); OED's field-based case study of Ethiopia; data on project implementation to date collected from current task team leaders,[2] SAP, and other internal data systems; interviews with task team leaders and with country directors on their views of key issues in program design and implementation (see Appendixes I and J); a desk review of national AIDS strategies in 21 MAP and 5 non-MAP countries; and OED's recent evaluation of community-based and community-driven development (CBD/CDD; CDD or CD, as applicable, for the remainder of this review) development (OED 2005a).

The Objectives, Design, and Risks of the Africa MAP

The overarching objective of the Africa MAP is to prevent HIV infection and mitigate its impact. According to design documents, the goal of the first phase of the 10–15 year program of support is "to intensify action against the epidemic in as many countries as possible," with two explicit objectives: (a) to scale up prevention, care, support, and treatment programs and (b) to prepare countries to cope with the impact of those who develop AIDS over the next decade.[3] The development objective of the first envelope of $500 million (MAP I), approved in September 2000, is to increase access to HIV/AIDS prevention, care, and treatment programs, with emphasis on vulnerable groups (such as youth,

Box 4.1: The Design and Eligibility Criteria of the Africa MAP

The first and second Africa MAPs were each a $500 million envelope from which individual countries or Regional programs could access IDA resources, provided that each country satisfied certain eligibility criteria. The projects are intended to represent the first phase of a 10-to-15-year commitment of assistance to fight HIV/AIDS on the continent.

The strategy and project template focus on putting into place the machinery to "get things done," and relatively less on what should be undertaken. The MAP attempts to accelerate implementation through project design that will ensure: enhanced political commitment; multisectoral activities and coordination; a substantial increase in financial resources; creation of the fiduciary infrastructure to accelerate disbursements, with contracting of key project management activities, when necessary; and channeling of a large share of project funds directly to NGOs and communities.

Countries that wish to participate in the Africa MAP must meet four eligibility criteria (World Bank 2000b):

- Evidence of a strategic approach to HIV/AIDS, developed in a participatory manner, or a participatory strategic planning process underway, with a clear roadmap and timetable
- Existence of a high-level HIV/AIDS coordinating body, with broad representation of key stakeholders from all sectors, including people living with HIV/AIDS

- Government commitment to quick implementation arrangements, including channeling grant funds directly to communities, civil society, and the private sector[a]
- Agreement by the government to use multiple implementation agencies, especially NGOs and CBOs.

Provided that these are met, the MAP is committed to finance the overall national HIV/AIDS strategy. In an annex, the MAP project appraisal document highlights different priorities for countries with concentrated and generalized epidemics, but there is no attempt to prioritize activities or objectives in implementation; this is already assumed to have occurred in the national strategy. The components in the vast majority of MAP projects are organized around the funding of an implementing entity—the public sector and civil society, for example—rather than the type of intervention or objective. Of the first two dozen Africa MAP projects, only four have components that reflect the type of activity or objective.[b]

The purpose of the project template approach is to expedite project preparation. To compensate, the projects are supposed to have a higher budgetary coefficient on supervision, strong M&E (representing 5–10 percent of project costs) that enhances "learning by doing," and mid-course adjustments.

a. During MAP II, this was strengthened to say that subcontracting of key implementation arrangements would be the norm and that government agrees "to channel grant funds directly to communities, civil society, and the private sector, and to have effective procurement mechanisms in place" (World Bank 2001b, p. 15).

b. The activity-oriented components are: knowledge management (Ghana); targeted interventions (Burkina Faso); orphans (Burundi); and three components in Malawi on prevention and advocacy, treatment, care and support, and impact mitigation. Malawi is also the only MAP with a component exclusively for monitoring, evaluation, and research. (In most of the other projects this function is embedded in the project management or coordination component.)

Most MAP design features and eligibility criteria seek to raise political commitment and mobilization.

women of childbearing age, and other groups at high risk). MAP II, approved in February 2002, had, in addition, the objectives of: (i) pilot testing antiretroviral therapy (ART); and (ii) supporting cross-border initiatives. Each individual country project also has specific development objectives "as stated in national strategic plans."[4] The MAP has combined the use of country "eligibility criteria" and a project

design template to meet these goals and objectives (see box 4.1).

The MAP strategy and mechanisms can be related to the elements of development effectiveness used by OED—relevance, efficacy, efficiency, institutional development, and sustainability (see table 4.1).[5] Most of the eligibility criteria and project design features attempt to ensure broad political commitment and mobilization (affecting both the relevance and sustainability of activities) and to engage civil society and actors in all sectors in implementation (effecting greater access to services). A

Table 4.1: Linking MAP Strategy and Mechanisms to Development Effectiveness

Measure of development effectiveness	Objective	MAP mechanisms to ensure the objective	
		Eligibility criteria	Project design feature
Relevance	Build political commitment	• Participatory approach to strategy development • High-level coordinating body • Commitment to quick implementation arrangements and multiple implementing agencies	• High-level policy dialogue • Multisectoral response (commitment from more sectors than health) • Enlist NGOs, CBOs, communities (political mobilization)
	Implement activities that are appropriate to the stage of the epidemic, locally adapted, technically sound, in agreement with policies.	• National AIDS strategy	• Learning by doing and strong M&E
Efficacy	Wider coverage of interventions		• More finance • More implementers (non-health sectors, civil society)
	Implement the most effective interventions	• National AIDS strategy[a]	• Monitoring, evaluation, research
Efficiency	Economize on scarce capacity in the short run while expanding it in the long run	• Commitment to quick implementation arrangements and multiple implementing agencies • HIV/AIDS coordinating body	• Tap capacity of other ministries, NGOs, CBOs • Capacity-building activities • Contracting out management functions
	Prioritize activities to ensure cost-effectiveness and allocative efficiency (financing public goods, addressing externalities)	• National AIDS strategy	• Learning by doing: monitoring, evaluation, research
Institutional development[b]	Improve intersectoral coordination	• Multisectoral HIV/AIDS coordinating body	
	Create mechanisms to enlist civil society	• Commitment to multiple implementing agencies	• Capacity building for civil society
	Ensure transparency and accountability		• Fiduciary mechanisms
Sustainability[c]	Political commitment and ownership by civil society	• [see political commitment above]	• [see political commitment above]
	Financial, economic, technical resilience	• National AIDS strategy	

a. It was also an assumption of the approach that pilot interventions have been shown locally effective.

b. The ability of a country to make more efficient, equitable, and sustainable use of its human, financial, and natural resources through: (a) better definition, stability, transparency, enforceability, and predictability of institutional arrangements and/or (b) better alignment of the mission and capacity of an organization with its mandate.

c. The resilience to risk of net benefit flows over time, including technical, financial, economic, social and environmental resilience, government and other stakeholder ownership, institutional support and resilience to exogenous influences.

The main risks identified by the MAP were slow implementation and low coverage, due to weak commitment and capacity.

number of mechanisms are designed to economize on scarce capacity—improving efficiency by contracting out management and fiduciary functions, for example. To assure technical efficacy, cost-effectiveness, and allocative efficiency, the MAP approach is highly dependent on three criteria and design features—the rigor of the national AIDS strategy, the assumption that pilot projects have been tested, and the implementation of intensive M&E and learning by doing. Unlike previous AIDS projects, the management or coordination of the MAP projects in most cases rests with a multisectoral body, and Ministry of Health activities are financed through that body.[6]

The Africa MAP was classified in design documents as a high-risk program, and efforts were made to mitigate the main risks through eligibility criteria and program design. The main risks were described as slow implementation and low coverage of interventions, due to low political commitment and implementation capacity.[7] The MAP II proposal also acknowledged a risk that the community-based component could reinforce existing inequalities, particularly with respect to implementation of antiretroviral therapy.

However, several risks with respect to technical efficacy, efficiency, and sustainability were not assessed in the MAP design documents. Among these are the risks that:

Other risks to efficacy, efficiency, and sustainability were not addressed in MAP design.

• National strategic plans, which are the blueprint for the activities to be financed, may not direct resources to activities with the largest impact or may not have assessed adequately the sustainability of the program. This could result in: (a) allocation of scarce capacity to less effective, efficient, or sustainable activities, including those that are the least politically objectionable and that do not address the main drivers of the epidemic; or (b) support of unsustainable ac-

tivities, with adverse consequences for the long-run support and viability of NGOs and civil society and, in the case of treatment programs, for development of viral resistance.

• Communities may not know "what's best" in terms of implementation of interventions, and thus select those with low efficacy, that do not exploit any comparative advantage in implementation, and for which they lack the technical expertise. Large transfers have the potential to result in maldistribution of resources within the community, the expectation of further transfers, and elite capture.

• Multisectoral AIDS commissions may attempt to implement rather than coordinate, and increase red tape, slowing the response and institutional development of key ministries that are already engaged, such as the Ministry of Health and the military. Scarce capacity in some sectors may be diverted from important poverty-reduction activities in which they have a mandate and capacity to low-impact anti-AIDS activities in which they have no capacity or comparative advantage in implementation.

• The intensified M&E and supervision that was to compensate for a more thorough technical analysis of activities during preparation may not be implemented—as has been the case in most previous AIDS projects—resulting in little learning by doing and reduced efficiency and efficacy.

Based on the poor performance of past AIDS and HNP projects on implementing M&E, the lack of experience of the Bank in working through multisectoral AIDS commissions,[8] and the findings of the OED evaluations of CBD/CDD and social funds on effectiveness and/or sustainability, all four of these critical risks should have been rated *high*. There were no design elements of the overall MAP to mitigate these risks, which could theoretically compromise effectiveness even if greater implementation is achieved.

Were the Assumptions Valid?

The focus of the MAP on rapidly scaling up interventions was based on the assumption, first, that past efforts to fight AIDS in Africa had been unsuccessful, and, second, that there are five principal reasons for this failure: (a) inadequate finance, (b) lack of political commitment, (c) failure to achieve broader coverage of successful pilot interventions, (d) inability to get resources to communities, and (e) too narrow a focus on the health sector as the main actor. Implicit in the third reason is a sixth assumption: that in each country, pilot interventions have been evaluated, found effective, and are suitable for wider replication.

Evidence from this evaluation strongly supports the assumption that the lack of political commitment was the most important constraint to action—not only in Africa, but in all developing regions. The lack of finance and failure to achieve broader coverage of services, cited as separate constraints by the MAP, were also valid, but fundamentally a reflection of low commitment. In the course of researching the Bank's response to AIDS, OED did not find any instance in which a client requested HIV/AIDS assistance and the Bank declined to provide it. Attempts to provide HIV/AIDS assistance to countries where commitment was weak (such as in Indonesia and Zaïre) were not successful. The MAP's heavy emphasis on commitment and political mobilization in design was warranted, based on the previously low success rate of engaging African countries.

However, several other assumptions are not well substantiated. The first of these was that past efforts to control the epidemic in Africa had been unsuccessful. On the one hand, there was not at that time, nor is there currently, much evidence concerning the extent to which the trajectory of the epidemic is different than what might have happened in the absence of government and donor action. Except for a few research settings, HIV incidence and AIDS morbidity and mortality have not been tracked in Sub-Saharan Africa, and there are few population-based surveys that have tracked behavior over time. No studies have convincingly linked outputs of government AIDS programs and donors to these outcomes on a national scale. On the other hand, the Bank's HIV/AIDS assistance in Burkina Faso, Chad, Kenya, and Zimbabwe largely achieved its objectives. Several key interventions were implemented nationwide, though in some cases they were judged not to be sustainable.[9] Substan-

tial institutional development was built in Burkina Faso (for the AIDS component), Chad, Kenya, and Uganda. There was clearly too little effort to control the epidemic across the continent, but at least in the countries studied by OED where the Bank was engaged on a national scale, usually in collaboration with other donors, it would not be correct to say that efforts have been "unsuccessful."

OED could find no evidence to support the assumption that lack of success in controlling AIDS in Africa has been caused by a failure to get resources to communities. The failure to mobilize political support from communities in some instances in the past may have been a missed opportunity in generating higher-level political commitment; however, most of the case studies of generating high-level commitment do not involve a push from the bottom or funding of communities. Brazil is the main exception. In that case, the bottom-up political mobilization for fighting AIDS emerged from an indigenous democratization movement of the 1980s; AIDS policy did not precipitate this movement. While there are certainly examples of successful HIV interventions implemented by communities, OED could find no evidence that community-driven AIDS interventions are systematically more effective or more cost-effective than those implemented by NGOs, government, or even the private sector.

Nor does OED find that an over-emphasis on the health sector was a reason for lack of success. While it may be the case that other key sectors could use more resources to fight the epidemic, OED found no evidence that reallocation from health to other sectors would have improved the effectiveness of the response in the countries studied. OED found no instances in which the response of other sectors was as

The MAP correctly focused on the lack of political commitment as the most important constraint to action in Africa.

OED found no evidence that failure to get resources to communities was responsible for lack of previous success in AIDS control.

powerful as that of the health sector, and in most cases health ministries have worked with the most critical government agencies in other sectors.[10] To the extent that the AIDS response is assigned to a low-level unit within the Ministry of Health with weak capacity, it reflects the low priority and political support of AIDS control. Bank assistance to strengthen the capacity of the health sector improved the AIDS response when political commitment was present. OED has not found examples of a strong response that bypassed the health sector or that was led by a sector other than health.

The assumption that there are many pilot activities that have been locally evaluated, found effective, and are suitable for wider replication is not well supported by task team leader interviews. In 42 percent of African MAP countries, the task team leaders were unaware of any previous local pilot testing of an HIV/AIDS intervention suitable for wider-scale replication. In the other 58 percent, they reported that fewer than four interventions had been locally tested. In more than half of these cases, only a single pilot project was cited. In about a third of the cases, one of the pilot projects was a CD-type intervention that did not necessarily directly address HIV/AIDS.

Fewer pilot projects have been evaluated than assumed by the MAP.

Two constraints to better performance were important in the first generation of assistance and are not among the explicit assumptions in the MAP design documents: (a) severely *limited capacity* within government and civil society; and (b) *conflict, political instability, and governance* problems. The MAP acknowledges capacity constraints by invoking mechanisms to accelerate disbursements and contract out some management activities and through project components that intend to build capacity on a large scale.[11] Conflict, political instability, and governance problems are responsible for unsatisfactory project outcomes in Haiti and Zaïre, and the failure of

Project preparation was shortened in MAP I, but the delay to effectiveness increased.

the fully prepared Nigeria STI project to be negotiated. Among completed projects, there are no examples to date of Bank support for an effective AIDS response in countries with civil conflict or that are in arrears, even though these countries may be those most susceptible to the rapid spread of HIV.

Evidence on Implementation to Date[12]

Project preparation—which normally might have taken one or two years for each project—was considerably shortened, but with consequences for the delay from project approval to effectiveness (see box 4.3). The MAP compensates for rapid preparation through a project design that relies on the technical rigor of the national strategic plan, learning by doing, and more intense supervision.[13] While more than 80 percent of MAP I and II task team leaders thought that the preparation time was sufficient for national ownership of the project, there is evidence that important activities were squeezed. Only 58 percent of MAP I task team leaders reported that the time was adequate to ensure quality project design, for example. The first joint World Bank and UNAIDS Progress Review in June/July 2001 found that the substantial delays between project approval and effectiveness in MAP I were in part the result of inadequate preparation (World Bank 2001c). The review recommended that operational manuals, first-year implementation programs, and the process for application and review of community grants should be finalized prior to project approval. These and other actions to improve project preparation resulted in a doubling of preparation time between MAP I and II, but a shortening of the time between preparation and effectiveness. MAP II task team leaders were more likely to report conducting an institutional analysis or an NGO capacity assessment during project preparation than were MAP I team leaders. Only 17 percent of task team leaders reported that analytic work was conducted prior to project approval for MAP I, and while this number rose to 42 percent among MAP II team leaders, it was still relatively low.

Box 4.2: Did the MAP Reduce Project Preparation Time?

One of the important rationales of the Africa MAP for using a project design template was to accelerate implementation by reducing the time it takes from project identification through Board approval (preparation). OED compared the preparation time and time from approval to effectiveness[a] of 56 completed and active AIDS projects (23 of which were Africa MAP projects) with 61 completed or active (non-AIDS) health projects in the same countries.

The six Caribbean MAP projects had the shortest total time from identification through effectiveness (14.8 months), followed by Africa MAP I (16.2 months, see figure). However, total time rose to 21.8 months in Africa MAP II. The 12 African MAP I projects had the shortest preparation time of any group of AIDS projects (7.7 months), but also the longest time from approval to effectiveness (8.5 months). Preparation time doubled during MAP II, to 16.5 months, although this seems to have reduced average time to ef-

fectiveness by about 40 percent. The total time from identification until effectiveness for MAP II projects is only about two months less than other African AIDS projects, and five months less than AIDS projects in other Regions. Three-quarters of non-MAP African AIDS projects were health or social protection projects with an AIDS component, requiring preparation for all activities, perhaps explaining the longer preparation time.

AIDS projects worldwide also had substantially lower total time from identification through effectiveness (21.7 months) than did (non-AIDS) health projects in the same countries (28.7 months, not shown). This is mainly due to a year's shorter preparation time for AIDS projects in Africa (13.9 months, compared with 25.6 months for African health projects). Excluding African AIDS projects and the Caribbean MAP projects, AIDS and health projects elsewhere in the world have roughly the same total time from identification to effectiveness (26–27 months).

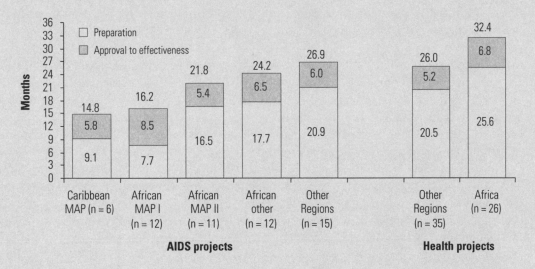

a. "Effectiveness" is a legal term that refers to the time when the borrower may begin to draw from World Bank loans. The borrower must approve the loan or credit agreement through its own government procedures, and any special conditions set by the agreement must be met.

It is difficult to say whether or not supervision of the Africa MAP projects has been more intensive than for regular projects.[14] On the one hand, supervision of the MAP I projects from the Bank's budget seems not to have been more intensive than for standard health projects. OED compared the Bank budget supervision expenditures for MAP I projects in 8 countries at one and two years after project

effectiveness with the supervision costs of 11 ongoing health projects in the same countries. On average, supervision costs within the first 12 months were 39 percent higher for the health projects than for the MAP projects.[15] After two years the cumulative supervision costs for the health projects were 10 percent higher than for the MAP projects. Comparing the projects country-by-country, in six of the eight countries

Supervision of MAP I projects has probably not been more intensive than that for other health projects, at least during the first two years.

MAP supervision costs since project effectiveness were similar to or less than those for health projects. These statistics do not include supervision from other sources, however, such as support from the ACT*africa* team or supervision activities financed from trust funds. Almost all of the MAP I task team leaders nevertheless reported that the Bank budget funds allocated for supervision were adequate to ensure minimum quality; however, only 7 of 12 task team leaders reported that supervision resources were adequate for MAP II countries.

Fewer MAP projects have contracted out key functions than anticipated, but where this has been done, team leaders believe it has accelerated implementation. Task team leaders reported that roughly half of the projects did not contract for financial management or procurement and about 70 percent did not contract for NGO management or M&E. However, among the projects that had completely or partially contracted-out these functions, 86 to 92 percent of team leaders reported that it had accelerated implementation of the project. Streamlined procedures and an operational manual have been developed for the prototype MAP project, with the potential for simplifying and accelerating implementation (Brown and others 2004). A comparison of the disbursement rates of MAP I and health, nutrition, and population projects in 11 countries suggests that, on average, the MAP projects have disbursed somewhat faster, although there is great dispersion around the trend lines for the two groups (see figure 4.1).[16] Comparing the disbursement rates country by country, in 6 of the 11 countries the MAP disbursed at a faster rate than the HNP projects, in 2 countries the disbursement rates were roughly the same, and in 3 countries the results varied depending on the elapsed time.[17]

MAP projects have helped to create mechanisms for governments to finance NGOs and CBOs and invested in capacity to implement HIV/AIDS interventions. Task team leaders reported that in 8 of 19 MAP projects, the government had not been funding NGOs or CBOs before the project, including one case in which mechanisms existed but had never been used. In seven of those cases the MAP reportedly created the mechanisms. Task team leaders for 58 percent of the 19 MAP projects reported that few or no indigenous NGOs had the capacity to design, manage, and evaluate HIV/AIDS programs before the project.

Large numbers of actors have been engaged for implementation. According to task team leaders, an average of 16 ministries are being supported among the first 24 Africa MAP projects; 10 of the 24 projects support between 20 and 30 line ministries, and two-thirds support 10 or more ministries. Further, in line with the Africa Region strategy, more than three-quarters of the African countries participating in the MAP have World Bank–supported projects in other sectors with AIDS activities and components. Most of these are not formal components and therefore are difficult to monitor; supervision resources may not be adequate to ensure their efficacy (see box 4.3). An analysis of AIDS and education projects found that MAP resources for the education sector are more likely to be used in countries that have AIDS components in ongoing education operations, though the supervision of both is weak (Bakilana and others 2005).[18] The number of NGOs and CBOs enlisted in the Africa MAP projects is substantially greater than in the first-generation projects (see table 4.2).[19]

Political commitment is reported to have increased, and it is likely that the Africa MAP played a role in some countries. Many international events since 1999–2000 have influenced political commitment, but the Africa MAP projects have delivered key inputs aimed at raising commitment in most cases. According to interviews with task team leaders and country directors for two dozen MAP I and II projects, the eligibility criteria for commitment were backed up with substantial high-level policy dialogue during project preparation and after approval.[20] In 44 percent of 19 African MAP projects, team leaders reported that political commitment at the highest levels of government has risen since the launching of the projects, and in 56 percent it has risen at the level of local government (see Appendix I). In about half of the cases, the task team leaders attributed the increase in commitment to the Bank's intervention; in other cases they expressed an opinion that increased commitment was only partially attributable to the Bank or the result of changes in government. According to OED's case study of Ethiopia, donors credited the Bank with opening up a frank dialogue about HIV/AIDS at the highest levels of government in 1999, including with the president, prime minister, and minister of economy and finance. The government agreed to borrow from IDA, raise the issue in public speeches, and incorporate HIV/AIDS into the Poverty Reduction Strategy Paper (PRSP). Increased awareness and political commitment were cited as the main achievements of the MAP to date by country directors for 82 percent of MAP I and 62 percent of MAP II countries. These reports will be followed up in depth by OED when the projects are completed, to understand whether they can be attributed to the Bank's actions. However, **the fact that two dozen or more countries have been willing to borrow (or accept a grant) for a national HIV/AIDS response is, in itself, indicative of a significant change in commitment and meets the goal of the first phase of the MAP of "intensifying action in as many countries as possible."**

Did the Unanticipated Risks Materialize?
Many of the anticipated risks in the project appraisal document linked to implementation—

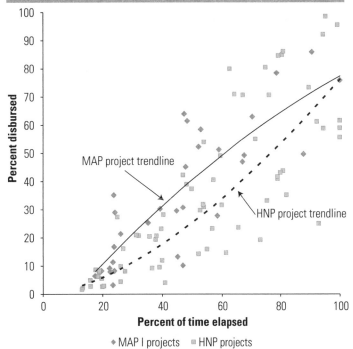

Figure 4.1: Africa MAP I Projects Disbursed More Quickly Than HNP Projects in the Same Countries, on Average

Source: World Bank data.

Note: Eleven MAP projects and 14 HNP projects.

such as low commitment and limited capacity—have been reduced through the MAP design mechanisms. However, as noted above, a number of risks affecting the program's development effectiveness were not assessed

The MAP is reported to have helped increase political commitment in many African countries.

Table 4.2: Number of NGOs and CBOs Supported by Africa MAP Projects, as of July 2004

Projects	Fiscal year approved	NGOs	CBOs
Africa MAP I (10–11 countries)[a] – mean	2000–2001	247	1,674
[minimum, maximum]		[5,700]	[40,6700]
Africa MAP II (11 countries)[b] – mean	2002–2004	46	157
[minimum, maximum]		[0,120]	[0,550]

Source: PPARs, ICRs, MAP TTL self-administered questionnaire.

a. Excludes Kenya for NGOs and Kenya and Nigeria for CBOs.

b. Excludes Mauritania.

Box 4.3: Embedding AIDS Activities in Education and Transport Projects

Adding AIDS activities or components to projects in sectors outside of health is one strategy for ensuring that key sectors become involved. Potential advantages are that they can address policy issues within that sector and may build ownership by the ministry involved over the longer term. However, these AIDS activities are rarely large enough to become a formal project component that can be monitored, and very few have been evaluated. When the activities are "retro-fitted" into an ongoing project, there is often little documentation of the objectives or performance when the project closes.

While there are a few exceptions, supervision of AIDS activities in non-health sector projects also is generally modest. OED identified 18 ongoing projects in the education sector and 16 in the transport sector that mentioned AIDS activities in project design documents; only 4 had formal AIDS components that exceeded $1 million.[a]

In reviewing the most recent status report for these 34 projects, AIDS was rarely mentioned in the development objectives (see table). Fewer than 40 percent reported on the status of AIDS activities and fewer than a third had AIDS indictors. Virtually all of the indicators were in terms of outputs. None of the status reports elicited comments of managers on AIDS.

Seminars, workshops, and analytic work on HIV/AIDS have been launched within the Bank's education and transport sectors to familiarize staff and government counterparts with AIDS impacts and how the sectors can help alleviate the problem.[b] However, in the context of a specific project, supervision resources are often too tight to be able to enlist a technical expert for these small and specialized activities for which the sectors themselves have little expertise. An exception is Ethiopia, where some transport projects have hired the expertise needed to ensure technical quality.

Supervision of AIDS Activities in Education and Transport Projects

Percent of projects for which the most recent Project Status Report...	Sector	
	Education (n = 18)	Transport (n = 16)
Mentioned AIDS in development objectives	11	6
Reported the status of AIDS activities	39	25
Had AIDS indicators	28	31

Source: Appendix C and the most recent Project Status Reports.

a. All of the education projects and 14 of the 16 transport projects are in Sub-Saharan Africa. Three education projects and one transport project have formal AIDS components greater than $1 million.

b. See, for example, Bundy and Gotur 2002; Valerio and Bundy 2004; World Bank 2003b.

Efforts to date have not been able to avoid unanticipated risks in the MAP design. and there are no mitigating mechanisms in the design. For example, the MAP relies heavily on the national AIDS strategy and rigorous M&E to promote learning by doing to ensure technical relevance, efficiency, and efficacy. If the national AIDS strategy is weak or M&E is not implemented, then effectiveness would be seriously compromised. Many of the unanticipated risks became apparent soon after approval of the first MAP projects and have been recognized in internal reviews by ACT*africa*. Additional resources have been brought to bear to address some of them.[21] Efforts may also have been made in individual country projects to mitigate these risks through other means. The findings to date, discussed below, suggest that in the aggregate the MAP design has not been able to avoid them.

Most national AIDS strategies do not cost or prioritize activities and are unlikely to ensure the technical relevance, efficiency, or efficacy of the Bank's assistance without additional analysis.[22] A background study for the OED evaluation reviewed the strategic plans of 21 African countries with MAP projects and 5 countries with conventional Bank HIV/AIDS projects. It concluded that, while there were some important exceptions, overall the strategies resembled a template with a complete or nearly complete menu of standard interventions and no prioritization (see box 4.4). There was also no clear relation between the content of many of the strategic plans and the stage of the epidemic.[23] The strategic plans tend to be oriented around implementation rather than behavioral or epidemiological outcomes. This suggests that the existence of a national strategy is not an adequate substitute for the standard analysis at project appraisal.

In the absence of strategic advice on prioritization, many of the programs being financed are not sufficiently focused on public goods and reducing high-risk behavior. The task team leaders for only 4 of 19 Africa MAP countries reported that the highest-risk behavior was being

---

Box 4.4: How Strategic Are National Strategic Plans?

OED reviewed national HIV/AIDS strategic plans from 21 countries participating in the Africa MAP[a] and the strategic plans of 5 non-MAP countries that were studied in depth for the OED evaluation—Cambodia, Chad, India, Indonesia, and Russia. Evidence of a strategic approach included: clear goals, explicit priorities; systematic planning, targets, timeframes, and indicators; clear plans for M&E; clearly specified implementation actors and responsibilities; and cost estimates and strategies for resource mobilization. Additional characteristics were the extent to which the plans are efficient, equitable, relevant, and feasible.

Strategic Plans in Africa MAP Countries

In most of the documents, the term "priority" is used to describe most, if not all, of the main components of an HIV/AIDS program, without any ranking according to importance or effectiveness. All of the national strategies set out similar broad areas of focus (prevention, care/treatment, mitigation, and enabling environment). Almost all of the reviewed strategies included all but a few of the standard (two dozen) areas of intervention, with no discussion of their relative importance or effectiveness. The only prioritization occurred around the inclusion of antiretroviral therapy (ART)—only a third of the 21 plans envisioned it on a large scale. Seventeen of the 21 included ART for prevention of mother-to-child transmission (MTCT). Only 10 of the plans were costed. While the overall documents did not prioritize, there were some implicit priorities embedded in the budgeting and implementation stages. But there was a lack of transparency in prioritization. Only seven of the documents provided baseline data for a significant share of targets and indicators. All but one plan (Uganda, 2000/01–2005/6) explicitly mentioned high-risk groups (HRGs) as targets for intervention. But only seven referred to HRGs in the statement of overall goals and objectives. The costing data did not provide adequate detail to judge whether these plans are really putting resources on HRGs. These strategies generally focused on process and implementation issues, rather than on the impact of programs on HIV.

In terms of overall strategic direction, with a lack of clear statements of priorities, the strategies are so similar that a generic package of HIV/AIDS areas of focus and interventions could have served just as well. This is important with regard to the question of what guidance is provided to the MAP projects by the national strategic plans.

Strategic Plans in Five Non-MAP Countries

The plans for Chad, Cambodia, India, Indonesia, and Russia also tended to have a core set of interventions that are assumed to be of equal importance, so that priorities should not be decided among them. However, all but the Russian document (which was actually a piece of legislation) emphasized targeting of HRGs and included a standard set of preventive interventions to address them. This was in contrast to many of the strategies in African countries with MAP projects, where HRGs are often placed at the same level of priority as large "vulnerable" population groups (such as youth and women) who are at risk of infection, but much less likely to spread HIV, on average. The strategies of the non-MAP countries also have less emphasis on underlying "root" causes and on the need for a multisectoral response, which is recognized but not operationalized to nearly the same extent. However, cost-effectiveness is not considered in any of the non-MAP strategies, nor is capacity treated as prominently. World Bank AIDS projects based in these five countries have clearly articulated objectives and priorities, however, in an attempt to ensure efficacy and efficiency.

Source: Mullen (2003a, b).

a. Plans for Gambia and Sierra Leone were not available at the time of the review, and the Malawi project had not yet been approved.

---

systematically addressed by the public sector; in half of the countries it is only being addressed to the extent that NGOs undertake these activities; in 5 cases (28 percent), no part of the project assures that high-risk behavior is systematically addressed. The OED case study on Ethiopia found that the MAP had insufficient support for public goods, especially surveillance, research, and M&E. No baseline data were established on the prevalence and behaviors of the general population in regions or high-risk groups. The under-financing of public goods and interventions for high-risk groups is greater in the more recent MAP II than in MAP I projects: Data obtained from task team leaders showed that MAP I countries were twice as likely as MAP II countries to support public sector operational research, targeted prevention interventions to high-risk groups (HRGs), and activities to mitigate the impact of AIDS to PLWHA. MAP II countries were substantially more likely to finance treatment of TB and other opportunistic infections, and slightly more likely to finance public antiretroviral therapy (see Appendix H). The MAP in only one country— Burkina Faso—has a special component to address high-risk behavior. There is often a strong reluctance to focus funds on the highest-risk behavior in generalized epidemics in Africa, in part because of the difficulty of identifying and reaching those at highest risk of HIV transmission. Recent research suggests that focusing prevention efforts on areas where people go to find new sexual partners may be less difficult than identifying specific risk groups, and more efficient than relying on interventions to the general population (see box 4.5).

Many MAP projects do not ensure that public goods and the highest-risk behaviors are addressed.

The overall record of the Africa MAP in implementing strong M&E to improve "learning by doing" is weak, similar to the M&E record of the portfolio of completed HIV/AIDS projects. If 5–10 percent of project costs had been allocated

The record of the Africa MAP in implementing M&E to date is weak, and no better than for first-generation AIDS projects.

for M&E, as proposed in MAP design documents, some $50–100 million would have been available for M&E in the two rounds of Africa MAP projects. However, except for the one project with a separate M&E component (Malawi, 8.3 percent of project costs), very little is known about M&E allocations, let alone actual expenditure.[24] Slow progress in designing and implementing M&E systems was recognized in the first joint World Bank and UNAIDS progress review mission in June/July 2001,[25] at which time it was recommended that M&E functions be outsourced and M&E plans be finalized during project preparation. In 2002, a generic M&E operational manual was prepared jointly with UNAIDS (World Bank and UNAIDS 2002) and a Global Monitoring and Evaluation Support Team (GAMET), based at the World Bank, was created to facilitate UNAIDS cosponsor efforts to build country-level M&E capacities and coordinate technical support.[26] Despite these additional inputs, the *Interim Review of the MAP* conducted in early 2004 found that most of the six projects visited had developed M&E plans, but in none had the plans been operationalized,[27] which made it difficult to assess what had been accomplished. As of the summer of 2004, task team leaders for 24 MAP I and II projects reported that M&E had been wholly or partially contracted out in a third of the projects, although outsourcing for M&E increased between MAP I and II (see Appendix H, table H.10). Team leaders for only two of the projects reported that the M&E systems were functioning well. The OED case study of Ethiopia found that the M&E framework was not developed until the third year of the project. In only a quarter of the Africa MAP countries has there been a national AIDS knowledge and risk behavior survey of the general population within a year of project approval.[28] In 9 of 28 countries with MAP projects, there has never been a population-based, nationwide survey to measure the patterns of AIDS knowledge and risk behavior among men and women. The recommendations of the *Interim Review* included making a functional M&E system a condition for future projects, putting it in a separate component with non-fungible resources, and building capacity.

Box 4.5: PLACE: Focusing Prevention Where People Go to Find New Partners

In countries with generalized epidemics where HIV is spreading substantially by casual sexual networks, reaching people with the highest rates of partner change with prevention services can be challenging. Approaches that focus on occupational groups at high risk of HIV transmission may not be sufficient to reach important populations with many casual sexual partners, particularly if the latter are difficult to identify, such as *migrant labor* or *out of school youth.* The PLACE approach—for Priorities for Local AIDS Control Efforts, developed by MEASURE Evaluation—attempts to systematically identify locations where people go to meet new partners, for the purpose of targeting prevention programs to areas that are likely to have high HIV incidence.

In South Africa, for example, the authors found more than 200 sites in each of three townships and 64 sites in one central business district where people go to meet new sexual partners (Weir and others 2003). The male-to-female ratio was 2:1, and almost half of all men and women interviewed had a new sexual partner in the past 4 weeks. Commercial sex was rare in the townships but available at 31 percent of the sites in the business districts. Yet fewer than 15 percent of the township sites and 20 percent of the business district sites had condoms. PLACE has also been applied in Burkina Faso (Burkina Faso PLACE Study Group 2002 and Nagot 2003), India (Bhubaneswar PLACE Study Group 2002), Madagascar, Mexico (Mexico PLACE Study Group 2002), Tanzania (Tanzania PLACE Study Group 2002), and Uganda (Ssengooba and others 2003 and Uganda PLACE Study Group 2002).

However, the experience of completed HIV/AIDS projects suggests that none of these measures is sufficient to ensure that M&E takes place or that the results are used to improve performance. No additional incentives have been incorporated into the MAP program design to overcome these problems. Disbursements, for example, are not tied to the existence of baseline studies or intermediate evaluations.

The MAP projects, like past HIV assistance, are also neglecting to collect HIV and behavioral data on groups most likely to contract and spread HIV. In Ethiopia, where years ago the government was monitoring HIV among sex workers in many different parts of the country, they are no longer monitored; epidemiological surveillance is almost entirely among pregnant women attending antenatal clinics. According to the task team leaders, about 58 percent of governments of the first two dozen African MAP countries are collecting HIV prevalence data and 75 percent are collecting behavioral information on at least one high-risk group. Nevertheless, 10 countries were not monitoring HIV in any high-risk group and six were not monitoring behavior.

The engagement of a large number of sectors in implementation, many of them with no apparent comparative advantage in addressing AIDS, has increased the complexity and coordination problems of the national response, with substantial risks for efficiency and efficacy. As noted earlier, two-thirds of the first two-dozen Africa MAP projects are supporting the response of 10–30 ministries, according to task team leaders. There are many potential objectives of such engagement (see box 4.6), but in the case of programs supported by the MAP, the objectives for different sectors are not well differentiated. It may be helpful to the objective of *political mobilization* to engage as many sectors as possible, for example, but it is unclear whether widespread engagement in *implementation* will enhance efficacy or efficiency. Although the AIDS epidemic has wide-ranging impacts and societal determinants, this does not mean that all sectors are equally relevant or competent in launching an effective response. Enlisting all sectors in implementation does not use the comparative advantage of sectors that are most critically involved effectively, and it encourages action in areas that are far removed from other ministries' mandates. The *Interim Review of the MAP* found that the implementation engagement of most ministries was around HIV prevention and care of their civil servant workforce, rather than sectoral programs on

Box 4.6: The Objectives and Modalities of Multisectoral Approaches

For well over a decade, the international community, including the World Bank, has emphasized the need for an AIDS response that goes beyond the health sector, with two main objectives: improving the efficiency and effectiveness of programs on the ground and mobilizing the public. To the extent that multisectoral activities were launched in the first phase of the Bank's response, they tended to address the first of these objectives. In the hardest-hit countries, adult mortality from AIDS was affecting all sectors of the economy, generating the need for plans to mitigate the impact. There are also many AIDS activities that require multisectoral collaboration in implementation to be effective. For example, changing the behavior of sex workers requires not only involvement of the Ministry of Health and the acquiescence of sex workers, but the cooperation of law enforcement, brothel owners, and local government.

The Bank's HIV/AIDS assistance has addressed either or both of these objectives through five main approaches: (1) building the capacity of the Ministry of Health to work selectively with other priority sectors;[a] (2) supporting establishment of national multisectoral commissions, usually under the president or prime minister, either to coordinate or implement a national multisectoral response;[b] (3) supporting a response coordinated by a ministry with multisectoral responsibilities, like planning;[c] (4) supporting AIDS components or activities in non-health sectors, such as education, transport, or social protection; and (5) facilitating a dialogue among key ministries.[d]

OED could find no evidence to suggest that any one institutional arrangement is more effective or efficient in producing results on the ground than the alternatives, if the political commitment is present. The multisectoral commission model supported widely by the Africa MAP seems to be based on experience in Uganda;[e] more than a decade after the formation of the Uganda AIDS Commission, the definition of multisectoral coordination and the best way of pursuing it is still being debated in that country (De Merode and others 2001). The MAP operational manual lists a number of theoretical responsibilities of these agencies but notes that, "in reality, [their] role is often ill-defined" (Brown and others 2004). The first MAP Progress Review noted a strong tendency for the secretariats of National AIDS Councils (NACs) to become implementation bureaucracies, as opposed to coordinating agencies, and reported that "Partner agencies in both the public sector and civil society remain unclear as to [their] responsibility…in supporting the implementation process" (World Bank 2001c, p. 5). The MAP *Interim Review* found that the NAC secretariats had grown to 50–70 professional staff in some countries and had little accountability (World Bank 2004). Evidence to support the effectiveness of institutions to manage the AIDS response outside of the Ministry of Health from the Bank's experience is scant.[f]

a. For example, in Bangladesh, Brazil, Cambodia, Eritrea, Guyana, India, Jamaica, Kenya (in the 1990s), Uganda, and Zimbabwe.

b. Most countries of the Africa MAP, as well as several in the Caribbean MAP.

c. For example, in Chad and Indonesia. This has often been the strategy in population programs, which also seek multisectoral action.

d. As in Russia, for example.

e. "Those few countries that have made significant progress in slowing the epidemic (such as Uganda) have placed the coordinating body of national HIV/AIDS efforts under the president's office, where it has the visibility, reach and authority to coordinate and mobilize all stakeholders" (World Bank 2000b, p. 11).

f. As presented in Chapter 3, the Ministry of Health in a number of Bank-supported projects did work successfully with a handful of the key sectors for results on the ground. The Indonesian AIDS project was launched by Bapenas without adequate support of the Ministry of Health, the main implementer. In Chad and Burkina Faso, AIDS and population projects were managed from the Ministry of Plan, which undermined support in the Ministry of Health.

the ground (World Bank 2004). The findings also suggest that activities may be occurring within ministerial "silos" rather than bringing critical sectors together to achieve jointly a specific objective.[29]

The overarching authority vested in institutions to coordinate the multisectoral response in many cases has resulted in the disengagement of the Ministry of Health, the lead technical agency for the long-run fight against AIDS. Task team leaders for roughly half of the African MAP projects reported

that the Ministry of Health was either initially or continues to be disengaged from the response as a result of the shift in responsibility to a national multisectoral commission. In one-fifth of the countries, the Bank's country director became involved in sorting out tensions between the Ministry of Health and the National AIDS Council or another agency. The experience to date indicates that building the capacity and political support for a strong response within the Ministry of Health is absolutely essential as the foundation for an effective national response across sectors.

The components for grants to civil society also pose substantial risks for the development effectiveness of the MAP projects. Considering that the average MAP project allocates 40 percent of resources to the civil society response, roughly $400 million has been committed for this purpose—from a low of $0.42 per capita (Ethiopia) to a high of $5.86 (Gambia, see figure 4.2).[30] This includes allocations of $2.53 per capita in Mauritania and nearly $1 per capita in Madagascar, both of which have *nascent* epidemics. There are many possible objectives of engaging civil society in general or specific NGOs, CBOs, or communities, including: (a) to improve the relevance, efficiency, or efficacy of service delivery or to exploit a comparative advantage in implementation; (b) to mobilize political support for AIDS control; (c) to empower communities or marginalized groups; or (d) to foster an indigenous, independent civil society response. The objectives and distinction between the roles of these different elements are not clearly articulated in the MAP design documents and will make them difficult to assess.

The use of civil society funds is generally demand-driven and, according to task team leaders, is not strategic from the perspective of the needs of the national program. According to 8 of 12 task team leaders, there is no process for prioritizing which interventions NGOs and CBOs undertake to ensure efficiency. In many if not most instances, any proposal that passes muster is being funded.[31] NGOs and CBOs can select from a broad menu of eligible activities; there is no assurance of systematic coverage. The OED case study on Ethiopia found that there had been no systematic evaluation of NGO or community projects. The task team leaders for 17 projects reported that none included provisions to evaluate the effectiveness or impact of NGO and CBO interventions. For about a third of the projects it was reported that there were no M&E

The emphasis on engaging all sectors in some cases reduced the engagement of the Ministry of Health.

A large share of MAP resources are for civil society, but the objectives and roles of civil society are not clear in the MAP design.

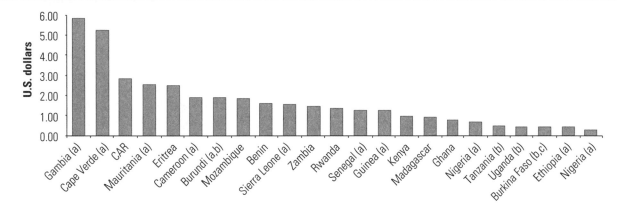

Figure 4.2: Budgeted per Capita Public Spending on Civil Society AIDS Interventions, Africa MAP Countries

Source: Project appraisal documents and World Bank 2003a for population.

Note: (a) Excludes value of serparate capacity-building component with CSO allocation; (b) Excludes other component with partial allocation to CSOs; (c) Combines financing for CSOs and provincial governments.

The impact and cost-effectiveness of community-driven approaches to AIDS were not evaluated relative to alternatives before being widely adopted.

mechanisms whatsoever for the civil society component; others, in effect, only monitored process and output indicators (47 percent) or were subjected to financial or management audits (24 percent).

Financing community-driven development (CDD) approaches for AIDS is a major new element of the MAP for which impact or cost-effectiveness was never formally evaluated before it was widely adopted. A pilot project of the approach was conducted in the Poni region of Burkina Faso in 2000–01, financed by the Population and AIDS Control Project. A process evaluation of the pilot about a year into implementation found that: "confusion persists on the specific objectives of the pilot project. This situation is a result of the lack of formal planning.... Likewise, the anticipated results and the indicators were not clearly specified and it is difficult to know if they were reached. The dominant impression is that each of the actors and promoters had their own version of what the pilot project was or should be and their own expectations in relation to results."[32] In the MAP design, it is unclear whether the objective of sending AIDS resources to communities is political mobilization, service delivery, or empowerment.[33] If some of these activities are being promoted purely to mobilize segments of civil society, there may be less costly, more efficient approaches. There are many ways of ensuring community participation that do not involve transfer of funds, for example.

The recently completed OED evaluation of the Bank's support for community-driven and community-based development (CBD/CDD) suggests additional risks for the efficacy and efficiency of CBD/CDD projects, a category that includes all of the Africa MAP projects.[34] CBD/CDD projects tend to be more successful on quantitative goals, such as infrastructure construction, than on qualitative goals, such as capacity enhancement. The evaluation found that the effectiveness of Bank CBD/CDD projects in enhancing social capital and empowering communities has varied widely, that the link between CBD/CDD and community capacity enhancement is weak, and that sustainability is lower in CBD/CDD than in non-CBD/CDD projects (OED 2005a). The results of CBD/CDD projects have depended on local political and social conditions, government commitment, and community capacity. They tend to be more successful when they support indigenously matured participatory efforts or when the Bank has provided sustained, long-term support to communities beyond the length of a single subproject. The evaluation also notes that, for the Bank, CBD/CDD interventions have been more expensive to prepare and supervise; for the borrower, there are substantial costs. Weaknesses in M&E (particularly with regard to monitoring progress on qualitative goals) and the short time span of the Bank's subproject cycle constrain the Bank's capacity to implement CBD/CDD projects (OED 2005a). Four issues are highlighted for special attention in future CBD/CDD interventions: (a) the need for clear articulation of expected achievements; (b) calculation of costs and benefits, including long-term poverty impact, of undertaking the CBD/CDD approach as a basis for comparison with alternatives; (c) increased focus on sustainability and long-term development; and (d) addressing constraints related to the Bank's mode of operation, its operational policies, and its M&E systems.

The lack of prioritization and costing in most of the national AIDS strategies also poses risks for the sustainability of the activities and benefits of the MAP projects. There are no eligibility criteria or program design features of the MAP that ensure sustainability of the response, aside from what is mentioned in the national strategic plan. Sustainability is especially relevant to the civil society components and to long-run expenditures on AIDS treatment. The MAP strategy did not specify whether the initial large share of expenditure on civil society was a one-time measure for mobilization or whether it is a permanent feature. The OED evaluation of the Bank's support to CBD/CDD found that "the

Bank's structure and mode of operation limit its ability to ensure sustainable outcomes from CBD/CDD projects: "...the process must be managed 'close to the ground,' but normally without direct Bank involvement at the local level....with its mode of operation, distance from implementation, and its current M&E system, the Bank has found it difficult to ensure...sustainability of development outcomes from its CBD/CDD projects" (OED 2005a). The MAP operations manual already cites an example in which failure to assess the sustainability of antiretroviral treatment in Nigeria resulted in a three-month lapse in the availability of drugs in 2003, compromising the effectiveness of the treatment and contributing to viral resistance (Brown and others 2004). The 10–15 year commitment of the Bank to these countries does not eliminate the need to consider the long-term sustainability of efforts and to encourage more efficient and effective use of the funds.

To summarize, the Africa MAP has succeeded in enlisting at least two dozen countries to launch major HIV/AIDS initiatives with $1 billion of new resources and appears to have contributed to heightened political commitment. This alone is an enormous accomplishment, given the lack of demand for AIDS assistance by most of these countries in the 1990s. There is evidence of broad mobilization of civil society, on a greater scale than most (but perhaps not all) of the completed HIV/AIDS projects, and of many more sectors of the economy. Mechanisms have been created to finance an AIDS response from civil society in many countries where this did not previously exist. The objective of scaling up interventions is being pursued.

However, the overarching objective of the MAP is to prevent HIV infection and mitigate its impact; broader implementation and political commitment are a means to that end. Since these projects are all still in the field, it is too early to assess whether this is being accomplished. The MAP approach relies heavily on the technical and strategic guidance of the national strategic plan, coupled with strong M&E, heavier than normal supervision, and the existence of proven, locally evaluated pilot projects to ensure the efficiency and efficacy of the Bank's assistance. The risks associated with these factors were not assessed during preparation of either MAP I or II, and because of the emphasis on rapid preparation of the projects, less analytic work and fewer baseline assessments were conducted. The strategic input of the Bank—which might have provided some insurance against these risks—was much less than in previous HIV/AIDS projects. While there are no doubt examples of countries in which these risks have been mitigated by project-specific features, the evidence to date suggests that in many cases the national strategic plans are not sufficiently prioritized, that weak M&E has not produced the anticipated learning by doing, and that many activities are being scaled up that have never been evaluated locally. Supervision appears to be no greater than in health lending, while the complexity of the projects and the number of activities are far greater. There is a risk that many of the actors that have been mobilized politically behind the fight against HIV/AIDS are engaged in implementing activities for which they have no technical expertise or comparative advantage, diverting scarce capacity from other poverty-reduction activities and diverting resources from actors that can use them effectively. The mid-term reviews of these projects and the next phase of lending provide an opportunity to develop mechanisms to minimize these risks and improve the effectiveness of the Bank's assistance.

Weaknesses in national AIDS strategies pose risks for the sustainability of MAP activities.

It is too early to assess whether the MAP projects are meeting their objective of preventing HIV infection and mitigating its impact, efficiently and sustainably.

Chapter 5: Evaluation Highlights

- AIDS requires both rapid action and determined, long-term building of capacity and sustainability.
- International assistance for AIDS has dramatically increased, especially for treatment.
- The Bank's comparative advantage is in helping to build institutions, assessing alternatives, and improving the performance of national AIDS efforts.
- While it is important for the Bank to engage with partners, its most important partners remain the developing countries themselves.

Conclusions

A **new and unprecedented disease.** AIDS was a completely new and unprecedented disease—one that spread silently and rapidly, and then killed its victims 10 years later. It was and still is enormously stigmatized because of the way it is spread. Even as neighboring countries were hit, there was denial virtually everywhere and insistence that the conditions were different in "my country." At the same time, while HIV was spreading rapidly, weak health systems in developing countries were faced with enormous demand from afflictions and people who were dying now.

Without a better understanding of the true levels of infection and risk behavior, AIDS was assumed to be primarily an urban disease in Africa, where two-thirds of the population was rural. Many in the Bank were deeply concerned that a call for AIDS programs might divert scarce resources from programs to strengthen weak health systems. They did not fully realize the impact that this epidemic would eventually have on mortality and on the health system itself. Despite important developments in treatment, AIDS was—and remains—an affliction that is incurable and expensive to treat. This adds to the stigma surrounding it and the reluctance to allocate resources to treatment.

Lessons of the first generation of World Bank assistance. During the first phase of the Bank's response, projects were developed based on client demand and the initiative of concerned staff, often in collaboration with the Global Program on AIDS. The Bank committed more than $500 million to countries on four continents for free-standing AIDS projects, large AIDS components, and many activities embedded less formally in health projects. In many of the countries where it was active, the Bank helped to build national institutions for the long-run response to AIDS, strengthened the activities of Ministries of Health, and assisted governments in strategic thinking, while keeping an eye on prevention and the main drivers of the epidemic, even when the latter was controversial. Awareness was raised, condoms were provided, NGOs were enlisted, health staff was trained. But both commitment and implementation capacity often were overestimated, reducing efficacy below what might have been achieved. Important information-oriented activities on HIV infection, behavior, and the efficacy of interventions were often delayed, poorly supervised, or not implemented because of the perceived urgency of the problem and the need to get disbursements going. This not only reduced the learning and possible improvements in efficiency, but in many instances delayed policy makers' awareness of the problem. Many innovations were "tested," but few if any were evaluated, limiting learning by doing.

The main impediments to more effective global action by the Bank in containing the spread of HIV in the 1990s were low demand by the Bank's borrowers and the delay by health sector management in recognizing the longer-run threat of AIDS to health and to fragile health systems in the countries that were hardest hit. **Two main lessons coming out of the first phase pertained to the importance of generating and sustaining political commitment and the need to produce information to reduce the uncertainty surrounding the disease and to lead to locally adapted responses.**

Preliminary lessons from the Africa MAP. The concept underlying the Africa MAP of a line of credit for well-prepared programs to fight AIDS is sound, and the announcement of a significant envelope of potential funds for AIDS may have been an important signal to reluctant governments of the Bank's commitment. In the late 1990s, Bank management came to understand the bottleneck of low commitment by clients and the severity of the disease, which reduced life expectancy in the hardest-hit countries to levels from the 1950s. As a result, the MAP placed enormous emphasis in its eligibility criteria and its program design on the mobilization of top leaders, all sectors of the economy, and civil society. This was backed by strong commitment and engagement from within the Bank, as AIDS became much more prominent in CASs. There has been a tremendous turnaround in the willingness to act, not only in the countries and the Bank, but also among the international community. The demand constraint was further eased by the approval of IDA grants in September 2002.

The sense of urgency led the MAP to rely heavily on "template" strategies and institutions, and to focus on mobilization and implementation over content. The project design addressed the risks associated with weak political commitment and implementation capacity, but neglected other important risks linked to relevance, efficiency, and efficacy of the Bank's assistance. Individual projects may have reduced these risks, such as by enhancing the role of the Ministry of Health or creating components on priority activities. The Bank's ACT*africa* team identified many of these unanticipated risks and has intervened to minimize them. The extent to which these efforts have succeeded will not be known until ongoing projects can be assessed after their completion.

There is evidence for some concern about these risks in the implementation to date, however. The emphasis on quick preparation often resulted in delays in implementation—a lesson that has been well learned throughout the Bank's broader portfolio, and even in previous AIDS projects.[1] National strategic plans—the blueprint for how MAP resources are to be spent—in many cases have not been sufficiently prioritized to guide the allocation of scarce human resources. Stronger M&E and "learning by doing" that were supposed to ensure efficacy and efficiency have not fully materialized. By and large, what is being scaled up has not been locally evaluated. The objectives of the engagement of the wide array of mobilized actors—central ministries, local government, NGOs, CBOs, the private sector, and communities—are not always clear. The activities supported do not necessarily reflect programmatic priorities or a comparative advantage in implementation. To date, there is little information about the coverage and quality of services, the extent to which they compete with or complement efforts by local government, or the sustainability of activities. Like the portfolio of completed projects, preventive programs for the general population are being supplied, while public goods and prevention among the epidemiologically most relevant populations are not being addressed to the extent that they should be. The mechanisms used to mobilize the population have dramatically increased the complexity of the projects and, in some cases, failed to strengthen or even alienated the Ministry of Health, the lead agency in the response.

In parallel with the Africa MAP, other Regions of the Bank have expanded HIV/AIDS assistance to countries with nascent and concentrated epidemics, largely without the signaling effect of a MAP or the need to shorten preparation.[2] These efforts have benefited from an international environment that has put more pressure on governments to address AIDS. In large countries, such as Brazil, China, India, and Russia, the Bank's assistance is small in relation to total health spending, but has been used to encourage emphasis on public goods, prevention, and the need to extend access to those most likely to contract and spread the virus.

AIDS is a long-run problem. The AIDS epidemic is wreaking havoc in the hardest-hit countries now, but it is a long-run problem. It demands a mix of actions, some designed for rapid impact and others focused on building long-term capacity and sustainability. Immediate action is imperative to prevent future infections—the only way at present to reduce the scope of the epidemic and its impact—and to ensure care and support for those who have fallen ill. Most of the people who will fall ill over the next decade have already been infected. This presents a predictable impact on health care needs, although the treatment environment is rapidly changing.

In addition to efficient and effective short-run responses, developing countries need support for creating strong national and subnational institutions and mechanisms to respond to the long-run problem, not only by dramatically expanding HIV/AIDS prevention (which remains politically difficult), but also by strengthening the ability of health systems to deliver care to AIDS patients and to address other health problems, by strengthening social safety nets to help those affected, and by ensuring sustainability of these efforts. There will be a continuing need to develop and maintain

political commitment within countries at all levels and across all sectors.

AIDS demands both short-run action and long-term capacity building.

Future directions of the Bank's HIV/AIDS assistance. Throughout the 1990s and up to the present, the World Bank has been the largest external provider of AIDS assistance to developing countries. This is about to change. Since 2000, there has been an enormous mobilization of resources for AIDS by the international community, primarily for treatment. Not only have the Bank's commitments dramatically increased, by nearly $2 billion; the Global Fund to Fight AIDS, TB, and Malaria (GFATM) has committed $1.6 billion[3] to financing anti-AIDS efforts in developing countries—roughly doubling AIDS assistance in African countries where the Bank is already active (see table 5.1).

In addition, the U.S. government has announced its intent to direct a total of $15 billion over 5 years to 15 countries in Africa, Asia, and the Caribbean, primarily for treatment and care. The Gates and Clinton Foundations have pledged hundreds of millions of dollars. Indeed, the concern of the health community in the early 1990s that AIDS might sideline broader health sector development may be coming to pass in the most severely affected countries. The GFATM AIDS commitments to Rwanda and Uganda on an annual basis exceed the recurrent budget of the Ministry of Health.[4] The Bank and the President's Emergency Program for HIV/AIDS Relief (PEPFAR) are also financing these countries. Although in some cases the pledged resources from other donors have not yet been received, the ability to absorb this level of resources and to use them effectively needs critical examination, as does the balance between AIDS and health spending and the sustainability of the investments being made. While most donors are investing in long-run capacity building, in the short run they are all drawing on the same pool of relatively fixed capacity. The prioritization of scarce national capacity in the short run needs to be addressed in every country.

With its long-run commitment to poverty alleviation, its unique relationship with national governments, its analytic strengths, and its multisectoral reach, the Bank's comparative advantage is to help countries build robust institutions adapted to local political and social realities; to assess alternatives; and help to improve the efficacy, efficiency, and sustainability of AIDS efforts in the long term. The crucial importance of political commitment is now recognized, though the need to constantly renew and broaden commitment may still be underestimated. The vital needs for timely information; prioritization of activities; and information to design, monitor, evaluate, and improve programs are still not fully appreciated.

To be effective, the Bank will need to focus on greater use of information and evaluation, helping governments to link decisions to evidence and to assess alternatives and set priorities. Programmatically it must continue to press for broadened political commitment and maintain a focus on public goods and prevention, particularly among those most likely to contract and spread HIV, in countries at all stages of the epidemic. In the hardest-hit countries, the Bank must act to improve the efficiency and sustainability of AIDS treatment in health systems and strengthen programs to integrate orphans and other severely affected groups into national safety net and anti-poverty measures.

Bank and borrower efforts need to be more evidence-based, to enhance development effectiveness.

Partnerships. The Bank worked closely with the WHO/GPA in the early years for technical input and currently is collaborating with UNAIDS, as well as agencies such as the U.S. CDC. Much of the Bank's ongoing assistance to governments is parallel to, in coordination with, and often cofinanced with bilateral and multilateral donors. Increasingly, supervision is conducted through joint reviews with other donors and government.

Harmonization of procedures at the country level will reduce the burden on governments of dealing with the different reporting requirements of multiple international agencies. The World Bank has endorsed the "Three Ones" policy of one national authority, one strategy, and one M&E system. It is not enough to obtain agreement, however; what is agreed upon must also be shown to improve the efficiency and impact of programs in each country. The Bank and its international partners bear some responsibility, for example, for promoting template national multisectoral coordinating institutions

---

Table 5.1: GFATM Approvals and World Bank Commitments in Countries Receiving Both ($US millions)

Country groupings	GFATM approved (2 years)	Total active World Bank commitments (5 years)
African MAP countries, of which:	544.59	959.1
MAP I countries[a] (n = 12)	316.99	462.9
MAP II countries[b] (n = 11)	227.60	496.2
Other countries[c] (n = 13)	200.49	468.7
Total	745.08	1,427.8

Source: GFATM Web site, accessed November 5, 2004.

a. Benin, Burkina Faso, Cameroon, CAR, Eritrea, Ethiopia, Gambia, Ghana, Kenya, Madagascar, Nigeria, Uganda.

b. Burundi, Congo DR, Guinea, Guinea-Bissau, Malawi, Mozambique, Niger, Rwanda, Senegal, Tanzania, Zambia.

c. Bangladesh, Cambodia, Chad, China, Dominican Republic, Guyana, Honduras, India, Jamaica, Moldova, Pakistan, Russian Federation, Ukraine.

Coverage: All countries with approved and signed GFATM proposals for HIV/AIDS and in which the Bank is also providing HIV/AIDS assistance. In instances where several GFATM proposals have been approved, only the value of grant agreements that have been signed are included. GFATM approvals generally include only approvals for HIV/AIDS. The exception is projects labeled HIV/AIDS/TB, where the two parts could not be separated. In these cases the entire amount was attributed to AIDS.

that are in many cases experiencing great difficulty in exercising their basic functions.

The most important partners from the Bank's perspective must remain the developing countries themselves. Efforts to harmonize and collaborate among donors are important to the extent that they are client-oriented and help governments to improve the relevance, efficiency, and efficacy of their response. There remains a risk that harmonization at the country level will expand the scope of activities to include the priorities and monitoring conventions of all donors. This is already the case in the U.N. family: the *Five-Year Evaluation of UNAIDS* concluded that the Integrated Work Plan and U.N. Development Assistance Framework at the country level "[lack] strategic perspective and are not responsive to country needs" (Poate and others 2002, p. xv).

The Bank's most important partners are the developing countries themselves.

The Bank is serving its clients best when it exercises its comparative advantage in helping governments to set priorities and sequence activities based on evidence. It can do this through policy dialogue, participatory analytic work, and the design of projects that focus scarce capacity on the highest priority activities—those likely to have the largest impact—with an eye on the sustainability of the response.

Recommendations

In the next phase of its response, the Bank should help governments use human and financial resources more efficiently and effectively to have an impact on the HIV/AIDS epidemic. The Bank should focus on improving the efficiency, efficacy, and sustainability of national AIDS programs by building capacity; developing strong national and subnational institutions; investing strategically in public goods and the activities likely to have the largest impact; and creating incentives for monitoring, evaluation, and research based on local evidence that is used to improve program performance.

For All Bank HIV/AIDS Assistance

1. Help governments to be more strategic and selective, to prioritize, using limited capacity to implement activities that will have the greatest impact on the epidemic. Greater prioritization and sequencing of activities will improve efficiency, reduce managerial complexity, and ensure that the most cost-effective activities are implemented first. In particular, the Bank should ensure that public goods and prevention among those most likely to spread HIV are adequately supported.

- The Bank should help governments prioritize and sequence the implementation of activities likely to have the greatest impact and that enlist sectors and implementers according to their comparative advantages to work collaboratively toward specific epidemiological outcomes. Costs, cost-effectiveness, impact, equity,

human resource requirements, and sustainability of alternative AIDS prevention, treatment, and mitigation strategies should be assessed.

- With respect to prevention, projects in countries at all stages of the epidemic should be systematically mapping high-risk behavior; monitoring HIV and behavior in populations most likely to contract and spread HIV; assuring high coverage of information and preventive interventions to them; and taking action to reduce stigma and legal barriers to prevention and care among marginalized groups. A country-by-country assessment of the extent to which this is currently taking place and an action plan to improve performance would satisfy this recommendation.

- With respect to treatment and care, in high-prevalence countries the Bank should work with government and other partners to assess the costs, benefits, affordability, sustainability, and equity implications of different types of treatment for AIDS patients, on the basis of which to make rational decisions in the allocation of health resources. This should be a priority even if Bank resources will not be financing this care. A population-based HIV prevalence survey is critical to understanding the scope and distribution of demand for treatment and for designing efficient treatment and care strategies in hard-hit, low-income countries.

2. Strengthen national institutions for managing and implementing the long-run response, particularly in the health sector. Expanded responses among other priority sectors are important, but should not come at the expense of investments in the capacity of the health sector to respond to AIDS. In addition:

- Bank assistance should distinguish between institutions and strategies for raising political commitment (mobilization) and those for efficient and effective implementation of activities on the ground. Both objectives have been shown to be critical, but experience shows that a single institution may not be able to satisfy both objectives efficiently.
- Bank HIV/AIDS assistance needs to consider strategies for building, broadening, and sustaining political commitment in specific settings.
- Greater use of institutional and political analysis should be made to enhance the local relevance and effectiveness of national and subnational institutions (including multisectoral institutions and those in the Ministry of Health) in relation to local capacity, political realities, and the stage of the epidemic.

3. Improve the local evidence base for decision making. The Bank should create incentives to ensure that the design and management of country-level AIDS assistance is guided by relevant and timely locally produced evidence and rigorous analytic work.

- The Bank should launch immediately—within the next 6 months—an in-depth inventory and assessment of the extent of implementation of

all planned M&E activities and the availability and comparability over time of input, output, and outcome data relevant to assessing program effectiveness, in all countries with freestanding HIV/AIDS projects and significant components. This assessment should serve as the basis for a time-bound action plan to improve the incentives for M&E in the Bank's HIV/AIDS assistance, with explicit targets in terms of improved monitoring and periodic use of evaluation to improve program effectiveness.
- Ongoing projects and those in the planning stage should pre-identify a program of commissioned research and analytic work on issues of priority to the AIDS program.[1]
- Pilot programmatic interventions should be independently evaluated before they are replicated or expanded; those that have been scaled up without the benefit of evaluation should be evaluated within the next 12 months as a condition for continued finance.
- The Bank should become an "AIDS knowledge bank" by: maintaining a central database of Bank-sponsored or managed analytic work on AIDS—including evaluations—that is complete, up to date, and accessible to staff, clients, researchers and the public; developing a mechanism for the routine dissemination of findings from the Bank's analytic work on AIDS to internal and external audiences; translating key products; and investing in priority cross-national analytic work and research that is an international public good.[2]

For the Africa MAP

The Africa MAP is designed to mitigate risks concerning political commitment and implementation, but there are few structural mechanisms to assure efficiency or efficacy. These risks can be reduced through the following actions (in addition to the recommendations above, which apply to all projects):

- **A thorough technical and economic assessment of national strategic plans and government AIDS policy and an inventory of the activities of other donors should become a standard part of MAP project prepa-**

ration. When national strategic plans are found inadequate as a basis for prioritization and sequencing of activities, the Bank should engage government in strategic discussions, informed by analytic work, to identify programmatic priorities that reflect the stage of the epidemic, capacity constraints, and the local context. Follow-on projects should be structured to ensure that those priority activities, including public goods and prevention among those with high-risk behavior, are pursued.

- **The objectives of the engagement of different segments of civil society need to be clearly articulated to distinguish between the actors enlisted for purposes of political mobilization and those with the expertise and comparative advantage to implement activities with a direct impact on the epidemic.** The results of ongoing CDD-type AIDS activities should be rigorously evaluated with respect to their effectiveness in changing behavior or mitigating impact before they are renewed, in line with the recommendations of the OED CBD/CDD evaluation. The complementarity or competition between CDD AIDS activities and the decentralized public sector response should be assessed as part of this effort.

- **The Bank should focus support for implementation on the sectors whose activities have the greatest potential impact on the epidemic and with some comparative advantage in implementation—such as the Ministry of Health, the military, education, transport, and others, depending on the country—and ensure that the resources to supervise their activities are forthcoming.** The objectives of multisectoral action against AIDS—particularly in terms of political mobilization and implementation—also need clearer articulation; the key actors with respect to each of these two objectives need to be more clearly defined. A country-by-country assessment of the relation between MAP support for line ministries and the AIDS activities in non-health sector assistance and their relative effectiveness should be conducted, with an eye on improving their complementarity and using supervision resources efficiently.

APPENDIXES

Evaluating the development effectiveness of the Bank's HIV/AIDS assistance is challenging because, first, there are many determinants of the spread of HIV beyond the activities of the Bank, donors, and governments. Individual and household behavior ultimately determines the course of the epidemic and is conditioned on factors such as culture, political institutions, educational levels, the status of women, and the macroeconomic environment. Second, the Bank is only one of many actors in HIV/AIDS, and all Bank-supported projects are implemented by government, directly or indirectly, often in collaboration with other co-financiers. While the Bank can influence policies, responsibility for key policy decisions and the implementation of programs rests with the government. Thus, the development effectiveness of the Bank's activities is strongly linked to the effectiveness of government.

Figure A.1 presents a schematic diagram of the channels through which World Bank HIV/AIDS assistance affects government outputs, behavioral outcomes, and epidemiological impacts at the country level. The Bank's policy advice, analytic work, and lending can affect government policy directly by influencing government strategies, policies, and public spending on activities relevant to the HIV/AIDS epidemic. Collectively, these are indicators of government commitment. In countries where decision making has been decentralized, **government commitment** is reflected in the strategies and expenditure decisions of many levels of central and local administration. The Bank can affect commitment indirectly through its influence on the behavior of other donors and effective coordination with their activities. Unlike other donors, which can interact both with government and directly with the private sector and nongovernmental organizations

(NGOs) as implementers, the Bank affects the behavior of the private sector and NGOs through its impact on government policies and spending.

Government policies and public spending influence HIV/AIDS through strengthening the government's resources and capacity to provide public goods, service coverage and quality, and the strengthening of institutions to manage the response to HIV/AIDS, both in the public health system and in other public services, such as education, transport, and social protection. Government also affects the response of the private sector and NGOs through the regulatory and legal environment, public subsidies for certain activities, and subcontracting management and implementation. The capacity and activities of the private sector and NGOs also affect the activities of the public health system, in some countries augmenting it. The two-way arrow in figure A.1 between the public health system and other public services reflects the degree of multisectoral coordination of activities. *The outputs of this middle tier of public and private agencies represent the* **implementation** *of government strategies, policies, and activities, some of which may be financed by the Bank.*

Ultimately, the epidemiological impact of Bank-supported government policies and programs on HIV/AIDS depends on the behavior of households and individuals. Within the constraints of their income, human capital, and physical endowments (such as wealth), as well as the cultural and macro environment, households and individuals process public information, make decisions on the allocation of their own time and resources across activities that raise or lower their risk of contracting HIV, and decide whether to consume public and private services (preventive and curative care, schooling, other social services). For ex-

Figure A.1: Channels Through Which World Bank Assistance Affects HIV/AIDS Outcomes

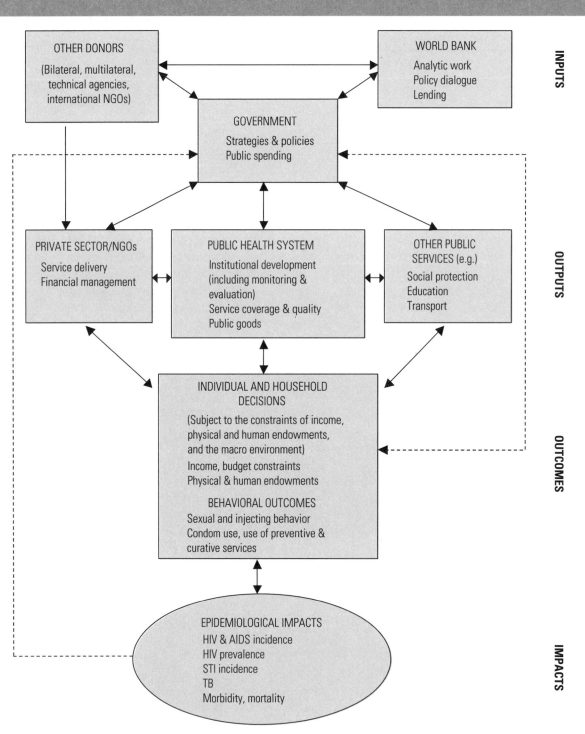

ample, they decide with whom to associate, their number of sexual partners, whether to use condoms, or whether to seek medical treatment for a sexually transmitted infection (STI). *Thus, individuals and households, to the extent that they are affected by public policies and services, may change* **behavior** *(an outcome) that, in interaction with the epidemiological macro environment, results in changes in* **epidemiological impacts** *in terms of HIV infection, other STIs, morbidity from AIDS opportunistic infections (like TB), and AIDS mortality.*

The focus of this evaluation is on documenting and assessing these key elements of the response of the Bank and the government, including:

- The *activities of the Bank and donors,* their interactions or coordination with each other, and with the government and civil society.

- The *government's commitment* to HIV/AIDS, as measured by the policies and strategies adopted and the level and distribution of public expenditure relevant to the problem.
- The *implementation* of policies and programs, in terms of the coverage and quality of services, provision of public goods, and institutional development. Vital to an understanding of the inputs and outputs is the extent of *multisectoral* collaboration within government and the *modalities and effectiveness of interactions between the public and private/NGO sectors.*

The activities of the Bank and donors can be thought of as **inputs**, and both government commitment and implementation as **outputs**. The evaluation will attempt to link the inputs to outputs and, where possible, to **behavioral outcomes** and **epidemiological impacts** at the individual level.

APPENDIX B1:   TIMELINE OF PROJECT APPROVALS AND HIV/AIDS STRATEGIES

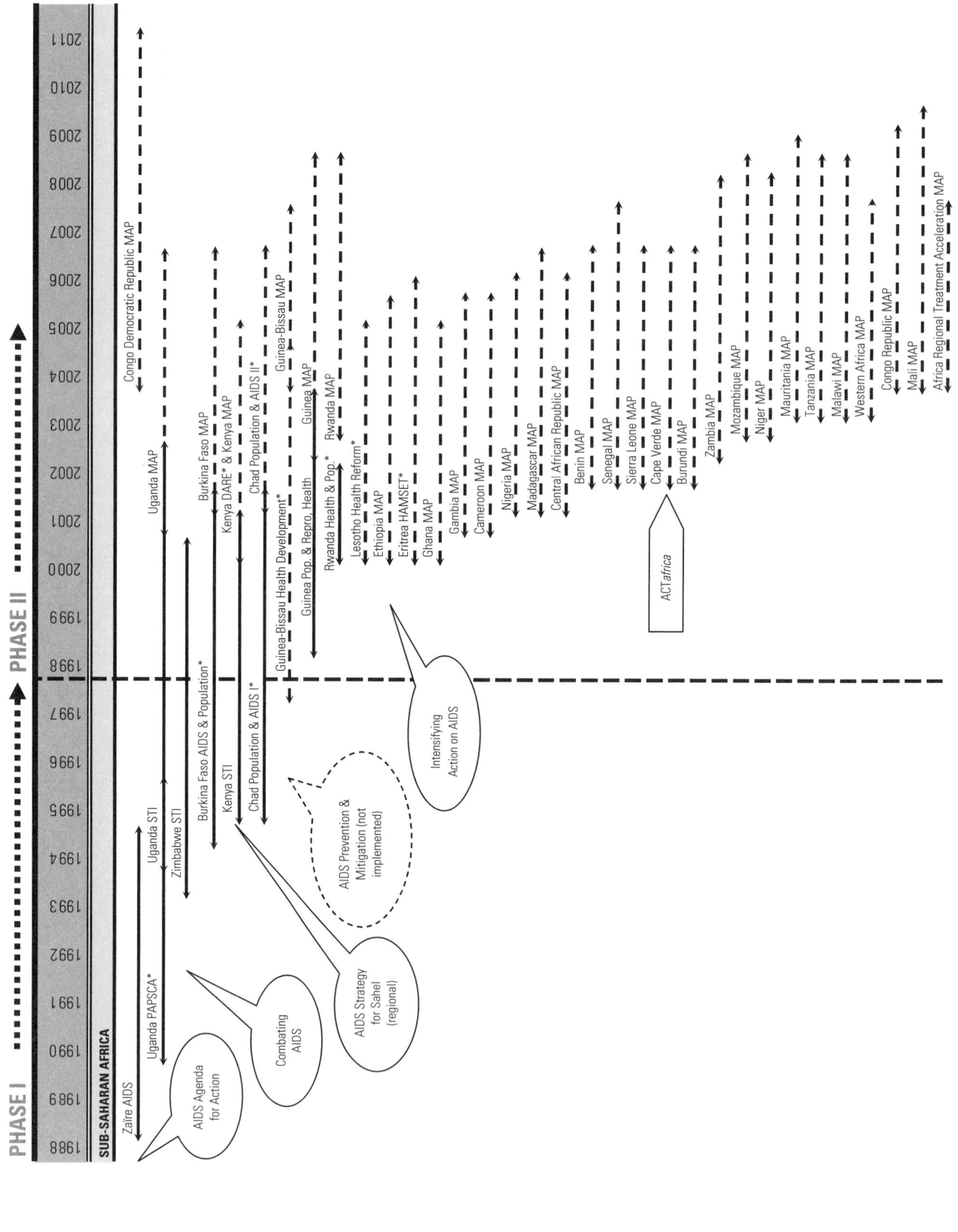

*AIDS component

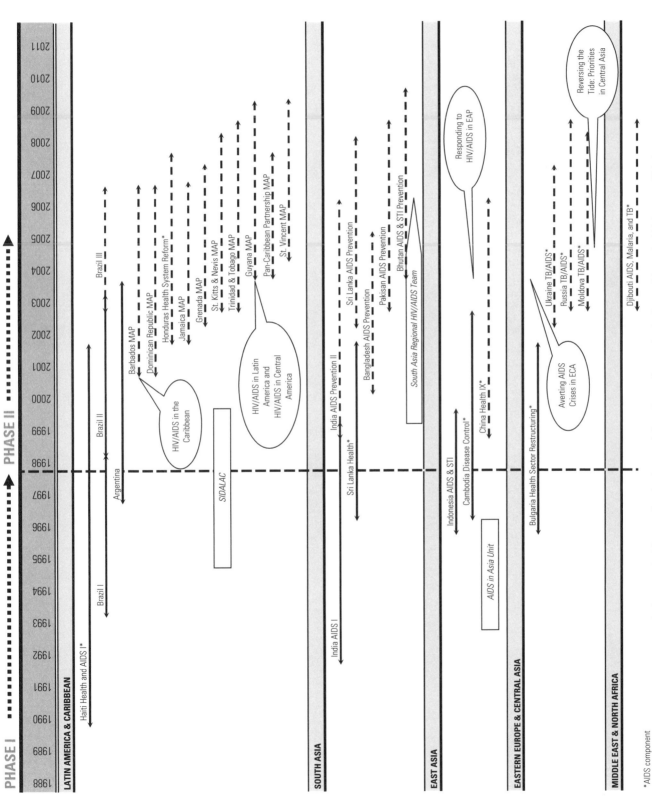

APPENDIX B2: AN ANNOTATED TIMELINE OF THE WORLD BANK HIV/AIDS
RESPONSE

Year	Analytic work	Strategy and institutional response	Lending	World Bank events
1986		At the start of this timeline, Population, Health, and Nutrition (PHN) is a centralized Department of the World Bank.	At the start of the timeline, the Bank has been lending directly for health projects only since 1980.	Barber Conable becomes the 7th president of the World Bank (July). In October, President Conable announces that an internal reorganization will take place with assistance from professional management consultants.
1987	At the request of WHO/GPA, a Bank economist is sent to Geneva in mid-1987 to estimate the economic impact of AIDS. World Bank demographers initiate modeling of the demographic impact of AIDS in select countries (Tanzania, Zaïre) using the PRAY model, which demonstrates the potential impact of greater condom use.	*Financing Health Services in Developing Countries* placed health financing at the center of policy dialogue with borrowers, focusing on improved efficiency and equity. Key reforms: user charges at government health facilities; insurance; effective use of nongovernmental resources; and decentralized planning, budgeting, and purchasing. The reorganization substantially changes the way that PHN is organized. (1) At the central level, Population, Health, and Nutrition becomes a division of the Population and Human Resources Department. (2) Technical departments are created within each Region, including PHN units. (3) Within Regions, country departments are created, combining the functions formerly divided between programs and projects departments.	World Bank issues a press release announcing approval of the Burundi Health and Family Planning Project ($14 million), with a $1.9 million component supporting the National AIDS Control Program (December). The component includes blood screening, IEC, health worker training, surveillance, STD control, and research & evaluation. Immediately after negotiation, the government wants to renegotiate the AIDS component because it is financed by a credit (not a grant). The component was never formally dropped; $715,000 was spent for equipment, furniture, and IEC using funds from another project component. WHO/GPA financed most of the planned activities through $4.76 million in grants, along with other donors. The AIDS component funds were reallocated to rehabilitate health facilities and build additional health infrastructure.	On May 8, Mr. Conable announces that implementation of the reorganization will begin, and will be completed by September. In his address to the Annual Meetings of the World Bank and the IMF, President Conable says "We will support the World Health Organization's worldwide effort to combat AIDS, a disease that has potentially grave consequences for some countries in Africa." (September)[a] As part of the reorganization, two Africa vice presidencies (East and Southern, and Western) are merged. Edward Jaycox is appointed Vice President for Sub-Saharan Africa.
1988	Bank research article on the direct and indirect costs of AIDS in Tanzania and Zaïre is published.	*Acquired Immunodeficiency Syndrome (AIDS): The Bank's Agenda for Action (1988)* is prepared by the Africa Technical Department. If called for the Bank to assist countries through: • Policy dialogue on prevention & control	First free-standing AIDS project approved in Zaïre, building on research by *Projet SIDA*, headed by Jonathan Mann. This is also the first health project in that country and the first approved freestanding Bank project for a single disease. The press release notes	The staff newsletter, *The Bank's World*, features an article on the spread of HIV and its impact on health systems and the economies. It announces that AIDS control components are planned for 10 health projects. Only 5,000 cases of AIDS have

- Analytic work on current & projected spread of HIV & STDs
- Financing priority activities via free-standing AIDS projects and components, restructuring active health projects
- Mobilizing donor resources
- Training Bank staff
- Launching Regional studies/programs
- Assisting governments to establish sub-Regional AIDS research & training centers

However, this strategy was not formally adopted by Bank management and was issued as a working paper.

that average lending for population, health, and nutrition globally is $220 million annually.

Northeast Endemic Disease Control Project in Brazil is approved, with a $6.6 million AIDS component. (Most of this money was used later to prepare the first Brazil AIDS project.)

Bank offers to lend to Thailand for AIDS, but government declines to borrow.

World Bank press release on World AIDS Day (December) reports that the Bank is supporting AIDS-related project components in 7 countries and preparing components in 9 more.

been reported in Sub-Saharan Africa, but an estimated 1 million Africans are infected (March).

1989

"Guidelines for Rapid Estimation of the Direct and Indirect Costs of HIV Infection in a Developing Country," by Over, Bertozzi, and Chin, is published.

World Bank releases Sub-Saharan Africa: From Crisis to Sustainable Growth. A box on AIDS notes that the epidemic "is likely to strain the capacity of already weak health sectors in the countries to which it spreads during the next decades. The potential cost of caring for AIDS patients is high, in addition to the indirect cost to society of the loss of labor and family caretakers. It is also likely to divert resources from the treatment and control of other diseases." (p. 65) The most affected countries are Burundi, Kenya, Rwanda, Tanzania, Uganda, and Zaire. "Strategies... depend on the specific epidemiology of AIDS within the country concerned." Four priorities:

- Integration of AIDS with primary health care and family planning programs, MCH, and STD services

The staff newsletter, The Bank's World, features an article on AIDS in the workplace, how HIV/AIDS can and cannot be transmitted.

(Continued on the following page.)

Year	Analytic work	Strategy and institutional response	Lending	World Bank events
1989 (cont.)		• Counseling of people who test positive for HIV, "to reinforce behavioral patterns that could reduce the spread of infection." • Rapid diagnosis and treatment of STD patients and targeted condom distribution to prostitutes. • IEC targeted to "school-age populations, sexually active people and prostitutes."		
1990	World Bank demographers include AIDS mortality in population projections for all countries. World Bank Research Committee approves funding of research proposal to study the impact of adult mortality on households in Kagera, Tanzania. A longitudinal survey is fielded from 1991 to 1994. Co-financed by USAID and DANIDA. Bank economist gives plenary speech at the International AIDS Conference in Africa (Kinshasa) on the economic impact of AIDS. Background work launched on the *Tanzania AIDS Assessment & Planning Study*, not formally published until December 1992. Background studies on: • Demographic impact (Bulatao 1990) • Survivor assistance (Bertozzi 1990; Ainsworth & Rwegarulira 1992) • Managing OIs (Pallangio 1990) • Cost-effectiveness of alternative IEC interventions (Foote 1990) Sector work on the impact of AIDS in Uganda is launched (December), updated in		First Health and AIDS project approved in Haiti (January), including a $3.3 million component for AIDS. By the time the project closed, $10 million had been spent on AIDS. PAPSCA project for alleviating the social costs of adjustment in Uganda is approved, with $3.3 million for a major component for widows and orphans from war and AIDS. In 1990–91, projects with AIDS components are approved in three countries with low HIV prevalence—Morocco (1990), Mali, and Madagascar (>$1 million but <10% of project costs).	

1993 with Uganda Census numbers, published in 1995. Background work included the food security impact of AIDS.

1991	Bank economist gives plenary speech at the Vth International Conference on AIDS in Africa in Dakar on "The economic impact of AIDS: Shocks, responses, and outcomes." Additional *Tanzania AIDS Assessment* Background papers are produced: • Projected mortality (Chin 1991) • Costs & effects of STD treatment, blood screening, & condoms (Over 1991)	HIV/STD specialist joins the Africa Technical Department, financed for nearly 3 years by the U.S. Centers for Disease Control (June). Returning from a workshop on the economic impact of AIDS in South Africa, a staff member notes that the consensus of the meeting was that South Africa is in a position to act earlier than other African countries and can learn from the experience of the North. The workshop estimated that there would be 400,000 AIDS cases by 2000.[b]	Lewis T. Preston becomes the 8th president of the World Bank (September).
1992	Researchers publish three studies of the economic impact of AIDS, both macro and micro. The *Tanzania AIDS Assessment and Planning Study* is published. Bank demographers publish the *1992–93 World Population Projections* incorporating the demographic impact of AIDS in all countries. They predict that life expectancy will decline in Uganda from 48 in 1985 to 44 in 2000–05, and in Zambia from 53 to 46 over the same time frame. With limited knowledge of the spread of HIV in South Africa, life expectancy is expected to increase.	HIV/STD specialist in Africa is designated the Region's coordinator of HIV/AIDS activities in the Region, with an informal working group of technical and operational staff. The Africa Region issues its second AIDS strategy: *Combating AIDS and other Sexually Transmitted Diseases in Africa: A review of the World Bank's Agenda for Action* (1992). It articulates a country-level agenda to: • Develop multisectoral policies for coping with the impact of the epidemic • Allocate prevention resources to groups with low HIV but high STD infections and on "core transmitter" groups • Set priorities for prevention • Integrate HIV and STD responses • Strengthen health infrastructure	The India National AIDS Control Project is approved, the second free-standing AIDS project. Creates NACO, the National AIDS Control Organisation. By the project's close in 1999, the government will have spent substantially more of its counterpart funds than was originally agreed, a sign of government commitment. Division chief of the HNP division of the Africa Technical Department gives presentation on HIV/AIDS to the Africa Regional Management Team, including managers of non-health departments.

(Continued on the following page.)

Year	Analytic work	Strategy and institutional response	Lending	World Bank events
1992 (cont.)		And a *Bank-level agenda* to: • Assess impact of AIDS on development, on health and non-health sectors • Include HIV/AIDS overviews in non-health sector studies • Analytic work on the effectiveness of STD/HIV interventions • Raise priority of lending for parts of health system critical to STD/HIV prevention & control • Increase involvement of NGOs and CBOs • Improve information of Bank staff within and outside the health sector • Continue collaboration with WHO/GPA ↑ AIDS should *not* dominate the HNP agenda in Africa.		
1993	*Disease Control Priorities in Developing Countries* increased Bank support for project lending for disease control. The chapter on HIV/AIDS and STDs, by Mead Over and Peter Piot, highlighted the role of "core transmitter groups" in launching and sustaining an STD epidemic and the theoretical efficiency of targeting prevention resources to those groups. *World Development Report 1993: Investing in Health* highlights the role of government in the health market. It advocates a 3-pronged approach: fostering an environment that enables households to improve their health; improving the cost-effectiveness of government health care and expanding basic public health programs; and encouraging diversity and competition in provision of health services and insurance.	The first Regional AIDS support unit is set up, the *AIDS in Asia* unit in the East Asia and Pacific Region.	The Brazil *AIDS & STD Control Project* is approved ($250 million, of which $160 million is Bank loan), emphasizing prevention among those most likely to contract and spread HIV. The IBRD loan disburses faster than projected. The first of three sexually transmitted infection (STI) projects is approved, in Zimbabwe, a country with perceived high political commitment. The project mainly supports drug purchases. Following economic and political chaos from 1991 onward, disbursements of all lending to Zaïre are suspended in 1993 and the Bank's first free-standing AIDS project is cancelled in 1994. Only $3.3 million of the $8.1 million credit was disbursed. Low capacity and problems with local management of implementation led to slow	Africa Region Vice President Jaycox chairs a session on the economic impact of AIDS at a one-day symposium at the Annual Meetings of the African Development Bank, in Abidjan, Côte d'Ivoire. World Bank President Preston attends the meeting of the heads of U.N. agencies, the Administrative Committee on Coordination, chaired by the U.N. Secretary General, on the "Joint and Cosponsored United Nations Programme on HIV/AIDS," October 28.

It recommends a cost-effective package of basic health services that includes low-cost HIV prevention. Early and effective HIV prevention is essential because:

- HIV is widespread and spreading rapidly
- The cost-effectiveness of prevention drops when infections move out of high-risk groups into the general population
- The consequences of AIDS are severe and costly
- Prevention is politically charged because it involves sex and drug use.

Priority interventions are:

- Public information on protection
- Encouraging condom use
- Reducing blood-borne HIV transmission
- Integrating HIV prevention and STD services
- Encouraging voluntary anonymous testing
- Developing public health surveillance systems

Research on the macroeconomic impact of AIDS in Tanzania is published in the *World Bank Economic Review*.

disbursements even before these problems, however.

Preparations are initiated for a $19.2 million HIV/AIDS prevention project in Nigeria (to be funded with a $13.7 million IDA credit), with strong support from the Minister of Health. The proposed project featured a research and evaluation component. A $1 million PHRD grant is made available for studies during preparation, including a household survey with HIV and STD prevalence modules, a study of the feasibility of condom production, and a pilot study of social marketing of male urethritis kits.

| 1994 | "AIDS and African Development" is published in the *World Bank Research Observer*. Bank demographer projects child mortality rates through 2005, with and without AIDS. The Bank publishes *World Population Projections 1994–95*, including the impact of AIDS, immediately before the International Conference on Population and Development (ICPD) in Cairo. | Africa Region HIV/AIDS specialist becomes staff member (February). Global focal person for HIV/AIDS, Debrework Zewdie, joins the central Population, Health, and Nutrition Department. *Better Health in Africa* sets forth practical strategies for health improvement in Africa. HIV/AIDS is labeled the most dramatic new health threat. HIV prevalence, vulnerable | An STI project is launched in Uganda and the first of three population projects with substantial AIDS components, in Burkina Faso. | Sven Sandstrom, Managing Director of the World Bank Group, delivers a keynote address to the AIDS in the World Conference, on "AIDS and Development: A shared concern, a shared vision," in Stockholm. The conference is sponsored by the Government of Sweden. |

(Continued on the following page.)

Year	Analytic work	Strategy and institutional response	Lending	World Bank events
1994 (cont.)		groups, transmission modes, and economic impacts are discussed and potential AIDS treatment costs as a share of total and government health expenditures presented. Recommendations are in a box: The public policy response must start with prevention. The top priority is carefully targeted public education and condom promotion campaigns; and for the detection and treatment of other STDs. There is also recognition of the growing needs of AIDS patients as their diseases progress and the strain on African hospitals, underscoring the importance of health system reform. However, overall, the AIDS epidemic is given scant treatment in the document and is not featured in the report's recommendations.		
1995	World Bank discussion paper on *Uganda's AIDS Crisis: Its implications for development* is published.	The *Regional AIDS Strategy for the Sahel* is issued for a set of extremely poor countries with relatively low HIV prevalence. It calls for: (1) Country-level support for: • Medium- to long-term strategies to develop sustainable policies and programs • Strengthened communications • Accelerated condom social marketing • Expanded clinical management of STDs • Assisting NGO & private sector initiatives • Broad-based policy analysis and program coordination (2) Regional support for: • Advocacy and capacity building with grant financing from the donor commu-	The Kenya *STI* and *Chad Population and AIDS Control* projects are approved. After two years of preparation and a final project appraisal document, the Nigeria AIDS prevention project is cancelled for reasons that have nothing to do with the project's merits. At the time, there were many governance problems, only social sector projects were being approved and several of them had been cancelled after approval. The $1 million PHRD grant for preparatory research is still approved for execution. However, it too is eventually not pursued following a one-year struggle within the government over who would be the signatory for the PHRD account.	James Wolfensohn becomes the ninth World Bank president (June). Bank funds a high-level OAU delegation, accompanied by Africa region AIDS coordinator, to talk with 4 African presidents on the AIDS agenda, in preparation for the 1996 OAU assembly.

nity, by mobilizing political & opinion leaders

- Pilot projects
- Studies and research
- Technical support and training

The Latin America and Caribbean Region proposes to support a Regional AIDS Initiative for Latin America and the Caribbean (SIDALAC), based in the Mexican Health Foundation (FUNSALUD) in Mexico City. SIDALAC is funded through earmarked contributions of the Bank to UNAIDS. Its main objectives are to conduct analytic work for strategic planning, and to disseminate results and promote exchange of country experiences in the Region.

1996

AIDS Prevention and Mitigation in Sub-Saharan Africa: An Updated World Bank Strategy.

(1) Findings:

- Household and sectoral impacts
- Slow progress with multisectoral policies
- Pilot projects needed to be expanded in depth and breadth
- Interventions need to be targeted early in the epidemic to the highest-risk groups to be most cost-effective
- Care of AIDS patients needs to be integrated into the health system

(2) New areas for the Bank:

- Generating political commitment
- Changing risk behaviors
- Mobilizing resources to intensify the breadth and depth of programs

The Cambodia *Disease Control and Health Development Project* is approved, the first Bank-supported health project in that country, with components to strengthen government infectious disease programs for AIDS, TB, and malaria.

The Indonesia *HIV/AIDS and STD Prevention and Management Project* is approved, the first free-standing AIDS project in a country with a nascent epidemic.

Health projects with AIDS components in Bulgaria and Sri Lanka are approved. The Bulgarian project finances only blood safety.

President and Mrs. Wolfensohn travel to India, visit the Dharavi red-light district of Mumbai and meet with prostitutes and NGOs. He discusses AIDS with the Prime Minister, President, Minister of Finance, and the Chief Ministers of Maharashtra, Karnataka, and Orissa (October).

In his speech to the Annual Meetings, President Wolfensohn calls for creation of the "Knowledge Bank" (October).

Africa VP Jaycox retires. He is replaced by two Vice Presidents for Africa — Messrs. Callisto Madavo and Jean-Louis Sarbib.

(Continued on the following page.)

Year	Analytic work	Strategy and institutional response	Lending	World Bank events
1996 (cont.)		• Improving design and implementation of cost-effective measures to mitigate the epidemic However, because this strategy was developed and disseminated immediately prior to an internal restructuring within the Africa Region, it is never published or disseminated. World Bank joins UNAIDS as one of six co-sponsors. *AIDS in Asia* unit is disbanded.		
1997	*Confronting AIDS* is published by the research department of the Bank, in a press conference led by the Bank's Chief Economist and Senior Vice President, Joseph Stiglitz. The report assembles evidence on the economic and societal determinants of the epidemic, its economic impact, and the effectiveness of interventions in developing countries. It identifies principles for priority-setting by policy makers, makes the economic case for government involvement in fighting AIDS, and highlights government's unique role in providing public goods and ensuring that people most likely to contract and transmit HIV engage in safer behavior. It advocates access of AIDS patients to cost-effective health care and the integration of AIDS mitigation programs and policies with poverty reduction programs and emphasizes the need to intervene early in countries with nascent epidemics, highlighting India, China, and Eastern Europe, where epidemics can still be averted. Preface of the book is	The *HNP Sector Strategy* is released, emphasizing the Bank's objectives to improve HNP outcomes of the poor, enhance the performance of health systems, and secure sustainable health care financing. Mentioned emergence of new epidemics and the infectious disease burden, mentioning AIDS, TB, and malaria in an annex. No specific strategy for HIV/AIDS. The global AIDS coordinator is hired to lead AIDS activities in the Africa Region (September). A 1997 reorganization of the Bank tried to strike a better balance between "country focus" and "sectoral excellence." Sector staff are grouped into larger Regional sector units or departments and worked with country departments in a matrix relationship. Sector Boards (including the HNP Sector Board) were created to bring together the Regional managers working in the same sector. Bankwide "anchor" units were put in place to provide quality support to the Regions.	The *AIDS and STD Control Project* in Argentina is approved.	East Asian economic crisis unfolds in the summer of 1997. Senior Vice President and Chief Economist Joseph Stiglitz addresses the European Parliament on the need to confront AIDS in developing countries, in Brussels (November 25).

co-signed by the Bank, UNAIDS, and the European Commission.

World Bank economists deliver plenary speeches on *Confronting AIDS* at the International Conference on AIDS and STDs in Latin America (Lima, Peru) and at the International Conference on AIDS and STDs in Africa (Abidjan, Côte d'Ivoire). (December)

"Setting priorities for government involvement in antiretrovirals" is published in a WHO volume, based on work on mother to child transmission in Thailand.

The first of several pieces of country-level economic and sector work sponsored by the AIDS in Asia unit is completed.

1998

Eighteen background papers for *Confronting AIDS* are published by the European Commission in a background paper volume. The original report is disseminated widely in Latin America and Asia, translated into Spanish, French, Russian, Vietnamese, Japanese, and Chinese.

World Bank discussion paper, "World Bank HIV/AIDS interventions: Ex-ante and ex-post evaluation," is published, reviewing the design and performance of Bank-sponsored projects to date.

Two more outputs of the AIDS in Asia unit are issued.

Joint symposium of World Bank and UNAIDS in Washington on the demographic impact of AIDS, chaired by Africa Region VP Callisto Madavo (January). The shocking statistics on reduced life expectancy lead to dramatically increased commitment by Africa Regional management to mainstream AIDS in all of the Region's work.

Institution-wide AIDS Vaccine Task Force is initiated by the Chief Economist's office and the Vice President for Human Development, chaired by the head of the health sector, to develop new and innovative mechanisms for the Bank to encourage more rapid development of an HIV/AIDS vaccine for developing countries (April).

The second *Brazil AIDS & STD Control Project* is approved. By project closing in 2003, the government has spent more counterpart funds than it originally committed to the project.

The Guinea *Population and Reproductive Health Project* is approved.

In an address to the Economic Commission for Africa in Addis Ababa, President Wolfensohn puts education and health at the top of the African agenda and urges delegates to "vigorously and straightforwardly pronounce the words 'AIDS' and 'AIDS prevention'." He says that AIDS "needs to be put front and center and we need to emphasize prevention." (February) Africa VP Callisto Madavo delivers a speech at the 12th World AIDS Conference in Geneva (June 30, 1998), on "AIDS, Development and the Vital Role of Government." He speaks of the impact on development and the impact of development on AIDS, and the contribution of partners/donors: (a) keep AIDS in the policy agenda; (b) supplement country resources; (c) "broadly disseminate the latest information (biological, technical, policy and

(Continued on the following page.)

Year	Analytic work	Strategy and institutional response	Lending	World Bank events
1998 (cont.)				facilitate cross-country sharing of experience"; (d) facilitate international public goods, like vaccine research and evaluation. While saying that the Bank has not done enough, he notes the demand problem—"Because our resources are loans to governments, we cannot start programs on our own. Governments must first seek our support."
1999	Four more papers from the AIDS in Asia unit are issued (including a newsletter). Sector work is forthcoming on Brazil and Uganda, linked to projects. Study of the AIDS vaccine industry's perceptions of the market for an AIDS vaccine in developing countries is completed for the AIDS Vaccine Task Force.	New Africa Region Strategy, *Intensifying Action Against HIV/AIDS in Africa*. Noting that many interventions have been shown cost-effective, the strategy focuses on creating an enabling environment and mobilizing resources to increase coverage of interventions. The four pillars of the strategy are: • Advocacy to strengthen political commitment • Mobilization of resources • Support for HIV/AIDS prevention, support, treatment • Expanding the knowledge base. The paper advocates a "decentralized participatory approach." In low-prevalence countries (defined as less than 7% HIV prevalence), it advocates focusing on prevention among groups at highest risk for transmitting HIV. In high-prevalence countries (7% prevalence or higher), "the program must address wider objectives and reach all vulnerable groups, while reinforcing sustainable behavior change among those at highest risk." AIDS Campaign Team for Africa (ACT *africa*) unit is created to provide resources and technical support to country teams to "main-	The first *India AIDS Control project* is concluded, with the government disbursing more counterpart funds than were in the plan, a sign of heightened political commitment. A second *India AIDS Prevention Project* is approved. Following poor implementation experience and the East Asian crisis, the *Indonesia HIV/AIDS & STD Prevention and Management Project* is cancelled, with only $4.5 million of the $24.8 million commitment expensed. A health project with a major AIDS component is approved for China. Preparation of a TB/AIDS control project in Russia is launched, with much policy dialogue. Discussion and project development continue through 2002. The AIDS project pipeline for Africa is dry; there are no preparations underway for new AIDS projects.	Africa VP Madavo addresses the International Conference on AIDS in Africa in Lusaka, Zambia, calls for "A new compact on AIDS" and launches the new Africa region strategy to "intensify" the fight against AIDS (September). Madavo visits Ethiopia to discuss HIV/AIDS with the Prime Minister and encourage project development. Vice President for South Asia, Mieko Nishimizu, speaks on the impact of AIDS and the need to confront the epidemic at the International Conference on AIDS in Asia and the Pacific (ICAAP), in Kuala Lumpur. (October) Following up on the ICAAP meeting, President Wolfensohn sends letters to the heads of state of South and East Asia pointing out the economic impact of AIDS on urging them to act. (December) President Wolfensohn travels to Nigeria and raises AIDS in the policy dialogue.

"stream" HIV/AIDS activities in all sectors, headed by the Africa Region AIDS Coordinator.

The South Asia Health Unit forms a small HIV/AIDS team supported by funds from the Regional Vice President's office.

2000

Thailand Social Monitor series publishes study "Thailand's Response to AIDS," documenting the evolution of the epidemic, AIDS policy, programs, and evidence of effectiveness.

The AIDS Vaccine Task Force produces recommendations on how the Bank can accelerate an AIDS vaccine (May). However, no action is taken by management on the recommendations. The European Commission offers to co-finance with Development Economics one of the recommendations, namely additional research on the demand for and cost-effectiveness of AIDS vaccines in developing countries.

The Bank drops earmarking of support to SIDALAC; funding reverts to UNAIDS where it competes with other proposals.

First *Multi-Country AIDS Program* (MAP) is approved by the Board to provide a $500 million envelope for financing HIV/AIDS projects (September). The first four projects are in Kenya, Ethiopia, Eritrea, and Ghana. The Ethiopia project is identified, appraised, and negotiated in only six weeks. The Eritrea project departs from the template, is based in the MOH and has AIDS, TB, and malaria components.

Free-standing AIDS project is approved for Bangladesh, which has a nascent epidemic; health projects with major AIDS components are launched in Kenya and Lesotho.

President Wolfensohn becomes the first President of the World Bank to address the UN Security Council. He calls for a "War on AIDS" and asserts that the resources and effort being devoted to the epidemic are grossly inadequate. (January) He estimates that $1–$2.3 billion is needed for prevention in Africa, against $160 million in existing official assistance.

At the spring meetings of the Bank and the Fund in Washington D.C., AIDS is placed as the first item of business before the Development Committee, in addition to trade & development and debt relief. (April) No country that wishes to act will be unable to implement it for lack of resources.

In response to a concept note from ACT*africa* asking for several hundred million dollars for African AIDS lending not subject to IDA caps, senior Bank managers approve an even greater amount ($500 million) on condition that the Africa team bring two fully negotiated projects to the Bank's Board by the Annual Meetings, in September (June).

At the International AIDS Conference in Durban, South Africa, the Bank pledges $500 million to assist with AIDS prevention and care in Africa. (July).

(Continued on the following page.)

Year	Analytic work	Strategy and institutional response	Lending	World Bank events
2000 (cont.)				At the Caribbean AIDS Conference the Bank pledges to dramatically increase the scale of its assistance to AIDS in Caribbean countries by $85–100 million In his speech to the Annual Meetings, President Wolfensohn underscores the huge increase in resources made available to Africa ($500 million), with AIDS assistance overall at $1 billion. He calls for exploring "innovative instruments," including grants, for such pressing issues as HIV/AIDS" (September, in Prague, Czech Republic). Mr. Wolfensohn again travels to India and raises AIDS as an issue.
2001	Numerous sector studies and operational background papers are issued. Two clusters of research studies are published that focus on: (a) the potential demand for an AIDS vaccine in developing countries; and (b) the economic impact of adult AIDS mortality on children, the elderly, and households in Tanzania.	*HIV/AIDS in the Caribbean: Issues and Options*, the sub-regional strategy for the Caribbean, is produced. World Bank Institute launches the Leadership Program on AIDS.	Seven country-level African MAP projects are approved, one of them in Madagascar, a country with a nascent AIDS epidemic. The $155 million Caribbean Multi-Country AIDS Project is approved, with the first two loans for Barbados and the Dominican Republic. Agreement is reached to allow financing of anti-retroviral treatment in Barbados, an upper-middle income country (June). The second Chad Population and AIDS project is approved, outside of the MAP (July).	
2002	The Bank releases the *Economic Consequences of HIV/AIDS in Russia* in May 2002, updated in November. It seems to have a positive impact on government commitment, in conjunction with contacts with President Wolfensohn.	The Global HIV/AIDS program is created. The Global Monitoring and Evaluation Support Team (GAMET) is created, housed at the World Bank, to facilitate UNAIDS cosponsor efforts to build country-level M&E capacities and coordinate technical support (June).	Second $500 million multi-country AIDS program envelope is approved (February). The second MAP allows finance of antiretroviral treatment. Seven country-level African MAP projects are approved, including two financed by the first IDA grants (Guinea and Zambia).	Debrework Zewdie is appointed as the first Global HIV/AIDS adviser, under the Vice President for Human Development. Bank President Wolfensohn meets with President Putin of Russia, discusses commitment to borrowing for AIDS control.

	Education and AIDS: A Window of Hope launches the Bank's efforts to engage the education sector in the response to AIDS. *Africa's Orphans and Vulnerable Children*, a working paper, is published by the social protection family in the Africa Region, engaging yet another sector. An AIDS toolkit for transport projects is published.	HIV/AIDS is featured as one of the main themes at a meeting in Beirut on "The public health challenges in the 21st century in the Middle East and North Africa," sponsored by the Bank/MENA, WHO, the National Institutes of Health, U.S. Centers for Disease Control and Prevention and American University of Beirut. The meeting is attended by delegates from 22 countries, including 11 ministers of health or finance. Three sessions address the need to confront AIDS in the Middle East and North Africa Region, one of them by Peter Piot, head of UNAIDS (June).	A national AIDS prevention project is approved for Sri Lanka (an IDA grant), with a nascent epidemic, and health projects with major AIDS components are approved in Honduras and Ukraine. The latter is the first large AIDS commitment in Eastern Europe other than for blood safety. IBRD loans for two Carribbean MAP projects are approved, for Jamaica and Grenada.	IDA grants become a new instrument for use against AIDS (September).
2003	A research paper on the *Long-run Economic Costs of AIDS* in South Africa is released at the Nairobi AIDS conference, with dramatic conclusions that increase the pressure to act in South Africa.	*Averting AIDS Crises in Eastern Europe and Central Asia*, a Regional strategy, is published.	Eight African MAP projects are approved, financed by IDA grants, including the first regional project on the Abidjan-Lagos transport corridor. A first AIDS project is approved for Pakistan, which has a concentrated epidemic, and the third Brazil AIDS project is approved. New AIDS/TB projects are approved in Russia, following many years of dialogue and analytic work, and in Moldova. IBRD loans are approved for two additional Caribbean MAP projects, in St. Kitts and Nevis and Trinidad & Tobago.	
2004	Large study on modeling the costs and consequences of HIV/AIDS treatment and prevention in India is completed, conducted to inform Indian government of treatment policy options. Report by the Middle East and North Africa	East Asia and the Pacific Region publishes a Regional strategy, *Addressing HIV/AIDS in East Asia and the Pacific*.	By the end of the fiscal year (June 2004), five African MAP projects are approved, including a regional Treatment Acceleration Program (TAP) covering several countries, all IDA grants. Three additional Caribbean MAP projects are approved—country-level projects in	The World Bank, GFATM, UNICEF, and Clinton Foundation reach an agreement that allows countries supported by the three institutions to gain access to ARV drugs and diagnostic prices negotiated by the Clinton Foundation (April).

(Continued on the following page.)

Year	Analytic work	Strategy and institutional response	Lending	World Bank events
2004 (cont.)	Region highlights the cost of inaction with respect to HIV/AIDS.		Guyana and St. Vincent & the Grenadines and a regional Caribbean project. All receive some element of grant financing. An AIDS and STI Prevention and Control project is approved in Bhutan.	Human Development Network Vice President Jean-Louis Sarbib participates in a high-level panel discussion on accountability for results of HIV/AIDS assistance at the 13th International Conference on AIDS, in Bangkok (July).

a. There were no references to AIDS in the speeches of either President Clausen (1981–86) or Preston (1991–95) in the World Bank Archives' collection.

b. "Although the full economic impact of the disease is not completely clear, it is apparent that we are not facing a 'doomsday' scenario."

c. Wolfensohn statement to the Development Committee, April 17, 2000.

APPENDIX B3:   TIMELINE OF GLOBAL AIDS EVENTS

Year	Events			Technology/"best practices"	Epidemiology
	International	Industrialized world	Developing world		
1981		U.S. Centers for Disease Control (CDC) issues first warning about occurrence in gay men of rare form of pneumonia that is later determined to be AIDS-related. (1) First reported case of gay-related immunodeficiency disease (GRID) in France. (2) *New York Times* publishes first news story on AIDS. (1)			
1982		U.S. CDC formally establishes the term "Acquired Immune Deficiency Syndrome (AIDS)." (1) Gay Men's Health Crisis (GMHC) founded in U.S.—first community-based AIDS service provider in U.S. (1)	First AIDS case diagnosed in Brazil. (3) Tuberculosis (TB) is the major cause of death of AIDS patients in Port au Prince, Haiti. (2)		AIDS cases reported from blood transfusions and possible mother-to-child transmission (MTCT). (4) U.S. CDC identifies four risk factors for AIDS: male homosexuality, intravenous drug abuse, Haitian origin, hemophilia A. (1)
1983	Start of global surveillance of AIDS cases by World Health Organization (WHO). (4)		Reports of deaths from "wasting disease" in the Ugandan border village of Lukunya. (2) Peter Piot and officials from the U.S. CDC identify 38 AIDS cases in Kinshasa, Zaïre, half of which are women. Results not accepted by journals for a year because reviewers would not believe in heterosexual spread—not published until July 1984 in *The Lancet*. (2) Unusual patient deaths observed in Lusaka, Zambia, hospitals. (2)	U.S. government issues recommendations for preventing HIV transmission through sexual contact and blood transfusions, including: avoiding sexual contact with persons with AIDS; risk groups refraining from donating plasma and/or blood; evaluating blood screening procedures. (5)	AIDS cases in children incorrectly believed to be from casual household transmission. (4) U.S. CDC adds fifth risk factor: female sexual partners of men with AIDS—suggests general population at risk. (1)

1984	AIDS tabulated as a "notifiable disease" for the first time in U.S. (6)	Zairian government supports establishment of Projet SIDA (jointly supported by the Belgian Institute of Tropical Medicine, the U.S. CDC, and the U.S. National Institute of Infectious Diseases) to start a systematic long-term study of HIV/AIDS: HIV infection rate in Kinshasa estimated at 4–8%. (7) Link between HIV and increased TB noted by Projet SIDA (Zaïre) researchers. (2) First AIDS case diagnosed in Thailand, among gay men returning from abroad. (8)		Isolation of the human immunodeficiency virus (HIV). (1) U.S. CDC states that abstention from intravenous drug use and reduction of needle-sharing should also be effective in preventing HIV transmission. (1)	13,143 AIDS cases reported worldwide to WHO, cumulatively, from 1979–1984. (9)
1985	1st International AIDS Conference in Atlanta, Georgia, hosted by U.S. Health and Human Services and WHO. Reports that there was an older AIDS epidemic in Africa that may have originated in monkeys, resulting in blame and "finger-pointing" to Africa as the source of the epidemic. African leaders upset at the insinuation, and resistance develops to foreign researchers. (2)	Reported cases of wasting disease ("Juliana's disease") in Kagera, Tanzania. Tanzanian doctors identify these as AIDS cases, based on comparisons with published symptoms in the medical journals in the U.S. AIDS cases are confirmed by Walter Reed Army Hospital among hospital patients (a year earlier) in Lusaka, Zambia.	U.S. blood banks begin screening for HIV. (1) U.S. teen Ryan White is barred from school because he has AIDS; speaks out against stigma and discrimination. (1) U.S. actor Rock Hudson dies from AIDS. (1) Germany distributes 27 million leaflets on AIDS and promotes condom use. (2)	U.S. government licenses commercial production of first blood test for AIDS. (4) New Bangui definition of AIDS adopted to reflect clinical symptoms. (4) Australian researchers report AIDS case from breastfeeding. (10)		15,202 new AIDS cases worldwide reported to WHO. (9)
1986	U.S. President Reagan first mentions the word "AIDS" in public. (1)	First AIDS cases diagnosed in India and Ethiopia. (11, 12) Projet SIDA (Zaïre) finds 1985 infection rate in the general population of Kinshasa is about 1/3 that of gay men in San Francisco. Key		HIV-2, a second strain of HIV, is identified, prevalent in West Africa. (2) U.S. Surgeon General issues report on AIDS calling for education and condom use. (1) Early results of clinical test show AZT (zidovudine) slows down attack of HIV. (13)		28,791 new AIDS cases worldwide reported to WHO. (9)

(Continued on the following page.)

Year	Events				Epidemiology
	International	Industrialized world	Developing world	Technology/"best practices"	
1986 (cont.)			risk factors identified as multiple heterosexual partners, injections with unsterilized needles, and foreign travel. (2)		
1987	WHO-Global Program on AIDS (GPA) established. (1) AIDS is first disease debated on the floor of the United Nations General Assembly. Resolution is passed supporting coordinated response by the UN system. (14) World Health Assembly passes "Global Strategy for the Prevention and Control of AIDS" put forth by GPA, which established the principles of local, national, and international action to prevent and control HIV/AIDS. (2) 81 countries have passed laws against HIV+ people or other social groups at high risk. (2) 3rd International AIDS Conference, Washington, D.C.—U.S. and French researchers denounce discriminatory and irrational policies of the U.S. and governments worldwide. (2)	U.K. Secretary of State for Social Services visits U.S. and shakes hands with an AIDS patient. (4) AIDS Coalition to Unleash Power (ACT UP) founded in U.S.—in response to proposed cost of AZT. (1) Princess Diana opens first AIDS hospital ward and shakes hands with AIDS patients. (4) *And the Band Played On: People, Politics and the AIDS Epidemic* by Randy Shilts published—details U.S. response to AIDS epidemic. (1) First AIDS case diagnosed in the Soviet Union. (15) U.S. President Reagan made first major speech on AIDS, saying abstinence hasn't been adequately stressed and pointing out that "medicine and morality teach the same lessons." (2)	President Kaunda of Zambia announces his son has died of AIDS. (4) The AIDS Support Organization (TASO) founded in Uganda. (4) Uganda Red Cross begins HIV/AIDS control activities by working alongside rock musician, Philly Lutaya—the first famous Ugandan to go public about his HIV status.	WHO-GPA calls for establishing national AIDS programs in every country and implementing prevention programs including preventing sexual transmission through education, preventing parenteral transmission by keeping blood supplies safe, preventing intravenous drug abuse and educating and treating intravenous drug abusers, ensuring that injecting equipment is sterile, and preventing perinatal transmission. (16) U.S. government approves AZT as the first antiretroviral drug for AIDS treatment. (1)	54,741 new AIDS cases worldwide reported to WHO. (9) WHO-GPA develops modeling software program, Epimodel, to estimate current HIV infections and number of AIDS cases. (17)
1988	World Summit on Ministers of Health meet in London to discuss common AIDS strategy, "endorsed the GPAs 15-point declaration that called for openness and candor between governments and scientists, opposed AIDS-related discrimina- the Soviet Union. (2)	First comprehensive needle exchange program established in U.S. in Tacoma, Washington. (1) Outbreak of HIV in medical institutions infects over 300 infants in the Kalmykia and Rostov regions of	HIV infection rate among IDUs in Bangkok, Thailand, jumps to 40%. (8) HIV infection rate among sex workers in Addis Ababa, Ethiopia, found to be 20%. (8)		75,975 new AIDS cases worldwide reported to WHO. (9)

	tion, gave primacy to national education programs as a means to limit the spread of AIDS, and reaffirmed the GPA's role in international leadership." (2) However, many representatives ignored the message of favoring educational rather than repressive measures to fight the epidemic. First Annual World AIDS Day. (1) GPA increasingly links human rights issues with the spread of HIV/AIDS. (2) Halfdan Mahler resigns as head Director-General of WHO, replaced by Hiroshi Nakajima.	Estimated global external assistance for HIV/AIDS is on the order of $60 million. (18)		
1989	U.S. government creates National Commission on AIDS. (1) AIDS activists stage several major protests about the high costs of AIDS drugs in the U.S. (1)	HIV infection rate among sex workers in Chiang Mai, Thailand, found to be 44%; 0.5% in army conscripts. (8) "100% condom" program among CSWs piloted in one province in Thailand. (8)	WHO issues statement about link between HIV/AIDS and TB, both growing epidemics. (19)	97,243 new AIDS cases worldwide reported to WHO. (9)
1990	Jonathan Mann resigns as head of WHO GPA. (4) Michael Merson replaces Mann. 6th International AIDS Conference in U.S.: NGOs boycott conference to protest U.S. immigration policy. (1) International AIDS Society announces it will not hold conference in country with travel restrictions. (4)	Ryan White dies; U.S. government passes Ryan White Care Act, providing federal funds for community-based care and treatment services.	U.S. government approves AZT for treatment of pediatric AIDS. (1)	102,289 new AIDS cases worldwide reported to WHO. (9)

(Continued on the following page.)

Year	Events				
	International	Industrialized world	Developing world	Technology/"best practices"	Epidemiology
1991		U.S. basketball star Magic Johnson announces he is HIV positive. (1)	New Thailand Prime Minister Anand launches AIDS prevention and control program as national priority, including massive public information campaign and national launch of 100% condom program among CSWs. (8) Imperial College (UK) modelers predict that AIDS would generate negative population growth in Africa. (20)	WHO develops guidelines for the clinical management of HIV infection in adults. (21)	125,779 new AIDS cases worldwide reported to WHO. (9)
1992	WHO sets priority target for prevention: availability of condoms. (4) The World Health Assembly (WHA) endorses WHO's global strategy for prevention and control of AIDS and calls upon member states to: intensify prevention and raise political commitment; adopt the updated global strategy, with particular attention to action directed at women, children and adolescents; integration of AIDS prevention and control with STD activities; improve prevention due to blood and blood products; mobilize national resources for a multisectoral response for prevention and mitigation; adopt measures to oppose discrimination; overcome denial on the scope of the epidemic; and educate health professionals to care for AIDS patients. (22) *AIDS in the World* published. (23)		*AIDS in Africa: Its Present and Future Impact* by Tony Barnett and Piers Blaikie published—predicts grave economic outcomes, dissolution of households and families in Eastern Africa. (25) U.S. State Department releases "White Paper" with predictions of life expectancy at birth reduced by 15 years and infection rates of 10–30% of sub-Saharan Africa. (24)	First successful use of (dual) combination drug therapy. (26) Concern that TB was not only increasing among HIV-positive people, but that this could be raising the risk of acquiring TB in the rest of the population.	149,799 new AIDS cases worldwide reported to WHO. (9)

1993		Russian ballet star Rudolf Nureyev dies from AIDS. (1) Russian government adopts first post-Soviet AIDS legislation. (15) HIV infection rate in army conscripts in Thailand peaks at 4%, after peaking among Northern Thai conscripts the previous year at more than 12%. (8)	Reports of transmission of drug-resistant HIV. (4)	308,353 new AIDS cases worldwide reported to WHO. (9)
1994	The International Conference on Population and Development (ICPD) in Cairo, September 5–13, endorses a plan of action that calls for: (a) reproductive health programs to increase efforts to prevent, detect, and treat STDs; (b) specialized training for health care providers, including family planning providers, for specialized training in prevention, detection, and counseling for STDs, including HIV/AIDS; (c) incorporating information, education, and counseling for responsible sexual behavior and prevention of STDs and HIV into all reproductive health services; and (d) promote reliable supply and distribution of high-quality condoms as integral components of all RH services. "All relevant international organizations, especially the WHO, should significantly increase their procurement." (23)	Condom use among CSWs in Thailand rises to more than 90%, up from 14% in 1988; reported STDs among men decline to about 10% of former levels. (8) Researchers show that the incidence of HIV in Thailand among young army conscripts has declined following increased use of condoms and decline in use of sex workers. (28) Incidence of HIV declines in female Zaïrian sex workers following targeted condom promotion and STD treatment. (29)	AZT is shown to reduce the risk of mother-to-child transmission of HIV by 67.5 percent. (30) Median time from HIV infection until development of AIDS is measured, drawing on data from homosexual men in hepatitis B vaccine trial cohorts in Amsterdam, New York City, and San Francisco over the period 1978–91: 122 months (10.2 years) from infection until AIDS and 20 months (1.7 years) from initial AIDS diagnosis to death. (31) Median survival time from CD4 T-cell count of 200 among homosexual men in San Francisco increased from 28 months in 1983–86 to 38 months in 1988–93, due primarily to prevention and treatment of pneumocystis carinii pneumonia (PCP); AZT had no effect on survival time. (32) A double-blind randomized controlled trial finds that there's no significant difference in clinical outcome or progression of HIV	152,911 new AIDS cases reported worldwide to WHO. (9)

(Continued on the following page.)

Year	International	Events Industrialized world	Developing world	Technology/"best practices"	Epidemiology
				disease among HIV positive people treated immediately with AZT and those for whom treatment is deferred. (33)	
				Two-drug anti-retroviral regimens found only moderately effective in reducing morbidity, add less than one year of disease-free survival and have no real benefit on length of life. (34)	
1995	7th International AIDS Conference for PLWHA is held in Durban, South Africa, first time in Africa. (4)		Results of 1995 Demographic and Health Survey in Uganda show reduction in percent of young adults who have ever had sex, increase in condom use, and decline in the percent with a casual partner, which could account for evidence of decline in HIV incidence in Uganda. However, it is not clear whether these changes can be attributed to public policy or the huge toll of AIDS mortality on families in Uganda.	U.S. CDC issues first guidelines on prevention of opportunistic infections (OIs). (1)	WHO estimates 4.7 million new infections; 1.8 million new AIDS cases. (9)
				Results of a randomized controlled trial in Mwanza, Tanzania, find that treatment of symptomatic STDs reduces the incidence of HIV by more than 40%. (35)	
				Researchers present evidence of the impact of harm-reduction programs on maintaining low HIV prevalence among injection drug users. (36)	
				Research suggests treatment should be aggressive and early on in the course of HIV infection, i.e., "hit early, hit hard." (37)	
				U.S. FDA approves first protease inhibitor drug, saquinavir, for treatment of HIV. (38)	
1996	Joint United Nationals Programme on HIV/AIDS (UNAIDS) established	External assistance for HIV/AIDS to low- and middle-income countries	Brazil government begins national ARV distribution. (1)	Results from clinical trials show effectiveness of combination ther-	UNAIDS estimates 3 million new infections; 23 million infected as

(Continued on the following page.)

with 6 co-sponsors (UNDP, UN-ESCO, UNFPA, UNICEF, World Bank, WHO). Peter Piot named head. (1) 11th International AIDS Conference in Vancouver, Canada, highlights effectiveness of HAART. (1) International AIDS Vaccine Initiative (IAVI) founded, launched to accelerate development of preventive AIDS vaccine in developing countries. (1) *AIDS in the World II* published. (9)

amounts to $300 million. (39) Short-course AZT is shown effective in preventing mother to child transmission in Africa. (40) Researchers document changes in sexual behavior and a decline in HIV infection among young men in Thailand. (41) Community-based trial of mass treatment of STDs in the population in Rakai, Uganda, finds that STD treatment reduces incidence of STDs but not HIV. (42) These results are diametrically opposite those found in Mwanza, Tanzania, and launch a discussion of conditions under which reduction in conventional STDs will lower HIV incidence.

apy using protease inhibitors, ushering in new era of HAART. (43) Viral load becomes central piece of information for decisions on beginning and modifying treatments. (44)

of the end of 1996 and more than 6 million had already died from AIDS. Total of 30 million have contracted the virus since the beginning of the epidemic. (47)

1997

U.S. CDC reports that U.S. AIDS death rate decreased in 1996. (6)

Domestic spending on AIDS in Thailand peaks at $82 million. (8)

U.S. government issues draft guidelines recommending early, aggressive treatment of HIV-infected individuals with triple-drug therapy—including those who are asymptomatic and otherwise healthy. (45) Annual cost of HAART per patient in Western countries is on the order of $20,000, including drugs, monitoring, outpatient visits. (45) Survival time after HIV infection in developing countries is thought to be less than in the industrialized world—perhaps 7 years—but not much evidence. (46)

UNAIDS reports that as of the end of 1997 (17):
- 5.8 million new infections in that year, of which 590,000 are children under 15
- 30.6 million PLWHA
- 2.3 million deaths from AIDS in that year

Year	Events			Technology/"best practices"	Epidemiology
	International	Industrialized world	Developing world		
1998	UNAIDS issues its first report on the Global HIV/AIDS Epidemic. (17) 12th Annual World AIDS Conference, Geneva: Reports of potential problems with HAART, including side effects, treatment adherence, high costs, resistant strains.	14 of the largest donors in OECD/ Development Assistance Committee provide $300 million. (18)	Treatment Action Campaign (TAC) forms in South Africa. (1)	Several reports indicate growing signs of treatment failure and side effects from HAART. (1) AZT prices cut 75% after results of MTCT trial in Thailand. (4) AIDSvax starts first large-scale human trial of AIDS vaccine. (4) U.S. CDC issues guidelines suggesting caution in initiating treatment too early. (48)	As of the end of 1998, UNAIDS estimates 5.8 million new infections, of which 590,000 were children under 15; 33.4 million were currently infected worldwide, and 13.9 million died since the beginning of the epidemic. (49)
1999	World AIDS Day focuses on people under 25. (4)		South Africa wins first round in battle with U.S. and pharmaceuticals to force cut in drug prices. (4) Kenyan President Moi declares AIDS a national disaster. (4)	First human vaccine trial begins in developing country, Thailand. (1) Nevirapine found to be more affordable and effective in reducing MTCT. (4)	UNAIDS estimates 34.3 million infected as of the end of 1999, of which 1.3 million are children under 15. 5.4 million new infections in 1999, 2.8 million AIDS deaths, and 18.8 million deaths since the beginning of the epidemic. (18)
2000	Millennium Development Goals announced, including reversing the spread of HIV/AIDS, malaria, and TB. (1) 13th International AIDS Conference is held in South Africa, first time in developing country. (1) UN Security Council meeting held on the issue of AIDS.	U.S. government formally declares AIDS a threat to national security. (1) G8 leaders acknowledge need for additional HIV/AIDS resources. (1) Evidence emerges that HIV incidence is on the rise among gay men in San Francisco and that risk behavior is increasing there and in Sydney, Melbourne, London, New York. (18)	Reports emerge that South African President Mbeki consulted two "dissident" researchers to discuss their views that HIV is not the cause of AIDS. (4) Botswana announces that new contributions from donors will provide ARV therapy for all HIV-infected pregnant women and children. (4)	Disappointing results emerge from nonoxynol-9 studies as microbicide for women. (4)	UNAIDS reports that as of the end of 2000: <ul><li>5.3 million new infections</li><li>36.1 million PLWHA</li><li>3.0 million deaths from AIDS in that year. (50)</li></ul>
2001	African Summit in Nigeria calls for tenfold increase in AIDS spending for developing countries—"war chest." (1)		Indian drug company Cipla offers to make AIDS drugs available at reduced prices to Médecins sans Frontières. (4)		UNAIDS reports that as of the end of 2001: <ul><li>5.0 million new infections</li><li>40.0 million PLWHA</li><li>3.0 million deaths from AIDS in that year. (51)</li></ul>

	Global Fund to Fight AIDS, Tuberculosis, and Malaria (GFATM) established. (4) Stephen Lewis appointed as U.N. Special Envoy for AIDS in Africa. (4) U.N. convenes first ever special General Assembly session on AIDS (UNGASS). (1)			39 pharmaceutical companies withdraw case against South Africa over lower drug prices. (4) Reports emerge from Thailand that new infections are plummeting through widespread condom use.	
2002	GFATM receives applications for more than six times the amount anticipated. (4) Available external AIDS assistance to developing countries $1.7 billion. (39)	WHO publishes guidelines for providing ARV drugs in resource-poor countries, including list of 12 essential AIDS drugs. (4)	South Africa announces free nevirapine to reduce risk of MTCT. (4)		UNAIDS reports that as of the end of 2002: • 5.0 million new infections • 42.0 million PLWHA • 3.1 million deaths from AIDS in that year. (53)
2003	U.S. President Bush proposes spending $15 billion in combating AIDS in Africa and Caribbean over the next five years (PEPFAR). (1) WHO announces 3x5 initiative with the goal of providing treatment for 3 million people by 2005 in resource-poor countries. (1) Clinton Foundation secures price reductions for drugs from generic manufacturers. (1) Available external assistance for HIV/AIDS in low- and middle-income countries jumps to $4.7 billion. (39)	WHO declares that the failure to deliver treatment to nearly 6 million people is a global health emergency. (4)	South Africa government announces provision of free ARV drugs in public hospitals. (1) Russian President Putin mentions AIDS in address in Parliament. (15) Chinese Premier Wen shakes hands with AIDS patients for the first time. (52)	Vaxgen vaccine trials show no effect on HIV. (4)	UNAIDS reduces estimates of PLWHA, citing improved tools, fresh data, and U.N. census information showing some countries in Africa have smaller populations than previously thought. (54) UNAIDS estimates that as of the end of 2003, 38 million (range 35-42 million) people living with HIV/AIDS, 4.8 million newly infected in 2003, and 2.9 million AIDS deaths. Since the beginning of the epidemic, 20 million have died. (39)
2004			Brazil government reaches agreement with pharmaceutical companies to reduce prices of AIDS drugs by one-third. (4)		UNAIDS estimates that as of the end of 2004, 39.4 million (range 35.9-44.3 million) are living with HIV/AIDS, 3.1 million died in 2004 (range 2.8-3.5 million) and 4.9 million newly infected in 2004 (range 4.3-6.4 million). (55)

(Continued on the following page.)

Sources:

1. Kaiser Family Foundation Web site (www.kff.org/hivaids/timeline/).

2. Garrett 1994.

3. OED 2004b.

4. AVERT Web site (www.avert.org/historyi/htm).

5. US CDC, 1983.

6. As reported in Sepkowitz 2001.

7. World Bank 1988 and Zaïre project documents.

8. World Bank 2000e.

9. Mann and Tarantola 1996.

10. Ziegler and others 1985.

11. OED 2003.

12. Vaillancourt and others 2004.

14. UN General Assembly Resolution A/RES/42/8, 26 October 1987.

13. Fischl and others 1987.

15. Twigg and Skolnik 2004.

16. Mann 1987.

17. UNAIDS 1998.

18. UNAIDS 2000a.

19. WHO/GPA, INF/89.4, "Statement on AIDS and Tuberculosis." See also Harries 1989.

20. Anderson and others 1991.

21. WHO, "Guidelines for the clinical management of HIV infection in adults," WHO/GPA/IDS/HCS/91.6, Geneva 1991.

22. Forty-fifth World Health Assembly, Geneva, May 4–14 1992, WHO 45.35, *Global strategy for the prevention and control of AIDS.*

23. *Programme of action of the UN ICPD.* Section on Sexually transmitted diseases and HIV infection, "Actions." http://www.iisd.ca/Cairo/program/p07010.html.

24. Gellman 2000.

25. Barnett and Blaikie 1992.

26. Delta Coordinating Committee 1996.

27. Horner and Moss 1991.

28. Carr and others 1994.

29. Laga and others 1994.

30. Connor and others 1994.

31. Hessol and others 1994.

32. Osmond and others 1994.

33. Concorde Coordinating Committee 1994.

34. As reported in World Bank 2000e.

35. Grosskurth and others 1995.

36. Des Jarlais and others 1995.

37. Ho 1995.

38. Food and Drug Administration, "FDA approves first protease inhibitor drug for treatment of HIV," press release, December 7, 1995.

39. UNAIDS 2004b.

40. Mansergh and others 1996.

41. Nelson and others 1996.

42. Wawer and others 1996.

43. See, for example, National Institutes of Health, "Study Confirms that Combination Treatment Using a Protease Inhibitor Can Delay HIV Disease Progression and Death," press release, February 24, 1997.

44. Mellors and others 1996.

45. World Bank 1997a, p. 179.

46. World Bank 1997a, Box 1.2, p. 21.

47. UNAIDS data, as cited in World Bank 1997a.

48. CDC 1998.

49. UNAIDS 1998.

50. UNAIDS 2000a.

51. UNAIDS 2001a.

52. "Chinese Premier in Landmark Meeting with AIDS Patients," *Agence France-Presse*, December 1, 2003.

53. UNAIDS 2002b.

54. "UN cuts AIDS estimates, but warns pandemic still worsening," *Agence France-Presse*, November 25, 2003.

55. UNAIDS 2004a.

APPENDIX C1:   HIV/AIDS PORTFOLIO DATA

1. Closed AIDS Projects and Components as of June 30, 2004[a]

Country	Project name	Date approved	Date closed	Type[b]	Total project cost[c] ($ million)	Amount committed by Bank ($ million) Total	Amount committed by Bank ($ million) AIDS	AIDS Actual ($ million)
Free-standing projects								
Zaïre	National AIDS Control Program	9/8/1988	12/31/1994	CR	21.9	8.1	8.1	3.3
India	National AIDS Control	3/31/1992	3/31/1999	CR	99.6	84	84	84
Zimbabwe	STI Prevention and Care	6/17/1993	12/31/2000	CR	87.3	64.5	64.5	63.6
Brazil	AIDS and STD Control	11/9/1993	6/30/1998	LN	250.0	160	160	160
Uganda	Sexually Transmitted Infections	4/12/1994	12/31/2002	CR	73.4	50	50	48.7
Kenya	Sexually Transmitted Infections	3/14/1995	6/30/2001	CR	65.5	40	40	37.1
Indonesia	HIV/AIDS and STD Prevention and Management	2/27/1996	9/30/1999	LN	35.2	24.8	24.8	4.5
Argentina	AIDS and STD Control	5/22/1997	12/31/2003	LN	30.0	15	15	15
Brazil	Second AIDS/STD	9/15/1998	6/30/2003	LN	286.5	165	165	161.5
Subtotal	9 projects				949.4	949.4	611.4	611.4
Project components								
Haiti	First Health & AIDS	1/16/1990	3/31/2001	CR	33.7	26.3	3.3[d]	10.0[e]
Uganda	Costs of Adjustment (PAPSCA)	2/2/1990	9/30/1995	CR	37.1	28.1	3.3	3.5
Rwanda	Health and Population (including supplement)[f]	6/19/1991	6/30/2002	CR	33.45	28.8	5.1	4.8
Burkina Faso	Population and AIDS Control	5/31/1994	9/30/2001	CR	34.5	26.3	12	11.2
Chad	Population/AIDS Control	3/23/1995	12/31/2001	CR	27.2	20.4	12.9	12.7
Bulgaria	Health Sector Restructuring	4/9/1996	12/30/2001	LN	47.1	26	2.7	2.7[g]
Sri Lanka	Health Services	12/19/1996	6/30/2002	CR	22.6	18.8	7.6	6.8[d]
Cambodia	Disease Control and Health Development	12/24/1996	12/31/2002	CR	35.6	30.4	6.1	4.9
Guinea	Population and Reproductive Health	12/1/1998	12/31/2003	CR	12.0	11.3	2.1[d]	2.1[g]
Subtotal	9 components				283.25	216.4	55.1	58.7
Total	18 projects/components				1,232.65	827.8	666.5	636.4

a. Free-standing AIDS project or project with an AIDS component >$1 million and at least 10% of total project costs.

b. Type: LN (IBRD loan); CR (IDA credit); G (IDA grant); BL (Blend of IBRD and IDA).

c. Includes the Bank's funding commitment, borrower counterpart funding, and any co-financing by others.

d. Total project cost for the AIDS component, this includes loan or credit disbursement plus government and/or other donor contribution.

e. TB and AIDS lending together.

f. Includes $7 million IDA supplement approved 12/21/2000. Both the original project (after restructuring) and the supplement had AIDS allocations and any co-financing by others, as planned in the appraisal document.

g. Based on commitment; actual not yet available.

2. Active Portfolio of World Bank AIDS Lending as of June 30, 2004[a]

(a) AIDS Projects and Components

Country	Project title	Approval date	Projected closing date	Type[b]	Total project cost[c] ($ million)	Amount committed by Bank ($ millions)	
						Total	AIDS
Free-standing projects							
India	Second National HIV/AIDS Control	6/15/1999	3/31/2006	CR	229.8	191	191
Bangladesh	HIV/AIDS Prevention	12/12/2000	6/30/2005	CR	52.6	40	40
Sri Lanka	National AIDS Prevention	12/22/2002	6/30/2008	G	20.9	12.6	12.6
Pakistan	HIV/AIDS Prevention	6/5/2003	12/31/2008	G/CR	47.8	37	37
Brazil	AIDS and STD Control III	6/26/2003	12/31/2006	LN	200.0	100	100
Bhutan	HIV/AIDS and STI Prevention and Control	6/17/2004	12/31/2009	G	5.9	5.8	5.8
Project components							
Guinea-Bissau	National Health Development	11/25/1997	12/31/2004	CR	66.1	11.7	2.9
China	Health IX	5/4/1999	6/30/2006	BL	93.9	60	20
Lesotho	Health Sector Reform	6/8/2000	6/30/2005	CR	20.4	6.5	2
Kenya	Decentralized Reproductive Health and HIV/AIDS (DARE)	12/12/2000	6/30/2005	CR	117.3	50	29.5
Chad	Second Population and AIDS	7/12/2001	9/30/2006	CR	33.1	24.6	19.5
Honduras	Health System Reform	4/25/2002	7/31/2007	CR	31.0	27.1	6.8
Ukraine	Tuberculosis and HIV/AIDS Control	12/19/2002	6/30/2007	LN	77.0	60	32.2
Russia	TB/AIDS Control	4/3/2003	12/31/2008	LN	286.2	150	46.9
Moldova	TB/AIDS	6/10/2003	7/31/2008	G	5.7	5.5	5.5
Subtotal	15 projects/components				1,287.7	781.8	551.7

(Continued on the following page.)

111

2. Active Portfolio of World Bank AIDS Lending as of June 30, 2004[a] (continued)

(b) African Multi-Country AIDS (MAP) Projects[a]

Country	Project title	Approval date	Projected closing date	Type[b]	Total project cost[c] ($ million)	Amount committed by Bank ($ millions)	
						Total	AIDS
Free-standing projects							
Ethiopia	Multisectoral HIV/AIDS	9/12/2000	12/30/2005	CR	63.4	59.7	59.7
Kenya	HIV/AIDS Project (umbrella)	9/12/2000	6/30/2005	CR	52.4	50	50
Ghana	AIDS Response Project (umbrella)	12/28/2000	6/30/2005	CR	27.8	25	25
Gambia	HIV/AIDS Rapid Response	1/16/2001	12/31/2005	CR	16.2	15	15
Uganda	HIV/AIDS Control	1/18/2001	12/31/2006	CR	50.0	47.5	47.5
Cameroon	Multisectoral HIV/AIDS	1/21/2001	12/31/2005	CR	60.0	50	50
Burkina Faso	HIV/AIDS Disaster Relief	7/6/2001	12/31/2006	CR	23.5	22	22
Nigeria	HIV/AIDS Response	7/6/2001	6/30/2006	CR	96.3	90.3	90.3
Madagascar	Multisectoral STI/HIV	12/13/2001	12/31/2006	CR	21.0	20	20
CAR	HIV/AIDS	12/14/2001	6/30/2006	CR	18.0	17	17
Benin	HIV/AIDS Multisectoral	1/04/2002	9/15/2006	CR	25.4	23	23
Senegal	HIV/AIDS Prevention	2/7/2002	9/30/2007	CR	32.2	30	30
Sierra Leone	HIV/AIDS Response	3/26/2002	12/31/2006	CR	15.3	15	15
Cape Verde	HIV/AIDS	3/28/2002	12/31/2006	CR	9.6	9	9
Burundi	HIV/AIDS and Orphans	6/27/2002	12/31/2006	CR	36.7	36	36
Guinea	Multisectoral AIDS	12/19/2002	7/31/2008	G	22.3	20.3	20.3
Zambia	HIV/AIDS (ZANARA Project)	12/30/2002	2/28/2008	G	46.0	42	42
Mozambique	HIV/AIDS Response	3/28/2003	12/31/2008	G	64.0	55	55
Rwanda	Multi-Country HIV/AIDS	3/31/2003	10/30/2008	G	32.0	30.5	30.5
Niger	HIV/AIDS Prevention and Care	4/4/2003	6/30/2008	G	27.5	25	25
Mauritania	HIV/AIDS Multi-sector Control	7/7/2003	3/31/2009	G	23.4	21	21
Tanzania	Multisectoral AIDS	7/7/2003	9/30/2008	G	82.0	70	70
Malawi	Multi-sector AIDS Program	8/25/2003	12/31/2008	G	274.74[d]	35	35
Western Africa	HIV/AIDS Abidjan-Lagos	11/13/2003	7/1/2007	G	17.9	16.6	16.6
Congo, DR	Multisectoral HIV/AIDS	4/16/2004	1/31/2011	G	102.4	102	102
Congo, Rep. of	HIV/AIDS and Health	4/20/2004	6/30/2009	G	21.4	19	19
Guinea-Bissau	HIV/AIDS Global Mitigation Support	6/2/2004	12/31/2007	G	7.0	7	7
Mali	Multisectoral HIV/AIDS	6/17/2004	7/31/2009	G	28.0	25.5	25.5
Africa	Regional HIV/AIDS Treatment Acceleration	6/17/2004	9/30/2007	G	61.5	59.8	59.8
Project components							
Eritrea	HAMSET (HIV/malaria/TB/STI)	12/18/2000	3/31/2006	CR	50.0	40.0	13.9
Djibouti	HIV/AIDS, Malaria, and TB Control	5/29/2003	9/30/2008	G	15.0	12	9
Subtotal	31 projects/components				1,422.9	1,090.2	1,061.1

(c) Caribbean Multi-Country AIDS (MAP) Projects[e]

Country	Project title	Approval date	Projected closing date	Type[b]	Total project cost[c] ($ million)	Amount committed by Bank ($ millions)	
						Total	AIDS
Barbados	Caribbean APL AIDS Prevention	6/28/2001	12/31/2006	LN	23.6	15.2	15.2
Dominican Rep.	Caribbean APL AIDS Prevention	6/28/2001	12/31/2006	LN	30.0	25	25
Jamaica	HIV/AIDS Prevention and Control	3/29/2002	12/15/2006	LN	16.5	15	15
Grenada	2nd Phase APL HIV/AIDS Prevention and Control	7/25/2002	6/30/2007	LN	7.2	6	6
St. Kitts and Nevis	HIV/AIDS Prevention and Control	1/10/2003	6/30/2008	LN	4.5	4	4
Trinidad & Tobago	HIV/AIDS Prevention	6/27/2003	12/31/2008	LN	25.0	20	20
Caribbean	Pan-Caribbean Partnership Against HIV/AIDS	3/25/2004	12/31/2007	G	9.9	9	9
Guyana	HIV/AIDS Prevention and Control	3/30/2004	6/30/2009	G	11.0	10	10
St. Vincent and Grenadines	HIV/AIDS Prevention & Control	7/6/2004	6/30/2009	LN/G	8.8	7	7
Subtotal	9 projects				136.5	111.2	111.2
Total active portfolio	55 projects				2,897.1	1,983.2	1,727.0

Source: WB Project Portal (Web page) as of 7/9/2004.

a. Free-standing AIDS project or project with an AIDS component >$1 million and at least 10% of total project costs.

b. Type: LN (IBRD loan); CR (IDA credit); G (IDA grant); BL (Blend of IBRD and IDA).

c. Includes the Bank's funding commitment, borrower counterpart funding, and any co-financing by others.

d. Includes other donors and the Global Fund.

e. All are free-standing AIDS projects.

3. World Bank Projects with AIDS Components of >$1 Million but <10% of Total Project Costs as of June 30, 2004

Country	Project title	Date approved	Projected closing date	Type[a]	Status	Amount committed by Bank ($ million)		AIDS Actual ($ million)
						Total	AIDS	
Health[b]								
Brazil	NE Endemic Disease Control	3/31/1988	30/06/1996	LN	Closed	109	6.6	7.4[c]
Morocco	Health Sector Investment	2/20/1990	12/31/1998	LN	Closed	104	8	8[d]
Mali	Health/Population/Rural WS	3/19/1991	12/31/1998	CR	Closed	26.6	1.4	1.4[d]
Madagascar	National Health Sector	5/28/1991	12/31/1999	CR	Closed	31	2	2[d]
Honduras	Nutrition and Health	1/5/1993	6/30/2001	CR	Closed	25	2.2	2.2[d]
Zambia	Health Sector Support	11/15/1994	6/30/2002	CR	Closed	56	1.8	1.8[d]
Cameroon	Health/Fertility/Nutrition	3/7/1995	6/30/2001	CR	Closed	43	2	2[e]
Benin	Population and Health	5/30/1995	12/31/2002	CR	Closed	27.8	1.2	1.2[d]
China	Disease Prevention	12/12/1995	6/30/2004	CR	Closed	100	5	5[d]
Cote d'Ivoire	Integrated Health Services Development	6/27/1996	12/31/2004	CR	Active	40	2.1	
Niger	Health Services Development	9/5/1996	12/31/2003	CR	Closed	40	1.7	1.7[d]
Eritrea	National Health Development	12/16/1997	12/31/2004	CR	Active	18.3	1.7	
Gambia	Participatory Health Population and Nutrition	3/31/1998	6/30/2005	CR	Active	18	1.5	
Bangladesh	Health & Population	6/30/1998	12/31/2004	CR	Active	250	5.8	
Ethiopia	Health Sector Development	10/27/1998	6/6/2005	CR	Active	100	2	
India	Maharashtra Health Systems Development	12/8/1998	3/31/2005	CR	Active	134	1.3	
India	Uttar Pradesh Health Sector Development	4/25/2000	12/31/2005	CR	Active	110	3	
Chad	Health System Support	4/27/2000	12/31/2005	CR	Active	41.5	1.9	
Tanzania	Health Services Development	6/15/2000	12/31/2003	CR	Closed	22	2	2[d]
Bulgaria	Health Sector Reform	6/22/2000	9/30/2005	LN	Active	63.3	3	
Mexico	Mexico III Basic Health Care	6/21/2001	6/30/2007	LN	Active	350	18	
Venezuela	Caracas Metro Health	6/21/2001	12/31/2006	LN	Active	30	1.6	
El Salvador	Earthquake Emergency Reconstruction & Health Services	12/4/2001	4/30/2007	LN	Active	142.6	1.4	
China	Tuberculosis Control	3/21/2002	3/15/2010	LN	Active	104	3.9	
Nigeria	Second Health Systems Development	6/6/2002	7/1/2007	CR	Active	127	4	
Cambodia	Health Sector Support	12/19/2002	12/31/2007	CR/G	Active	27	2	
Subtotal	26 Projects					2,140.1	87.1	34.7

Education								
Malawi	Secondary Education	3/24/1998	12/31/2004	CR	Active	48.2		1.4
Nigeria	Second Primary Education	5/11/2000	12/31/2004	CR	Active	55		1.2
Rwanda	Human Resources Development	6/6/2000	6/30/2006	CR	Active	35		3.3
Subtotal	3 Projects					138.2		5.9
Transport								
Kenya	Northern Corridor Transport Improvement	6/17/2004	12/31/2009	CR	Active	276.5		4.4
Subtotal	1 Project					276.5		4.4
Social Protection								
Pakistan	Social Action Program II	3/24/1998	6/30/2002	CR	Closed	250		1.5[d]
Thailand	Social Investment Program	11/13/1998	4/30/2004	LN	Closed	300		1.5[d]
Subtotal	2 Projects					550.0		3
Other sectors								
Ethiopia	Emergency Recovery	12/5/2000	12/31/2005	CR	Active	555.0		3.0
Congo DR	Emergency Early Recovery	7/31/2001	1/31/2005	GR	Closed	50.0		8.0
Subtotal	1 Project					605.0		11.0
Total	33 projects					3,709.8	111.4	37.7

Source: WB Project Portal (Web page) and ImageBank as of 7/9/2004.

a. Type: LN (IBRD loan); CR (IDA credit); G (IDA grant); BL (Blend of IBRD and IDA).

b. The Ghana Second Health Program Support Project ($90 million) is supposed to finance the AIDS activities of the Ministry of Health. However, the TTL was unable to provide information on the amount allocated to HIV/AIDS. It may exceed $1 million, but no documentation is available.

c. Total project cost for the AIDS component, this includes loan disbursement plus government and/or other donor contribution.

d. Based on commitment; actual not available.

e. $24 million of the original credit was cancelled. Figure based on commitment; actual not available.

4. Non-Health Sector World Bank Projects with AIDS Commitment for $1 Million or Less or Unknown as of June 30, 2004[a]

Country	Project title	Approval date	Closing date	Type[b]	Status	Amount committed ($ millions)	
						Total	AIDS
Education							
Madagascar	Education Sector Strategic Program	3/10/1998	3/30/2005	CR	Active	65.00	
Ethiopia	Education Sector Development Program Support	5/26/1998	12/31/2006	CR	Active	100.00	
Zambia	Basic Education Subsector Investment Program (BESSIP)	4/8/1999	6/30/2005	CR	Active	40.00	
Senegal	Quality Education for All	4/11/2000	12/31/2004	CR	Active	50.00	
Benin	Labor Force Development	6/9/2000	6/30/2005	CR	Active	5.00	0.10
Zambia	Technical Education, Vocational and Entrepreneurial	6/14/2000	12/30/2006	CR	Active	25.00	
Mali	Education Sector Expenditure Program	12/20/2000	12/31/2005	CR	Active	45.00	
Mozambique	Higher Education	3/7/2001	5/31/2007	CR	Active	60.00	
Guinea	Education for All Program (Phase I)	7/24/2001	12/31/2005	CR	Active	70.00	
Burkina Faso	Basic Education Sector	1/22/2002	12/31/2006	CR	Active	32.60	
Nigeria	Universal Basic Education	9/12/2002	6/30/2008	CR	Active	101.00	
Chad	Education Reform	3/18/2003	6/30/2007	CR	Active	42.34	
Niger	Basic Education	7/17/2003	12/31/2007	CR	Active	30.00	
Lesotho	Second Education Sector Development	7/17/2003	12/31/2007	CR	Active	21.00	0.25
Ghana	Education Sector	3/9/2004	10/31/2009	CR	Active	78.00	1.00
Subtotal	15 Projects					764.94	1.35
Social Protection							
Cameroon	Social Dimensions of Adjustment (SDA)	5/24/1990	6/7/1994	LN	Closed	35.7	
Zambia	Social Recovery	6/19/1991	7/31/1998	CR	Closed	20.0	0.4
Rwanda	Food Security and Social Action	6/17/1992	12/31/2000	CR	Closed	19.1	
Malawi	Second Social Action Fund	10/15/1998	11/30/2003	CR	Closed	66.0	0.1
Brazil	Social Protection Special Sector Adjustment Loan	1/7/1999	6/30/1999	LN	Closed	252.5	0.2
Zambia	Social Investment Fund	5/25/2000	12/31/2005	CR	Active	64.7	
Zambia	Mine Township Services	6/20/2000	12/31/2004	CR	Active	37.7	0.2
Tanzania	Social Action Fund	08/22/2000	06/30/2005	CR	Active	71.8	
Senegal	Social Development Fund	12/20/2000	12/31/2005	CR	Active	161.5	
Eritrea	Emergency Demobilization and Reintegration	5/16/2002	12/31/2005	CR	Active	60.0	
Malawi	Third Social Action Fund	06/10/2002	12/31/2006	CR/GR	Active	78.1	

Country	Project	Date	Date	Type	Status	Amount	
Sierra Leone	National Social Action	04/24/2003	12/31/2008	CR	Active	42.0	
Congo, Democratic Rep.	Emergency Demobilization, Reinsertion and Reintegration Program	5/25/2004	3/31/2008	GR	Active	100.0	
Subtotal	13 Projects						0.9
Transport							
Mozambique	First Roads and Coastal Shipping (ROCS)	6/2/1992	12/31/1999	CR	Closed	74.30	
Ethiopia	Road Sector Development Program	1/15/1998	5/31/2005	CR	Active	309.20	
Malawi	Roads Rehabilitation and Maintenance	06/10/1999	03/31/2005	CR	Active	39.5	
Senegal	National Rural Infrastructure	01/27/2000	06/30/2005	CR	Active	42.9	
Senegal	Urban Mobility Improvement Program	05/25/2000	12/31/2005	CR	Active	103.0	
Djibouti	International Road Corridor Rehabilitation	6/22/2000	08/31/2005	CR	Active	15.00	
Chad	National Transport Program Support	10/26/2000	7/31/2006	CR	Active	67.00	0.5
Uganda	Second Phase of the Road Development Program	7/3/2001	6/30/2006	CR	Active	64.52	
Mozambique	Roads and Bridges Mgmt. and Maintenance	7/19/2001	6/30/2005	CR	Active	162	
Ghana	Road Sector Development Program	7/26/2001	6/30/2006	CR	Active	220.00	
Djibouti	International Road Corridor Rehabilitation (supplement)	5/6/2003	n/a	CR	Active	6.00	
Ethiopia	Second Road Sector Development Support Program	6/17/2003	6/30/2009	CR	Active	127.00	0.13
Cambodia	Provincial and Rural Infrastructure	9/11/2003	9/30/2007	CR	Active	21.00	
Madagascar	Transport Infrastructure Investment	12/8/2003	06/30/2008	CR	Active	842.5	
Zambia	Road Rehabilitation and Maintenance	3/9/2004	6/30/2007	CR	Active	50.00	
Burundi	Road Sector Development	3/18/2004	12/31/2009	CR	Active	51.20	0.2
Subtotal	16 Projects					2,195.1	0.83
Other sectors[c]							
Cameroon	Petroleum Environmental Capacity	6/6/2000	12/31/2005	CR	Active	5.77	
Mali	Agricultural Services and Producer Organizations	12/11/2001	12/31/2005	CR	Active	43.5	1.0
Nigeria	Community-Based Urban Development	06/06/2002	06/30/2009	CR	Active	137.5	0.2
Tanzania	Participatory Agricultural Development	05/27/2003	12/31/2008	CR	Active	69.9	
Subtotal	2 Projects					256.67	1.2
Total	46 Projects					2,637.11	3.75

Source: WB Project Portal (Web page) and ImageBank as of 7/9/2004.

a. This list of projects with small AIDS components should be considered a conservative estimate of the true number of small AIDS components in these three sectors, as it is based on the formal presence of an AIDS component or mention of project-sponsored AIDS activities in the Project Appraisal Document (PAD). Both early on in the response to the AIDS epidemic as well as recently, project managers were urged to "retrofit" or "restructure" ongoing projects by adding AIDS components and activities, many of them quite small. Since they were added after project approval, the documentation in terms of objectives, disbursements, and outcomes is not easily accessible—in any of the sectors, including in the health sector (which is not presented here).

b. Type: LN (IBRD loan); CR (IDA credit); G (IDA grant); BL (Blend of IBRD and IDA).

c. OED did not do a systematic search for AIDS components in sectors other than education, transport, and social protection.

APPENDIX C2:   PERFORMANCE RATINGS FOR COMPLETED AIDS PROJECTS

OED Ratings[a]

Country[b]	Project name	Project period	Project outcome	Institutional development	Sustainability	Bank performance	Borrower performance
Free-standing projects							
Zaïre	National AIDS Control Program	1988–1994	U	N	U	U	HU
India	National AIDS Control	1992–1999	S	S	L	S	S
Zimbabwe	STI Prevention and Care	1993–2000	MS	M	U	U	U
Brazil	AIDS and STD Control	1993–1998	S	S	L	S	S
Uganda	Sexually Transmitted Infections	1994–2002	MU	S	L	S	S
Kenya	Sexually Transmitted Infections	1995–2001	MS	S	L	S	S
Indonesia	HIV/AIDS and STD Prevention	1996–1999	U	N	U	U	U
Argentina	AIDS and STD Control	1997–2003	MS	S	L	S	S
Brazil	Second AIDS and STD	1998–2003	S	S	HL	S	S
Project components							
Haiti	First Health and AIDS	1990–2001	U	M	U	U	U
Uganda	Costs of Adjustment (PAPSCA)	1990–1995	MS[c]	P	UC[d]	S	S
Burkina Faso	Population and AIDS Control	1994–2001	MU	M	L	S	S
Chad	Population/AIDS Control	1995–2001	MS[c]	S	L[e]	S	S
Bulgaria	Health Sector Restructuring	1996–2001	HS	H	L	S	S
Sri Lanka	Health Services	1996–2002	S	M	L	S	S
Cambodia	Disease Control and Health Development	1996–2002	S	H	L[5]	S	S
Guinea	Population and Reproductive Health	1998–2003	U	M	U	U	S
Rwanda	Health and Population (suppl) and Management	2000–2002	MS	N	U	S	S

a. Explanation of ratings: Outcomes, Bank and Borrower Performance: HS (highly satisfactory); S (satisfactory); MS (marginally satisfactory); MU (marginally unsatisfactory); U (unsatisfactory); HU (highly unsatisfactory). Institutional Development: H (high); S (substantial); M (modest); P (partial); N (negligible). Sustainability: HL (highly likely); L (likely); U (unlikely); UC (uncertain); NE (not evaluable).

b. Ratings for projects in italics are based on OED Project Performance Assessments (PPARs) undertaken in the field. Ratings for all other projects are based on an OED desk review of the project's Implementation Completion Report, which is a document prepared by the implementation team (the Bank and the Borrower) that includes the team's own ratings.

c. While the overall project was rated MS, the AIDS components were informally assessed to be S in OED's PPARs of these projects.

d. The sustainability of the activities comprising this project (primarily recurrent assistance to widows and orphans) was rated either uncertain or unlikely.

e. Sustainability of the AIDS component was similar to that of the overall project.

COVERAGE OF HIV/AIDS IN COUNTRY ASSISTANCE
STRATEGIES AND POVERTY REDUCTION STRATEGY PAPERS

Country Assistance Strategies

The Country Assistance Strategy (CAS) is a broad development framework, planned and developed by the Bank in collaboration with the government and other stakeholders, and tailored to the country's needs. The CAS is the central tool of Bank management and the Board for reviewing and guiding country programs, and the vehicle for assessing the impact of the Bank's work. CASs have always been prepared alongside a project. Through fiscal year 1994, CASs were not stand-alone documents, but were included as a major section in the project documentation that was presented to the Board ("Memorandum and President's Report"). Beginning in fiscal year 1995, CASs began to be produced as stand-alone documents.

Sample

All CASs for two time periods were reviewed with respect to their coverage of AIDS: fiscal 1994–95 (96 CASs for 84 countries) and fiscal 2000–02 (49 CASs for 48 countries). A list of all CASs reviewed is in Attachment 1.

Reference to HIV/AIDS

There was a significant increase in the percentage of CASs that include a reference to HIV/AIDS over this time period. An electronic text search was conducted to determine whether the terms "HIV" or "AIDS" appeared in the main text, tables, boxes, or annexes. The search found that in fiscal 1994–95, 27 CASs (28.1 percent) and in fiscal 2000–02, 40 CASs (81.6 percent) contained the terms HIV or AIDS.

The CASs were reviewed to determine whether HIV/AIDS was identified as a critical issue by the government or the Bank, or both, based on the reference to or discussion of AIDS in the government's development agenda and/or the Bank's proposed assistance strategy for the country (see table D.1).[1] AIDS is recognized as a priority by the Bank more often than by the government. In addition, there is a significant increase in the percentage of CASs that identify HIV/AIDS as a critical issue for the Bank, the government, and both Bank and government.

Table D.1: Recognition of HIV/AIDS as a Critical Issue

	Fiscal years 1994–95	Fiscal years 2000–02[a]
Critical issue for the Bank	14 (14.6%)	23 (46.9%)
Critical issue for the government	7 (7.3%)	17 (34.7%)
Critical issue for both	4 (4.2%)[a]	15 (30.6%)[b]

a. Burkina Faso, Burundi, Kenya, Mali. The following countries had generalized epidemics but did not mention AIDS as a priority by the government or the Bank in the CAS: Republic of Congo, Côte d'Ivoire, Ethiopia, Guyana, Lesotho, Mozambique, Uganda, Zimbabwe.

b. Armenia, Bangladesh, Belarus, Burkina Faso, Djibouti, Ethiopia, Guyana, India, Latvia, Mauritania, Mozambique, Pakistan, Tanzania, Uganda, and Zambia. There were no countries with generalized epidemics for which the FY2000–02 CAS did not mention AIDS as a priority for both the Bank and the government.

HIV Prevalence Rates and AIDS Prioritization in the CAS

The countries with higher HIV prevalence rates or at more advanced stages of the epidemic are more likely to have HIV/AIDS identified in the CAS as a government or Bank priority. In fiscal years 1994–95, HIV/AIDS is identified as a Bank priority more often than as a government priority, regardless of the stage of the epidemic. However, in fiscal years 2000–02, it is identified as a priority equally by the Bank and the government for countries at the generalized stage, but more often as a Bank priority in countries at less advanced stages.

Among the 35 countries that produced CASs in both time periods, almost half (17) had a "heightened" prioritization in the later time period. In these cases, either (i) the earlier CAS had no mention or only context information on AIDS but the later CAS had government and/or Bank prioritization, or (ii) only the government or Bank prioritized AIDS in the first period but both did so in the second period.[2]

Link Between CAS and AIDS Lending

Twenty-seven CASs in the review (18.6%) proposed a project with either a main component or a subcomponent on HIV/AIDS.

- Seventeen CASs proposed a freestanding AIDS project or a project with a major component on AIDS.[3] In 13 of those CASs, AIDS was identified as a critical issue by both the government and the Bank.
- Ten CASs proposed a project with a subcomponent on AIDS. In 7 of those CASs, AIDS was identified as a critical issue by the Bank but not the government.

Poverty Reduction Strategy Papers (PRSP)

PRSPs describe a country's macroeconomic, structural, and social policies and programs to promote growth and reduce poverty, as well as associated external financing needs. They are prepared by governments through a participatory process involving civil society and development partners. The time period reviewed was fiscal years 2000–02 (13 full PRSPs). All PRSPs in this period were included in the review (Attachment 2).

Twelve out of the 13 PRSPs (92.3%) referred to HIV/AIDS. Nine of the 13 PRSPs (69.2%) included strategic actions specifically addressing HIV/AIDS.[4] Some also included HIV/AIDS-related indicators and anticipated budget allocations. The countries at more advanced stages of the epidemic were more likely to include strategic actions on HIV/AIDS in the PRSP.

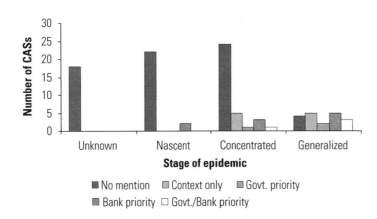

Figure D.1: Stage of the Epidemic and CAS Prioritization, FY1994–95

Figure D.2: Stage of the Epidemic and CAS Prioritization, FY2000–02

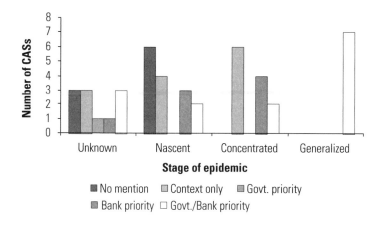

Figure D.3: Stage of Epidemic and Prioritization of AIDS in the PRSP, FY2000–02

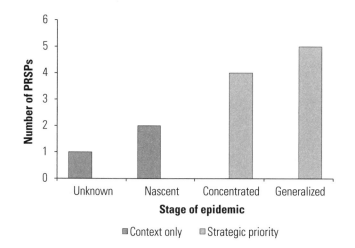

Attachment 1: Country Assistance Strategies Reviewed

Africa

	FY94	FY95	FY00	FY01	FY02
Benin	x				
Burkina Faso	x			x	
Burundi		x			
Cameroon	x				
Comoros	x				
Congo, Republic of	x				
Côte d'Ivoire	x				
Ethiopia	x	x		x*	
Gabon	x				
Ghana	x	x	x		
Guinea	x				
Kenya	x				
Lesotho	x				
Madagascar	x				
Malawi	x				
Mali		x			
Mauritania	x				x
Mauritius	x				x
Mozambique	x		x		
Niger	x				
São Tomé and Principe				x	
Senegal		x			
Sierra Leone	x				
Swaziland		x			
Tanzania	x	x			
Togo		x			
Uganda	x	x		x	
Zambia	x	x			
Zimbabwe	x				

Eastern Europe and Central Asia

(cont.)

	FY94	FY95	FY00	FY01	FY02
Romania	x			x	
Russia	x	x	x		x
Slovak Republic	x			x	
Slovenia	x				
Turkey				x	
Turkmenistan				x	
Ukraine				x	
Uzbekistan		x			

Latin America and the Caribbean

	FY94	FY95	FY00	FY01	FY02
Argentina	x	x		x	
Barbados	x				
Belize				x	
Bolivia	x				
Brazil		x	x		x
Chile		x			
Colombia	x				
Dominican Republic		x			
El Salvador	x				x
Guatemala		x			
Guyana	x				
Honduras	x		x		x
Jamaica				x	
Mexico	x	x			x
Nicaragua	x				
Panama		x			
Paraguay	x	x			
Peru		x			
Trinidad and Tobago			x		
Uruguay	x				
Venezuela	x				

East Asia and the Pacific

Cambodia	x					
China	x	x		x		
Indonesia	x	x			x	
Korea	x					
Mongolia	x	x		x		
Papua New Guinea	x	x		x		
Philippines	x					x
Thailand		x				
Vietnam	x	x				

Eastern Europe and Central Asia

Albania	x	x				
Armenia		x		x		
Azerbaijan		x				
Belarus	x	x				x
Bosnia and Herzegovina		x				x
Bulgaria		x				
Croatia		x				
Czech Republic	x					
Estonia		x				
Hungary		x				
Kazakhstan	x				x	
Kyrgyz Republic		x				
Latvia		x				
Lithuania		x				
Macedonia	x	x				
Moldova	x	x				
Poland		x				

Middle East and North Africa

Djibouti	x					
Egypt	x	x				
Iran	x					
Jordan				x		
Lebanon	x					
Morocco	x	x		x		
Tunisia						

South Asia

Bangladesh	x	x				
Bhutan	x	x		x		
India	x	x	x			
Maldives		x	x			
Nepal	x	x				
Pakistan	x	x				

* Interim

Attachment 2: Poverty Reduction Strategy Papers Reviewed

	FY00	FY01	FY02
Africa			
Burkina Faso	x		
Gambia			x
Mauritania		x	
Mozambique			x
Niger			x
Tanzania		x	
Uganda	x		
Zambia			x
East Asia and the Pacific			
Vietnam			x
Eastern Europe and Central Asia			
Albania			x
Latin America and the Caribbean			
Bolivia		x	
Honduras			x
Nicaragua			x

Background

An inventory was undertaken of the Bank's AIDS-related nonlending products—both completed and in the pipeline—as of the end of fiscal year 2004, including economic and sector work (ESW) and other research, analytical, or dissemination products. These products reflect a variety of activities, including research projects, strategy documents, and project background documents. The inventory contains the following information for each item (if applicable): type of activity, project ID, title, author, Bank task leader, date completed, country, region, source of funding (i.e., Bank budget, trust fund), originating Bank unit.

The initial work on the inventory was done by the Bank's Health, Nutrition and Population Team (HDNHE), including information collected through survey questionnaires and inquiries sent to Bank-managed trust fund units. OED followed up this work with further research through: (i) search of existing publications and document databases maintained by the Bank (that is, Bank intranet, Business Warehouse, ImageBank); (ii) input from relevant Bank staff; and (iii) search of Project Appraisal Document bibliographies.

The inventory, which is posted in full on the OED evaluation Web site (www.worldbank.org/oed/aids), is an indicative list of HIV/AIDS-related items produced by the Bank, rather than a definitive list. Caution is in order because: (i) there are potential double-entries, especially as some activities are disseminated in more than one form, and (ii) OED believes that many pieces of non-lending work are not reported. This is particularly the case before SAP was implemented in fiscal year 2000. Further, many products are only captured under the catch-all category of "Internal Order" rather than as itemized products. Of particular note, although the ESW category existed before fiscal year 2000, there is no systematic way of searching for these products in the Bank's information systems.

Findings

There are 254 items in the inventory (230 completed by fiscal year 2004 and others in the pipeline), based on information collected as of the end of October 2004.

Analytic Work: Sector Work and Research. There has been an increasing number of AIDS-related research and sector work at the Bank since fiscal year 1989. With regard to Regional coverage, Sub-Saharan Africa has had by far the highest number of products. While all Regions currently have work being done on AIDS, only Africa had coverage before fiscal year 1996, aside from multi-regional studies.

"Official" ESW Products. A systematic search found 19 ESW products for fiscal years 2000–04. Most of these are country-level or subregional assessments of the HIV/AIDS situation. Others cover more specific sectoral areas, such as poverty reduction, transport, manufacturing, or education. All Regions except East Asia and the Pacific completed official ESW products on AIDS during this period (see table E.3). Again, by far, the Africa Region has had the highest number of official ESW products.

Table E.1: World Bank Sector Work vs. Research on AIDS, before and since Fiscal Year 2000

Region	Sector work [of which "official" ESW]		Research		Total
	Before FY00	Since FY00	Before FY00	Since FY00	
Sub-Saharan Africa	23	61 [10]	19[c]	14	117[d]
East Asia and Pacific	7	8 [0]	3	2	20
Eastern Europe and Central Asia		9 [2]	1	1	11
Latin America and Caribbean	2	7 [3]	2	1	12
Middle East and North Africa		4 [1]	0	1	5
South Asia	1	2 [1]	0	3	6
Multi[a]	1	1 [0]	3	3	8
Global[b]	4	20 [2]	23	4	50
Total	38	112 [19]	51	29	229

a. Product focuses on more than one specific region.

b. Product is not focused on specific regions, but rather is globally applicable.

c. Of note from the earlier years are *Tanzania AIDS Assessment and Planning Study* (1992) and *Uganda AIDS Crisis: Its Implications for Development* (1995). The final papers and background papers comprise 10 of the 23 sector work papers before fiscal year 2000.

d. Of the 33 research products for Sub-Saharan Africa, 14 were from a single research project in Tanzania.

Table E.2: World Bank–Managed Analytic Work on AIDS by Fiscal Year

Activity	Fiscal year															
	1989	1990	1991	1992	1993	1994	1995	1996	1997	1998	1999	2000	2001	2002	2003	2004
Research	1	1	1	2	7	3	1	0	0	31	2	7	7	4	8	4
Sector work	1	3	5	2	5	1	1	3	4	4	8	8	16	45	18	25
Total	2	4	6	4	12	4	2	3	4	35[a]	10	15	23	49	26	29

a. Twenty-one items are separate studies that were compiled into one book.

Table E.3: "Official" Bank-Financed Economic and Sector Work by Region and Year of Completion, Fiscal Years 2000–04

Fiscal year	AFR	EAP	ECA	LAC	MNA	SAR	Global	Total
2000	2							2
2001	4			1				5
2002	3		1	1	1			6
2003	1							1
2004			1	1		1	2	5
Total	10	0	2	3	1	1	2	19

Note: AFR = Africa, EAP = East Asia and the Pacific, ECA = Eastern Europe and Central Asia, LAC = Latin America and Caribbean, MNA = Middle East and North Africa, SAR = South Asia.

Figure E.1: Trends in Analytic Work by Fiscal Year of Completion

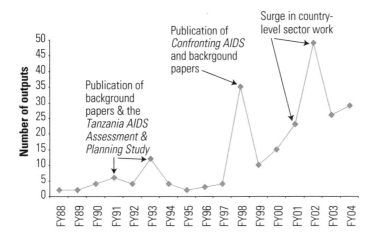

Figure E.2: Number of Analytic Products by Fiscal Year of Completion: Africa vs. Other Regions (or Global)

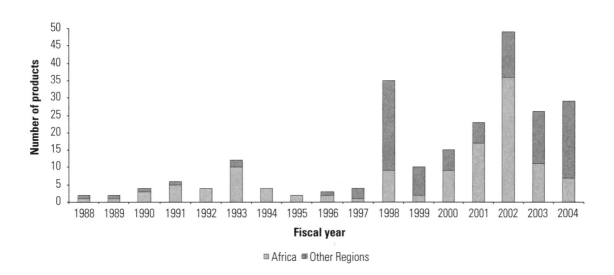

APPENDIX F: THE REACH, QUALITY, AND UTILITY OF THE BANK'S ANALYTIC WORK IN HIV/AIDS

This appendix presents the findings of surveys of the reach, quality, and utility of the World Bank's analytic work on HIV/AIDS among two audiences: (1) participants at the 13th International Conference on AIDS and STDs (ICASA), in Nairobi, Kenya, September 21–26, 2003; and (2) Bank staff in the health, nutrition and population (HNP); education; and social protection sectors, surveyed at the Human Development (HD) Forum, at the University of Maryland, November 17–19, 2003.

The objectives of the two surveys were: (i) to assess the reach of Bank reports to several key audiences and identify lessons regarding dissemination; and (ii) to assess the technical quality and usefulness of the Bank's analytic work.

Sample and Methodology

Both surveys used self-administered questionnaires distributed to event participants in their registration packets. At the Nairobi AIDS Conference, a two-page questionnaire was put in each of the 6,000 registration packets and an additional 113 were distributed to delegates without packets. A total of 466 questionnaires were returned for an estimated response rate of 7.6 percent.[1] Similarly, for the Bank staff survey a short questionnaire was placed in 800 registration packets. Approximately 550–650 individuals actually registered. A total of 212 questionnaires were returned for a response rate of 33–38 percent. A complete description of the methodology for the two surveys is contained in background papers prepared for this study and is available on request.

The survey of Nairobi AIDS Conference participants asked about respondents' demographic characteristics, including age, sex, nationality, education, employer, ability to read technical articles in English, and access to the Internet. The Bank staff survey asked for similar demographic characteristics, as well as professional affiliations at the Bank, including whether they were based in headquarters or the field, their Regional affiliation, their primary sectoral affiliation, their professional background (economist, specialist, administrative staff, or other), whether they had been a task manager of an HIV/AIDS project in the Bank, and whether they had provided technical support or analytic work for HIV/AIDS projects and activities at the Bank. The surveys also gathered information about respondents' access to the Internet and use of the World Bank's AIDS Web site (www.worldbank.org/aids) and the World Bank-sponsored International AIDS Economics Network (IAEN) Web site (www.iaen.org).

Nairobi AIDS Conference respondents were presented with a list of 12 global or Africa-related Bank reports on HIV/AIDS. Bank staff were presented with a list of 18 global and regional reports and 7 toolkits on HIV/AIDS. The reports included in each survey are listed in Attachment 1. In both surveys, respondents were asked whether they had heard of a report and whether they had read it. If they had read a report, they were asked to rate its technical quality and its usefulness to their work on HIV/AIDS.

Results from the Nairobi AIDS Conference

Background characteristics. The average age of respondents was 40 years and the majority of respondents were male (62 percent) and African (85 percent). Ninety-four percent of respondents were residing in Africa. Education levels were high: 43 percent of respondents had at least a graduate degree; 27 percent had obtained up to a university degree. With regard to employment, about a third (32 percent) of respondents worked for a national or local NGO or CBO, one in five (21 percent) worked in government, 17 percent worked for an international NGO, 9 percent for a university, and 8 percent for a donor agency or the United Nations.

Most respondents completed the English-language questionnaire (88 percent). Of those who completed the French questionnaire, 29 percent reported that they could read technical articles in English with no difficulty and 59 percent could read them only with some difficulty.

Recognition and Readership. Figure F.1 shows the percentage of respondents who had heard of a report and read each of the reports. The reports with the highest recognition were also usually those with the highest readership. One-quarter of respondents had heard of none of the reports.

Closer examination of the data by occupation (table F.2) reveals that the reports have not been very successful at reaching respondents

working for the government, presumably a primary audience, and even fewer of them had read the reports. For 9 out of the 12 reports, donors (bilaterals, multilaterals, U.N.) had the highest percentage of respondents who had heard of the report, followed by academics. Fewer than half of government staff had heard of any of the reports. For 11 out of the 12 reports, either donors or academics were most likely to have read the report. Among the two policy reports read by the largest share of respondents working for government, "Breaking the Silence" was published in *The Lancet*, an international medical journal, and *Intensifying Action Against AIDS in Africa* was disseminated at a previous African AIDS conference in Lusaka, Zambia.[2] Both were published in 2000. Respondents working for government were most likely to have read the technical paper, "HIV Infection and Sexually Transmitted Diseases," a chapter in the reference volume, *Disease Control Priorities in Developing Countries*, published in 1993.

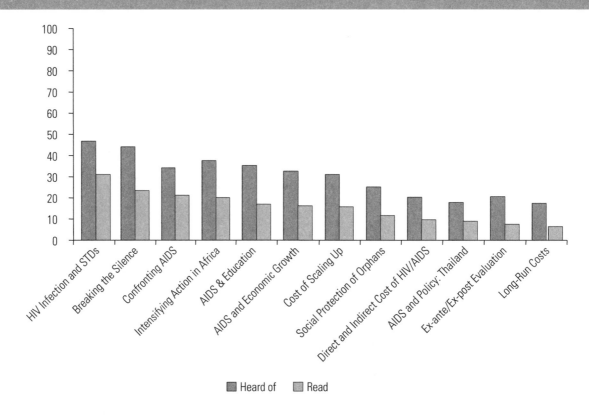

Figure F.1: Nairobi AIDS Conference: Percentage of Respondents Who Had Heard of and Read the Report

Table F.2: Nairobi AIDS Conference Participants: Audience Reach of World Bank Analytic Work on HIV/AIDS[a] (percent)

Report	Government (n = 95) Heard	Read	Donor (n = 35) Heard	Read	University (n = 40) Heard	Read	National/ local NGO (n = 146) Heard	Read	International NGO (n = 78) Heard	Read	Other (n = 62) Heard	Read	Total (n = 456) Heard	Read
Policy														
Breaking the Silence: Setting Realistic Priorities for AIDS Control in Less-Developed Countries	43	20	52	30	53	36	50	26	38	18	31	18	44	24
Intensifying Action Against HIV/AIDS in Africa: Responding to a Development Crisis	41	19	50	39	38	15	36	17	32	22	37	21	38	20
AIDS & Education: A Window of Hope	36	16	47	29	28	13	39	18	30	14	31	16	35	17
Confronting AIDS: Public Priorities in a Global Epidemic	32	15	44	44	49	38	32	17	29	22	35	18	34	21
Social Protection of Africa's Orphans and Vulnerable Children: Issues and Good Practice	22	9	35	21	31	15	29	11	21	10	18	11	25	12
AIDS and Public Policy: Lessons and Challenges of Success in Thailand	19	11	24	15	15	5	21	10	20	11	5	2	18	9
Technical														
HIV Infection and Sexually Transmitted Diseases	48	28	51	34	43	38	45	28	51	40	43	26	47	31
Evaluation														
World Bank HIV/AIDS Interventions: Ex-ante and Ex-post Evaluation	18	4	33	15	23	5	25	11	13	5	15	5	21	8
Economic														
HIV/AIDS and Economic Growth: A Global Perspective	34	16	37	15	28	23	36	15	29	15	30	16	33	16
Cost of Scaling up HIV Program Activities to a National Level in Sub-Saharan Africa	31	14	38	18	28	20	32	13	30	17	29	19	31	16
The Direct and Indirect Cost of HIV Infection in Developing Countries: The Case of Zaïre and Tanzania	21	10	26	12	28	18	17	6	19	8	19	13	20	10
The Long-run Economic Costs of AIDS: Theory and an Application to South Africa	16	5	35	21	18	5	14	3	16	5	19	10	17	6

a. Sample size shown is maximum for each group across all reports.

Nearly 13 percent of respondents completed a French questionnaire. Among the reports issued in French, recognition was higher among those completing the French questionnaire (table F.3). Among reports issued only in English, recognition among francophone respondents was considerably lower. However, readership of the reports by Francophone respondents—even when the report was issued in French—is less than half that of Anglophone respondents. This may point to particular problems in distribution or access to those translations; it is a problem that merits further investigation.

Technical Quality and Utility. The survey asked respondents who had read a report to rate its technical quality. The possible ratings were: 1-Very low; 2-Low; 3-Average; 4-High; 5-Very high; 6-Don't know. The survey also asked respondents who had read the report to rate its usefulness to their work on HIV/AIDS. The possible ratings were: 1-Not useful; 2-Useful; 3-Very useful; 4-One of the most useful. The ratings on technical quality and usefulness for each report are shown in table F.4.

For all 12 reports, more than 60 percent of the respondents gave the reports a technical quality rating of "High" or "Very High." For half, 70 percent or more gave a rating of "High" or "Very High." The majority of respondents rated all 12 reports as "Very Useful" of "One of the Most Useful." For five reports, at least 70 percent found the report to be "Very useful" or "One of the Most Useful."

Internet Use. Internet access of some form was available to 90 percent of respondents, but only 58 percent had "regular" access (connection at

Table F.3: Nairobi AIDS Conference Participants: Percentage Who Had Heard of and Read Report—Anglophone Versus Francophone Respondents[a]

Report	Heard of report		Read report	
	English (n = 399)	French (n = 58)	English (n = 399)	French (n = 58)
Published in both English and French				
Intensifying Action Against HIV/AIDS in Africa: Responding to a Development Crisis	37	41	21	17
Confronting AIDS: Public Priorities in a Global Epidemic	34	38	22	14
Cost of Scaling Up HIV Program Activities to a National Level in Sub-Saharan Africa	31	34	16	14
Published only in English				
HIV Infection and Sexually Transmitted Diseases	49	28	33	18
Breaking the Silence: Setting Realistic Priorities for AIDS Control in Less-Developed Countries	46	29	25	16
AIDS & Education: A Window of Hope	38	20	19	2
HIV/AIDS and Economic Growth: A Global Perspective	36	12	18	5
Social Protection of Africa's Orphans and Vulnerable Children: Issues and Good Practice	25	25	12	8
The Direct and Indirect Cost of HIV Infection in Developing Countries: The Case of Zaïre and Tanzania	21	17	10	9
World Bank HIV/AIDS Interventions: Ex-ante and Ex-post Evaluation	21	14	8	4
AIDS and Public Policy: Lessons and Challenges of Success in Thailand	19	12	9	9
The Long-run Economic Costs of AIDS: Theory and an Application to South Africa	18	10	7	2

a. Sample size shown is maximum for each group across all publications.

Table F.4: Nairobi AIDS Conference Participants: Quality and Usefulness of Analytic Work

Report	Sample size	Technical quality (% rating high or very high)	Usefulness (% rating very useful or most useful)
The Long-Run Economic Costs of AIDS: Theory and an Application to South Africa	29	79	75
HIV Infection and Sexually Transmitted Diseases	134	76	74
Breaking the Silence: Setting Realistic Priorities for AIDS Control in Less-Developed Countries	102	75	71
The Direct and Indirect Cost of HIV Infection in Developing Countries:			
The Case of Zaïre and Tanzania	43	72	67
Intensifying Action Against HIV/AIDS in Africa: Responding to a Development Crisis	91	71	67
Confronting AIDS: Public Priorities in a Global Epidemic	96	70	74
Cost of Scaling Up HIV Program Activities to a National Level in Sub-Saharan Africa	69	65	59
AIDS & Education: A Window of Hope	73	64	69
AIDS and Public Policy: Lessons and Challenges of Success in Thailand	39	64	61
Social Protection of Africa's Orphans and Vulnerable Children: Issues and Good Practice	50	62	64
HIV/AIDS and Economic Growth: A Global Perspective	71	61	57
World Bank HIV/AIDS Interventions: Ex-ante and Ex-post Evaluation	33	61	72

home and/or office). It was more common for non-Africans (94 percent) than for Africans (52 percent) to have regular Internet access. Respondents who work for donors were most likely to have regular access to the Internet (94 percent), followed by those who worked for international NGOs (80 percent) and universities (65 percent). Those who worked for national or local NGOs/CBOs had the least access to the Internet (42 percent).

Thirty-seven percent of respondents had visited the Bank's AIDS Web site at least once and 15 percent had visited the IAEN site at least once. Males and non-Africans were more likely to have visited both sites than females and Africans. Respondents working for donors and international NGOs were more likely to have visited both sites, compared to respondents working for other employers.

Results: World Bank Human Development Staff

Background characteristics. The average age of respondents was 43 years, and 60 percent were fe-

male. Almost all respondents were Bank staff (98 percent). Among Bank staff, 69 percent were based at headquarters and 30 percent were based in the field. Forty-seven percent of respondents identified themselves as "Specialists," 22 percent as "Economists," 20 percent as "Other" (i.e., Operations Officers), and 11 percent as "Administrative." Fourteen percent of respondents (29 individuals) had been a task manager (TTL) of an HIV/AIDS project (stand-alone or component), while 44 percent had provided technical support or analytic work for HIV/AIDS work in the Bank.

Recognition and Readership. Figure F.2 shows the percentage of respondents who had heard of each report and who had read each report. Figure F.3 shows the same for the toolkits. The reports with the highest recognition were not necessarily the same as those with the highest readership.

Additional analysis of the data found that report recognition was balanced between headquarters staff and field staff regardless of whether the report was global or Region-specific. However, Region-specific reports were more likely to be rec-

Figure F.2: Bank Human Development Staff: Percentage of Respondents Who Had Heard of and Read the Reports

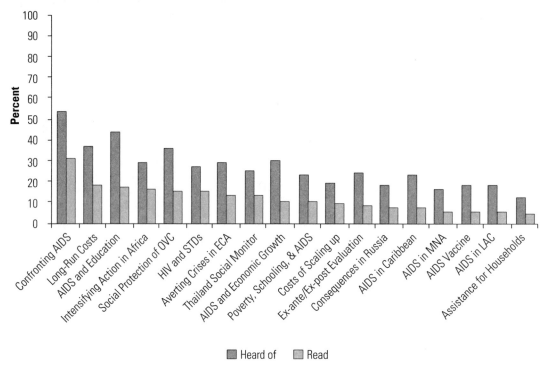

Note: MNA = Middle East and North Africa; LAC = Latin Anerica and the Caribbean.

Figure F.3: Bank Human Development Staff: Percentage of Respondents Who Had Heard of and Read the Toolkits

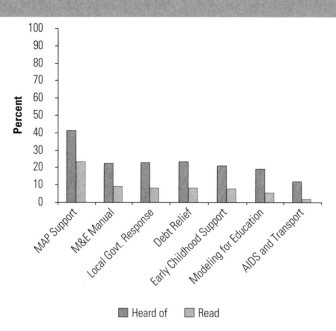

ognized and read by those who were affiliated with the Region that was the focus of the report.

For all reports and toolkits, recognition was higher among task team leaders of HIV/AIDS projects and those who had provided technical support or analytic work to HIV/AIDS projects and activities than all Bank-staff respondents. Even so, among task team leaders, fewer than half had read most of the reports, and fewer than a third had read most of the toolkits (table F.5).

Staff from the health, nutrition, and population (HNP) sector had the highest recognition and were more likely to have read a report (table

F.6). Among the reports not most read by HNP staff, four were focused on non-HNP sectors and were more likely to be recognized and read by staff of those sectors. Only one AIDS report each was recognized by at least half of the staff in each of these sectors.

Technical Quality and Utility. The survey asked Bank staff respondents who had read a report or toolkit to rate its technical quality according to the following scale: 1-Very low; 2-Low; 3-Average; 4-High; 5-Very high; 6-Don't know. Respondents were also asked to rate the usefulness of the re-

Table F.5: Recognition and Readership among World Bank AIDS Task Team Leaders (n = 29)

Report or toolkit	Percent who had heard of it	Percent who had read it
Confronting AIDS: Public Priorities in a Global Epidemic	82	82
HIV Infection and Sexually Transmitted Diseases	59	41
The Long-Run Economic Costs of AIDS: Theory & Application to South Africa	59	26
Intensifying Action Against AIDS in Africa: Responding to a Development Crisis	58	54
AIDS and Education: A Window of Hope	56	28
Costs of Scaling up HIV Program Activities to a National Level in Sub-Saharan Africa	52	37
Social Protection of Africa's Orphans & Vulnerable Children	52	37
Thailand's Response to AIDS: Building on Success, Confronting the Future	44	28
World Bank HIV/AIDS Interventions: Ex-ante and Ex-post Evaluation	40	29
Averting AIDS Crises in Eastern Europe and Central Asia	40	24
HIV/AIDS in the Caribbean: Issues and Options	40	12
AIDS and Economic Growth	36	16
The Epidemiological Impact of an AIDS Vaccine in Developing Countries	36	8
HIV/AIDS in the Middle East and North Africa: The Costs of Inaction	33	19
HIV/AIDS in Latin America: The Challenges Ahead	33	15
Poverty, AIDS, and Children's Schooling: A Targeting Dilemma	31	19
The Economic Consequences of HIV/AIDS in the Russian Federation	27	23
Preparing and Implementing MAP Support to HIV/AIDS Country Programs in Africa: Guidelines and Lessons Learned	79	57
AIDS, Poverty Reduction, and Debt Relief	56	26
Local Government Responses to HIV/AIDS: A Handbook	52	33
National AIDS Councils Monitoring and Evaluation Operations Manual	46	27
Operational Guidelines for Supporting Early Childhood Development in Multisectoral HIV/AIDS Programs in Africa	35	19
AIDS and Transport in Africa: A Quick Reference Guide	35	9
Modeling the Impact of HIV/AIDS on Education Systems—A Training Manual	27	12

Table F.6: What Have Sectoral Staff Heard of and Read? (percent)

Report	Health, nutrition, and population (n = 85)		Education (n = 41)		Social protection (n = 29)	
	Heard	Read	Heard	Read	Heard	Read
Confronting AIDS	65	52	45	14	34	14
HIV & STDs	45	31	16	7	3	0
AIDS and Education	38	18	66	31	31	0
Modeling for Education Toolkit	21	6	30	9	7	0
Poverty, Schooling & AIDS	17	2	30	16	21	14
Social Protection of OVC in Africa[a]	29	14	38	7	59	41
Early Childhood Development Toolkit	21	6	22	11	31	10

a. OVC: orphans and vulnerable children.

Table F.7: What Have Regional Staff Heard of and Read? (percent)

Report	Africa (n = 38)		East Asia (n = 25)		South Asia (n = 17)		Eastern Europe and Central Asia (n = 31)	
	Heard	Read	Heard	Read	Heard	Read	Heard	Read
Non-Regional								
Confronting AIDS	50	43	76	32	65	56	55	29
AIDS and Education	53	20	35	8	44	29	31	4
HIV & STDs	42	22	29	17	41	28	23	10
Thailand's Response to AIDS	17	9	48	32	59	33	26	7
Ex ante/Ex post Evaluation	36	18	25	4	25	18	19	7
Poverty, AIDS and Schooling	36	28	17	8	19	0	16	6
Regional								
Intensifying Action on AIDS in Africa	62	46						
Social Protection of Africa's OVC	63	38						
Costs of Scaling up in Africa	42	26						
Averting an AIDS Crisis in ECA							81	43
Consequences of AIDS in Russia							68	30

port or toolkit to their work on HIV/AIDS. The possible ratings were: 1-"Not useful;" 2-"Useful;" 3-"Very useful;" 4-"One of the most useful." The percentage of Human Development staff rating a report high or very high for quality and very useful or one of the most useful for usefulness is shown in table F.8.

For 8 of the 10 reports or toolkits read by at least 20 people, half of respondents or more rated quality "High or "Very high." For 4 of those reports, at least 70 percent of respondents rated quality "High" or "Very high." For virtually all reports, 85 percent or more of those who read them found the report "Useful" or higher. In 3 of the 10 cases, respondents found them "Very useful" or "One of the most useful."

Table F.8: Human Development Staff: Quality and Usefulness of Analytic Work

Report or toolkit	Sample size	Technical quality (% rating high or very high)	Usefulness (% rating very useful or most useful)
Thailand's Response to AIDS	23	83	65
Confronting AIDS	63	76	51
HIV and STDs	29	76	46
The Long-Run Costs of AIDS	34	74	38
Averting an AIDS Crisis in ECA	26	69	50
Social Protection of Orphans & Vulnerable Children	29	59	31
MAP Support Toolkit	45	56	48
AIDS and Education: A Window of Hope	31	55	39
Intensifying Action Against AIDS in Africa	33	49	41
AIDS and Economic Growth	20	35	35

Note: Results are presented only if at least 20 respondents read the report.

Web site Use. The survey found that the World Bank AIDS Web site had been visited by 56 percent of all human development staff respondents and 77 percent of respondents who had provided support to HIV/AIDS work. The IAEN Web site had been visited by 23 percent of all respondents and 40 percent of those who had provided support to HIV/AIDS work.

Quality and Utility of Reports Common to Both Surveys

With only one exception, the Nairobi AIDS Conference participants generally gave the reports ratings on technical quality that were equal to or higher than the technical ratings by Bank staff (table F.9). The Nairobi participants were far more likely to report that the reports were very useful or one of the most useful than were Bank staff.

Table F.9: Comparison of Quality and Utility Ratings of Nairobi AIDS Conference Participants and Bank HD Staff

Report	Nairobi AIDS conference participants		Bank Human Development staff	
	Technical quality (% rating high or very high)	Usefulness (% rating very useful or most useful)	Technical quality (% rating high or very high)	Usefulness (% rating very useful or most useful)
The Long-Run Economic Costs of AIDS:				
Theory and an Application to South Africa	79	75	74	38
HIV Infection and Sexually Transmitted Diseases	76	74	66	46
Intensifying Action Against HIV/AIDS in Africa:				
Responding to a Development Crisis	72	67	49	41
Confronting AIDS: Public Priorities in a Global Epidemic	70	74	76	51
AIDS & Education: A Window of Hope	64	69	55	39
HIV/AIDS and Economic Growth: A Global Perspective	61	57	35	35
Social Protection of Africa's Orphans and Vulnerable Children:				
Issues and Good Practice	62	64	59	31

Attachment 1. Reports and Toolkits Used in the Surveys

Table A.1: Reports Used for Survey of Nairobi AIDS Conference Participants

Intensifying Action Against HIV/AIDS in Africa: Responding to a Development Crisis. World Bank, August 1999.

Confronting AIDS: Public Priorities in a Global Epidemic. *World Bank Policy Research Report*, World Bank, 1997 and 1999 (rev.). Oxford University Press, New York.

Education and HIV/AIDS: A Window of Hope. World Bank, 2002.

Social Protection of Africa's Orphans and Other Vulnerable Children: Issues and Good Practice. K. Subbarao, A. Mattimore, K. Plangemann. *Africa Region Human Development Working Paper* No. 9, World Bank, August 2001.

Breaking the Silence: Setting Realistic Priorities for AIDS Control in Less-Developed Countries. M. Ainsworth, W. Teokul. *The Lancet*, July 2000, 356(9223), pp. 55-60.

AIDS and Public Policy: Lessons and Challenges of Success in Thailand. M. Ainsworth, C. Beyrer, A. Soucat. *Health Policy*, April 2003, vol. 64, No. 1, pp. 13-37.

HIV Infection and Sexually Transmitted Diseases. M. Over, P. Piot, from *Disease Control Priorities in Developing Countries*, D. Jamison and others, eds. pp. 455-527. Oxford University Press, New York, 1993.

World Bank HIV/AIDS Interventions: Ex-ante and Ex-post Evaluation. J. Dayton. *World Bank Discussion Paper* No. 389, June 1998.

Costs of Scaling HIV Program Activities to a National Level in Sub-Saharan Africa: Methods and Estimates. World Bank, March 2001.

The Direct and Indirect Cost of HIV Infection in Developing Countries: The Case of Zaïre and Tanzania. M. Over, S. Bertozzi, J. Chin from *The Global Impact of AIDS*, A. Fleming, M. Carballo, D. Fitzsimmons, M. Bailey, J. Mann, eds. Alan R. Liss, New York, 1988.

HIV/AIDS and Economic Growth: A Global Perspective. R. Bonnel. *The South African Journal of Economics*, 2000, Vol. 68, No. 5, pp. 820-855.

The Long-Run Economic Costs of AIDS: Theory and an Application to South Africa. C. Bell, S. Devarajan, H. Gersbach. *Policy Research Working Paper* No. 3152, October 2003.

Table A.2: Reports and Toolkits Used for Bank Staff Survey

Reports

Confronting AIDS: Public Priorities in a Global Epidemic. *World Bank Policy Research Report*, World Bank, 1997 and 1999 (rev.) Oxford Univ. Press, New York.

Education and HIV/AIDS: A Window of Hope. World Bank, 2002.

Social Protection of Africa's Orphans and Other Vulnerable Children: Issues and Good Practice. K. Subbarao, A. Mattimore, K. Plangemann. *Africa Region Human Development Working Paper* Series No. 9, World Bank, August 2001.

Poverty, AIDS, and Children's Schooling: A Targeting Dilemma. M. Ainsworth, D. Filmer. *Policy Research Working Paper* No. 2885, World Bank, September 2002.

Breaking the Silence: Setting Realistic Priorities for AIDS Control in Less-Developed Countries. M. Ainsworth, W. Teokul. *The Lancet*, July 2000, 356(9223), pp. 55-60.

Sources of Financial Assistance for Households Suffering an Adult Death. P. Mujinja, M. Lundberg, M. Over. *Policy Research Working Paper* No. 2508, World Bank, December 2000.

Table A.2: Reports and Toolkits Used for Bank Staff Survey (continued)

The Long-Run Economic Costs of AIDS: Theory and an Application to South Africa. C. Bell, S. Devarajan, H. Gersbach. *Policy Research Working Paper* No. 3152, World Bank, October 2003.

HIV/AIDS and Economic Growth: A Global Perspective. R. Bonnel. *The South African Journal of Economics*, 2000, Vol. 68, No. 5, pp. 820-855.

The Epidemiological Impact of an HIV/AIDS Vaccine in Developing Countries. J. Stover, G. Garnett, S. Seitz, S. Forsythe. *Policy Research Working Paper* No. 2811, World Bank, March 2002.

World Bank HIV/AIDS Interventions: Ex-ante and Ex-post Evaluation. J. Dayton. *World Bank Discussion Paper* No. 389, June 1998.

HIV Infection and Sexually Transmitted Diseases. M. Over, P. Piot from *Disease Control Priorities in Developing Countries*, D. Jamison and others, eds. pp. 455-527. Oxford University Press, New York, 1993.

Intensifying Action Against HIV/AIDS in Africa: Responding to a Development Crisis. World Bank, August 1999.

Costs of Scaling HIV Program Activities to a National Level in Sub-Saharan Africa: Methods and Estimates. World Bank, March 2001.

Thailand's Response to AIDS: Building on Success, Confronting the Future. *Thailand Social Monitor*, World Bank, November 2000.

Averting AIDS Crises in Eastern Europe and Central Asia: A Regional Support Strategy. World Bank, 2003

The Economic Consequences of HIV/AIDS in the Russian Federation. C. Ruehl, Pokrovsky, Viniogradov. World Bank, 2002.

HIV/AIDS in Latin America: The Challenges Ahead. A. Abreu, I. Noguer, K. Cowgill. *Health, Nutrition, and Population Paper* Series, World Bank, 2003.

HIV/AIDS in the Caribbean: Issues and Options. P. Marquez, V. Sierra, J. Gayle, R. Crown. World Bank, June 2000.

HIV/AIDS in the Middle East and North Africa: The Costs of Inaction. C. Jenkins, D. Robalino. World Bank, 2003.

Toolkits

Preparing and Implementing MAP Support to HIV/AIDS Country Programs in Africa: The guidelines and lessons learned. World Bank, July 2003.

National AIDS Councils Monitoring and Evaluation Operations Manual. World Bank, UNAIDS, 2002.

Operational Guidelines for Supporting Early Child Development in Multisectoral HIV/AIDS Programs in Africa. World Bank, UNAIDS, UNICEF, 2003.

AIDS, Poverty Reduction and Debt Relief: A Toolkit for Mainstreaming HIV/AIDS Programs into Development Instruments. O. Adeyi, R.. Hecht, E. Njobvu, A. Soucat. World Bank, UNAIDS, March 2001.

Modeling the Impact of HIV/AIDS on Education Systems – A Training Manual. World Bank, UNAIDS, June 2002.

AIDS and Transport in Africa: A Quick Reference Guide. World Bank, July 2003

Local Government Responses to HIV/AIDS: A Handbook. World Bank, Cities Alliance, UNDP/UN Habitat, AMICAALL, September 2003.

Brazil

Chris Beyrer, Varun Gauri, and Denise Vaillancourt

The objectives of this study are to: (a) assess the impact of the World Bank's HIV/AIDS assistance to Brazil relative to the counterfactual of no Bank assistance; and (b) distill lessons for future HIV/AIDS activities.

Previous experience in campaigns against the military government and for expanded access to health care inspired civil society in Brazil to mobilize aggressively against AIDS when domestic cases first appeared in 1982. The epidemic first spread rapidly among men who have sex with men (MSM) and then among injecting drug users (IDUs), after which a wave of heterosexual transmission took off. Several states, particularly São Paulo, led the response. By 1989, the federal government had established a national program, regulated the blood supply, and established a national AIDS commission composed of government and nongovernmental representatives.

The World Bank provided important assistance to Brazil's response in the form of two projects totaling $550 million (funded in part by $325 million in loans from the Bank) that were in operation from 1993 to 2003. A third, $200 million project was approved in June 2003. In addition, the Northeast Endemic Disease Control Project financed $7.4 million toward media campaigns on HIV/AIDS, the establishment of the National AIDS and STD Control Program (NASCP), and the preparation of the first AIDS project. It was Brazil that approached the Bank about an interest in borrowing to support its HIV/AIDS program in the early 1990s, a time when the Bank did not have an explicit AIDS strategy for Brazil,

nor was it already engaged in AIDS policy dialogue with the government. In 1993, when the first AIDS project began, prevention was not yet active outside selected major metropolitan areas, nor among certain high-risk groups. Brazil had not developed the laboratory network that would facilitate its testing and (especially) its treatment programs. The National Coordination on HIV/AIDS/STDs was reconstituting after a difficult period from 1990 to 1992, and many states and municipalities did not have HIV/AIDS programs at all. The Bank's implicit assistance strategy focused on preventive efforts, institutional strengthening (especially surveillance, monitoring, and evaluation), and public goods to promote cost-effectiveness in treatment. These emphases were, and remain, relevant.

The efficacy of the World Bank's assistance was high in some areas. The partnerships with NGOs and community service organizations (CSOs) mobilized effort in prevention at a critical time and expanded the geographic and functional coverage of the program significantly. Bank financial and technical assistance also supported the local design and implementation of 27 state and 150 municipal HIV/AIDS action plans, under the supervision of local STD/HIV/AIDS coordination units, many of which had been established with project assistance. The Bank's efforts to assist Brazil in development of HIV epidemiological surveillance were less successful—eventually, a substantial amount of data on HIV prevalence and risk behavior on some key populations (pregnant women and military recruits) did become available, but not until after 1997. Systematic HIV surveillance remains a challenge. Similarly, a comprehensive strategy for the monitoring and evaluation of program impact was not developed until well into the second project, in preparation for the third. The capacity to use epidemiologic, behavioral, and program data for program decision making and coordinating prevention activities remains weak in Brazil, particularly outside of key metropolitan areas. Brazil failed to undertake cost-effectiveness analyses planned under Bank support, with the consequence that there is little empirical basis for the prioritization of program activities and for the allocation of human and financial resources. Although the projects did develop a system for promoting local initiatives, the latter (like many health initiatives in the country) were not integrated with other local health sector programs. The absence of an effective framework for health sector decentralization in Brazil until late in the 1990s hampered that effort.

As of the end of 2003, a total of 310,310 AIDS cases had been reported in Brazil since the beginning of the epidemic and an estimated 0.65 percent of the adult population was thought to be living with HIV/AIDS. A 2002 study of MSM in 10 state capitals found that 70 percent reported always using condoms with every sex partner in the previous six months. By that year, there were 160 needle and syringe exchange programs in operation in Brazil. A study of 3,000 sex workers in five cities in 2001 found that 74 percent consistently used condoms with clients. Coverage of prisoners with a basic set of educational and condom promotion efforts was reportedly 65 percent nationwide. Annual sales of male condoms have increased from 5 million in 1985 to 395 million in 2001. Brazil passed a law guaranteeing universal access to antiretroviral drugs to AIDS patients free of charge in 1996. In 2004, some 175,000 AIDS patients were under care: 135,000 in treatment with ARV drugs and 40,000 in other care. Brazil has built a national laboratory network for HIV viral load and CD4/CD8 immunologic monitoring to guide therapy. The impact on mortality, morbidity, survival after AIDS diagnosis, hospitalizations, opportunistic infection rates, and quality of life has been substantial.

Government commitment to fighting HIV/AIDS preceded Bank involvement, and general prevention programs almost certainly would have occurred even without the projects. The evaluation team nevertheless found four critical

areas in which the Bank likely had an impact relative to the counterfactual of no involvement:

- The projects helped safeguard prevention resources during a period of macroeconomic and financial instability in which there was a dramatic increase in demand for AIDS treatment and protected HIV/AIDS funds from political interference at the local level.
- The national response has been more focused on HIV prevention among groups with high-risk behavior, including very marginalized groups such as IDUs and sex workers, because of the legitimacy conveyed by the Bank's support.
- The creation and support of state and municipality-level HIV/AIDS and STD coordination units (in all 27 states and 150 municipalities), the development and implementation of local-level work program proposals that would be the subject of formal agreements (contracts) between these units and the NASCP, the financing of staff costs and cofinancing of other costs by local government, and the training of local-level program staff all are likely to have happened earlier than would have been the case without Bank assistance. The Bank's support helped to create local program capacity and propelled local government involvement that would ultimately facilitate program decentralization.
- The Bank's engagement encouraged early development of mechanisms for government to finance NGOs as implementers of AIDS programs, improving the efficiency and effectiveness of the prevention program, empowering marginalized groups that are key to success, and expanding the base of stakeholders to reinforce government commitment.

While many of the activities financed by the two projects likely improved the efficiency and effectiveness of treatment and care, the team cannot dismiss the strong likelihood that they would have been undertaken by the government even in the absence of the Bank's involvement. Unfortunately, due largely to the failure of government to adopt systematic surveillance of HIV and risk behavior—and the inability of the Bank to ensure that these planned activities in the two projects were implemented—it is not possible to assess the impact of either the government's prevention efforts or the Bank's contribution to them on the epidemic or the behaviors that spread it. There has been very little evaluation of the cost-effectiveness of any of the innovative prevention interventions sponsored by these projects. The attempt to encourage monitoring and evaluation in the Brazilian AIDS program is arguably one of the areas in which the Bank's assistance has had the least impact.

The evaluation has also highlighted numerous lessons from the Bank's engagement with Brazil on AIDS: the need to foster political commitment at all levels of policy formulation and implementation; the Bank's role in lending legitimacy to controversial prevention programs; the need to address constraints in the health system that are critical to the AIDS response; opportunities for the Bank to invest in public goods that improve the efficiency of treatment; the critical contribution of NGO involvement in reaching high-risk groups, but the need to invest in implementation capacity to make sure this happens; concerns about the long-run sustainability of the NGO response that is dependent on Bank-sponsored projects; the need to incorporate adequate preparation and incentives for M&E into projects; and the feasibility of working with high-risk groups in a concentrated epidemic when interventions are developed by and with communities at risk and respecting their human rights.

Ethiopia

Denise Vaillancourt, Sarbani Chakraborty, and Taha Taha

The objective of this case study is to evaluate the impact of the World Bank's assistance–policy dialogue, analytic work, and lending—on Ethiopia's national response to HIV/AIDS, and to derive lessons from that experience. This case study is based on a review of published and unpublished documents on HIV/AIDS in Ethiopia; structured interviews with various stakeholders representing the government, civil society, World Bank, donors, and nongovernmental, community-based, and faith-based organizations; field visits to selected regions of Ethiopia in August 2003; and analysis of epidemiological and behavioral data.

AIDS Epidemic
The first cases of HIV infection in Ethiopia were reported in 1984, and the first AIDS cases in 1986. Heterosexual transmission is the major mode of HIV infection. HIV spread rapidly among sex workers and other populations with high rates of sexual partner change. In its second phase, HIV spread to the sexual partners of high-risk populations, including monogamous partners and those with much lower rates of partner exchange. In rural Ethiopia, the epidemic began in the early 1990s. National adult HIV prevalence was estimated at 6.6 percent in 2002— 13.7 percent in urban areas (15.6 percent in Addis Ababa) and 3.7 percent in rural areas. About 219,400 Ethiopians were estimated to be living with AIDS. The Ethiopian HIV/AIDS epidemic is now 'generalized,' with average HIV prevalence in the general population of 5 percent or higher. However, there is considerable geographic heterogeneity in the epidemic, with some regions at an earlier stage.

Ethiopia's Early Response
Ethiopia's initial response, launched in 1987, was one of the first in Africa. Under the Department of AIDS Control (DAC) within the Ministry of Health (MOH), the HIV/AIDS program centered on a strategic plan that emphasized the provision of public goods (surveillance, research, monitoring, evaluation, laboratory capacity) and prioritized prevention interventions both for high-risk groups and for the general population. In its earliest years, the program was decentralized to 14 regions, collaborated with key sectors, and financed NGO activities. The initial response was launched under the Derg government (1974–91), when bilateral donor assistance for AIDS was limited, as many but not all bilateral donors withdrew support to the Marxist regime. Although the World Bank had been active in other sectors in Ethiopia since 1950, and the first health project was approved in 1985, it did

not provide financial or technical support to these early HIV/AIDS program efforts. In addition to public budget allocations, the early program received technical and financial support from the World Health Organization's Global Program on AIDS (WHO/GPA).

In the early 1990s, with the ousting of the Derg, the new government had an overwhelming and pressing agenda of competing development and political priorities. The rapid decentralization of resources and decision-making autonomy to new regions dramatically reduced the size and mandates of federal-level agencies. One consequence of this upheaval was a weakening of the national HIV/AIDS response. The government was facing an ambitious and under-funded agenda to improve and expand basic health care services. Although HIV infection was believed to be high at that point in time—especially in Addis Ababa and other urban areas—other diseases, such as malaria, caused more illness and death and predominated in rural areas, where over 80 percent of the population lives. In 1996, a new medium-term AIDS strategy was prepared and a national conference on "Breaking the Silence" was held, both a result of strong lobbying and support of UNAIDS and bilateral donors.

Initiation of World Bank HIV/AIDS Dialogue, 1996–99

In 1996 the World Bank launched a dialogue on the social sectors with the government, underpinned by a large and participatory social sector analysis published in 1998. This marked the initiation of the Bank's dialogue on HIV/AIDS. AIDS was one of many diseases subjected to a burden of disease analysis, and the study projected future HIV infections and AIDS cases. The Social Sector Report culminated in 10-year development plans for both the health and education sectors, provided the basis for the design of sector-wide approach (SWAp) operations, and significantly improved social sector donor coordination under the leadership of the Bank. It strengthened both the credibility of the Bank and its working relationship with the government and donors. The Health Sector Development Program (HSDP, $100 million, Credit No. 3140) was approved by

the Board in 1998 and became effective in 1999. The control of sexually transmitted diseases (STDs), including HIV/AIDS, is one of 9 programs included in the 10-year health sector development program. The World Bank financial support to the HSDP focused on strengthening and expanding basic health services, which are critical for HIV/AIDS activities within the health sector. The Bank's country director and resident representative have persisted in raising the issue of HIV/AIDS at every opportunity.

In 1999, the World Bank prepared a new Africa Regional AIDS strategy, *Intensifying Action Against HIV/AIDS in Africa*, and created an AIDS Campaign Team for Africa (ACT*africa*) to guide the Region in implementing this strategy. Intensified dialogue in Ethiopia, with support from the Regional vice president for Africa and the president of the World Bank, culminated in an agreement to undertake a rapid preparation of an HIV/AIDS operation, the Ethiopia Multisectoral HIV/AIDS Project (EMSAP, $59.7 million, Credit No. 3416), one of the first two projects under the new Multi-Country AIDS Program (MAP) for Africa. In addition, HIV/AIDS components were integrated into new or restructured projects in other (non-health) sectors.

Ethiopia Multisectoral AIDS Project

To satisfy the Bank's eligibility criteria for the Ethiopia Multisectoral AIDS Project (EMSAP), the government established in early 2000 a National AIDS Council (NAC) and a National AIDS Council Secretariat (NASC) placed within the Prime Minister's Office. The EMSAP channeled funds to four components: capacity building for government and civil society; expanding governmental multisectoral response; expanding the response of NGOs and communities; and project coordination and management. Forty-four percent of project funds ($28.1 million) were allocated for NGO and community-based activities. The NASC assumed responsibility for coordination of HIV/AIDS programs, a responsibility previously assigned to the MOH. The project was prepared and negotiated in only six weeks because Bank management considered that the AIDS crisis warranted an emergency response and committed to seeking Board approval by the time of the annual meetings in September 2000. Preparation focused on setting up implementation arrangements that would accelerate the flow of funds and not on the content of the AIDS response that would be supported. It did not appraise the government's five-year strategic framework from technical, economic, financial, social, or institutional perspectives. Consultation with donors and NGOs during project preparation was extremely limited. A number of preparation tasks were postponed until the implementation phase of the project.

The EMSAP became effective in early 2001 and has now been active for three years. By the end of 2003 (six months short of the original closing date), less than half of the credit had been disbursed. The closing date of the project has been extended by 18 months, until December 2005. To date, the public sector multisectoral response has been weak, both in funds committed and spent and in the quality of the proposals submitted by ministries. The transfer of coordination of the HIV/AIDS program to the NASC initially resulted in the alienation of the MOH. The EMSAP has financed important health inputs (drugs for opportunistic infections, voluntary counseling and testing centers, new surveillance sites), but these have not yet translated into improved services and products. The civil society and community response component has stimulated action among these actors. NGOs have prepared and launched projects, many of them focused on information, education, and communication activities. Other prevention activities include the setting up and support of thousands of anti-AIDS clubs across the country for in-school and out-of-school youth. The number of local-level HIV/AIDS councils established and work programs prepared and financed have exceeded plans. The coordination of these activities and their coherence with the needs and demands of diverse regions and multiple target groups are not yet fully developed.

Impact of World Bank Assistance

Government commitment. The main impact of the World Bank's assistance has been to raise the profile of AIDS as a development issue and increase resources available to government and civil society to fight the epidemic. The 1998 Social Sector Report and accompanying dialogue was not successful in convincing the social sector leadership of the urgency of the HIV/AIDS epidemic. However, intensive work by high-level Bank officials in 1999–2000 succeeded in opening dialogue with the highest levels of government. Government spending on HIV/AIDS has since increased through project lending as well as counterpart financing of the new HIV/AIDS Prevention and Control Office (HAPCO). Regional budget allocations are financing Regional-level HAPCO staff and operating costs.

Institutional response. The eligibility criteria for EMSAP leveraged the efforts of UNAIDS and other partners to create a multisectoral institution for HIV/AIDS coordination. EMSAP has supported the establishment and functioning of the federal and 11 regional HAPCOs. However, the new institutions were interpreted by the MOH as a lack of confidence in its leadership on HIV/AIDS and its capacity in health. The consequence had been a disengagement of the MOH—the key ministry in the fight against HIV/AIDS. This situation is reported to have improved with the recent nomination of the Minister of Health as chair of NAC Board. HIV/AIDS components of non-health sector projects have supported more ownership and quality interventions than have public sector work programs in non-health ministries financed under EMSAP.

HIV/AIDS and the Health Sector. The two health projects have contributed to strengthening health system capacity for prevention and treatment of many conditions, including STDs, but with little direct support for HIV/AIDS activities. IDA financing made available for HIV/AIDS has not been fully exploited by MOH.

Strategic choices. The World Bank has not had significant impact on the content of national policy, adopted in 1998, or on the 2000–04 strategy. The 1996–98 Social Sector Report did not review the HIV/AIDS medium-term plan and the EMSAP committed to support whatever activities were already in the national strategic plan without engaging in a discussion of priority activities for the public sector.

Civil society engagement. The EMSAP has supported a major shift in the environment of NGO and CBO participation in HIV/AIDS activities by supporting contracts between government and NGOs on an unprecedented scale. To date, there has been no systematic evaluation of NGO or community projects, so their impact is unknown. Cumbersome mechanisms for disbursement and replenishment of funds have affected the timeliness and reliability of financial flows to NGOs, causing stronger NGOs to turn to other financing sources and leaving the EMSAP resources to weaker NGOs. Civil society capacity has been utilized in part and modestly strengthened through applied experience and some training. However, capacity building remains a critical priority of the project.

Monitoring and evaluation. The Bank's collaboration with other partners to strengthen surveillance, monitoring and evaluation capacity has had modest impact to date. EMSAP has invested in expanding the number of ante-natal clinic surveillance sites, especially in rural areas. There is no systematic HIV surveillance of high-risk groups and data on pregnant women are not regular or reliable as of yet. There was no monitoring and evaluation framework at the project's outset, limited baseline data was available at the time EMSAP was developed, and efforts have been insufficient to develop a proper baseline. An M&E framework was not produced until the end of the third year of project implementation.

Impact on outcomes. Available data show that, while awareness of HIV/AIDS was already over 90 percent in 2000, knowledge of specific prevention methods in 2001–02 was limited (50 percent of key target populations report knowing the three main ways to prevent HIV infection), and risky behaviors persist despite such knowledge. As there was no baseline measurement of many of the key outcome indicators, it is not possible to assess any changes that might have occurred during the course of the project to date, let alone evaluate the attribution of those changes

to the project. The bulk of prevention interventions supported to date were for information, education, and communication, and not for targeted behavior change.

Findings and Lessons

The Bank was late in launching a dialogue and in providing support. It missed an opportunity to launch a dialogue on HIV/AIDS during the restructuring of the Family Health Project in 1993 ($33 million, Credit No. 1913), at which time enough information about the progression of the disease was available to warrant a stronger approach. When it did initiate a policy dialogue in 1998, the Bank succeeded in getting AIDS on the agenda on a par with other key infectious diseases. However, it did not succeed in convincing government about the momentum and consequences of the infection and of the urgent need to halt further spread. Bank management was persistent and ultimately successful in opening up a dialogue with the highest levels of government. The two new channels of Bank support for HIV/AIDS—introduction of HIV/AIDS components in non-health projects and the EMSAP— were generated very recently as a result of the Africa Region's intensified strategy.

A number of lessons emanate from the World Bank's experience in Ethiopia that are relevant to other HIV/AIDS efforts.

- The adoption of HIV/AIDS coordinating institutions to satisfy eligibility criteria established by the Bank does not automatically ensure deep or sustained commitment by the multitude of actors necessary for an effective response.
- Project design and implementation that focus primarily on process rather than results undermine the effectiveness and efficiency of the Bank's financial support.
- The creation of a multisectoral institution does not necessarily foster a multisectoral approach and, if not founded on local institutional analysis, risks alienating key actors, like the Ministry of Health. Within the context of a multisectoral approach, the prominence of the health sector as a major leader and implementer in the fight against HIV/AIDS is unequivocal.

- Financial allocations and disbursements are necessary but insufficient conditions for successful NGO participation in the fight against HIV/AIDS. A number of factors can undermine NGO contributions, even when funding is accessible, including: the absence of a capacity-building strategy based on in-depth assessments, the lack of baseline knowledge about the numbers and coverage of target populations, inadequate monitoring and evaluation of NGO activities, and the absence of viable mechanisms for coordination of public-private partnerships, in line with their comparative advantages.

- Failure to establish key baseline data and to design a monitoring and evaluation framework during project design is a missed opportunity for creating a targeted, results-based approach.

Indonesia

A. Edward Elmendorf, Eric R. Jensen, and Elizabeth Pisani

The HIV/AIDS epidemic, until recently, was at very low levels in Indonesia. The first case of HIV was identified in a foreign homosexual tourist in Bali in 1987. Systematic sentinel surveillance of sex workers in Jakarta and Surabaya began in 1988. In 1993/1994, sentinel surveillance reported the first positive sample among sex workers and the first positive blood samples were identified among blood donors. HIV prevalence was still sufficiently low in 1997 that MOH statistics refer specifically to a small number of cases in Irian Jaya as "Thai fishermen, who have since left the country," and this relatively small adjustment accounted for a significant share of all AIDS cases in the country at the time.

Projections of the possible course of the HIV/AIDS epidemic were generated by expatriate consultants and researchers beginning in the early 1990s. They did not take existing surveillance data as their starting point, were largely based on the Sub-Saharan African and Thai experiences of the late 1980s and early 1990s, and showed rapid acceleration of the epidemic. In hindsight, the projection models were ill suited to the purpose to which they were put in In-

donesia. HIV cases were projected to rise to roughly 500,000 in 2000 and to 700,000 in 2005, assuming that effective prevention efforts were launched during the mid-1990s. If prevention efforts were less successful, the model predicted that the number of cases would increase to an estimated 700,000 in 2000 and 1.2 million in 2005. This turned out to be dramatically wrong, as HIV prevalence barely increased through most of the 1990s. Since 1999, the HIV epidemic has emerged concurrently with an epidemic of intravenous drug use (IDU). IDU was rare before 1997 and has made a significant contribution to the HIV/AIDS epidemic. Without its contribution, more current projection models show virtually no epidemic taking place in Indonesia.

Before the AIDS epidemic and since its advent, the World Bank has had a long, active, and largely successful engagement in health in Indonesia. Starting with a population project in 1972, the Bank financed 13 health, nutrition, and population projects previous to its engagement on HIV/AIDS in the country in 1996. Nonetheless, much remains to be done to improve health services and outcomes. Compared to neighboring countries, Indonesia showed high infant and maternal mortality levels throughout the 1990s (including the period prior to the financial crisis), and UNDP data suggest that health indicators in Indonesia improved at a slower rate than would be consistent with Indonesia's per capita economic growth.

A $24.8 million IBRD loan for the Bank-financed HIV/AIDS and STDs Prevention and Management Project was negotiated in January 1996. The project was designed to support behavioral interventions and to finance laboratory and testing support. Some of this was accomplished—more HIV screening among sex workers is one example. However, project execution was problematic from the outset. The Project Appraisal Document (PAD) sometimes budgeted substantial funds for expenditures that were unnecessary for Indonesia's situation. Clients at antenatal clinics were counseled about HIV/AIDS, even though HIV prevalence among married women was (and remains) virtually zero. Labs were equipped to speed processing, under the faulty assumption that supply bottlenecks were the cause of testing delays. About 20 percent of the loan was programmed for test kits already in the possession of the government at appraisal. Many of the problems stemmed from a weak project management unit. Many also sprang from inappropriate project design, but these issues could have been handled by a more effective project management unit through reprogramming of the use of Bank funds. The projections should have been subjected to more searching scrutiny by specialists on HIV modeling. The failure of dire outcomes to materialize may have hurt political commitment as the project unfolded. The weaknesses in design and especially in project management led the project to be designated a problem project in the Bank's Indonesia portfolio only two years into its three-year planned execution. At the time of the East Asia financial crisis in 1997 and 1998, when the Bank's portfolio was restructured, 80 percent of the loan was cancelled. The HIV/AIDS project failed to achieve its development objectives, and was correctly judged by Regional staff as unsatisfactory in the implementation completion report.

The behavioral interventions of the Bank-financed project were to be implemented largely by NGOs. This required granting them tax-free status. The collapse of an agreement with the Ministry of Finance (MOF) to facilitate NGO involvement in turn made this a lengthy process. Eventually, some NGOs did work on the project, but we found little evidence that NGOs new to HIV/AIDS work before working with the project have continued to work in this area. To a number of observers, a meaningful contribution of the project was finally to gain acceptance of the idea and practice of government funding of NGOs for the provision of health services. The project may have helped to raise HIV/AIDS awareness at an early stage of the epidemic. However, it did so in alarmist fashion, and there appears to have been a period of complacency, perhaps backlash, during project implementation.

Except for the cancelled loan, there has been little HIV/AIDS-specific activity by the World Bank in Indonesia. Since 1999, the epidemic among intravenous drug users (spreading to their sexual

partners) has helped fuel a growing sense of urgency regarding HIV/AIDS. Little if any of this increase can be attributed to Bank activities, as until very recently the Bank has hardly been involved in AIDS-related dialogue or programs since the close of the HIV/AIDS loan.

On net, the impact of the Bank on the progress of the HIV/AIDS epidemic in Indonesia has been minimal. The most direct intervention, the HIV/AIDS and STDs Prevention and Management Project, accomplished little before most of the loan was cancelled. Outside of that loan, there have been some informal high-level contacts between Bank staff and government officials that may have helped to raise awareness. However, given the nature of the epidemic at that time, the lack of information about its course, and the demonstrated lack of response by the government, it is difficult to attribute any impact to the Bank on this score. The funding mechanisms for NGOs are in place, and one lasting result may be the relative ease of incorporating civil society in future Bank-funded health and AIDS work in Indonesia.

The Indonesian case underscores the essential tension between early (and cost-effective) intervention and intensity of commitment. This tension was heightened by the unwillingness of the Government of Indonesia to focus resources on the social periphery, at appraisal, during the early stages of project implementation, and especially as health resources were stretched to the breaking point by the financial crisis. Commitment also may have been diminished by the nature of the project relative to needs perceived by stakeholders. In a context where little is known about the extent of the epidemic and the behaviors that spread HIV, as was the case in Indonesia in the early to mid-1990s, more appropriate interventions would have aimed at increasing public health monitoring and surveillance capabilities and behavioral studies. As understanding of the nature of the epidemic and the behaviors that spread it increased, this information could have been used for evidence-based advocacy and policy dialogue to create an environment that would support effective work with groups at risk for HIV.

Russian Federation

Judyth L. Twigg and Richard Skolnik

The Operations Evaluation Department (OED) of the World Bank is evaluating the impact to date of the World Bank's work on HIV/AIDS. The Russian Federation was selected for a case study because it has one of the fastest-growing HIV/AIDS epidemics in the world and the Bank has invested heavily in non-lending HIV/AIDS assistance and project development. This study examines: whether or not the Bank did the "right thing" in its HIV/AIDS work with Russia; whether or not it did it "the right way"; and whether or not the Bank's work made any difference to the way Russia addresses HIV/AIDS, compared to what it would have done in the absence of the Bank's involvement.

This assessment was based on a review of literature on HIV/AIDS globally and in Russia, a review of the World Bank's files, and over forty interviews with an array of stakeholders from Russia, the Bank, development partners, academia, and NGOs. The report examines the context of the epidemic, the government response to HIV/AIDS, and the Bank's HIV/AIDS activities in support of Russia. It then assesses the impact of the World Bank's assistance on the Russian response to date relative to what might have happened if the Bank had not been involved.

HIV/AIDS Epidemic

The first reported case of AIDS in Russia was in 1987 and the first AIDS death in 1988. HIV initially spread primarily among men who have sex with men, with the exception of an outbreak of pediatric infections in health facilities in 1989. Profound and unprecedented social changes since the break-up of the Soviet Union, however, have rendered Russia fertile ground for an HIV/AIDS epidemic. From 1987 to 2002, syphilis rates, for example, rose from 4 to 144 per 100,000 and peaked at 278 per 100,000. New HIV cases began to increase rapidly in 1996, with the vast majority among injecting drug users (IDUs). The rate of increase from 1999 to 2002 was among the highest in the world. As of October 2003, 255,350

HIV-positive persons had been officially reported in Russia since the beginning of the epidemic, of which 817 had AIDS, and 4,065 people had already died from AIDS-related causes. The true figure for HIV infection may be 3-5 times higher.

Government Response

During the Soviet period, there was no overarching national program to coordinate activity related to HIV/AIDS. In 1993, after the Soviet collapse, the Russian government developed the "Federal Program for the Prevention of the Spread of AIDS in the Russian Federation from 1993–95." In practice, this program was overwhelmingly oriented toward a medical approach that stressed epidemiology and the biomedical sciences over prevention, education, social services, and legal support for HIV and AIDS patients. In August 1995, the legislature passed a Federal Anti-AIDS law that provides current federal guidelines for HIV/AIDS prevention, care, and support. It brought almost all activity in the country relating to HIV and AIDS under the authority and supervision of the federal government. The 1998 Federal Law on Narcotic and Psychoactive Substances criminalized all drug consumption or possession not prescribed by physicians and prohibited substitution therapy of opiate addiction with methadone. Its provisions could easily be interpreted as defining needle or syringe exchange programs as illegal. The government has established a Federal AIDS Center, 86 Regional AIDS Centers, and 6 Territorial AIDS centers. In addition, there is a Federal Clinical AIDS Center in St. Petersburg. The system of regional AIDS centers includes over 1,000 screening laboratories and 500 offices for anonymous testing.

The highest levels of the government have been nearly silent on HIV. The government's early response, much like that to other STIs, was dominated by mass testing and contact tracing. The approach to prevention is highly medicalized and not focused on those at greatest risk of contracting and spreading HIV. The federal government spends less than $4 million a year on its earmarked federal HIV/AIDS program for a country of 144 million people. It continues to have great difficulty dealing with groups engaging in high-risk behaviors, and many government practices on both HIV and STI stigmatize people. There is very little treatment of AIDS patients with antiretroviral therapy, and the approach that is taken is based on two drugs rather than three.

World Bank Response

From the early 1990s, the World Bank recognized the need to ensure that the government had appropriate safety nets and a health system that was effective and protected the poor. By the mid-1990s, an explicit part of the Bank's Country Assistance Strategy was to help Russia deal with its most pressing health problems and to address TB and HIV. In response to a government request, in 1999 the Bank began to develop a TB project with the Ministries of Health and Justice, to which HIV was added. WHO, DFID, CIDA, Soros/Open Society Institute (OSI), USAID, Médecins sans Frontières, and local NGOs were already involved in helping Russia to pilot better approaches to HIV. The Bank initially worked closely with these groups in designing a project that would take their efforts to scale and raise the government's HIV/AIDS program to the level of international best practice. OSI was especially helpful to the Bank's work, by facilitating high-level interest in HIV and TB in Russia, by helping to get harm reduction on the agenda, and by encouraging Russia to consider new approaches to the difficult harm reduction issue. DFID was also particularly helpful in inspiring and financing a number of critical parts of project preparation, analytical work, and policy dialogue.

Over four years, the Bank engaged in high-level policy dialogue and co-sponsored training and analytic work in parallel with preparation of the TB and AIDS Control Project. In 2000–01, project development ground to a halt due to government concerns about the DOTS approach to TB control being advocated by the Bank and the effect of international competitive bidding requirements on the domestic manufacturers of TB drugs. During the 9-month pause, the Bank sought, first, to restore its relationship with the government by reducing the perception of pressure to borrow and supporting public health seminars and, second, to maintain focus and

raise commitment to HIV/AIDS by jointly producing with a Russian scientist a model of the economic impact of HIV and by planning a high-level meeting on vaccines that took place just after approval of the project by the Bank. In addition, the Bank worked with the government to keep the project out of the media, as well as to take an approach to TB that acknowledged and built on Russia's own efforts and institutions.

The TB and HIV/AIDS Control Project was finally negotiated in December 2002, approved by the Board of Directors of the Bank in April 2003, and became effective in December 2003. The objectives of the HIV/AIDS component of this assistance were to help the government to: (i) improve its national strategy, policies, and protocols on HIV and STI; (ii) promote public education on HIV and STI; (iii) improve surveillance, monitoring, and evaluation; (iv) strengthen laboratories and blood safety; (v) prevent mother-to-child transmission; and (vi) engage in targeted prevention programs for HIV and STI in both the civilian and prison population.

Development Effectiveness of the Bank's Assistance

In terms of development effectiveness, the Bank's HIV/AIDS assistance to Russia has been relevant to the epidemiological situation, Russia's institutions, and the Bank's country and health strategies, although a better understanding of the borrower at the outset through institutional analysis would have improved the relevance of the early dialogue on project development. In addition, the Bank avoided the tendency to try to do too many things in the TB and HIV/AIDS Control Project and focused on those areas that would avert the maximum number of HIV cases if the project were implemented effectively. The Bank might have acted on HIV somewhat earlier, but to its credit, it did act as it became clear that Russia faced a rapidly growing epidemic.

The Bank's assistance tried to influence the Russian HIV/AIDS program in ways that would make it more effective, more efficient, and more in line with emerging global experience. Its policy dialogue, analytic work, and project preparation activities were most effective in three areas: (a) improving the efficiency and technical quality of the response; (b) working with government to create a vehicle—the project— for systematic expansion of coverage of interventions nationally; and (c) raising high-level government commitment to address HIV/AIDS.

Impact of the Bank's HIV/AIDS Assistance

The timeline of events related to HIV/AIDS in Russia reveals some temporal linkages between World Bank activities and government actions. Correlation, however, does not prove causation, and therefore due caution must be exercised in drawing conclusions about the Bank's role. The evaluation team finds that the Bank has had an impact on the Russian government commitment to fighting HIV/AIDS along three critical dimensions:

- The quality and quantity of information government officials possess
- The capacity and will of some constituencies to act on this information
- The way of thinking about HIV/AIDS.

In the absence of World Bank engagement on HIV/AIDS, the government's approach would have been less targeted to the main drivers of the epidemic and less in tune with international best practice in key areas. It would also have paid less attention to capacity building, to laboratory strengthening, and to making the blood supply safe. In addition, the government would not be planning to take its HIV/AIDS efforts to scale in a timely way. Rather, many such efforts would remain small, local, and not in step with the imperative to move ahead forcefully against the epidemic. The World Bank has served as a facilitator to coordinate better and more expansive activities that were already taking place, and to catalyze thinking in new directions that bring the government program closer to international standards of prevention and treatment.

Lessons Learned

This case study highlights a number of lessons for the Bank.

- It underscores the importance of understanding the country context and embedding project development carefully in that context.
- It demonstrates how to build government commitment through reducing the pressure to borrow and engaging clients through highly relevant joint analytic work and selected high-level contacts with Bank policy makers.
- The approved project illustrates the important leverage of a small operation in large countries in potentially improving the effectiveness, efficiency, and coverage of the response.
- The Bank's involvement on HIV/AIDS in Russia highlights the value of policy and project dialogue, analytical work, and technical assistance to help build country capacity for addressing key health issues in more effective and efficient ways.
- Finally, there were important lessons for the Bank concerning the need to match the skills of task managers with the variety of demands placed on staff in that position. The placement of senior staff in Moscow, in conjunction with the very able non-specialist already working on health there, might have reduced problems in the relationship and speeded project development. The placement of senior technical staff in Moscow during project implementation could also be very helpful.
- The AIDS epidemic is a long-run problem in Russia; effectively helping the government to address this issue will require flexibility by the Bank and a long time horizon.

OED used a self-administered questionnaire to collect basic data on the preparation and implementation of all 24 country-level African MAP projects approved by December 31, 2003, from task team leaders (TTLs). The survey was sent to those who were TTLs at preparation as well as to the current TTL. A total of 32 TTLs completed questionnaires for the 24 countries, as in several cases the current TTL was the same as the TTL at preparation and in others the same TTL was or had been responsible for more than one country. The questionnaires were distributed in early June 2004. The response rate was 100 percent, although in some instances the TTLs missed or did not answer a question, so the sample size is not uniformly 24. Table H.1 lists the MAP I and II countries covered by the survey.

Table H.1: Country Coverage of the TTL Self-Administered Questionnaires

MAP I (n = 12)	MAP II (n = 12)
Benin	Burundi
Burkina Faso	Cape Verde
Cameroon	Guinea
Central African Republic[a]	Malawi
Eritrea	Mauritania
Ethiopia	Mozambique
Gambia	Niger
Ghana	Rwanda
Kenya	Senegal
Madagascar	Sierra Leone
Nigeria	Tanzania
Uganda	Zambia

a. At the time the questionnaire was distributed, the CAR was in non-accrual status and the project's effectiveness had been delayed. The responses on design relate to pre-effectiveness activities, some of which occurred after approval, using funds from other sources.

TTL Background

The technical background of MAP TTLs involved in project preparation has remained fairly consistent: about a quarter of projects had TTLs who are medical doctors and half (which may include the M.D.s) have TTLs with some public health training (see table H.2). However, during implementation only 38 percent of the projects had TTLs with a public health background.

The same pattern is evident with sector affiliation: about 71 percent of projects had TTLs for preparation who were mapped to Health, Nutrition, and Population (HNP), compared to a smaller share (58 percent) among current TTLs. About one in five projects was managed in either preparation or implementation by a TTL affiliated with the Environmentally and Socially Sustainable Development (ESSD) network (including agriculture, rural development, and operations). Overall, 42 percent of MAP projects under implementation have TTLs from a sector other than HNP.

TTLs who prepared MAP I projects had about 9 years of HIV/AIDS experience and in MAP II about 8 years.[1] At the time of the interview, the preparation TTLs for one of the MAP I and four of the MAP II projects had had three years or less of HIV/AIDS experience. Among the preparation TTLs, 54 percent had managed another free-standing AIDS project or one with a major HIV/AIDS component.

The current TTLs for MAP II projects have more HIV/AIDS experience (10 years) than those for MAP I projects (6 years). However, current TTLs of 3 MAP I and 4 MAP II projects had 3 years or less of HIV/AIDS experience. For only a third of MAP I projects did the current TTL have experience managing another HIV/AIDS project, compared with TTLs for about half of the MAP II projects.

On average, TTLs for both MAP I and II projects had a decade or more of Bank experience.

The Bank's AIDS Portfolio in African Countries with MAP Projects

Lending

According to the TTLs, among these 24 countries with multisectoral HIV/AIDS projects, 83 percent also had at least one project in a sector other than health (such as education, transport, or social protection) with an HIV/AIDS component (table H.3). The share of countries with HIV/AIDS components in other sectors has increased between MAP I and II (from 75 percent to 92 percent), as has the mean number of components (from 1.7 to 2.4).

Policy Dialogue

Policy dialogue occurred almost universally in both MAP I and II projects both during preparation and since approval (table H.4).

However, there were some notable differences between MAP I and II countries and between preparation and implementation in terms of the content of policy dialogue (table H.5).

- Overwhelming attention was given to institutional development, including the multisectoral response and role of the Ministry of Health (MOH), during preparation (83 percent of projects). This continued at a lower level during implementation (43 percent—but particularly in MAP I projects, 50 percent).
- There was extraordinarily little attention to: (a)

Table H.2: TTL Characteristics

	Preparation			Implementation		
	MAP I (n = 12)	MAP II (n = 12)	MAP I & II (n = 24)	MAP I (n = 12)	MAP II (1) (n = 12)	MAP I & II (n = 24)
Training: Percentage of projects with TTLs who studied…[a]						
Medicine	25	25	25	25	33	29
Public health	58	50	54	33	42	38
Demography	17	8	13	17	17	17
Economics	17	25	21	42	25	33
Sector mapping: Percentage of projects with TTLs mapped to…[b]						
HNP	75	67	71	58	58	58
Education		8	4		8	4
Social Protection				17	17	13
ESSD	25	17	21	25	17	21
Infrastructure		8	4		9	4
Previous experience, in number of years: mean [range]						
HIV/AIDS	9.3 [3,18]	7.9 [2,20]	8.6	6.3 [1,18]	10.1 [2,20]	8.2
Bank	11.8 [6,27]	15.9 [7,28]	13.9	10.3 [5,16]	15.4 [4,29]	12.8
Management of other HIV/AIDS projects (percent)	58	50	54	33	50	42

Source: Self-administered questionnaire.

Note: Unit of observation is the *project* (not the individual); some individuals are mapped to more than one project.

a. Other fields of study: nutrition, development studies, urban planning, public policy, sociology, business and law, international relations.

b. HNP (Health, Nutrition & Population), ESSD (Environmentally and Socially Sustainable Development).

strategic discussions (only 17 percent of projects) or (b) technical issues (13 percent prevention, 17 percent treatment) during preparation.

- The most common issue for policy dialogue during implementation was antiretroviral therapy—policy, technical, and implementation issues (56 percent of projects)—among both MAP I and II projects.
- Policy dialogue on technical issues surrounding prevention was very low, both during project preparation and implementation—only one in four countries. And during implementation, prevention discussions were much lower in MAP II (9 percent, where ARV treatment was allowed) compared with MAP I (42 percent, where ARV could only be funded retroactively).

Thus, institutional issues dominated the policy dialogue during project preparation; during implementation, the dialogue on institutions continued, but technical discussion of antiretroviral therapy dominated in both MAP I and II projects. Very little policy dialogue was conducted on strategy or on technical aspects of prevention.

Analytic Work

The share of projects for which analytic work was conducted before project approval more than doubled between MAPs I and II, from 17 percent to 42 percent (table H.6). The MAP I countries do not catch up after effectiveness, with a relatively low percentage conducting analytic work.

The main topics for analytic work were:

- Analyses of the HIV/AIDS situation, policy responses, risk behavior (4 countries)
- Analysis of the orphan situation (3 countries)
- Macro- and microeconomic impact of AIDS (2 countries)

Table H.3: AIDS Components in Projects in Other Sectors

	MAP I (n = 12)	MAP II (n = 12)	MAP I & II (n = 24)
Percent of countries with at least one project in another sector w/an AIDS component	75	92	83
Percent w/an HIV/AIDS component in an education project	58	66	66
Percent w/an HIV/AIDS component in a transport project	50	50	50
Percent w/an HIV/AIDS component or activities in a CDD or social fund or social action project	0	50	42
Mean [min,max;total] projects with AIDS components per country	1.7	2.4	1.8
	[0,4;20]	[0,5;26]	[0,5;46]

Source: Self-administered questionnaire.

Note: This table includes 5 projects in MAP I countries and 6 in MAP II countries that were reported to have AIDS components by the TTL but for which there is no mention of AIDS in the project appraisal document. If these are excluded, then 79 percent of all MAP countries had at least one non-health sector project with an AIDS component, and the mean number is 1.3, 1.9, and 1.6 for MAP I, MAP II, and both, respectively. Other sectors with AIDS components included: urban development (3); emergency demobilization or rehabilitation (2); agriculture (2); rural infrastructure (1).

Table H.4: Percent of Projects in Which Policy Dialogue on HIV/AIDS Was Conducted with Client Government

	MAP I (n = 12)	MAP II (n = 12)	MAP I & II (n = 24)
During preparation	92	92	92
Since approval	83	91[a]	87[a]

Source: Self-administered questionnaire.

a. Excludes Sierra Leone.

Table H.5: Trends in Policy Dialogue During Preparation and Implementation (percent of projects)

Stage of project cycle	N	Advocacy/ political commitment	Strategies	Institutional development[b]	Monitoring and evaluation	Donor interaction/ coordination	Prevention	Treatment
Preparation								
MAP I Total	12	25	17	75	0	17	8	8
MAP II Total	12	0	17	92	0	17	17	25
Both - Total	24	13	17	83	0	17	13	17
Implementation								
MAP I Total	12	0	17	50	17	0	42	58
MAP II Total	11[a]	0	9	17	9	17	9	55
Both - Total	23[a]	0	13	43	13	9	26	56

Source: Self-administered questionnaire.

a. Excludes Sierra Leone.

b. Institutional development includes multisectoral AIDS body, institutional framework and linkages, the health sector role in the multisectoral response, civil society role and mobilization, fiduciary issues, the local response, and monitoring and evaluation.

- Analysis of ARV supply and/or modeling (2 countries)
- Public expenditure analyses of HIV/AIDS programs and of ARV drugs (2 countries)
- Mapping of high-transmission areas (1 country)
- Study of migrants (1 country)
- Child needs assessment toolkit (1 country).

Project Preparation

The share of projects that have benefited from institutional analyses and NGO capacity assessments has increased over time; the share that conducted needs assessments has declined (table H.7).[2] In any event, analyses of these sorts are only being undertaken systematically for two-thirds to three-quarters of all projects.

About 80 percent of TTLs for both MAP I and II countries reported that the time allowed for preparation (which was, on average, 7.8 months for MAP I and 16.6 months for MAP II[3]) was sufficient to ensure national ownership of the project. However, substantially fewer MAP I TTLs at preparation reported that there was adequate time (58 percent) or Bank budget (67 percent) to ensure a quality project design. These figures on adequacy of preparation time and funds have risen to three-quarters in MAP II projects, but still, one in four TTLs of a MAP II project reported that preparation resources were inadequate.

Implementation

Overall, three-quarters of the projects' TTLs reported that the Bank budget funds provided for supervision were adequate to ensure some minimum level of implementation quality (table H.9). The adequacy is much lower for MAP II

Table H.6: Percent of Projects in Which Analytic Work Was Conducted

	MAP I (n = 12)	MAP II (n = 12)	MAP I & II (n = 24)
Prior to approval	17	42	29
Since approval	25	17	21

Source: Self-administered questionnaire.

Note: Excluded from "analytic work" are baseline surveys (which are surveys, not analysis, and measured elsewhere in the SAQ); needs, beneficiary, institutional, and NGO capacity assessments (measured elsewhere in the SAQ); and preparation of the national AIDS strategies.

Table H.7: Percent of Projects in Which Preparatory Assessments Were Conducted

	MAP I (n = 12)	MAP II (n = 12)	MAP I & II (n = 24)
Institutional analysis	67	92	79
Stakeholder analysis	75	75	75
NGO capacity assessment	58	75	67
Needs assessment	92	67	79

Source: Self-administered questionnaire.

countries (only 58 percent) than for MAP I countries (92 percent).

One aspect of the MAP template that was intended to expedite project implementation where there was limited government capacity was a provision for contracting out key management functions—financial management, procurement, NGO management, and monitoring and evaluation (M&E). The current TTLs for the 24 MAP projects were asked the extent to which these functions had in fact been contracted to others—completely, partially, or not at all.

TTLs reported that roughly half of the projects did not contract financial management or procurement and about 70 percent did not con-

tract out NGO management or M&E (table H.10). MAP II projects were more likely to at least partially contract out financial management, procurement, and M&E, compared with MAP I projects. However, over both MAPs the share that completely contracted out ranged from 4 to 29 percent. None of the projects contracted out all four tasks, while seven did not contract out any of them.

Among the projects that had completely or partially contracted out these tasks, 86 to 92 percent of TTLs reported that the arrangement had accelerated implementation of the project.

The most common reason for not contracting out financial management, procurement, and

Table H.8: Percent of Projects in Which Resources Were Adequate to Achieve Aims

	MAP I (n = 12)	MAP II (n = 12)	MAP I & II (n = 24)
Sufficient preparation time for national ownership of project	83	82 [a]	83
Sufficient preparation time for quality project design	58	75	67
Sufficient Bank budget funds for preparation adequate to ensure quality project design	67	75[a]	71

Source: Self-administered questionnaire.

a. Excludes Mauritania.

Table H.9: Percent of Projects with Bank Budget Funds Adequate for Supervision

	MAP I (n = 12)	MAP II (n = 12)	MAP I & II (n = 24)
Sufficient Bank budget funds for supervision to ensure minimum quality	92	58	75

Source: Self-administered questionnaire, as reported by current TTLs.

NGO/civil society management, cited by half or more of TTLs, was that adequate capacity existed to do this in government, including existing mechanisms (table H.11). In contrast, the most frequently cited reason for not contracting out M&E functions was the reluctance of the government (38 percent), including cases in which the government wanted to build its own capacity, and the absence of a suitable contractor (25 percent).

Interventions Supported by the MAP

The African MAP projects are supporting a large number of public sector activities and interventions, according to TTLs from 18 of the 24 projects under study (see figure H.1).[4] Among these activities, likely a subset of all of the activities supported in multiple sectors, are many that are public goods, prevention interventions targeting the general public or those most likely to spread HIV, care and treatment, and support to mitigate the impact of HIV/AIDS.

- The interventions most likely to be supported are **information and preventive interventions for the general public**, such as STD treatment, prevention of mother-to-child trans-

Table H.10: Extent to Which MAP Projects Contracted Out Key Management Functions (percent)

Function		Complete	Partial	Not at all
Financial management	MAP I	17	33	50
	MAP II	42	17	42
	Both	29	25	46
Procurement	MAP I	0	25	75
	MAP II	33	33	33
	Both	17	29	54
NGO management	MAP I	25	0	75
	MAP II	8	25	67
	Both	17	13	71
Monitoring and evaluation	MAP I	8	17	75
	MAP II	0	42	58
	Both	4	29	67

Source: Self-administered questionnaire, as reported by current TTLs.

Note: Sample size is MAP I (12), MAP II (12), Both (24).

Table H.11: Reasons for Not Contracting Out Key Management Functions (percent)

Management function	Adequate capacity/ existing mechanisms	No suitable contractor	Government reluctant	Other arrangements have been made	Don't know or no answer
Financial management (n = 11)	64	0	18	9	9
Procurement (n = 13)	54	8	8	15	15
NGOs (n = 17)	53	6	24	12	6
M&E (n = 16)	19	25	38	13	6

Source: Self-administered questionnaire.

mission (MTCT), condoms (including through social marketing), and voluntary counseling and testing (VCT), all supported by more than 80 percent of projects.

- Financing **of public goods**, such as blood safety, HIV surveillance, universal precautions for health workers, and behavioral surveillance, is somewhat less common. Only a third of projects supported operational research.
- Financing of several types of **care and treatment interventions** was equally as high as financing for public goods. This included treatment of TB and other opportunistic infections (OI), palliative care, and antiretroviral treatment. However, only half of the projects supported home-based care (HBC) for AIDS patients and only about a third supported prophylaxis for TB and other opportunistic infections among HIV-positive people.

- Roughly three-quarters of the projects financed public sector support programs to **mitigate the impact of AIDS** among people with HIV/AIDS (PLWHA) and orphans.
- **Preventive interventions targeted** to high-risk groups (HRG)—those most likely to contract HIV and spread it to others, such as sex workers, transport workers, the military, and police, are, as a group, the least likely to be supported and were covered by roughly half to two-thirds of the projects.

There were important differences in terms of some of the types of activities supported by MAP I and MAP II projects (figure H.2). MAP I countries were about twice as likely as MAP II to support public sector operational research, targeted prevention to high-risk groups, and mitigation of the impact of AIDS to PLWHA. MAP II countries were sub-

Figure H.1: Public Sector Activities and Interventions Supported by African MAP Projects

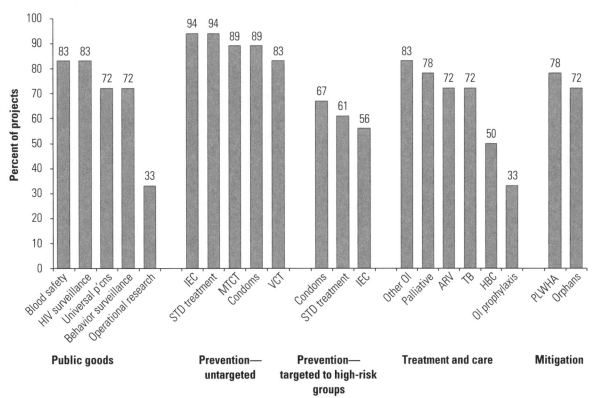

Source: Current TTLs, 18 African MAP projects.

Note: Excludes CAR, Ghana, Kenya, Malawi, Mauritania, and Senegal.

stantially more likely to finance treatment of TB and other opportunistic infections and slightly more likely to finance public antiretroviral treatment. However, they were less likely to finance palliative care and home-based care for AIDS patients.

Multisectoral Approach

TTLs reported a very large number of ministries or sectors involved in the national multisectoral response supported by the MAPs—an average of 16 ministries in each country, equally high for MAP I and II countries (table H.12). In 10 of the 24 projects, the project was supporting a response of 20 or more ministries, and in two-thirds, 10 or more ministries.

Nongovernmental Organizations and Community-Based Organizations

Overall, a mean of 143 different nongovernmental organizations (NGOs) and 921 community-based organizations (CBOs) had been financed per project through the civil society components, with substantially more of each financed to date by MAP I projects, compared with the more recently launched MAP II projects (table H.13).[5] The number of CBOs is some six times larger than the number of NGOs, on average, and ranges from none up to 6,700.

Monitoring and Evaluation

Baseline Surveys

The respondents for three-quarters of projects reported that at least one baseline survey was undertaken during preparation, either financed by the Bank or by others (table H.14).

Governments of three-quarters of MAP I countries and nearly two-thirds of MAP II countries had conducted national risk/sexual behavior surveys, even if not financed by the MAP

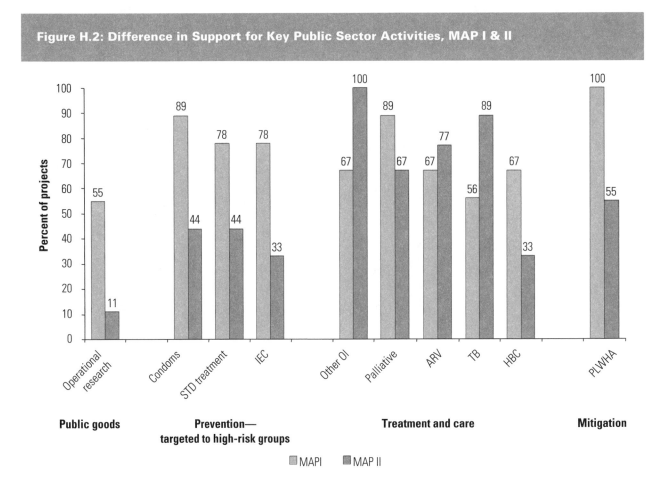

Figure H.2: Difference in Support for Key Public Sector Activities, MAP I & II

Table H.12: Ministries Officially Enlisted in MAP-Supported Multisectoral Response

	MAP I (n = 12)	MAP II (n = 12)	MAP I & II (n = 24)
Ministries officially enlisted in MAP-supported multisectoral response: mean [min,max]	17 [6,30]	16 [4,30]	16 [4,30]
Distribution of projects by number of ministries supported:			
Fewer than 10	3	5	8
10–19	4	2	6
20 or more	5	5	10

(table H.15). Since no additional information was collected, we do not know the extent to which the respondents counted Demographic and Health Surveys, as opposed to those explicitly investigating risky behavior, knowledge of transmission and prevention, and the adoption of preventive behaviors. While more MAP I countries had such a survey than not, one in four still did not. At the time of this survey, most of the MAP I projects had reached or passed the midpoint of the project.

Evaluation of Pilot Projects that Could Be Scaled Up

In both MAP I and II, in 58 percent of the countries, the preparation TTLs cited at least one pilot intervention that had been evaluated in the client country and that was suitable for replication on a larger scale (table H.16). In more than half of these cases (8/14 projects), only a single pilot project was cited. In 5 of the 14 projects, at least one of the pilot projects cited was a community-driven development (CDD) type inter-

Table H.13: The Number of NGOs and CBOs per Project Financed by the Project to Date

	MAP I		MAP II		MAP I & II	
	Mean [min,max]	n	Mean [min,max]	n^d	Mean [min,max]	n^d
Excluding double-counts [a]						
NGOs	247 [5,700]	11[b]	46 [0,120]	11	143 [0,700]	22[b]
CBOs	1674 [40,6700]	10[b,c]	157 [0,550]	11	872 [0,6700]	21[b,c]
Including double-counts						
NGOs	351 [5,1500]	12	46 [0,120]	11	212 [0,1500]	23
CBOs	1659 [40,6700]	11[c]	157 [0,550]	11	944 [0,6700]	22[c]

Source: Self-administered questionnaire.

a. In one country, the TTL could not separate the number of NGOs from CBOs, citing a combined total of 1,500. The top panel excludes this observation and in the bottom panel 1,500 is attributed to both NGOs and CBOs.

b. Excludes Kenya.

c. Excludes Nigeria.

d. Excludes Mauritania.

Table H.14: Percent of Countries in Which Baseline Surveys Were Conducted During Preparation or Implementation

Baseline surveys	During preparation			During implementation		
	MAP I (n = 12)	MAP II (n = 12)	MAP I & II (n = 24)	MAP I (n = 12)	MAP II (n = 12)	MAP I & II (n = 24)
Any baseline	75	75	75			
→ financed by others	33	67	50			
→ financed by project/Bank	42	33	38	75	50	63

Table H.15: Percent of Governments that Had Conducted National Risk/Sexual Behavior Surveys

	MAP I (n = 12)	MAP II (n = 12)	MAP I & II (n = 24)
National risk/sexual behavioral survey (even if not financed by MAP)	75	67	71

Source: Self-administered questionnaire.

vention that did not necessarily deal specifically with HIV/AIDS.[6] There were, in fact, very few interventions that had been previously evaluated in these countries—in 42 percent of the projects, none, and in the other 58 percent, only 1 to 3 each. OED was not able to establish the quality of the evaluation of the interventions that were cited.

Monitoring

The monitoring indicators in the Project Appraisal Documents (PADs) for 42 percent of all MAP projects had been revised; this was more likely to have happened in the MAP I countries (half of projects) than in MAP II (a third of projects). The mid-term review (MTR) is a major opportunity to do this, though none of the MAP II countries had reached the MTR as of the date of the survey.

Given the way that HIV spreads from people with the highest-risk behavior (who are often the first to be infected) to their sexual partners and children, many national AIDS programs seek to change the behavior and the infection rates among "high-risk groups" (HRG), defined in the questionnaire as "the populations most likely to spread HIV." Examples include sex workers, transport workers, the military, po-

lice, prisoners, miners, and so on. Prevention and lower infection rates among these groups are not only indicative of the success of project activities aimed at them, but are likely to have a larger impact on slowing infection in the lower-risk population.

According to current TTLs, about 58 percent of governments are collecting HIV prevalence data and 75 percent are collecting behavior information on at least one high-risk group (table H.17). The group most likely to be monitored in both cases is sex workers, followed by the military and transport workers. The share of countries monitoring at least one HRG and the number of groups being monitored was slightly higher in MAP II countries, which showed a greater diversity in the types of groups monitored as well. Nevertheless, 10 countries were not monitoring HIV and 6 were not monitoring behavior in any high-risk group.

Donor Coordination

The MAP I projects differ significantly from MAP II projects in the extent to which the Bank was the major HIV/AIDS donor at the time of preparation. According to TTLs, in three-quarters of the MAP I countries the Bank was the major donor for HIV/AIDS, compared with only 17 percent of

Table H.16: Evaluations of Potentially Replicable Pilot Projects in Client Country

	MAP I (n = 12)	MAP II (n = 12)	MAP I & II (n = 24)
At the time of project preparation	58	58	58
Since project approval, have any pilot projects been formally evaluated, even if not by project?	25	8	17

Table H.17: Percent of Governments (Irrespective of Whether Financed by MAP) Monitoring HIV and Behavior among High-Risk Groups and Mean [min, max] Number of High-Risk Groups Monitored

	HIV			Behavior		
	MAP I (n = 12)	MAP II (n = 12)	MAP I & II (n = 24)	MAP I (n = 12)	MAP II (n = 12)	MAP I & II (n = 24)
At least one high-risk group	58	58	58	83	67	75
Sex workers	58	58	58	83	67	75
Military	25	33	29	25	42	33
Transport workers	17	33	25	42	25	33
Fishermen	0	17	8	0	17	8
Police	0	17	8	0	17	8
Prisoners	8	0	4	0	8	4
Miners	0	17	8	8	17	13
STI patients	8	0	4	0	0	0
TB patients	0	8	4	0	0	0
Factory workers	0	0	0	8	0	4
Displaced persons (number)	0	0	0	0	8	4
Mean [min,max]	1.2	1.7	1.4	1.7	1.8	1.8
Number of high-risk groups	[0,3]	[0,4]	[0,4]	[0,4]	[0,4]	[0,4]

the MAP II countries, where the Bank was most likely a relatively minor donor (table H.18a). Many of the African countries that had had previous AIDS projects or components were in the MAP I group: Kenya and Uganda (with former STI projects and Uganda with the PAPSCA); Burkina Faso (with an AIDS and population control project); and Benin, Cameroon, Eritrea, Ethiopia, Gambia, Madagascar, and Nigeria (with AIDS components of health projects).

In contrast, none of the MAP II countries previously had Bank-sponsored free-standing AIDS projects and only a few had AIDS components of health projects (Niger, Tanzania, Zambia). This meant that the Bank was really starting from a much lower level of dialogue on AIDS in the MAP II countries.

Over time, other donors appear to have stepped up assistance to the MAP I countries where the Bank previously dominated, while in the MAP II countries the Bank stepped up its presence relative to other donors. As a result, at the time of the survey, the TTLs reported that the Bank was the major donor on HIV/AIDS in half of the countries of both MAP I and II, and in most of the rest it was one of several major donors (table H.18b).

With respect to coordination with other donors, during preparation the reported extent was very high in half of the countries and only moderate in a third for MAP I, but by MAP II, the level of coordination at preparation was reported as either high or very high in all countries. This may also reflect the fact that the Bank was coming from a less dominant position in terms of HIV/AIDS assistance in the MAP II countries. In terms of coordination during implementation, TTLs reported on average slightly less coordination with other donors in MAP I than in MAP II. Nevertheless, the TTLs reported for two-thirds of MAP I and three-quarters of MAP

II countries that the level of coordination was high or very high. OED did not interview representatives of other donors in these countries to assess their views on collaboration.

In terms of the change in engagement of other partners over time, the most notable change is the entrance of the Global Fund, which was not named as a donor during preparation of any of the 24 projects, but was reported to be present in two-thirds of the countries at the time of the survey in mid-2004 (table H.19).

Table H.18a: Relative Importance of the Bank as AIDS Donor and Extent of its Consultation with Other Donors at the Time of *Project Preparation*

	MAP I (n = 12)	MAP II (n = 12)	MAP I & II[a] (n = 24)
Percentage of client countries in which the Bank was…			
…the major donor	75	17	48
…one of several major donors	8	25	17
…a relatively minor donor	8	42	22
…not financing HIV/AIDS activities	8	8	9
…one of several minor donors	0	8	4
Percentage of projects in which consultation was…			
…very high	50	58	54
…high	17	42	29
…moderate	33	0	17

Table H.18b: Relative Importance of the Bank as AIDS Donor and Extent of its Coordination with Other Donors During *Implementation*

	MAP I (n = 12)	MAP II (n = 12)	MAP I & II[a] (n = 24)
Percentage of client countries in which the Bank is currently…			
…the major donor	50	50	50
…one of several major donors	42	50	46
…a relatively minor donor	8	0	4
Percentage of projects in which coordination has been…			
…very high	33	50	42
…high	33	25	29
…moderate	25	25	25
…low	8	0	4

Source: Self-administered questionnaire.

Table H.19: Number of Client Countries in Which Other AIDS Donors Were Involved at Time of Project Preparation and Currently

	Involved at preparation			Currently involved		
	MAP I (n = 12)	MAP II (n = 12)	MAP I & II (n = 24)	MAP I (n = 12)	MAP II[a] (n = 12)	MAP I & II (n = 24)
African Development Bank				1		1
Belgium				1		1
Canada	2		2			
Denmark	1		1	1		1
EU	1	1	2	2	1	3
France	4	4	8	4		4
Germany	3		3	2	1	3
Global Fund				7	9	16
Ireland				1		1
Italy				1		1
Netherlands	2		2	2		2
Norway	0	1	1			
U.K.	4	1	5	3	1	4
U.N. agencies	7	6	13	5	2	7
U.S.	7	8	15	7	5	12

a. Excludes Sierra Leone.

Overview of the Methodology and Sample

Over the period June 1–August 12, 2004, the current task team leaders (TTLs) of 19 ongoing African MAP projects—11 MAP I projects and 8 MAP II projects—were interviewed in an open-ended question format. The objective of the survey was to obtain their opinions on some of the main substantive issue of the OED AIDS evaluation, in light of performance to date, and additional insights on the design and future of the MAP as an instrument. This information builds on the results of the self-administered questionnaires reported in Annex H.

The 19 projects and 18 TTLs[1] in this survey included all current TTLs of MAP I projects (as of the time of the interview), with the exception of Ethiopia, which was not covered because OED had conducted a case study in that country. It included all 8 MAP II projects that had been effective for at least a year, as of mid-August 2004.[2] The countries are listed below. In only four cases (Benin, CAR, Cape Verde, Kenya) was the current

MAP I (11 countries, 10 respondents)	MAP II (8 countries, 8 respondents)
Benin	Burundi
Burkina Faso	Cape Verde
Cameroon	Guinea
CAR	Mozambique
Eritrea	Rwanda
Gambia	Senegal
Ghana	Sierra Leone
Kenya	Zambia
Madagascar	
Nigeria	
Uganda	

TTL the same as the TTL at the time of project approval, and the CAR project was still not effective as of the end of fiscal year 2004 because the country was in non-accrual status.

Design Issues

What were the main constraints to a more effective national response before the MAP?

Among the 16 countries that responded (9 in MAP I and 7 in MAP II), the most frequently cited constraint was **weak capacity in the Ministry of Health (MOH)**, including a weak or understaffed health system (9 countries, or half), followed by a **lack of political commitment**/denial/stigma in 6 countries (table I.1). TTLs for 6 countries cited lack of activities in other sectors or multisectoral institutions. Surprisingly, the TTLs for only four countries (one-quarter) cited **lack of financing** as a constraint; in one country the TTL mentioned that financing was not a constraint, and in one country that the ample financing of HIV/AIDS by many donors was stretching administrative capacity to the breaking point.

Among the nine MAP I countries, the most frequently cited constraint was lack of political commitment/denial/stigma, while for MAP II countries, the majority cited weak MOH capacity as the major constraint. The fact that finance was not mentioned as the major constraint more frequently does not imply that there was sufficient finance to launch a program, but rather that there were other constraints that were more binding.

Are there any specific design features that set this MAP project apart from the MAP template?

The most common special design feature reported by TTLs was the special component—for targeted interventions (Burkina Faso), other com-

Table I.1: Main Constraints to HIV/AIDS at Project Preparation

Constraint	Percentage of countries (n = 16)	MAP I (# countries)	MAP II (# countries)
Weak MOH capacity, including weak health system, limited manpower	56	3	6
Lack of political commitment/denial/stigma	38	4	2
Lack of financing	25	2	2
Lack of multisectoral coordination/weak MS institution (like CNLS)	19	1	2
Lack of activities or coordination outside MOH, in other ministries	19	2	1
Lack of coverage of HRG, need to expand pilot programs more widely	13	2	0
Political unrest/conflict	13	1	1
Lack of strategic framework for donor coordination	6	1	0
No operational mechanism for funding non-public sector entities	6	1	0
Don't know	13	2	1

municable diseases (Eritrea), orphans (Burundi), the private sector (Guinea), and treatment (Rwanda) (table I.2). While all MAP II countries were eligible for financing of antiretroviral treatment, two MAP I countries also offered it : Benin for preventing mother-to-child transmission (MTCT) and Cameroon for treatment, with an amendment of the credit agreement.

Did the project design reflect any important country-specific design factors or lessons from previous health/AIDS experience in this country?

In 7 of the 19 projects (37 percent), the TTLs noted no design features that reflected lessons from previous experience in the country (table I.3a).

The TTLs for 12 countries (7 MAP I, 5 MAP II) identified lessons from previous projects that were

Table I.2: Specific Design Features

Design feature	Percentage of countries (n = 19)	MAP I (# countries)	MAP II (# countries)
Special components	26	2	3
• Targeted interventions			
• TB and malaria			
• Orphans			
• Private sector			
• Treatment			
ARVs in MAP I	11	2	0
Community components using existing CDD or SF mechanisms	11	1	1
Windows or components for different levels of public sector	11	1	1
MAP doesn't fund MOH	5	1	0
MAP funds only MOH	5	1	0
No contracting out	5	0	1
Separate window for CBOs, emphasis on decentralization	5	1	0
More preparation and analytic work than template	5	0	1
None	37	5	2

taken into account in the project design, the foremost, cited for 7 countries (37 percent), were lessons related to ***poor implementation capacity or ability to coordinate*** in the public sector more generally or in the MOH. In two countries, this resulted in prioritization of sectors within the multisectoral response, in two others to greater reliance on the private sector. In one case, the project administrative unit was put in the Ministry of Finance and, in another, a more gradual implementation strategy was pursued, to avoid exceeding limited capacity. In one additional case, the project design was reported to have taken into account the limited capacity, but to date none of these mechanisms was deemed successful. In contrast, in one country the ***relatively good performance of the MOH and local governments*** was cited as having contributed to project design.

In four countries (21 percent), the projects were able to use mechanisms or ***institutions*** developed through previous community-driven development, though in one case this was not working well for political reasons. Also, in one of these countries, the project was able to use a drug procurement agency that was set up by previous projects.

In addition to these lessons, TTLs from five countries noted ***country-specific considerations*** that did not arise from past projects but that affected project design, including: the early stage of the epidemic; complementarity of activities with an ongoing health project;[3] components that were tailored to decentralized government; large refugee and orphan populations; a strong NGO sector; and an ongoing antiretroviral treatment program.

Table I.3a: Lessons from Previous Projects

Lesson from previous project	Percentage of countries (n = 19)	MAP I (# countries)	MAP II (# countries)
Low capacity of MOH, public sector (n = 7)	37		
Stretched too thin to supervise all sectors/ministries; prioritized ministries w/previous WB experience		1	1
Weakness of MOH, bad performance w/previous project led to more private sector role		1	1
Project admin unit in MOF due to past poor experience w/MOH in previous health project		0	1
Gave project time to mature, didn't push beyond capacity		0	1
Lack of capacity to plan and implement; proposed solutions have been ineffective		1	0
Institutions (n = 4)	21		
Previous success w/CDD mechanisms		2	2
Used national drug procurement agency from previous project		0	1
Substantive issues (n = 2)	11		
Lessons from previous STI project, especially regarding government commitment		1	0
Lesson from previous health project on lessons for young people		0	1
Good implementation capacity (n = 1)	5		
Good implementation capacity in MOH and local governments		1	0
None/not answered (n = 7)	37		
None		1	3
Not answered		3	0

Note: Total is more than 19 because some countries gave multiple answers.

Table I.3b: Country Characteristics and Project Design

Country characteristic	MAP I (# countries)	MAP II (# countries)
Complementarity with ongoing health project	1	0
Low prevalence country led to emphasis on prevention, IEC	1	0
Decentralized components	1	0
Large refugee and orphan populations	0	1
Strong NGO sector	0	1
Ongoing ARV treatment program	0	1

Themes of the OED Evaluation

Strategic Approach

The MAP template funds virtually any activity in the national strategy and the latter tend to be exhaustive menus of all that can be done. How is it being decided in [country] which activities will be funded first? What's the prioritization process?

The TTLs for nine countries (47 percent) reported no real prioritization process by government: whatever conforms to the broad national strategy and/or is on the list of allowable activities (or not on the list of what can't be funded) is funded (table I.4).[4] In four countries (22 percent), some prioritization is enforced by project components on, for example, targeted interventions, orphans, treatment, or workplace interventions. In two countries, plus the public sector of a third, the projects set priorities as a function of what other donors are doing and according to various indicators. In four countries, the TTL reported exerting pressure for specific priorities (behavior change, IEC for high-risk groups, MOH activities) or to be selective.

The TTLs sometimes cited what the revealed priority of governments was (regardless of the process—targeted interventions, prevention, awareness raising) or noted that different levels of government set priorities independently (3 countries).

What, if any, interventions are being financed to ensure that transmission is being reduced among those with high-risk behavior? Is there any aspect of the proj-

ect that assures that this issue will be addressed?

In only four countries (22 percent) —all of them in MAP I—is the highest-risk behavior being systematically addressed by the public sector (table I.5); in nine countries (50 percent) it is only being addressed to the extent that NGOs undertake these activities; in five countries (28 percent) no part of the project ensures that high-risk behavior is systematically addressed (and four of the five are MAP II countries). Thus, to the extent that this is taking place, it is more organized in MAP I countries. It has largely been relegated to NGOs, and the countries in MAP II are less likely to have addressed this at all.

Government Commitment

Respondents were asked to characterize the level of commitment to addressing HIV/AIDS prior to the launch of the project, then—for projects that have been effective for at least 12 months—they were asked whether the level of commitment had risen, fallen, or stayed the same and, if it had changed, the current level. The questions asked about five levels of government: the highest levels; ministry of health; other sectors; parliament/ legislature; and local/regional offices. The responses were on a 6-point scale: very high, high, moderate, low, nonexistent, or hostile. Note that in most cases the respondents were not present during project preparation.

Was there an explicit strategy in the project to raise government commitment? If so, what was it?

The TTLs for only a third of the countries (6) re-

Table I.4: Prioritization Process

Process	Percentage of countries (n = 19)	MAP I (# countries)	MAP II (# countries)
No prioritization process (n = 9)	47		
There's a list of things that can't be funded or that can be funded, otherwise no prioritization. Whatever is demanded.		3	1
There's no real prioritization process by government; whatever conforms to the broad national strategy is funded.		1	4
Priority enforced by components/project design (n = 4)	21		
Priority to targeted interventions		1	0
Priority to workplace interventions		1	0
Priority to orphans		0	1
Priority on treatment		0	1
Revealed priorities by government decisions (n = 4)	21		
Priority to targeted interventions		1	0
Priority to prevention		2	0
Priority to awareness creation/IEC		0	2
Other prioritization principles (n = 9)	47		
Try to balance prevention and treatment		0	1
Consideration of what other donors are financing		0	2
Provincial/geographic coverage		2	0
All groups are required to set priorities in their own action plans.		2	1
Priority activities based on indicators, in collaboration with other donors		1	0
Pressure from TTL on content (n = 4)	21	2	2
Not answered (n = 1)	5	1	0

Note: Total is more than 19 because the TTLs for some countries gave multiple answers.

ported an explicit strategy for raising government commitment, including activities such as training or study tours for leaders, or advocacy as the objective of Rapid Results Initiative (table I.6). In two of these cases, the strategies were simply development of a national strategic plan and requiring each sector to prepare its own program—pretty standard in all of the projects.

Strategies:

Training for parliament, leaders: 2

IEC, study tours for officials, parliament, religious leaders: 1

Rapid Results Initiative w/advocacy as focus: 1

Development of national strategic plan, committees, after approval: 1

Required key sectors in NAC, preparation of sector programs[5] 1

If the project has been effective for at least 12 months, to what extent has government commitment risen or fallen since the start of the project among these groups?

At the **highest levels of government**, TTLs reported that political commitment had risen in half of the countries and fallen in one since the start of the project (table I.7a). Commitment at the highest levels primarily rose in MAP I countries (7 of the 8 with an increase were MAP I); in the majority of MAP II countries (5 of 7), commitment at the highest levels was reported to be unchanged. This reflects the lower commitment at the highest level in MAP I countries before the project was launched (2/11 rated very high and 3/11 rated high), compared with MAP II countries (5/8 rated very high before the project launch).

Table I.5: Systematic Attention to High-Risk Behavior

Intervention/policy	Percentage of countries (n = 19)	MAP I (# countries)	MAP II (# countries)
Being systematically addressed by public sector (n = 4)	21		
Major emphasis on targeted interventions to HRG by government		3	0
"Hot zones" identified via mapping exercises and include HRG activities. These are the priority		1	0
Not systematically addressed by public sector (n = 9)	47		
Being addressed by NGOs, but no special emphasis		2	2
An area of special emphasis for NGOs		0	1
NGOs, some ministries, a MAP request for one group (prisons), but NAC not addressing them systematically		3	1
Not being addressed (n = 5)	26		
Project is trying to identify high-risk groups		0	1
No part of the project assures that this will be addressed		1	3
Not available (n = 1)	5	1	0

Table I.6: Strategy to Raise Political Commitment

Answer	Percentage of countries (n = 19)	MAP I (# countries)	MAP II (# countries)
Yes	32	4	2
No	58	6	5
N/A	11	1	1

For the *MOH, other ministries, and Parliament*, commitment was reported to have risen in roughly half of the countries, and not differentially between MAP I and II. The level of government with the largest number of countries reporting an increase in commitment is **local or regional government** (10 of 14 reporting), also evenly in MAP I and II.

What is the current level of government commitment?

The current level of commitment at the highest level of government (president, prime minister) and among MOH officials was reported to be high or very high by 14 of the 17 reporting TTLs (82 percent) (table I.7b). Roughly two-thirds reported local/regional government officials and Parliament/legislators to have high or very high commitment. In most countries com-

mitment varied across ministries, with some registering high and others moderate. TTLs for three countries reported that commitment at the highest level and in the MOH was moderate or low, and four that local and Regional government commitment was at these levels. In one country, the commitment of parliament/legislature was characterized as non-existent.

To what extent can these changes (or mitigation of declines) be attributed to the Bank's intervention?

Among the TTLs for the 13 countries that reported a change in commitment during the projects, seven attributed it entirely to the Bank's intervention (of which five were MAP II) and three partially (table I.8). In three cases, the TTLs claimed the changes were not due to the project, of which two were due to changes in government.

Table I.7a: Changes in Level of Political Commitment

Trend	Highest levels			MOH			Other ministries			Parliament			Local government		
	I #	II #	Both %	I #	II #	Both %	I #	II #	Both %	I #	II #	Both %	I #	II #	Both %
Rose	7	1	44	5	3	44	4	3	38	4	3	38	5	5	56
Same	2	5	38	3	3	33	3	3	33	2	4	33	2	2	22
Fell	0	1	6	0	1	6	0	0	0	0	0	0	0	0	0
DK/NA	2	1	17	3	1	22	4	2	33	5	1	33	4	1	28

Note: DK/NA - don't know/no answer.

Table I.7b: Current Level of Political Commitment

Trend	Highest levels			MOH			Other ministries			Parliament			Local government		
	I #	II #	Both %	I #	II #	Both %	I #	II #	Both %	I #	II #	Both %	I #	II #	Both %
Very high	5	5	56	6	2	44	1	1	17	1	2	17	2	4	33
High	3	1	22	2	4	33	4	2	56	5	3	44	4	2	33
Moderate	1	1	11	0	2	11	1	2	17	1	2	17	2	1	17
Low	0	1	6	1	0	6	0	0	0	0	0	0	1	0	6
Non-existent	0	0	0	0	0	0	0	0	0	0	1	6	0	0	0
Hostile	0	0	0	0	0	0	0	0	0	0	0	0	0	0	0
DK/NA	2	0	11	2	0	11	2	1	17	4	0	22	3	0	17

Table I.8: Attribution of Changes in Commitment to the Bank

Answer	Percentage of countries (n = 19)	MAP I (# countries)	MAP II (# countries)
Yes	39	2	5
Partially	17	3	0
No	17	1	2
N/A or no answer	28	4	1
Don't know	6	1	0

Multisectoral Response/Institutional Issues

What were the main government institutions involved in the national response to HIV/AIDS before the MAP project?
Eleven of the 17 countries responding (65 percent) initially had an AIDS department in the Ministry of Health, at a low level (3), mid-level (5), or high level (3) (table I.9). Two had a multisectoral National AIDS Committee (NAC) based in the MOH and three had one not linked to a ministry, under the president or prime minister. A single country had no institutional arrangement for AIDS before the project.

Has the institutional set-up changed? If so, has it been influenced by the MAP eligibility criteria? If so, in what way?

In all 13 cases where the institutional set-up changed, the TTLs attributed it to the MAP eligibility criteria and, to some extent, UNAIDS recommendations. In two countries where there was already a NAC (and thus no change), it wasn't clear to the TTLs whether the NAC had been the result of Bank activities or pressures (such as a visit from Bank President Wolfensohn) before the project (table I.10a, b).

Comments:
Friction between MOH and the NAC (3)
MOH has been given a major role in the NAC (3):
- Minister of Health is chair of NAC
- Minister of Health is the first vice president of the NAC, Minister of Social Affairs is the second VP

Table I.9: AIDS Institutions before the MAP

Institutional arrangement	Percentage of countries (n = 19)	MAP I (# countries)	MAP II (# countries)
Mid-level department in MOH (*)	26	4	1
High-level department in MOH	16	1	2
Multisectoral unit not linked to a ministry, under the president or prime minister	16	1	2
Low-level department in MOH	16	1	2
Multisectoral NAC in the MOH	11	1	1
None	5	1	0
Both a unit in MOH and multisectoral unit outside MOH	0	0	0
No answer/ NA	5	1	0
Don't know	5	1	0

* This option wasn't offered—it was a write-in, but ended up being the most common.

Table I.10a: Change in Institutions Since MAP Effectiveness

Changed?	Percentage of countries (n = 19)	MAP I (# countries)	MAP II (# countries)
Yes	68	7	6
No	16	2	1
N/A	5	1	0
No answer/don't know	11	1	1

Table I.10b: How Institutions Have Changed

How changed?	Percentage of countries (n = 13)	MAP I (# countries)	MAP II (# countries)
NAC in office of the president or prime minister	92	7	5
Created Ministry of AIDS, NAC secretariat inside AIDS ministry	8	0	1

- Minister of Health is vice-chair of NAC, Minister of AIDS is rapporteur.

Well-functioning MOH program and/or despite NAC (4):

- NAC a strong, credible institution, complementary relation w/NACP—NAC focuses on prevention and NACP on treatment
- NAC strengthened ability to coordinate donors, civil society, local government
- AIDS program in MOH still exists and is an important source for technical support, with many activities still focused on the health sector. The NAC has enabled more autonomy for other ministries and NGOs to design activities and access funding
- MOH program still exists and is implementing a significant health component.

Ineffective NAC (1):

- NAC/NAS not very effective, as doesn't meet often enough.

Other problems noted with or improvements in NAC (4):

- Need to attract better-qualified staff.
- Number of staff rose from 6 to 20 after the MAP.
- NAC has become filled with more dedicated and knowledgeable staff, is now thinking more about developing specific guidelines and implementation policies for issues such as ARV.
- In the MOH, there's a new "national coordinator" for AIDS, plus a MAP person, plus potentially a TAP person, both of whom report to the national coordinator.

NGOs, CBOs, and Civil Society Response

Prior to the project, how conducive was the environment to enlisting NGOs through the government for the fight against HIV/AIDS? Was the government already supporting NGOs? Was there already a mechanism? If not, did the project result in developing one?

In about half of the countries (10, or 55 percent), the government was already funding NGOs through the MOH and/or other sectors (table I.11). In eight (44 percent), the government wasn't funding NGOs or CBOs at all, including one case in which mechanisms existed on paper but had never been used.

In all seven cases where the government was not previously supporting NGOs and there was no mechanism, TTLs reported that the MAP resulted in creating mechanisms for supporting them. In some countries where the government was already funding NGOs to work on AIDS, the project created or strengthened mechanisms for funding CBOs and civil society.

To what extent were there capable local/indigenous NGOs with capacity to design, manage, and evaluate HIV/AIDS programs?

In 11 of the 19 countries (58 percent), the TTLs reported few or no indigenous NGOs with capacity to design, manage, and evaluate HIV/AIDS programs (table I.12).

Table I.11: The Environment for NGOs before the MAP

Answer	Percentage of countries (n = 19)	MAP I (# countries)	MAP II (# countries)
Government wasn't funding NGOs or CBOs	37	3	4
Government was already funding NGOs to work on AIDS	26	3	2
Government was already funding NGOs through the MOH	16	1	2
Government was funding NGOs in health or other sectors, but not AIDS	11	2	0
Non-functional mechanisms existed but they hadn't been used	5	1	0
Don't know	5	1	0

How is it determined what type of intervention will be financed for a given NGO or CBO? Is there any prioritization?

Of the 12 countries for which the TTL answered, in 8 there is no prioritization, with virtually any proposal that passes muster being approved, and in 2 others proposals are approved provided they are on the long list of potential activities in the Project Apprraisal Document (PAD) or not on the short list of ineligible activities. In other words, there is no prioritization in 10 of the

12 that answered (53 percent of the total). In one case, the TTL said that priorities were defined at project launch, but the TTL did not explain if these were institutionalized. The respondents for the 7 countries with no response (37 percent) generally explained in detail the approval process but did not address prioritization, or they gave additional information on logistics (table I.13).

Have the implementation/funding mechanisms foreseen by the project been suc-

Table I.12: Extent of Capable Local NGOs

Answer	Percentage of countries (n = 19)	MAP I (# countries)	MAP II (# countries)
Many/some	42	4	4
Few/limited indigenous capacity	42	6	2
No local NGOs for AIDS	16	1	2

Table I.13: Prioritization of NGO Interventions

Response	Percentage of countries (n = 19)	MAP I (# countries)	MAP II (# countries)
No prioritization; nearly all proposals are approved	42	4	4
Must be on one of the list of activities in the PAD (or not on the list of excluded activities)	11	2	0
Prioritization by districts as a function of work program, prevalence rate, vulnerable groups	5	1	0
Priority activities defined at project launch—HIV/AIDS knowledge; raising commitment; mitigation	5	0	1
Not answered	37	4	3

Table I.14a: Success in Accelerating Funds to Civil Society

Response	Percentage of countries (n = 19)	MAP I (# countries)	MAP II (# countries)
Yes	68	7	6
For big NGOs, but less so for small NGOs	5	1	0
No	11	2	0
Too soon to tell	11	0	2
Not answered	5	1	0

Table I.14b: Bottlenecks in NGO/CBO Financing

Response	Percentage of countries (n = 19)	MAP I (# countries)	MAP II (# countries)
Financial & administrative aspects (n = 8)	42		
Special accounts and cash flow		1	0
Overly centralized disbursement & low administrative capacity		1	0
Poorly developed banking system in periphery		1	0
Slow processing		1	0
Slow replenishment of special acct at central level		1	0
Special account ran out of money		0	1
Adapting Bank procedures for smaller NGOs		1	0
Inadequate staff to enter cost estimates into MIS		0	1
Low NGO capacity/poor results (n = 5)	26		
Building capacity for smaller NGOs		1	0
Results indicators – lack of them introduces delay in approval		1	0
Low quality of NGO proposals ->revisions		0	1
Getting NGOs qualified to receive money		0	1
Poor results		1	0
Selection process (n = 4)	21		
Clarifying the selection process		1	0
Political interference in selection of subprojects		0	1
Long time for subcontracted agencies to review proposals		0	1
Large proposals that need approval from NAS take long time to approve		0	1
No bottlenecks (n = 4)	21	3	1

Note: Total is more than 19 because some countries gave multiple answers.

cessful in accelerating funds to civil society?

For the most countries (13) the answer was an unqualified yes, and in one other it was the case for large NGOs. In four cases, the funding mechanisms had not accelerated funds or it was too soon to tell (the latter two both MAP II countries).

What are the bottlenecks, if any?

Only 4 of the 18 projects reported that there were no bottlenecks (table I.14b). The predominant problems were **financial and administrative**, affecting 8 countries (44 percent, including 6 of the 7 MAP I projects that reported bottlenecks) —cash flow, overly centralized disbursement, low administrative capacity, poorly developed banking systems, slow replenishments of the special accounts, problems adapting Bank procedures to project needs. The second most com-

mon bottleneck, mentioned by five countries (28 percent), was **low capacity of NGOs.** A third common complaint had to do with difficulties in the **selection process for NGOs** or their proposals—political interference, long and cumbersome review times, and lack of transparency (4 countries, 22 percent).

AIDS and the Health Sector

What has been the impact of the MAP and the national institutional set-up on the engagement of the MOH?

In half of the 18 active MAP countries TTLs reported that there was some disengagement or tension with the MOH as authority was put in a multisectoral committee outside the MOH: Five initially had displeasure or tension, but this has been neutralized (table I.15). In four there con-

Table I.15: Extent of Disengagement of the MOH Due to MAP Institutional Requirements

Response	Percentage of countries (n = 19)	MAP I (# countries)	MAP II (# countries)
No disengagement (n = 9)	47		
No disengagement		2	1
Didn't change the institutional set-up		2	0
MOH is still the leader, with other sectors involved		1	0
Excellent ownership because 1/3 of MAP funds are allocated to MOH		0	1
MOH has largest action plan and is leading the treatment program		0	1
MOH is head of NAC.		0	1
Initial disengagement, overcome (n = 5)	26		
Initially MOH was not pleased, now responsible for health operations		2	2
Tension involving lack of clarity between role of MOH/NAC, but Minister is VP of NAC.		1	0
Continued disengagement (n = 4)	21		
Alienated the MOH, both because of NAC and because didn't get another health project		1	0
Very negative effect on MOH, struggles between MOH & NAC, exacerbated by ethnic differences, nationally and at state level		1	0
Adverse impact due to NAC and creation of Ministry of AIDS		0	1
Adverse impact because of rivalry between current health minister and former health minister chairing the NAC		0	1
No comments offered (n = 1)	5	1	0

tinues to be disengagement or tension, due to either institutional or personal rivalries. In the remaining half of the countries, there was no reported disengagement. This was due, in some cases, to the fact that the MOH was still leading the national AIDS response, a special component of the project had been carved out for MOH, the MOH had a leadership role in the NAC, or the institutional set-up of the response was not affected by the MAP.

What has been done, if anything, to address the tensions or problems with the MOH?

TTLs for nine countries responded that they had tensions/problems with the MOH, and eight of them offered solutions. At the top of the list was personal discussions with the TTL or a decision to discuss all health activities directly with the MOH (five countries). In three cases a new minister of health, director of health, or new government came in, solving the problem. In three countries, there was an attempt to raise the project respon-

sibility or authority of the MOH by creating a special account for the MOH or simply giving it more say (table I16.a).

Does the MOH have its own special account?

Most MOHs have accounts with the NAC and some have special accounts from other health projects. However, in only four countries did the MOH have its own special account in a MAP, including in Eritrea, where the government response is led from the MOH. (TTLs for five countries did not respond or did not know, however; table I 16.b).

If there's a concurrent health operation, what is the relation between the MAP activities and the health project (formal and informal)? Are they coordinated? Complementary?

At the time of the interview, seven countries had no concurrent health project and an eighth had a concurrent AIDS and reproductive health proj-

Table I.16a: Solutions to MOH-NAC Tensions

Solution	Number of countries
Personal discussions w/TTL; TTL discusses all health activities directly w/MOH	5
New director of health or minister of health	2
Got MOH its own special account, after MTR.	1
New government and new minister of health	1
Trying to get a treatment committee going and justify a special account on a volume basis	1
More project responsibility given to MOH	1

Table I.16b: Special Accounts for the MOH

Answer	Percentage of countries (n = 19)	MAP I (# countries)	MAP II (# countries)
Yes	21	2	2
No	53	6	4
Don't know/no answer	26	3	2

Table I.17: Relation Between MAP and Concurrent Health Operations

Response	Percentage of countries (n = 19)	MAP I (# countries)	MAP II (# countries)
Good coordination (n = 8)	42		
Counterparts for the two projects are the same		2	1
Bank TTLs or teams are the same		2	0
Projects are supervised together		1	0
Work programs shared between projects and with the Global Fund activities.		1	0
Finance complementary activities		2	0
Pharmaceuticals link the health and MAP projects. MOH reviews drugs.		0	1
Some crowding out of health by MAP (n = 1)	5		
SWAP finances district health plans; a little crowding out by MAP, which tends to top up district health plans by financing treatment.		0	1
Very little coordination (n = 1)	5	1	0
No concurrent health operation at the time of the interview (n = 7)	37	4	3
No response (n = 3)	16	1	2

Note: Total is more than 19 because TTLs for some countries gave multiple answers. SWAP = sector-wide approach.

ect that did not address the entire health system.[6] Almost all of the remaining countries (8 of 10) reported good coordination through measures such as sharing the same counterparts, joint su- pervision, and the same TTL for the two opera- tions. The TTL for one country suggested that the MAP had crowded out some of the district health plans financed by a SWAp and one additional

Table I.18: M&E Indicators Being Collected

Response	Percentage of countries (n = 19)	MAP I (# countries)	MAP II (# countries)
Same as in the PAD	37	4	3
Additional indicators being collected	16	2	1
Change in some indicators (some added, some dropped)	42	4	4
Not answered	5	1	0

country reported very little coordination between projects (table I.17).

Monitoring and Evaluation

Are the indicators actually being collected different from the PAD? If so, in what way?
In nearly half of the countries with active projects (8, or 44 percent), some of the PAD indicators had been dropped, and new ones had been added. In three countries, the PAD indicators had been kept but others had been added, and in seven the indicators were the same as in the PAD (table I.18).

What mechanisms are in place to evaluate the effectiveness of interventions implemented by NGOs and CBOs?

The TTLs reported that none of the projects included provisions to evaluate the effectiveness or impact of NGO and CBO interventions. Of the TTLs for 17 countries that answered this question, about a third (6, 35 percent) reported that there were no mechanisms whatsoever for evaluating the effectiveness of interventions by NGOs and CBOs. Others in effect only monitored process and output indicators (8 countries, 47 percent) or subjected them to financial or management audits (4 countries, 24 percent). External evaluations at the MTR and ad hoc field visits were also used (table I.19).

What technical inputs has the project received for M&E? How useful has this assistance been in setting up and implementing M&E for this project?

Table I.19: Evaluation Mechanisms for NGOs and CBOs

Response	Percentage of countries (n = 19)	MAP I (# countries)	MAP II (# countries)
None (other than, for example, completion reports) (n = 6)	32	4	3
Indicators (n = 8)	42		
Output/process indicators only		0	3
Reporting with core indicators (not clear if they are process or outcome)		3	2
Report cards		1	0
External audits (n = 4)	21		
Technical audits by consultants hired by NAS		1	0
Management & financial audits		1	2
External evaluations (n = 5)	26		
MTR will have an evaluation		2	1
Ad hoc field visits/supervision missions		1	1
No answer or N/A (n = 2)	11	2	0

Note: Total is more than 19 because some countries gave multiple answers.

Table I.20a: Technical Inputs for M&E

Response	Percentage of countries (n = 19)	MAP I (# countries)	MAP II (# countries)
GAMET	79	7	8
Consultants	21	4	0
Other donors	63		
UNAIDS		3	1
USAID consultant/MEASURE		4	0
Other donors		2	0
CDC	0	2	
Development Economics[a]	5	1	0
None	5	1	0
No answer/NA	5	1	0

a. The Bank's research department.

Table I.20b: Comments on Technical Assistance

Comment	Number of countries
GAMET was very helpful	3
GAMET useful, but reported to someone other than the TTL; M&E expert needs to be part of overall team	1
GAMET not very helpful	1
"Technically they are helpful, but there's no one around to implement recommendations"	1
M&E technical assistance was very useful, part of the 'one system' M&E system that has been set up	1
"There's sometimes been an overload (not necessarily from the Bank), with each donor consultant coming with their own thing. Not too little, just uncoordinated"	1
"Disappointing results" from consultant	1

Most of the projects did get some technical assistance on monitoring and evaluation, often from many sources. GAMET was the most frequently cited source, for 15 countries (table I.20a,b).

What are the key issues in this country for improving M&E and ensuring that these results are used to inform decisions?
The TTLs for only two countries reported that the M&E systems were functioning well. For all of the rest, myriad problems were noted, including: the need to collect and disseminate relevant data for decision-making at the periphery; the need to create incentives; the need to make M&E more results-oriented, as opposed to process oriented; the need to build capacity for M&E at both the center and in decentralized units; the tendency of each donor to have a different set of indicators; the need to monitor quality as well as coverage of services; the lack of impact evaluation (table I.21).

Impact

(If the project has been active for at least a year) what are the main constraints to improving the national response to AIDS today? Has the MAP project had an effect in easing any of the initial constraints? Which ones?
Low implementation capacity remains the predominant constraint, cited by TTLs in six countries—capacity of the health sector, the NAC, and NGOs, and civil society. Financial resources were cited as a constraint for four countries,

Table I.21: Comments on Key Issues for Improving M&E

Comment	Number of countries
Overall M&E system is not operational	4
Need to provide incentives for data collection and build capacity of provinces for M&E	2
Data go to the center, but there's no guidance or feedback to the local level	1
Lack of power of the NAC over all of the actors; each donor has its own indicators	3
Weak capacity of the NAS M&E unit, more skilled people needed	2
Every indicator needs its own collection system & NAC wants to put them all together themselves instead of supporting other agencies to do it	1
Need M&E for whole program, not just project	1
Need to focus on monitoring quality of services, not just coverage	1
Current M&E systems designed to assist national-level decision makers, which isn't useful for implementers at the local level	1
Simplify M&E and make it relevant to local decision makers, to make it a management tool	1
Too much output-based evaluation; need to focus on results	3
Too many indicators; need to get agreement across agencies/donors	1
Need good impact evaluation methodology and to enter data into system for use	1
Training in GIS to understand spatial coverage	1
M&E system is functioning well right now	2

while in four others the TTLs remarked that the influx of money had outstripped the capacity to absorb it, given the limited skilled manpower for implementation (table I.22).

What has been the impact of the Bank's assistance through the MAP as of today, relative to the counterfactual of no MAP/no Bank assistance, both positive and negative?

It should be kept in mind that the MAP I countries are basically at mid-term review (MTR) or almost closed, while many of the MAP II countries have barely been effective for a year. The main impacts cited by TTLs, relative to the counterfactual of no MAP, were greater political commitment and community mobilization (9 countries, 50 percent); greater awareness of HIV as a problem (8 countries, 44 percent); stronger institutions and capacity, including multisectoral institutions (8 countries, 44 percent); impacts on other donors in terms of attracting money or donor coordination (6 countries, 33 percent); expanding access to treatment/care (5 countries, 28 percent, of which 4 are MAP II); and pro-

ducing public goods in terms of surveys, surveillance, and strategic papers (table I.23). **None of the TTLs cited any positive behavior change, a reduction in new HIV infections (as opposed to changes in HIV prevalence), or lower morbidity or mortality.**[7] TTLs for three countries reported negative impacts, in terms of the resentment of other donors, antagonisms between the MOH and the NAC, and a lack of transparency in the NAC.

In your judgment, has the MAP been more or less effective relative to a standard investment project (SIP) on HIV/AIDS prepared on a non-emergency basis in this country?

The large majority of TTLs thought that the MAP was effective or much more effective than a standard HIV/AIDS investment project (12 countries), while two thought that they were equally effective, and a third wasn't sure what the difference is between a MAP and a standard investment project. One TTL noted that at the preparation phase the MAP was less effective because the projects held to a template and were unwilling

Table I.22: Current Constraints to the AIDS Response

Answer	Percentage of countries (n = 19)	MAP I (# countries)	MAP II (# countries)
Low implementation capacity (n = 6)	32		
Weakness, low implementation capacity of health sector		2	2
Strengthen capacity at NAC in terms of training, manpower, organizational			
effectiveness, or dedication		2	0
Lack of involvement of civil society		1	
NGO capacity		0	1
Money – too little (n = 4)	21		
Lack of financing for ARV		2	0
Money is about to run out, lack of money		0	2
Absorptive capacity – too much money in relation to people (n = 4)	21		
Politics surrounding the huge sums of money		2	0
Shortage of human resources/absorptive capacity		0	2
Institutional issues (n = 3)	16		
Isolation of MOH; Relation between MOH and MoHIV/AIDS, which will compromise			
treatment program		1	1
Institutional and organizational issues, federal, state		1	0
Programmatic issues (n = 3)	16		
Strengthen M&E and link program to results		1	1
Improve targeting/more strategic thinking		1	1
Need a way to make sure critical interventions are "scaled up"		1	0
ARV treatment issues (health facilities, staff training, drug supply)		1	0
Lack of coordination (n = 2)	11		
Scattered, uncoordinated activities		1	0
Lack of coordination within government and among donors, so much money			
is flowing		0	1
Social issues (n = 1)	5		
Stigma		1	0
No answer or NA (n = 3)	16	2	1

Note: Total is more than 19 because some countries gave multiple answers.

to adapt to local conditions, while they were more effective at the implementation phase because of the ability to adapt the project by amending the development grant agreement. Note that only four of the TTLs interviewed were around at project preparation, when the "template" and emergency preparations were being pushed, so most may not have been as familiar with the preparation phase, especially of the first MAP. The main reasons the MAP projects were believed to be more effective is that they allow a mul-

tisectoral approach to HIV/AIDS and support communities, and that adaptation is possible (table I.24).

The Future of the MAP

Has the availability of new financial resources from the Global Fund or PEPFAR influenced the content of the MAP? If so, how?
Of the 16 TTLs for the 18 active projects, seven (37 percent) remarked that these other sources

Table I.23: Impact of MAP to Date

Response	Percentage of countries (n = 19)	MAP I (# countries)	MAP II (# countries)
Positive impacts			
Commitment, mobilization (n = 9)	47		
Increased political commitment		0	1
Greater community/civil society mobilization		4	3
Empowered local government, local implementers, gave them info, coordination; decentralized		2	2
Greater awareness, acceptance of HIV as a problem		5	3
Institutions (n = 8)	42		
Multisectoral activities		3	1
Stronger institutions/capacity		1	3
Impacts on other donors (n = 6)	32		
Has made program more attractive to fund by other donors		1	2
Enhanced donor coordination, one M&E system		1	3
Treatment (n = 5)	26		
Access of the poor to ARVs, more access to treatment		1	1
Created institutional framework for more access to treatment/care		0	3
Public goods (n = 4)	21		
More information on the epidemic through surveys, surveillance		1	1
Revised strategic framework		1	1
Other (n = 8)	42		
Leveling off in HIV prevalence		2	0
Mobilized lots of money		1	0
More people tested, aware of status		1	0
Activities would not have been on this scale		1	0
Funding of commodities (others fund mainly TA)		1	0
Decreased stigma		0	1
Better medical waste management		0	1
Behavior change		0	0
Negative impacts (n = 4)	21		
Resentment of other donors		1	0
No impact on prevalence, care or behavior		1	0
Antagonism between MOH and NAC		0	1
Lack of transparency		0	1
No answer/ N/A (n = 2)	11	1	1

Note: Total is more than 19 because some countries gave multiple answers.

have had no impact on the content of the MAP to date (table I.25). In some of these cases, the other sources are funding things that the MAP does not finance. The other half (44 percent) said that it has influenced the content (3) or that they anticipated that it would, once the money started flowing (5). Among those already affected, comments included that the involvement of other financiers has lessened the Bank's financial leverage and forced it to focus on its

Table I.24: Effectiveness of the MAP Relative to a Standard Investment Project

Response	Percentage of countries (n = 19)	MAP I (# countries)	MAP II (# countries)
Much more effective	11	2	0
More effective	53	5	5
The same	11	1	1
Less effective	0	0	0
Much less effective	0	0	0
Don't know – What makes MAP different?	5	1	0
Less effective at preparation phase, because held to "template," unwilling to adapt to local conditions. More effective at the supervision phase because can be adapted by amending DGA & ACT Africa not involved in supervision.	5	0	1
N/A no answer	16	2	1

Table I.25: Influence of Other Funding on the Content of the MAP

Answer	Percentage of countries (n = 19)	MAP I (# countries)	MAP II (# countries)
No	37		
No		1	3
No, the others are funding things that MAP doesn't finance, complementing the MAP		2	1
Not yet, because the money hasn't started flowing	26	3	2
Yes	21		
Funding of treatment shifted to others		1	0
Highlights need to prioritize because of absorptive capacity		0	1
Has lessened the Bank's financial leverage		1	0
Has gotten Bank to focus on its comparative advantage		1	0
N/A – No other funding	5	0	1
Don't know	5	1	0
No answer	5	1	0

comparative advantages, that as a result the treatment financing could be shifted to other donors, and that the large amounts of money highlight the need for government and donors to prioritize activities because of limited absorptive capacity.

How has the much broader availability of funds affected the relevance of the MAP? Is the approach still relevant?

There were basically only two answers to this question—still relevant (two-thirds of respondents) and no answer (one third, table I.26). Those that reaffirmed the relevance gave reasons such as the great needs, the MAP's unique approach (focusing on the multisectoral response and the use of local governments and NGOs), and the concern by governments about the predictability and sustainability of other sources (in particular the Global Fund). In two cases, the respondents noted that while still relevant, the other new funders had focused more on treatment and that the MAP needed to return to a strong emphasis on prevention.

In what ways, if any, would you change the design or approach to the Bank's HIV/AIDS assistance in this country in the next round of lending?

A third of the TTLs (4 from MAP I, 2 from MAP II) indicated that changes were needed in the overall approach in terms of greater emphasis on prevention (in the light of other donors' financing of treatment), on policy dialogue and strategy, and on working with the countries to help them find their own solutions (instead of following a template) (table I.27). Five TTLs did not answer the question. Other suggestions touched on country-specific issues that could be grouped roughly into financing (4, 22 percent), multisectoral issues (2, 11 percent), and specific interventions (2).

Were the eligibility criteria for the MAP useful and appropriate?

Nearly half (8, 42 percent) said that the eligibility criteria were useful and appropriate, but an almost equal number did not answer the question (7, 37 percent). Two TTLs dissented, saying that the contracting out should not have been forced in all cases, as in some it was not appropriate, and that the eligibility criteria should have not been imposed without dialogue or explanation.[8] Two TTLs did not know if the eligibility criteria were useful or appropriate (table I.28).

How should they be revised, if at all, for the next round?

TTLs from only 9 countries answered this question, including two cases in which the respondent was not sure how they should be revised. Comments from the seven responding countries are in table I.29.

How many TTLs have there been for this country since and including preparation?

Only four MAP projects (three MAP I, one MAP II) had retained the same TTL since preparation (table I.30). This is surprisingly low for the MAP II projects, as most were recently approved. In fact, three MAP II projects have had 3 TTLs each in the course of 2 years, and a fourth has had 4 TTLs.

If the TTL is not from the health sector, what have been the difficulties managing this project as someone not based in the health sector? Are there any advantages to have non-health staff managing the project?

Seven of the respondents (39 percent) were not from the health sector. None felt they had any difficulty managing the project. Six of the seven noted heavy involvement of health specialists. One advantage of not being from the health sector is greater credibility in marketing a multisectoral approach (2 responses). Two of the TTLs said that they were able to lend expertise to the community-driven components, which an HNP colleague probably would not have been able to do.

Table I.26: Impact of Other Funding Sources on the Relevance of the MAP

Answer	Percentage of countries (n = 19)	MAP I (# countries)	MAP II (# countries)
Yes	63		
Still relevant		3	3
MAP requirements seen favorably in light of the GF, other donors		1	1
MAP still offers MS approach, use of local governments, and NGOs		3	0
Government & NGOs don't trust sustainability, predictability of GF, others		1	0
N/A	5	0	1
Not answered	32	3	3

Table I.27: Recommended Changes in the Design or Approach to the Bank's HIV/AIDS Assistance in the Next Round, MAP Countries

Answer	Total – MAP I & II		Number of countries	
		Number of countries	MAP I	MAP II
	Percent	(n = 19)	(n = 11)	(n = 8)
Overall approach	37	6		
Greater emphasis on prevention /leave treatment to the other donors			3	
Focus more on the larger response (as opposed to the project); emphasis on policy dialogue, strategy, evaluation of results			1	1
Should change approach – assist country to find its own solution by asking the right questions, sharing experiences, listening to all levels of stakeholders, not a template				1
More country ownership from the beginning				1
Financing	21	4		
Grant instead of credit			1	1
Pooled funding			1	
Reduce counterpart & community contribution requirements (in latter case, especially for mobilization and awareness interventions)				1
Multisectoral aspects	11	2		
Revisit line ministry component – too vertical, not integrated			1	
More sectoral implementation of subprojects in ministry of transport, MOH, etc, using special accounts where there are already Bank operations in that sector				1
Specific interventions	11	2		
More technical support for the MOH				1
More support to PLWHAs before they get sick, with food, etc.			1	
Other	5	1		
If other funding materializes, just focus on the community component			1	
Not answered	26	5	3	2

Any other comments or issues you'd like to raise in this evaluation? (number of TTLs)

Issues to examine

- How important is it to give money to every ministry? (1)
- What are the most efficient and effective institutional arrangements for NGO financing? (1) Write a paper on "stock-taking" for the community response (1)
- What is the most efficient way to scale up? (1)

- Paper on how to have an impact even when the country is in non-accrual (1)
- MAPs are not dealing well with the orphan problem (1)

Lessons & comments

- "There was a total lack of responsibility of advisers in the MAP on content," attention only to process. This was "chaotic and irresponsible," due partly to the haste imposed in preparation. (2)
- There was too much haste—we're now find-

Table I.28: Usefulness and Appropriateness of Eligibility Criteria

Response	Percentage of countries (n = 19)	MAP I (# countries)	MAP II (# countries)
Yes, useful and appropriate	42	4	4
Caveat – contracting out not useful/appropriate	5	0	1
Not appropriate – Criteria should have been suggested, not imposed, w/o dialogue or explanation	5	0	1
Don't know/not sure	11	2	0
Not answered	37	5	2

Table I.29: Suggested Revisions for the Eligibility Criteria

Comment	Number of countries
Require good M&E system	3
Criteria should be adaptable to country context, not a cookie cutter	3
More flexibility in procurement procedures by the Bank	1
Provision for ARV needs to be 'more open'	1
Commitment to the "three ones"	1
More program management (vs. outsourcing)	1
Need for substantive technical advice on HIV/AIDS	1
Genuinely strategic plans, with prioritization	1

Table I.30: Number of TTLs to Date

Number of TTLs	Percentage of countries (n = 19)	MAP I (# countries)	MAP II (# countries)
1	21	3	1
2	37	5	2
3	26	2	3
4	11	1	1
Not asked	5	0	1

ing "communities" of five people (1). The preparation of the MAP projects should not have been done as quickly as they were pressured to do. In [country] it didn't make much difference because there was a previous AIDS project. But elsewhere it resulted in low ownership and involvement in civil society, and inability to deal with fraud, corruption, and the experience of previous health projects (1, citing 2 additional countries).

- "Cannot address AIDS without improving health systems." Need to come back to this focus. (2)
- Most money has been spent on training and workshops, not on implementation (1)
- In smaller countries, where the money is not needed, it may be more appropriate to supply technical assistance (1)
- The huge amount of money coming in from the Global Fund is distorting the policy dialogue,

ownership, and demanding more time of everyone on the ground. If you consider that 75 percent of the MOH budget is salaries, then the amount coming in on AIDS is clearly larger than the non-salary recurrent budget of the MOH. (1)

- Don't understand what the "MAP approach" is. (1)
- Rapid Results Initiative (RRI) is bottom-up but with no agreement from the top to change the rules; the Bank can't waive the guidelines for local shopping for the 3-month timeline. The Accelerating Results Together (ART) model, used since 1992, also gets results in 100 days (1).

Recommendations

- All TTLs should have two weeks of training on substance (1, TTL not from the health sector)
- Major advantage to having TTL in the field (1)
- MOH is still in need of major assistance (1)
- Keep the next MAP simple (1)

APPENDIX J: SURVEY OF WORLD BANK COUNTRY DIRECTORS FOR AFRICAN COUNTRIES PARTICIPATING IN THE MULTI-COUNTRY AIDS PROGRAM

OED interviewed 16 current and former country directors (CDs) responsible for 26 of the 28 active country-level African Multi-Country AIDS Program (MAP) projects (see attachment). Whenever possible, the current country director and the country director at the time of project approval were both interviewed. In many instances, this was the same individual and any one country director might be responsible for anywhere from 1–4 countries. Overall, two country directors were interviewed for 7 countries and a single country director for 19 countries. Interviewing took place over the period June–July 2004.

The interviewer asked 10 open-ended questions covering the following themes:

- Country-level policy dialogue
- The relevance of the Bank's assistance (including the comparative advantages of the Bank's assistance and the past and present relevance of the MAP approach)
- AIDS and resource allocation in the country portfolio
- The effectiveness of the Bank's HIV/AIDS assistance through the MAP.

A final question allowed the respondents to raise any other issues they felt should be addressed in relation to the OED evaluation.

This annex synthesizes the responses of the country directors. In many cases, the responses are not mutually exclusive, because the respondent would make several points in a single answer. When this is the case, it is so noted at the bottom of the table. The respondents were asked questions in relation to each of the countries for which they are responsible and, whenever pos-

sible, the answers are presented at both the respondent level (maximum sample of 16) and the country level (maximum sample of 26) of observation. However, in a few cases the responses were too general to be attributed to specific countries, so the results are shown only for the sample of 16 country directors.

Inputs: Engagement of Country Directors in HIV/AIDS Policy Dialogue

The country directors were asked whether they had been involved in any policy dialogue on HIV/AIDS and, if so, the content, participants, and degree of success. Fifteen country directors responded, representing 25 of the 26 countries with MAP projects, and all reported some involvement in policy dialogue (table J.1). The overwhelming subject matter had to do with promoting the MAP as a concept, either with the country or among donors (or both)—an activity of three-quarters of the country directors in nearly two-thirds of the countries. Five of these country directors noted the participation of World Bank senior management (the president or Africa Regional vice president) or high-level officials from other donor agencies, in five countries (not shown).

In one-fifth of countries the country director became involved in sorting out tensions between the MOH and multisectoral National AIDS Councils (NAC) or other agencies, arising in part from the new institutions promoted by the MAP. The extent of country director involvement in dialogue on substantive issues, such as the relative importance of prevention and issues of treatment policy, was relatively low, affecting only a fifth of countries and country directors.

Table J.1: Country Director Involvement in HIV/AIDS Policy Dialogue

Issue	Country directors (n = 15)		Countries (n = 25)	
	Number	Percent	Number	Percent
Consciousness-raising, HIV in relation to country strategy, promoting government participation in MAP	11	73	16	64
Smooth collaboration w/development partners and reduce tense relationships or resistance around MAPs[a]	6	40	6	24
Resolution of operational problems	5	33	6	24
Tensions between MOHs and NACs or other agencies	4	27	5	20
HIV/AIDS prevention, treatment and care, including ARV dialogue	3	20	5	20

Note: Responses are not mutually exclusive.

a. One CD mentioned that donors had actively fought the MAP in one of the countries.

Relevance of the Bank's HIV/AIDS Assistance

Comparative Advantage of the Bank in Addressing HIV/AIDS

The country directors were asked what they see as the comparative advantage or "value added" of the Bank in addressing HIV/AIDS in the countries for which they are/were responsible. An overwhelming share (88 percent), representing about two-thirds of the countries, reported the Bank's main comparative advantage is in terms of access to senior officials, convening power, and the ability to set agendas and build awareness (table J.2). More than half cited the Bank's multisectoral perspective, its ability to work on a national scale, and to make AIDS a development issue. Other frequently cited strengths were the ability to mobilize money and expertise and to set up institutions and procedures, and to facilitate order and discipline in public sector decision making.

Table J.2: Comparative Advantage of the Bank in Addressing HIV/AIDS

Response	Country directors (n = 16)		Countries (n = 26)	
	Number	Percent	Number	Percent
Access to senior officials, convening power, ability to set agendas and build awareness	14	88	17	65
Multisectoral perspective, ability to work on a national rather than geographically or sectorally limited scale, make HIV a development issue	9	56	11	42
Ability to provide large amounts of money and facilitate access to knowledge	6	40	12	46
Ability to help set up institutions and operational procedures and to facilitate order and discipline in public decision making	6	40	7	27
Ability to act with speed and flexibility	2	13	5	19
Willingness to take risks	2	13	2	8
Prior engagement in the health sector	1	6	1	4

Note: Responses are not mutually exclusive.

Has the MAP Capitalized on These Comparative Advantages?

The directors were asked whether the MAP capitalized on these comparative advantages and whether they saw any inherent advantages or disadvantages in the MAP projects compared with alternative ways of addressing AIDS in the country work program and lending portfolio. This was essentially a two-part question, and only three country directors answered the first part: two (responsible for 6 countries) believed that the MAP definitely did address the comparative advantages of the Bank, while a third (referring to one country) said that the preparation was too rushed and the staff should have undertaken and used sector work.

The results for the second part of the question, on advantages and disadvantages relative to alternative ways of addressing HIV, are shown in table J.3. Slightly more than a third of the directors quibbled with the perceived premise of the question, that there are alternatives (interpreted by them as substitutes) for the MAP in addressing the comparative advantages of the Bank; they noted that there are many complementary activities that might be undertaken to achieve an ob-

jective. A quarter of the directors indicated that the MAP was a short-term activity, but the intent is longer term, for which budgetary support through a sector-wide operation or Poverty Reduction Support Credit (PRSC) that includes AIDS is a more appropriate choice. Finally, a quarter summarized what they felt were the advantages and disadvantages with the MAP approach (though they did not compare it with alternatives).

The Impact of Increased Donor Assistance on the Relevance of the MAP

Country directors were asked how (if at all) the availability of new international sources of funding for HIV/AIDS (the Global Fund, the U.S. government's PEPFAR initiative, foundations, and bilateral donors) affected the relevance of the MAP and the Bank's allocation of resources for HIV/AIDS. Is there still absorptive capacity to use the resources efficiently? Should the Bank regroup or adapt its approach and, if so, how?

Nearly two-thirds of the country directors felt that the Bank strategy would or should change, citing the opportunity to improve institutions and the efficiency of resource use, the need to complement funding of antiretroviral drugs with in-

Table J.3: Advantages and Disadvantages of the MAPs Compared with Alternatives

Response	Country directors (n = 16) Number	Percent
MAP and other instruments and sector work are complements, not substitutes; need to work against objectives and issues rather than sectors or instruments	6	38
In the longer term, a sector-wide approach (SWAP) with budgetary support for HIV would be the preferred option	4	25
Advantages of the MAP:	4	25
• High visibility		
• Entire portfolio to be re-engineered to be HIV sensitive		
• Better, faster procurement procedures		
• Quick preparation addressed the urgency of HIV		
Disadvantages of the MAP:	4	25
• The emergency approach raised problems; it should have been based on sector work but it wasn't		
• The MAP is not a long-term solution		
• Didn't get enough country ownership and damaged relations with development partners		
No response	3	19

Note: Responses are not mutually exclusive.

vestments in the health system, and the even more urgent need to harmonize procedures among donors (table J.4). Only one in four directors thought that no change would be needed.

Resource Allocation in the Country Portfolio

Allocation for AIDS relative to other priorities

Country directors were asked whether the current level of funding for HIV/AIDS in their countries was too much, too little, or just about right compared with other development issues in the portfolio. If too much or too little, they were asked to explain.

Three-quarters of the country directors, representing about two-thirds of the countries, felt that the current allocations were about right, while about a quarter of the directors felt that there was a risk of over-funding in relation to absorptive capacity or other priorities (table J.5). Related to this, several noted that the level of funding is irrelevant if absorptive capacity is the binding constraint. None of the directors indi-

Table J.4: The Impact of Increased Donor Assistance on the Relevance of the MAP

| Response | Country directors (n=16) | | Comments by country directors |
	Number	Percent	
Changes in Bank strategy or operational policies are warranted	10	63	The Bank should scale back on money and focus on institutions, fiduciary review, other expertise, and using the money well. The Bank needs to seek synergies between itself and the GFATM. The Bank needs to harmonize policy and procedures with other donors. If others decide to finance drugs, they will need Bank support for the health system, complementary support.
There's no need to change the Bank's approach	4	25	Even with the arrival of other donors, there will still be an unmet need to finance treatment. The lack of policy context in the Global Fund is a reason to stay engaged.
No response	2	13	
Additional comments			
Absorptive capacity remains limited and is the real issue; new financial resources will exacerbate this problem	6	38	9 countries
Not much of these additional external resources have actually been disbursed	4	25	11 countries
Bank can play a facilitating role in the use of GFATM money, as already shown	4	25	5 countries
The international institutions favor Anglophone countries, so there will continue to be a need in Francophone countries	1	6	

Note: The responses are mutually exclusive; the "additional comments" are not.

Table J.5: Allocation for HIV/AIDS in the Country Portfolio Relative to Alternative Uses

Response	Country directors (n = 16)[a]		Countries (n = 26)[a]	
	Number	Percent	Number	Percent
About right	11	69	16	62
Risk of overfunding in relation to absorptive capacity or other priorities	4	25	6	23
Whether or not it is too high doesn't matter; absorptive capacity is the main issue	2	13	3	12
Did not answer question	2	13	4	15
Additional comments				
Institutional/absorptive capacity and ability to use available funds effectively is a concern	8	50	9	35
Additional funds will be needed (especially if ARV funding becomes an issue)	2	13	3	12

Note: The response on country directors and countries adds to more than 16 or 26 (and more than 100%) because some directors answered differently for the two or more countries for which they were responsible and some countries had directors responding from different time periods with different views. Additional comments are not mutually exclusive.

cated that too little was being spent on HIV/AIDS in their countries.

Additionality of MAP Resources

At the time that MAP was proposed, it was also conveyed that IDA resources for HIV through the MAP would be additional to the country-level IDA allocations, therefore not reducing resources for other programs. The country directors were asked whether in their experience the resources for MAP were additional to the IDA allocation for each country and the evidence supporting it.

There were only three directors, responsible for as many countries, who could confirm the "additionality" of MAP resources. Forty-four percent of the country directors said they were sure that MAP resources were not additional and more than a third (38 percent) were not sure (table J.6). In any event, it seems that in many instances the additionality issue never arose because IDA resources were sufficient to accommodate the MAP (a spontaneous comment from 38 percent of country directors, linked to absorptive capacity). One remarked that it isn't money but rather the availability of Bank staff and preparation/supervision budgets that are the real constraint.

The MAP and Health Lending

Related to the issue of resource allocation within the IDA envelope, the directors were asked whether there was any evidence that MAP or other HIV/AIDS lending has "crowded out" health lending in the countries for which they are responsible. The overwhelming share (93 percent, responsible for 88 percent of the countries surveyed) maintained that MAP lending had had no adverse impact on the availability of funds for health projects (table J.7). In fact, a third remarked that in five countries, MAP and health operations co-exist and are complementary. However, several noted that, while the availability of funds from the Bank was not an issue, the MAP may be drawing Bank staff and managerial time or health personnel in-country away from health sector operations or activities.

The Effectiveness of the Bank's HIV/AIDS Assistance Through the Map

Main Achievements of the Bank's HIV/AIDS Assistance to Date

The country directors were asked what they see as the main achievements of the Bank's HIV/AIDS efforts to date in the countries for which they are responsible, *compared to the counterfactual of no Bank HIV/AIDS involvement.*[1] They were also asked to mention any problem areas. In interpreting the responses to these questions, it

Table J.6: Is MAP Funding Additional to IDA?

Response	Country directors (n = 16)		Countries (n = 26)[c]	
	Number	Percent	Number	Percent
No, MAP funding is not additional	7	44	9	39
Don't know	6	38	7	30
One country director said not additional; other didn't know			3	13
One country director said additional; other didn't know			1	4
Yes, was incremental or facilitated additional funding to overall country program	3	19	3	13
Additional comment:				
It didn't matter because there was no constraint in terms of availability of IDA funds	6	38	11	48

Note: Countries add to more than 23 because for two countries more than one Country Director responded and the answers did not agree.

Table J.7: Is MAP or HIV/AIDS Lending Crowding Out Health Lending?

Response	Country directors (n = 16)		Countries (n = 26)	
	Number	Percent	Number	Percent
No, not crowding out health lending	14	93	23	88
Yes, crowding out health lending	1	7	2	8
Not sure	1	7	2	8
Additional comments of those not finding crowding out:				
MAP and health lending are in parallel and complementary	5	33	5[a]	19
Availability of Bank staff and managerial time for both health and AIDS is a constraint	2	13	3	12
MAP may be drawing health personnel away from health system	1	7	3	12

Note: Responses for Country Directors are mutually exclusive. Total countries exceeds 26 (and 100%) because of two countries in which Country Directors at two points in time had different conclusions (one finding crowding out, the other not).

a. At least 5 countries (19%), and perhaps as many as 8 (31%). (The CD cited "several" of his countries.)

is important to keep in mind that some of the MAP II projects had only recently been approved, and the MAP I projects had been in operation for several years longer, on average. Thus, the results are broken down for MAP I and II countries separately.

Almost all of the achievements cited were in terms of implementation and intermediate outputs. Increased awareness and political commitment was cited in more than half of both MAP I and MAP II countries, 71 percent overall,

and improvements in the civil society response (in terms of enlisting NGOs and building their capacity) were cited by about one in four respondents for both MAP phases (table J.8). Directors for about half of the MAP II countries reported as a major achievement improvements in donor coordination or harmonization, including attracting resources from other donors. Directors for one in four countries cited expanded services. In three countries—all of them MAP I—the country directors maintained that

Table J.8: Main Achievements of the Bank's HIV/AIDS Assistance to Date

Response	MAP I (n = 11)		MAP II (n = 13)		Total (n = 24)	
	Number	Percent	Number	Percent	Number	Percent
Increased awareness and political commitment	9	82	8	62	17	71
Improved donor coordination, harmonization; attracted other donor resources	0	0	7	54	7	29
Improvements in civil society/NGO response	3	27	3	23	6	25
Reduction in HIV prevalence relative to counterfactual	3	27	0	0	3	13
Established Bank's institutional and technical credibility with donors	0	0	2	15	2	8
Country-level MAP institutional framework established	1	9	0	0	1	4
Other achievements	1	9	5	38	6	25
Expansion of condom distribution, VCT, orphan interventions						
Blood transfusion improvements						
Promotion of access to treatment						

Note: Responses are not mutually exclusive. The videoconference was cut short for one CD for two countries, so no response is available.

HIV prevalence was likely lower than it would have been in the absence of the project. They generally did not substantiate these claims.[2]

It is noteworthy that none of the country directors mentioned an impact of the Bank's HIV/AIDS assistance on behavior change—such as increases in condom use, reductions in casual or commercial sexual partners, or delayed onset of sexual relations. Behavior is the channel through which program outputs change HIV transmission and reduce HIV incidence. This is not to say that behavior change has not occurred; it might indicate, however: (a) a lack of association of changes in behavior with "impact" in the respondents' minds; (b) a lack of baseline and trend data on which to base an opinion; or (c) lack of specific knowledge in this area by the country director in question.

Problems mentioned in terms of implementation and impact of the Bank's HIV/AIDS assistance were reported for six countries:

- Low quality of subprojects and slow development of action plans outside of the Ministry of Health
- Limited capacity, both within the client countries and within the Bank

The following MAP-specific problems were noted:

- Little is yet happening on the ground. "This is a pure MAP problem" (in reference to two MAP I countries).
- The Bank rushed to prepare the MAP in 3 months, then it took 9 months to become effective. This "forced the pace and paid the consequences," while in non-MAP AIDS projects they worked in an "orderly, credible way."
- "The Ministry of Health (MOH) was very jealous of its prerogatives and we had huge battles with the minister. There's a real risk of less enthusiasm and engagement than there should be, among the officials most directly concerned."

Effectiveness of MAP Relative to Standard Investment Projects

Country directors were asked whether the MAP instrument has been more or less effective in pursuing the objectives of stopping the HIV/AIDS epidemic than would have been a standard investment project. A surprising finding was that one in four directors did not recognize any difference between these two types of operation (table J.9). Among those remaining who answered the question, equal numbers thought that the MAP was more effective, less effective, or equally effective compared with a standard investment project. Among the advantages of the MAP cited were its multisectoral dimension, the engagement of the president and civil society, the results orientation, greater supervision resources, and the ability to launch regional operations. Among the factors mentioned that were thought to make the MAP less effective than a standard investment project was a lack of project preparation and the failure of the template approach to take into account local conditions and priorities.

Table J.9: The Effectiveness of the MAP Compared with a Standard Investment Project

Response	Country directors (n = 16)		Comments
	Number	Percent	
MAP is more effective	3	19	Theoretically more effective because of results orientation, intensity of supervision, and greater resources. Signaling effect of the MAP
			Multisectoral dimension, engagement of the president and civil society in the face of public sector implementation constraints
			Ability to launch multi-country regional operations
MAP is less effective/significant disadvantages	3	19	Failure to take into account local conditions (Bank insistence not to treat HIV as a health issue and multisectoral entity in the Presidency, against strong local view to the contrary)
			Alienated donor and UN agency partners
			Because of too much "focus on disbursement, with a top-down approach, we lost some credibility and focus on the real priorities....it would have been better to devote resources to the top priorities"
Equally effective	3	19	Both types suffer from similar operational problems, like lack of counterpart funds
			"As for the template approach, this has not really accelerated anything"
			"The MAP has suffered as much as other projects....the problems were the lack of preparation and dependence on an institutional framework that remained to be created"
			"The key point is to get beyond the instrument ... into an appropriate definition of the problem"
Each has advantages & disadvantages	1	6	The MAP has lightened up the Bank's procurement requirements and are 'an extreme form of CDD,' an "inevitable evolution." But they are open to the abuse of per diems
Don't recognize the difference between MAP and a standard investment project	4	25	
No answer	2	13	

Note: Responses are mutually exclusive.

Impact of Grants on Bank Leverage with the Borrower

The directors were asked in what ways, if any, has the move from IDA credits (during MAP I) to grants for AIDS (during MAP II) changed the Bank's relation or leverage with the borrower or the borrower's ownership and accountability. Half of the country directors thought that it had changed the Bank's leverage—generally increasing the Bank's involvement—while the other half saw no change or the issue had not arisen in their experience or it was too early to tell. Very few respondents commented on the impact on borrower accountability and ownership, with two commenting that they were not affected and a third distinguishing between the effect on country ownership and government ownership (table J.10).

Other Issues Raised by the Country Directors

In concluding, the respondents were asked about any other issues or opinions that they would like to provide on the MAP projects or on AIDS assistance more generally in the countries for which they are responsible. Issues raised by the country directors included:

- *Accountability.* (1) There is a risk that the Bank is disbursing excessive funds with inadequate controls in connection with the MAP operations. The MOH in the country was reported to argue that the "good times" should roll, funds should be disbursed, and the "accountability approach" should be avoided. There is a problem of getting "value for money" and of enforcing accountability. (2) Accountability remains an issue and costs are rising; there are real issues in scaling up without cost increases.
- *Donor coordination and the international situation.* (1) "I find the international situation on HIV confusing. There are so many actors. If we could give the countries some broader, institutional guidance, agreed at the senior management level and among the international institutions concerned, that would be

Table J.10: Impact of IDA Credits on the Bank's Leverage and the Borrower's Accountability and Ownership

Response	Country directors (n = 16)		Countries (n = 26)	
	Number	Percent	Number	Percent
Has changed the relationship	8	50	11	42
No change in relationship	4	25	9	35
Grants v. credits not an issue, had not arisen, or too early to tell	4	25	6	23
Additional comments among those who believe the relationship has changed				
Will increase the Bank's leverage	3	19	6	23
Facilitated the Bank's involvement in AIDS tremendously	1	6	2	7
Ministry of Finance is worried that grants will make it easier for the Bank to push its own agenda	1	6	1	4
Facilitated involvement in cross-border issues	1	6	1	4
Did not reduce government ownership or responsibility (including one comment that grants also require counterpart contribution)	2	13	4	15
Grants could increase country ownership but not necessarily borrower ownership, since grants can be sent more quickly to civil society	1	6	1	4

Note: Responses are mutually exclusive; additional comments are not.

very beneficial for our countries." (2) The issue of donor coordination, harmonization, and simplification has to be raised at the level of senior management at donor headquarters, not just at the country level or among working-level staff. (3) The Bank should be able to scale down its AIDS efforts over time and pass the torch to the Global Fund, though it may be too early now. If the MAP prevents the Global Fund from mobilizing donor funding, then the Bank should pull back.

- *Multisectorality in practice.* The long preparation for [country x] was a function of the "top-heavy baggage of multisectorality." "This kind of thing takes months or years in bureaucracies." "Disbursements have been slow." "The message that HIV is a development problem is important, but we should work with governments, and then broaden during implementation."

- *Absorptive capacity constraints.* These are paramount in many countries as even larger sums of money are allocated to HIV/AIDS.
- *Monitoring and evaluation.* We need to promote and organize real-time M&E, to get beyond formal, long-term work.
- *Complacency.* How do we avoid complacency in the Bank and among our clients, now that HIV has become part of the landscape?
- *New instruments.* What will happen to HIV/AIDS as it is absorbed into PRSCs? What will or should be the sectoral base of task team leadership?
- *Supervision resources.* One director argued that because the MAP projects are not above average complexity and since there's no more "learning by doing" than in other projects, that supervision does not require the additional resources provided by the MAP.[3]

Attachment: Country Coverage

MAP I (12 countries)	MAP II (16 countries)
Benin	Burundi
Burkina Faso	Cape Verde
Cameroon	Congo, Democratic Rep.
CAR	Congo, Republic of
Eritrea	Guinea-Bissau
Ethiopia	Malawi
Gambia	Mali
Ghana	Mauritania
Kenya	Niger
Madagascar	Rwanda
Nigeria	Senegal
Uganda	Sierra Leone
	Tanzania
	Zambia

APPENDIX K: STATEMENT OF THE EXTERNAL ADVISORY PANEL

The External Advisory Panel welcomes this comprehensive evaluation of the World Bank's HIV/AIDS assistance. We note that while the World Bank has had involvement in HIV/AIDS–related assistance since 1986, it substantially increased its involvement after 1998. As such, this timely and important evaluation has been conducted after less than seven years since the World Bank expanded the amount of funding and number of countries receiving support for HIV/AIDS. Because it is still early, it is not surprising that it is difficult to assess the true country-level impact of the World Bank's assistance, particularly on the ultimate goals of reducing HIV incidence and mitigating the impact of the epidemic. However, there are important observations and recommendations in the report; if the recommendations are fully implemented, the World Bank's ability to demonstrate impact in the future will be significantly enhanced.

Although the World Bank has not always been viewed as a major source of development assistance for health, it has been one of the largest supporters of HIV/AIDS activities in developing countries. The Bank's HIV/AIDS–related strategies and actions have clearly evolved over time and it will be essential that they continue to do so into the future, as the world learns more about what works and as the landscape of the epidemic and the global response continue to shift. We hope this report will help to stimulate dialogue within the Bank. Particularly in light of the World Bank's new leadership, this is an important moment to use the evaluation's recommendations to further strengthen the Bank's response.

Overall, the Panel would like to emphasize our belief that the evaluation is sound and our support for its findings. Our comments below should be understood in this context.

The evaluation is missing perhaps the most important and compelling recommendation—the job is not finished. The Panel strongly believes that the World Bank must sustain its commitment to making HIV/AIDS a central priority of its poverty-reduction strategy. Even with the increased involvement of other actors (the Global Fund on AIDS, Tuberculosis, and Malaria, the government of the United States, the private sector, and so on), the World Bank continues to have both its own comparative advantage in responding to AIDS and a crucial role to play as a UNAIDS co-sponsor.

The Panel believes that the World Bank should adopt an overall HIV/AIDS strategy— something that it has not done to date, despite various Regional and sector strategies. The fact that the World Bank does not really have a true institution-wide strategy seems short-sighted. We believe that the development and adoption of such a strategy would be an important step and one that would help with both global- and country-level prioritization of activities. Such a strategy should respond to the lessons of the evaluation and the evolution of the epidemic, paying particular attention to the need for serious and sustained mitigation investments in the most heavily affected countries and the ongoing uncertainty and risk associated with the emergence of new epidemic hot-spots in other parts of the world. A new strategy must be rooted in a forward-looking analysis in addition to drawing lessons from the past. In particular, the World Bank must work with countries to support the institutionalization of HIV prevention, care, and mitigation into politically, financially, and institutionally sustainable structures: the overall health system, the education system, the social protection system, and so on. HIV will be with us for at least another generation.

The Panel notes that the evaluation has demonstrated that Bank projects have sometimes "failed to reach people with the highest-risk behaviors," which in turn has likely "reduced the efficiency and impact of assistance." As a result, the Panel agrees that the Bank should try to encourage and support governments to prioritize "public goods" and "prevention among those most likely to spread HIV." We have two caveats, however.

Not unreasonably, the evaluation's terms of reference were restricted to the HIV-related impact of HIV-related investments. Nevertheless, it is not unreasonable to speculate that cost-benefit analyses of different intervention strategies, and therefore selection of appropriate priorities, may be considerably different if other potential benefits are factored into the analysis: for example, achievement of other sexual and reproductive health objectives, control of tuberculosis, or strengthening of health systems. We therefore recommend that the World Bank indeed help governments prioritize and sequence activities with an emphasis on those likeliest to have the greatest and most efficient impact on the epidemic, but that the World Bank not use such a rationale to rule out appropriate integration of HIV into other health programs, especially those related to sexual and reproductive health and infectious disease control, as long as such investments can be defended as cost-effective as overall packages.

In addition, necessarily sequencing highest-impact or highest-efficiency interventions first would sometimes result in missed opportunities for relatively easy, quick, and appropriate investments, which could also help to create or sustain political support for the overall AIDS response in a country. Similarly, the highest-impact interventions in the short run might not be the most sustainable. For example, it may be politically more appropriate to combine important but controversial interventions (such as focused HIV prevention with drug users or sex workers) with other programs that command broader public support, such basic HIV education in schools, or a range of voluntary counseling and testing (VCT), care, and support services. However, this should not detract from the strength of the Bank's program focus on the populations at greatest risk for HIV. In addition,

we believe that the World Bank must recognize both political realities and shifting conceptions of "good practice" to accommodate a range of investments: the classic message applies that a good program supported and led locally is far superior to a perfect program that only has support from foreigners and "experts."

The Panel strongly supports the evaluation's second recommendation, regarding the strengthening of national institutions, especially in the health sector. In addition, however, special note must be made of the mitigation needs of the most heavily affected countries, especially those with a large and growing burden of orphans. Some mitigation needs can and should be addressed through the health sector (including, of course, provision of care and treatment). Many others require leadership from other sectors, however, especially social protection and education. There is not clear evidence from the evaluation about the relative merits of addressing mitigation concerns through specialized AIDS technical advice and programming (such as MAP), as opposed to addressing these issues through appropriate sector lending in education, social protection, and so on. What matters most, however, is that the Bank recognize and respond to the special needs and challenges of the most AIDS-affected countries, and gear up both analytic and country work to respond to these needs. In addition, given the Bank's special capacity to leverage political commitment and action across multiple ministries, it is important that the Bank continue to look for opportunities for HIV *prevention* in sectors beyond health: education, development of transport infrastructure, and defense are all obvious areas for action.

At a more detailed level, we note that the evaluation documents a number of important findings without clearly documenting a suggested way forward. Perhaps most significantly, the evaluation repeatedly points to capacity limitations as a key constraint to success, especially in its discussion of MAP, but also elsewhere, but the evaluation does not recommend a clear response to these constraints. Since this is key to building successful programs, this may be an area in which the Bank could develop models that could be replicated. Given the multisectoral reach of the

World Bank, this may be a unique contribution the Bank could make. The evaluation finds evidence of high-quality analytic work, but poor performance at dissemination and using such work to leverage others. The finding is not surprising, but we would like to see more concrete recommendations on how the Bank could have been more effective in these efforts to date, and how it could be more effective in the future. Similarly, the evaluation finds evidence of innovative and successful partnerships with NGOs and civil society (e.g., Cambodia, Brazil), and a willingness to take risks in the advancing such partnerships (e.g., MAP). However, the Bank's capacity to learn from its NGO-related successes and failures seems limited, and there is no clear central or country strategy for either analyzing or advancing appropriate government–civil society relationships. Finally, the evaluation points to some useful and innovative Bank involvement in public-private partnerships (such as the International AIDS Vaccine Initiative), but once again the Bank does not yet seem to have a well-developed logic for prioritizing such efforts. None of these comments is meant to be particularly critical of past performance or of the evaluation's findings—the Bank (like other actors) has been making it up as they go along. However, it is crucial in mapping the way forward to respond to these particular shortcomings with explicit strategies and new mechanisms of working.

The evaluation quite correctly notes that the World Bank departed from some of its traditional planning and prioritization processes as it developed its work in HIV/AIDS. While the Panel shares the implied conclusion of the evaluators that perhaps the Bank may at times have strayed too far from its operational niche, we also give credit to Bank staff working on HIV/AIDS for their willingness to be innovative and responsive and to foster action even as clear evidence of "what works" was not yet available. It is surely better to have gambled on a variety of strategies, some of which turned out to be successful, than to have waited for a clear evidence base and a thorough analysis before engaging. That said, we agree with the thrust of two of the evaluation's related recommendations: that previous work has insufficiently invested in systematic learning and evaluation, and that future work must both build on the current evidence base and continue to generate new learning.

Looking forward, we suggest that the World Bank prioritize its role as a key supporter of long-term, sustainable responses. This implies an increased focus on infrastructure, integration of programs, HIV/AIDS-related health system strengthening, and attention to key long-term mitigation strategies outside the health sector. At the moment at least, other donors are better placed to emphasize speed and emergency responses, roles that the Bank itself has played in the past.

Helene D. Gayle, M.D., M.P.H., Director, HIV,
TB and Reproductive Health
Bill and Melinda Gates Foundation,
Seattle, USA
Jeffrey O'Malley, M.A., Country Director,
Program for Appropriate
Technology in Health (PATH),
New Delhi, India
Senator Mechai Viravaidya,
Parliament of Thailand,
Founder and Board Chairman,
Population and Community
Development Association, Thailand

Note: The fourth member of the External Advisory Panel, Ms. Mary Muduuli of Uganda, provided very constructive advice throughout the preparation of the report, but had to step down from the Panel shortly before the evaluation report was finalized, and was therefore unable to participate in the statement.

Management welcomes the opportunity to comment on this OED report, which provides a very useful overview of the Bank's work on HIV/AIDS and the timelines of key events inside and beyond the Bank. The report aims to assess "the development effectiveness of the Bank's HIV/AIDS assistance against the counterfactual of no Bank assistance," looking at "policy dialogue, analytic work and lending." It describes two phases in the Bank's response to HIV/AIDS: projects and analytic work done from 1985 through 1997, and the hugely increased, and, in management's view, innovative efforts since 1998. The report summarizes prior evaluations of early projects. In addition, although (as the report notes) none of the projects under the Africa Multi-Country AIDS Program (MAP) has closed, it offers assessments, based on OED's reading of the evidence, of their design. The report mentions but does not assess the major efforts management is already making to address many of the concerns raised. (Some of these efforts are noted in the Management Action Record at the end of this response.)

Areas for Comment. Management appreciates the extensive work reflected in this review. Management agrees that it is important to recognize how the early HIV/AIDS projects contributed to greater political commitment to addressing HIV/AIDS, greater efficiency and scale of national AIDS programs, and stronger institutions and national capacity; and management agrees also with the judgment that the Bank's initial response was held back internally, measured against the scale and impact of the epidemic. With respect to the MAP, it is reassuring that many of OED's observations and recommendations echo the findings of management's own

three reviews (in 2001 and 2002, and the 2004 independent "Interim Review" that was shared with the Board and is summarized in box L.1). However, management would like to comment on some specific aspects of the report: the methodological difficulties the OED review faced, learning over time and the treatment of Bank support, the review's stance on the role of Ministries of Health, targeting high-risk groups in prevention efforts in generalized epidemics, the role of communities, and monitoring and evaluation.

Key Issues

This section presents management's comments on six key areas of concern it identified in the OED report.

A. Methodology and Evidence Base

Because of its timing, the review does not take into account the extensive evolution that has taken place with regard to Bank assistance. Additionally, management would mention two issues of methodology.

- The OED review of the MAP assesses a broad Bank program at an early stage of implementation.[1] The MAP program has evolved considerably during the more than two years since the OED review began, so that some of the report's findings, of course, do not reflect recent achievements and developments. Specifically, the 2004 Interim Review high-

---

1. OED notes that the OED review of the MAP encompasses all active MAP projects through the end of fiscal year 2004. Interviews with MAP TTLs and country directors for MAP projects were conducted in the summer of 2004 (that is, in fiscal year 2005).

Box L.1: The MAP Interim Review

In fall 2003, as part of its oversight of the MAP, ACT*africa* commissioned a review of the MAP program as a whole. A team comprising 3 Bank staff, 2 senior consultants, and 3 non-Bank staff (representatives from UNAIDS, a major bilateral HIV/AIDS donor, and a major international NGO) reviewed all MAP program documents, interviewed MAP task team leaders and staff of ACT*africa*, conducted field visits in a roughly representative sample of 6 MAP countries, and obtained input from more than 300 government officials, donor representatives, and stakehold-ers. The team submitted a draft to ACT*africa* for comment, and then prepared a final draft reflecting management feedback. By prior agreement, management did not edit the report except for clarity and minor factual corrections. The report was presented to the Africa Regional Leadership Team in May 2004 and to the executive directors in August 2004, and thereafter made public. Its conclusions and recommendations are being incorporated into ongoing MAP projects wherever possible, and they directly informed the design of the second generation of MAP projects.

lighted the need for more rigorous strategic planning, greater health sector engagement, better targeting of vulnerable groups, and stronger monitoring and evaluation. While it is reassuring that nearly all of OED's principal observations and recommendations reaffirm the findings of management's own reviews and consultations, management believes that the review would have given greater recognition to the intensive efforts underway to address these issues, which are also prioritized in the draft Global HIV/AIDS Program of Action.[2]

- Management notes OED's extensive use of existing reviews of the earlier AIDS projects, MAP documents, and interviews with task team leaders (TTLs) and country directors, but it also notes two issues with the evidence base used. OED conducted only one field case study of a MAP project—Ethiopia. Management recognizes that the choice of projects was constrained by the early timing of the review; however, as the first MAP project, Ethiopia's is in many ways the least typical, since the MAP has continually evolved since its inception. This project has also been among the more problematic in implementation. The Ethiopia project provided lessons that guided later operations, but it lacks many of the features that are now standard in the MAP.

- Given the importance of the MAP in stimulating a broader response to HIV/AIDS, it is somewhat surprising that, except in Ethiopia, OED consulted no country-level MAP stakeholders (including governments) or others in the donor community or civil society.

- Given the central role of sexual behavior in the HIV/AIDS epidemic and its complex social and cultural dynamics, the OED review might have given more attention to social, social psychological, and community development analysis.

B. Learning over Time and Implementation Support

The review's summary assessment of the nine completed "first generation" HIV/AIDS projects and nine project components is generally positive, noting their contribution to greater political commitment to addressing HIV/AIDS, greater efficiency and scale of national AIDS programs, and stronger institutions and national capacity. Management agrees that these efforts deserve recognition. However, OED's favorable comparison of the early AIDS projects with all health, nu-

---

2. OED notes that the OED evaluation does not support the finding in the Interim Review that "the objectives, approach, and design of the MAP program have generally been appropriate" (the evaluation finds that several key assumptions underlying the MAP design proved unfounded and identifies a number of critical risks that were overlooked).

trition, and population projects gives little cause for comfort, as there is little direct evidence—outside countries with significantly lower prevalence rates, relative to Africa—of the effectiveness of earlier AIDS projects in preventing infections.[3]

Analytic Work. It would have been useful for the report to include comparators or benchmarks against which to interpret the results of surveys asking Bank staff and African policy makers about key Bank documents on AIDS. Management wishes that more could have been learned from the surveys about how to do better in getting key Bank reports to intended audiences.

Ongoing Implementation Support for MAP. The OED review tends to discuss the MAP as if it were simply a set of traditional projects. The report's reliance on project documents, and in particular its focus on what were explicitly named as risks and constraints at the very beginning of the program, has produced an unduly static picture of the MAP. In reality, MAP projects are more dynamic than standard Bank-supported operations, allowing for ongoing risk assessment, learning, and alterations. In this sense, the design of MAP encompasses more than what is provided for in any individual project. It also includes the larger program of intensive implementation support and cross-country learning led by ACT*africa* and the Global HIV/AIDS Program. In fact, many of the most important aspects of MAP design and implementation have arisen in the course of experience, and have been integrated both prospectively and retroactively into

other MAP operations. For instance, the original MAP document may not have singled out weak monitoring and evaluation (M&E) as a risk, or limited capacity as a constraint, but in practice the Bank has recognized these priorities from the outset and has devoted an unprecedented amount of time and resources to strengthening both of these traditionally weak areas. Specifically, MAPs have benefited from:

- Direct support from specialists, including M&E specialists, in ACT*africa* and the Global HIV/AIDS Program
- Country visits from technical support teams to resolve implementation roadblocks
- Workshops for TTLs and country-level practitioners from government and civil society to derive and disseminate lessons of successful experience
- Guidelines and manuals on such subjects as financial management, M&E, and procurement
- Recourse to the Implementation Acceleration Team (IAT), which comprises the heads of all central Bank departments and is charged with removing internal barriers to rapid processing and implementation of HIV/AIDS projects
- The various MAP reviews.

Early Action. This kind of support and flexibility has enabled the Bank to identify and address problems at an early stage. For instance, as the OED review correctly notes, MAP projects frequently encountered delays in implementation, partly because of inadequate attention to institutional factors. When the MAP reviews identified this issue, management decided in 2002 that institutional issues would need to be resolved before any future MAP project could be approved. As a result, preparation time increased, and time from approval to effectiveness fell. Likewise, disbursements in many MAP projects began sluggishly, but concerted attention to the common obstacles has helped accelerate implementation, and MAP projects are now disbursing at or very near their planned ambitious target disbursement rates.

Implementation Support Efforts. The Bank has also been willing to take larger steps. The IAT was es-

---

3. OED notes that there is insufficient evidence to assess the impact of any Bank lending on HIV incidence because of the failure to collect necessary data. However, there is ample indirect evidence, in the form of behavior change or increased knowledge, of plausible influence of Bank assistance on new infections in Burkina Faso, Cambodia, Chad, India, and Kenya (see Chapter 3, "Outcomes and Impacts" and box 3.5). These are all low-income countries with significant AIDS epidemics. Management notes the relatively low prevalence rates, relative to the Sub-Saharan Africa average, for most of the countries cited by OED.

tablished in January 2003 to improve the Bankwide implementation of MAP and other HIV/AIDS projects. The Implementation Acceleration Team has (a) facilitated changes in and exceptions to Bank policies and procedures; (b) provided project task teams with prompt advice on solving individual and systemic preparation and implementation problems; and (c) worked with the Global HIV/AIDS Program and ACT*africa* to share knowledge and build capacity in project preparation and implementation (including in fiduciary areas) through shared learning by Bank staff and country counterparts.

Similarly, in 2002 the education team in AFR, with ACT*africa* and HDNED, launched an effort to "Accelerate the Education Sector Response to HIV/AIDS" by sharing information among client education teams, providing technical assistance, and supporting clients in accessing education sector and MAP resources for the education sector response. More than 33 ministries of education, along with teams from health ministries and national AIDS commissions, have participated in this program. An evaluation has shown that countries that participate actively in this effort are more likely to access both education sector and MAP support.

Conclusion. In sum, the Bank has in place robust mechanisms to identify and remedy issues that arise during the implementation of MAP projects. While management agrees with OED that implementation needs to improve still further, it knows of no comparable Bank effort in support of a single program.

C. Role of Ministries of Health and the Health Sector

MAP requires that, to be eligible for MAP projects, countries must have in place a high-level multisectoral coordinating body. The OED review states that this requirement has alienated ministries of health (MOHs) in some countries (box 4.6), that MOHs need a more prominent role as the natural lead agency, and that there is no example of a strong response that bypassed the health sector and was led by a sector other than health. On the other hand, the report also notes that "Commitment to fighting AIDS needs to be more widely entrenched across the political and institutional spectrum than in a head of state or Minister of Health" (p. 23). OED disagrees with the MAP premise that "too narrow a focus in the health sector as the main actor" was one reason why earlier efforts were unsuccessful against AIDS, and it does not find "that an *overemphasis on the health sector* was a reason for lack of success."

Role of MOHs. Management agrees that MOHs have a central role in addressing HIV/AIDS, and that their capacity and role need to be strengthened. Nothing in the multisectoral response is meant to supplant the functions that only an MOH can perform. The need to fully engage the health sector was a key recommendation in the Second MAP Review, is an explicit focus in the second generation of MAP projects ("MAP2"), and is emphasized in the *Warriors* manual (Brown, Ayvalikli, and Mohammad 2004). Progress in this area is evident from OED's survey of TTLs: in 18 countries for which TTLs responded on this issue, there was never a problem in 9, the initial problems had been overcome in 5, and problems of MOH disengagement persist in only 4 (Appendix I, table I.15; it is also worth noting that in 1 of the 4, the problems are for personal reasons).[4] In Appendix I, table I.17, for 10 countries with both MAP and health projects, only one TTL reports "little" coordination with MOH, and only one reports "a little crowding out" of MOH-planned activities by MAP activities, while 8 report good coordination. In addition, whatever the institutional frictions have been, they do not appear to have resulted in limits on MOH im-

---

4. OED notes that countries with no reported disengagement included several in which the MOH was still leading the national AIDS response, a special component had been carved out for the MOH, the MOH had a leadership role in the NAC, or the institutional set-up was not affected. The *Interim Review of the MAP* (2004) found that "Where resources for the Ministry of Health were treated as part of the multisectoral response ... rather than as a dedicated component managed by the MOH, the results have been generally poor."

plementation: across all MAP projects, MOHs have received roughly half of all MAP funds channeled to the public sector, and they are expected to have more than 60 percent by projects' end.

Beyond the Health Sector. At the same time, field-based HIV/AIDS experts say there *is* evidence that earlier overemphasis on the health sector contributed to lack of success in several ways. First, MOHs are seldom powerful enough to motivate the highest levels of political commitment, require other ministries to act, or support community responses effectively. While they naturally play a lead technical role in surveillance, treatment, and many key interventions, they have no particular advantage in coordinating other government entities. It seems logical that the necessary multisectoral response could be coordinated better through a high-level multisectoral AIDS authority than through the MOH. Indeed, the first two countries to successfully curb HIV, Uganda and Thailand, had high-level coordinating bodies chaired by a very senior political leader, and promoted multisectoral responses that extended far beyond the health sector (although of course the health sector played a strong role).[5] Second, as box L.2 illustrates and evidence from Uganda demonstrates, an overemphasis on MOHs has in some cases "professionalized" AIDS and discouraged community and religious leadership and involvement. Third, there are examples where health sector leadership has led to an over reliance on health interventions. When the health sector dominated AIDS responses, many programs, including several World Bank-supported projects supported sexually transmitted infection (STI) care as a key intervention to reduce HIV transmission (and did not emphasize promoting changes in sexual behavior). Although one trial had indicated that STI

care reduced HIV transmission, several more recent trials have since contradicted that finding, starkly underscoring the dangers inherent in a narrow health sector response that is based on what may be imperfect scientific evidence. By contrast, management believes and relevant literature indicates that the decline in HIV transmission in Uganda was driven by widespread mobilization and behavior change (Low-Beer and Stoneburner 2003). Also, by contrast, expanded health service interventions, including condoms and voluntary counseling and testing, came later, as shown in figure L.1. [6]

Conclusion. The experience of Uganda, the first African country to successfully curb its epidemic, powerfully illustrates the dangers of a narrow, technocentric health sector response to a disease that can only be addressed through sweeping changes in cultural, social, and gender norms. This lesson is not limited to Africa. Throughout large swathes of Central and Eastern Europe and Central, South and South-East, and East Asia, it is becoming clear how important the legal, justice, police, prisons, and social welfare ministries are in creating contexts conducive to effective AIDS responses among injecting drug users, prisoners, and sex workers, the communities most vulnerable to HIV infection in these regions. Crucial as the health sector is, it can be said without exaggeration that the course of epidemics in much of Europe and Asia will depend at least as much on these other ministries as on the health ministry.

D. Reaching High-Risk Groups
The OED review repeatedly comments on the importance and cost-effectiveness of reaching high-risk groups. It takes a strong stand on the need to prioritize preventive efforts among high-risk

---

5. OED notes that MAP internal reviews and an external review of the Uganda and Senegal experience find significant problems with the functioning of multisectoral AIDS authorities (see box 4.6 of this report and Putzel 2004). Management notes that it does not view that journal article as meeting the standards of a review.

6. OED notes that the PPAR on the Uganda STI Project (Report No. 32600) found that, while some behavior has changed in Uganda, it is not clear to what extent it can be attributed to public policy. It noted that other factors may also have played an important role (high AIDS mortality and personal exposure to AIDS suffering and death).

Box L.2: The Need for a Multisectoral Response

An analysis of the pitfalls of a health sector–led response is the subject of a growing scientific literature.[a] The need for a broader response is movingly captured in a very personal statement by one of the intellectual leaders in HIV/AIDS, Daniel Low-Beer:

> I have just been in Botswana and glimpsed the future of the expensively scaled global AIDS development programme—it scared me. Here was a remote, rural community where everything was scaled up—all the acronyms—routine ARV treatment, PMCT, friendly clinics, STD treatment, VCT, even ABC. Yet the HIV infection rate remains at 25 per cent, despite spending 10 times what Uganda spent since 1991. So I asked the local health worker 'Do you talk to a patient who comes in with AIDS about AIDS, do you confront it?' He said No, a six-week counseling course had told him not to. He had a tick box on a sheet of paper for notifiable conditions that did not include AIDS. Only two out of 10 AIDS patients wanted testing and got treatment. I asked about the village chief—he does not feel qualified to talk about AIDS. I asked about the church, no one mentions it at funerals. AIDS had not gone beyond the headspace of awareness, education and counseling to a lower centre of gravity between the gut and the heart of behavior change.[b]

a. For example, Allen and Heald 2004.

b. Daniel Low-Beer, *Financial Times*, November 28, 2003.

Figure L.1: Trends in Socially Marketed Condoms and HIV Prevalence, Uganda 1990–2000

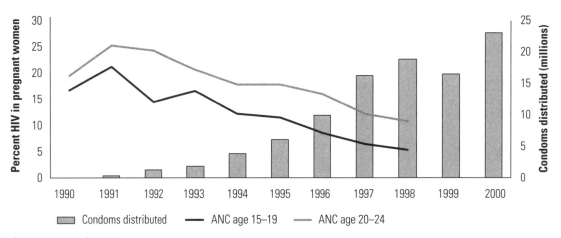

Source: Stoneburner and Low-Beer 2002.

Note: ANC = women attending ante-natal clinics.

groups even in generalized epidemics, while acknowledging a role, at later stages in the epidemic, for "additional society-wide prevention and awareness measures" and, in mature epidemics for treatment and care of people living with HIV/AIDS and programs and policies to help affected individuals and families (box 3.1). OED's document review concludes that few MAP projects are systematically addressing the highest risk behaviors.

Transmission Dynamics. All AIDS specialists agree with the need to begin by targeting individuals with the riskiest behavior. But the issue is more complex in a generalized epidemic than in a concentrated one. Some commentators argue that interventions among high-risk groups are always more cost-effective. But as the 1993 *World Development Report* notes, the cost-effectiveness of prevention declines as prevalence rates rise, and what has proven cost-effective in one setting is not necessarily transferable to others (box 3.1). Moreover, while it might always be more cost-effective in a narrow sense to target interventions to high-risk groups, the smaller the percentage of new infections for which these groups account, the less the impact targeting can have on the epidemic.[7] To understand the *specific* transmission dynamics in each context, it may be most important to first ask, What proportion of HIV infections arises from different populations and, more specifically, what proportion of infections may be attributed to high-risk groups?

Different Models. Behavioral and biological evidence and models for several African countries suggest that traditional risk groups may constitute a relatively small source of infections in highly generalized epidemics in Southern Africa; in East Africa, where mixed epidemics predominate, infections may arise roughly equally from traditional risk groups and the wider population; and in West Africa, sex workers and their clients undoubtedly play a major role in HIV transmission. In Swaziland, for example, as figure L.2 shows, behavioral data from the highly generalized epidemic suggest that most new infections arise from casual, rather than commercial, sex (there are similar data from Lesotho). These data are reinforced by other mapping and population estimation studies in numerous southern African countries, which have identified very small numbers of sex workers. They are also consistent with two recent studies estimating the contribution of high-risk sex to HIV transmission in Zimbabwe and Zambia (Cowan and others 2005; Cassalls 2005): in Zimbabwe, only 11 percent of adult male infections were likely to have arisen from commercial sex; and in Zambia, only about 2 percent of new adult HIV infections could be ascribed to traditional high-risk groups such as sex workers, truckers, and soldiers, and about 97 percent of new infections ap-

peared to have occurred in the general population among groups not considered to be at high risk (figure L.3).

Appropriate Targeting. Thus, the many major AIDS initiatives that have targeted sex workers in Swaziland, Lesotho, and elsewhere in Southern Africa have addressed behaviors that seldom happen and so are unlikely to contribute significantly to HIV transmission. Epidemiological data and models from highly generalized epidemics in southern Africa suggest that a Ugandan-type response, which focuses on sweeping changes in sexual norms and in the widespread adoption of safer sexual behaviors, may be vital. It is significant that Uganda's AIDS response during the decisive phase in the late 1980s, when incidence began to fall, emphasized behavior change in the general population and did not specifically target high-risk populations (Green 2003). There is no evidence that focusing primarily on high-risk groups has curbed generalized epidemics anywhere.[8] Indeed, evidence from Uganda, and to some extent, specific cities and regions in Ethiopia, Kenya, and Rwanda, suggests that significant and widespread reductions in the number of sexual partners among men in the general population was primarily responsible for declines in HIV prevalence and incidence. [9]

Relevance to the MAP. Since most of the population of MAP-supported countries, and most of MAP money, is in countries with generalized epidemics, the above findings are of particular rel-

---

7. OED notes that the OED evaluation neither states nor implies that it is always more cost-effective to target interventions to high-risk groups, nor does it recommend that programs focus primarily on high-risk groups in generalized epidemics.

8. OED notes that the OED report does not suggest that programs focus primarily on high-risk groups in generalized epidemics, but rather that coverage of high-risk groups be assured.

9. While OED agrees that there has been a decline in HIV incidence in Uganda, it notes that the article by Shelton and others (2004) referenced by management does not discuss any change in HIV outcomes in either Kenya or Rwanda, and only mentions evidence of a decline in HIV *prevalence* in Ethiopia. As noted in box 3.4 of the OED report, trends in HIV prevalence are not meaningful as an indicator of prevention success in mature epidemics.

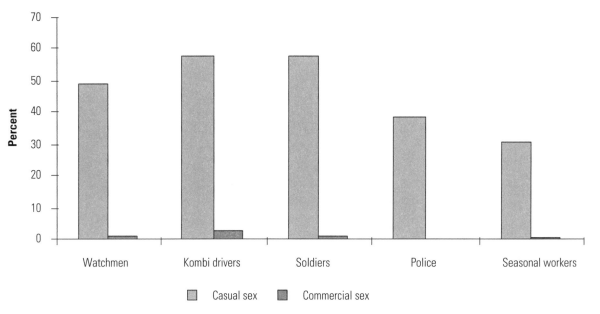

Figure L.2: Sex Partnerships in Swaziland

Source: Family Health International, Behavioral Surveillance Survey, 2002.

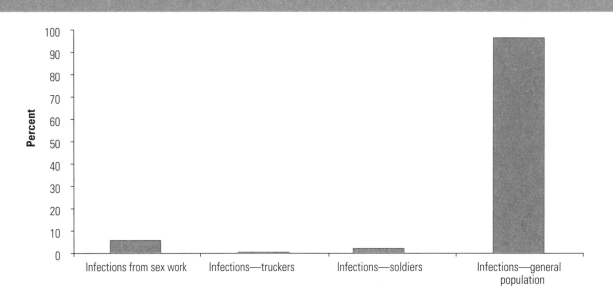

Figure L.3: New HIV Infections in Zambia, 2004

evance to the MAP.[10] Management suggests that OED's position does not reflect recent improved understanding of HIV transmission dynamics in different contexts and effective responses in generalized epidemics. While the MAP must undoubtedly sharpen its emphasis on understanding transmission patterns and adjust programming accordingly, its focus on changing sexual norms through large-scale social and community mobilization is consistent with this body of analysis and evidence—far more so than programs targeting narrowly defined risk groups.[11]

Who Can Reach High-Risk Groups? The review notes the important role played by nongovernmental organizations (NGOs) and community-based organizations (CBOs) in expanding access to prevention and care among high-risk groups in many of the completed projects, but it cautions that "NGOs may not always be better placed than government to work with high-risk groups" and cites an example from Indonesia to illustrate that some government agencies have regular contact with sex workers. However, even in Indonesia, much of the most important work among injecting drug users and prisoners, who have considerably higher HIV rates than sex workers, is done by NGOs. In Thailand government agencies have also played an important role in prevention among sex workers, but have been less effective in reaching injecting drug users. Government agencies in most countries lack the expertise needed and the channels through which to reach sex workers, injecting drug users, prisoners, and men who have sex

with men. Such groups tend to avoid (and sometimes fear) many government agencies. Moreover, it is often formal institutions such as health facilities and schools that have the most difficulty overcoming the stigma and social barriers to dealing with socially sensitive issues surrounding AIDS (Campbell 2003).

Context-Specific Strategy. The issue, therefore, is how best to reach high-risk populations and areas, in different contexts. For example, in Africa most sex workers do not work in establishments or clearly identified red-light districts, where they would be relatively easy to identify and target on a large scale. Government-led programs to promote 100 percent condom use in sex establishments, which helped to check HIV infection in Thailand and to a lesser extent in Cambodia, are much harder to introduce in Africa, India, or anywhere sex work is largely informal and widely dispersed. One way to reach widely dispersed informal and part-time sex workers, as well as highly sexually active men and most men who have sex with men and do not identify themselves as gay, is by prevention campaigns for the entire population in which it is not necessary for them to self-identify. Given the importance that high-risk behaviors play in driving the epidemic, it is essential to reach as many people as possible who engage in them. The OED review weighs whether it is better to rely on government agencies or on NGOs, but clearly both have important roles to play to ensure comprehensive coverage.

The PLACE Methodology. OED comments on the PLACE methodology, which asks people where others go to meet new sexual partners, and develops lists and maps of locations where efforts could be focused. It is an interesting new effort, but there are caveats. In Andhra Pradesh and West Africa, for example, it is unlikely that PLACE populations have rates of partner changes, STIs, and HIV near the levels confirmed among sex workers. PLACE studies in Central Asia exaggerate the importance of sexual transmission and divert crucial attention from injecting drug use. Nor is there any rigorous evidence of the effectiveness of interventions based on the PLACE

---

10. OED notes that two-thirds of the countries participating in the African MAP have levels of HIV prevalence in the general population of less than 5 percent.

11. The importance of changing social norms in the general population as a foundation for more specific and focused action is well illustrated by lessons from other health promotion and behavior change fields. For example, the smoking cessation literature underscores the importance of changing overall social norms as an essential prerequisite for more targeted behavior change campaigns. See also Cassalls 2005 and Pisani, Garnett, and Grassly 2003.

method, or reliable indications of the size of populations identified by the PLACE methodology. OED's statement about the possible efficiency of the approach is too strong for an unproven methodology.

Conclusion. Management agrees that the MAP must do more to support improved understanding of national transmission dynamics, as it is doing in current MAP operations. But the MAP principle that each AIDS response must be nationally owned and rooted in an understanding of the distinctive character of each epidemic remains wholly valid. As the OED report notes, there remains "great uncertainty and rapidly changing information about a totally new disease." Emerging research has cast into question some earlier articles of faith and research findings that inform some of the assumptions and judgments in the OED review.

E. The Role of Communities and Civil Society
The OED review contains several statements on the role of NGOs, CBOs, and other civil society groups—a role emphasized in the MAPs and other AIDS projects. For example, it states that "there is little evidence about the conditions under which NGO service delivery is more cost-effective than government services;" "Communities may not know 'what's best'…and …may select (interventions) with low efficacy… and for which they lack the technical expertise;" "there is no evidence that community-driven AIDS interventions are systematically more effective or more cost-effective than those implemented by NGOs, government, or even the private sector." The review also calls for precise delineation of the roles of various nongovernmental entities, in order to focus on those with the "expertise" to implement "activities with a direct impact on the epidemic." Management does not see in the OED review evidence that civil society activities pose "substantial risks" and it would like to raise four issues in this regard.

1. Limited Role of Formal Interventions
In management's view, adopting all of OED's conclusions would require a presupposition that there are clear, proven, tried, and tested in-

terventions to reduce HIV infection in the generalized epidemics in which many MAP projects operate. Management does not believe that the weight of evidence supports this presupposition. Uganda's national experience, the clearest positive example, underscores the central importance of political commitment, community engagement, and sweeping normative and behavioral change. In contrast, the evidence for specific interventions in generalized epidemics is remarkably weak: many first-generation Bank AIDS projects were STI projects and owed their inspiration to a single STI trial in Mwanza, Tanzania, in 1992 (Grosskurth and others 1995). A few years later, three major trials all found that STI treatment had no effect on HIV transmission (Wawer and others 1995; Kamali and others 2003). Similarly, voluntary counseling and testing is widely promoted as a prevention priority. It is obviously important as a platform for treatment, but the only rigorous trial of the approach found no evidence of any impact on STI or HIV markers, and a recent meta-analysis concluded there was little evidence that it reduces HIV transmission (Weinhardt and others 1999; Wolitski and others 1997). A recent adolescent sexual health trial in Mwanza, Tanzania, found that intensive education and health sector interventions did not reduce pregnancy, STIs, or HIV among adolescents, and it concluded that the failure to engage the wider community and in particular to change sexual norms and behaviors among older men, as Uganda had done, may have been a major reason for the trial's failure to achieve biological impact (Obasi 2003). Campbell's rigorous evaluation of why an intensive, carefully designed intervention among sex workers and their clients in South Africa had so little impact on new infections reached a similar conclusion (Campbell 2003). These findings caution against excessive reliance on formal interventions and underscore the centrality of the community engagement and normative changes championed by the MAP projects.

2. Role of Communities and Institutions
In management's view, the review does not give sufficient weight to the central role that com-

munities and their institutions play in creating the enabling environment to foster behavior change. Communities have a unique function that no other entity can perform, and that is not intervention-based. Most of the determinants of sexual behavior are deeply rooted in cultural norms, beliefs, roles, and practices that are established, maintained, enforced, and amended at the local level; they cannot be influenced by government alone. Stigma and silence, in particular, can be overcome only where civil society contributes to a deeply participatory process of social empowerment and social diffusion. In this realm of social change, knowing "what's best" is not a matter of technical expertise, but of local knowledge and local involvement. By definition, this can be supported—but not directed—from the outside. This is what some leading HIV/AIDS researchers have concluded:

> The likelihood that people will engage in health-promoting behaviors is influenced by…the extent to which they live in a supportive social environment. [Campbell 2000.]

> Individuals cannot change their behavior in a vacuum, but are heavily influenced by their social networks and group norms. Their very perceptions of risk are ordered and nurtured by the peer group and social context within which they operate. [B]ehaviors have to be supported and reinforced by the value system

of the society within which [people] function. [Ray and others 1998.]

Supportive Environment. The best-designed technical interventions cannot succeed if the social environment is unsupportive. In treatment programs around the world, for instance, it is common for a significant share of people diagnosed with HIV to decline antiretroviral treatment, even when it is free of charge. Quite literally, they would rather die than face the stigma or social isolation of admitting their HIV status. The most influential theories of behavior change recognize the centrality of community influence. For example, social diffusion theory (an outgrowth of diffusion of innovation theory in agriculture) notes that individuals are more likely to be positively influenced by the testimonies and examples of close, trusted neighbors and friends than external experts. Thus, it is vital to work with and through communities (box L.3).

MAP Model. Many of the mechanisms by which social norms evolve are unforeseeable, organic, and even ineffable. This is why the MAP has adopted a demand-driven model for civil society support. Management acknowledges that this approach poses a challenge to monitoring, and agrees that MAP projects should do a better job of supporting local assessments of impact. But embracing uncertainty is part of the unprecedented challenge of addressing AIDS, which the Bank must do. As the leading technical agencies

---

Box L.3: Experience of Uganda

In Uganda, social communication at the community level helped to pierce denial, promote personal risk perception, instill personal proximity to the epidemic, and thus change community norms and reduce HIV transmission. Activities were locally led by political, religious, and community leaders who promoted changes in community norms, not just individual actions, and created enabling and protective environments long before the concept gained currency. The involvement of faith-based communities is especially noteworthy: the founding leaders of Uganda's AIDS Commission were Catholic and Anglican bishops. All of this was accomplished without large-scale involvement by specialist agencies, and most of the country's gains preceded the growth in formal HIV services. As a result, even today, surveys reveal far more openness about AIDS in Uganda than in neighboring countries, where people are just as likely to personally know someone who has died as a result of AIDS. The cumulative effect of this cultural shift ultimately had a far greater direct impact on the epidemic than did any specific activities.

working on AIDS have recently stated, "All the components of a national response cannot be measured easily. For many components, such as reducing stigma and protecting human rights, indicators are still being developed and tested." (USAID and others 2004).

3. Competition with Government Services

The OED review states that it could find no evidence that community-driven AIDS interventions are systematically more effective or more cost-effective than those implemented by NGOs, government or the private sector. Management believes that international experience in contexts as diverse as San Francisco, Rio de Janeiro, and Rakai shows the vital role of communities in complementing government initiatives (McKusick, Horstman, and Coates 1985). No government can meet all the prevention, care, support, and treatment needs of the HIV-affected population, especially in countries with widespread epidemics. Even in middle-income countries, households and communities provide the vast majority of care and support. While a few services are so technical that they should be undertaken only by specialist institutions, many of the basics of HIV/AIDS interventions are well within the competence of even small organizations, with proper oversight.

Example. In the Poni pilot in Burkina Faso, for example, the OED report does not cite the evaluation's finding that more than 60 percent of the population of the province in all 500 villages received face-to-face HIV/AIDS education, and more than 2,000 people were trained. By contrast, the previous reproductive health project had trained fewer than 100 people in the provincial capital and was planning to reach no more than 20 villages. The use of community-based mechanisms helped expand this coverage substantially, relative to classical health projects.[12]

---

12. OED notes that the *cost-effectiveness* of the Poni pilot project has not been rigorously evaluated. An interim external evaluation remarked that even if effective at raising awareness, the project may be more costly than alternatives and less sustainable (CCISD 2001). It also questioned the wisdom of linking community mobilization to transfer of funds.

There is wide agreement that coverage is both a critical proxy for overall program implementation and a prerequisite for behavior change.

4. Community Mobilization

The OED report underestimates how much work has been done to prepare and guide community mobilization and to evaluate and document impact. The report *Rural Workers' Contribution to the Fight against AIDS: A Framework for District and Community Action* (Royal Tropical Institute and others 2001) laid the foundation for the community mobilization process, presenting objectives, costs, and lessons from 10 years of experience in Tanzania and elsewhere. It was reviewed by 400 workshop participants from 30 African countries and facilitated by a global authority on participation. Participants visited communities that had taken actions against AIDS, revised the paper, and used it as a basis for a strategy for community mobilization against AIDS. They then assessed the cost-effectiveness of community action compared to action by NGOs, government, and the private sector. Various other reports also assessed the impact of community mobilization, as did the MAP *Interim Review,* many supervision missions, and technical support missions (for example, Delion, Peters, and Bloome 2004). [13]

Results. The actions undertaken by communities and some of their concrete results are beginning to be documented. A growing number of communities are conducting situation analyses, using community maps to identify where the epidemic is spreading and reflect on factors within the community's control. Such actions have closed brothels and bars near secondary schools in Benin, changed the village laws to punish men who force girls to have sex in Tan-

---

13. OED notes that Working Paper #79, referenced above (Delion, Peters, and Bloome 2004), also states that "While communities can measure some progress, such as the number of people tested, ... and the number of people cared for, there is a need to develop instruments to compare impact of local response between different communities and regions, including a cost-effectiveness analysis"(p. 16).

zania, and organized "food baskets" each week at the market to support chronically ill patients. As one community member reported:

> Before [the MAP] nobody was really speaking of AIDS, outside information meetings. Now everybody talks about it, inside families, schools, shops, etc. Before, nobody dared to be tested, now many people were tested, testing is the normal thing to do. Before, nobody knew exactly what to do in case of AIDS, now many families have People Living with AIDS, there are many associations of PLWHA.

Measuring Results. Simple instruments and indicators are being used to measure results, and M&E tools have been developed to assess results and insert lessons systematically into operations. For example, "report cards" are being used in Benin and Cameroon. As a result of these assessments, many communities have made significant changes in their community action plans.

F. Monitoring and Evaluation

The OED evaluation states that "notwithstanding the piloting of innovative monitoring approaches in several countries, the overall record of the Africa MAP in implementing strong M&E to improve 'learning by doing' is weak, similar to the M&E record of the portfolio of completed HIV/AIDS projects." Management agrees that MAP M&E needs improving, but wishes to highlight two additional points (a) the review does not adequately acknowledge the ongoing intensive efforts to improve M&E that are beginning to achieve considerable improvement on the ground, although this is a difficult and slow process; and (b) it cannot be assumed that learning by doing does not occur in the absence of formal M&E, as the MAP was intended to provide small amounts of funding to huge numbers of actors with latent capacity, to enable them to learn by doing while executing their own small projects.

MAP Approach. Given the Bank's experience with weak M&E in projects in Africa, including in previous AIDS and health projects, the Bank decided within the first year of MAP implementation to assist TTLs and country counterparts by (a) developing an operational guide for program M&E (drafted in 2001, widely reviewed by stakeholders and technical partners, and published in 2002); and (b) creating special M&E country assistance capacity in the World Bank. One of the first things the Global HIV-AIDS Program did was create the Global AIDS Monitoring and Evaluation Team (GAMET). By early 2003 GAMET had three full-time staff paid by the Bank and 15 M&E consultants in the field,[14] helping countries with and without MAP projects to establish and maintain program M&E systems. By April 2005, GAMET's consultants had made 115 M&E support visits to 33 countries, about 75 percent of which were in Africa. While this effort has taken some time to show results on the ground, the latest assessment of M&E frameworks in MAP countries (attached as Annex A) shows a much more promising picture than the OED report.

Harmonization and M&E. Having one program M&E system for a country supported by all donors, rather than many separate systems, is one of the "Three Ones," a major harmonization effort led by UNAIDS that the Bank helped to launch in September 2003, and that was endorsed by all the major financial donors in Washington in April 2004.[15] The Bank has reinforced this approach by toughening its MAP access criteria with regard to M&E for second-generation MAP projects.

---

14. GAMET had its own budget line item in the 2004/05 UBW of $2.1 million that will increase to $3.66 million in 2006/07.

15. On 25 April 2004, UNAIDS, the United Kingdom and the United States co-hosted a high-level meeting at which key donors reaffirmed their commitment to strengthening national AIDS responses led by the affected countries themselves. They endorsed the **"Three Ones" principles**, to achieve the most effective and efficient use of resources, and to ensure rapid action and results-based management: **One** agreed HIV/AIDS Action Framework that provides the basis for coordinating the work of all partners. **One** National AIDS Coordinating Authority, with a broad-based multisectoral mandate. **One** agreed country-level Monitoring and Evaluation System. Accessible at www.unaids.org.

Conclusions. The lessons learned are that getting M&E established on the ground takes multifaceted special efforts (which the Bank has supported), and that it takes time. And it takes even more time to ensure that the monitoring turns into evaluation that affects program decision making. It also requires incentives to ensure that M&E is considered to be as indispensable as, for example, sound financial management and reporting. This is a long-standing issue in Bank-supported projects, noted in numerous other OED evaluations, and it will be interesting to see what future OED evaluations of completed MAP projects find, and what broad lessons can be drawn from GAMET efforts. Management would welcome more specific suggestions from OED on how to improve M&E.

OED Recommendations

Management agrees with the principles and broad goals underlying most of OED's recommendations, and indeed is already implementing some of them. For example, the Global HIV/AIDS Program of Action that is now being prepared singles out greater support for country strategic planning and prioritizing, for implementation, and for monitoring and evaluation as priority areas. However, management notes problems with some of OED's recommendations (a) some are relatively general and sweeping; (b) they relate to challenges that the Bank has long been grappling with that are intrinsically very hard to fix; (c) they require concerted action with other donors, and cannot be addressed by the Bank alone; and (d) they are not amenable to quick, top-down fixes, but require the long, slow process of building capacity in countries. The attached Management Action Record provides detailed responses to OED's recommendations.

Annex: GAMET Monitoring and Evaluation Status, by Country, April 2005

Country	Classification	M&E framework — Written doc presented to stakeholders: Conceptual plan mentioned	M&E plan — Operational plan with Gannt Chart with responsibilities mentioned	M&E costed plan/budget	M&E NAC staff — Central NAC staff	M&E implementation staff — Decentralized staff	M&E in country TA — Enlisted local TA through TWG or consultant	TWG/M&E working group	Database active — National Indicator Dataset: output, outcome	Surveillance—biological captured in ANC — Already processed data	Surveillance—behavioral — DHS, BSS, MICS, LQAS	Surveillance—health facility — Anything to do with quality	Program activity monitoring — Grantees reporting in a structured format on outputs	Evaluation research — Targeted assessments to improve programming	Evidence decision making — Using data for decision making
Angola	3														
Benin															
Burkina Faso	2	YES	YES	YES	YES	INT	INT	YES	NO	YES	INT	YES	YES	YES	NO
Burundi	1	YES	YES	YES	YES	YES	NO	NO	YES	YES	YES	NO	YES	NO	YES
Cape Verde	1	YES	YES	YES	YES	YES	YES	YES	YES	YES	YES	YES	YES	YES	YES
CAR	3	YES	NO	NO	YES	N/D	N/D	YES	NO	YES	N/D	N/D	NO	NO	NO
Congo Brazaville	2	YES	YES	YES	YES	NO	YES	YES	NO	NO	NO	NO	NO	NO	NO
Congo, D. R.	3	YES	YES	YES	YES	NO	YES	YES	NO	NO	NO	NO	NO	NO	NO
Côte d'Ivoire	2	YES	YES	YES	YES	NO	INT	YES	NO	YES	YES	INT	INT	INT	NO
Ethiopia	1/2	YES	YES	YES	YES	YES	NA	YES	INT	YES	YES	YES	INT	YES	INT
Gambia	2	YES	YES	YES	YES	NO	NO	YES	YES	YES	YES	NO	YES	NO	NO
Guinea Buisau	3	NO	NO	NO	NO	NO	NO	NO	NO	NO	NO	NO	NO	NO	
Guinea	2	YES	YES	YES	YES	INT	YES	YES	INT	YES	YES	YES	YES	NO	NO
Kenya	2	YES	YES	NO	YES	NO	YES	YES	NO	YES	YES	YES	YES	NO	NO
Lesotho	3	NO	NO	NO	NO	YES	YES	YES	NO	NO	YES	NO	NO	NO	NO
Madagascar	1	YES	YES	YES	YES	YES	YES	YES	YES	YES	YES	N/D	YES	YES	YES
Malawi	1	YES	YES	YES	YES	INT	YES	YES	YES	YES	YES	YES	YES	NO	YES
Mali	3	INT	NO	NO	YES	INT	YES	YES	NO	YES	YES	INT	NO	N/D	NO
Mauritania	2	YES	NO	NO	YES	NO	NO	YES	NO	YES	YES	N/D	N/D	N/D	N/D
Mozambique	2	YES	NO	NO	YES	INT	INT	YES	INT	YES	YES	NO	INT	NO	NO
Namibia	1	YES	YES	YES	YES	YES	YES	YES	YES	YES	YES	YES	INT	YES	NO

(Continued on the following page.)

Annex: GAMET Monitoring and Evaluation Status, by Country, April 2005 (continued)

Country	Classification	M&E framework: Written doc presented to stakeholders: Conceptual plan	M&E plan: Operational plan with Gannt Chart with responsibilities mentioned	M&E costed plan/budget	M&E NAC staff: Central NAC staff	M&E implementation staff: Decentralized staff	M&E in country TA: Enlisted local TA through TWG or consultant	TWG/M&E working group	Database active	National Indicator Dataset: output, outcome	Surveillance—biological captured in ANC: Already processed data	Surveillance—behavioral: DHS, BSS, MICS, LQAS	Surveillance—health facility: Anything to do with quality	Program activity monitoring: Grantees reporting in a structured format on outputs	Evaluation research: Targeted assessments to improve programming	Evidence decision making: Using data for decision making
Niger	3	INT	INT	NO	YES	YES	YES		NO	NO	INT	YES	N/D	NO	NO	NO
Nigeria	2	YES	YES	NO	YES	YES	YES	YES	NO	NO	YES	YES	INT	NO	YES	NO
Rwanda	1	YES	YES	YES	YES	INT	YES	YES	YES	YES	YES	YES	NO	YES	YES	YES
Senegal	1	YES	YES	YES	YES	YES	YES	YES	YES	YES	YES	YES	YES	YES	YES	NO
Sierra Leone	2	YES	YES	YES	YES	NO	NO	YES	YES	YES	YES	YES	NO	YES	NO	NO
Swaziland	2	INT	INT	NO	YES	INT	INT	YES	NO	NO	YES	YES	NO	INT	NO	NO
Tanzania	2	YES	YES	YES	YES	NO	INT	YES	NO	NO	YES	INT	NO	INT	NO	NO
Togo	3	NO	NO	NO	NO	NO	NO	NO	NO	NO	NO	NO	NO	NO	NO	NO
Uganda	2	YES	YES	YES	YES	YES	YES	YES	NO	NO	YES	YES	YES	INT	YES	YES
Zambia	3	YES	YES	YES	YES	YES	YES	YES	NO	NO	YES	YES	YES	INT	NO	NO
ARCAN	2	YES	YES	YES	YES	YES	N/A	N/A	NO	N/A	N/A	N/A	N/A	INT	NO	NO
GLIA	2	YES	YES	YES	NO	YES	YES	N/A	NO	YES	YES	Pilot / Done	NO	INT	NO	NO
IGAD	1	NA	NA	NA	NA	NA	NA	NA	NA	NA	N/A	NA	NA	NA	NA	NO
LACP	2	YES	N/D	INT	YES	YES	YES	N/A	N/D	N/A	N/A	N/A	N/A	N/A	N/A	N/A
TAP	3	YES	NO	N/A	N/A	N/A	N/A	N/A	N/A	N/A	N/A	N/A	N/A	YES	YES	N/D

1 = Successfully attained overall: framewrk doc., database populated, active operating program monitoring.

2 = Partially attained:national framewk adopted, database defined and partial developed, indicators agreed, system not operating properly.

3 = Not attained.

INT = in transition, N/D = no current data, ARCAN = Africa Regional Capacity Building Network Project, GLIA = Great Lakes Initiative on HIV/AIDS, IGAD = Inter-Governmental Authority on Development, LACP = Pan-Caribbean Partnership Against AIDS, TAP = Regional HIV/AIDS Treatment Acceleration Project.

Management Action Record

OED Recommendation	Management Response

For All Bank HIV/AIDS Assistance

1. **Help governments to be more strategic and selective, to prioritize, using limited capacity to implement activities that will have the greatest impact on the epidemic.** In particular, the Bank should ensure that public goods and prevention among those most likely to spread HIV are adequately supported.

   a) The Bank should help governments prioritize and sequence the implementation of activities likely to have the greatest impact and that enlist sectors and implementers according to their comparative advantages to work collaboratively toward specific epidemiological outcomes. Costs, cost-effectiveness, impact, equity, human resource requirements and sustainability of alternative AIDS prevention, treatment, and mitigation strategies should be assessed.

   b) Projects in countries at all stages of the epidemic should be systematically mapping high-risk behavior; monitoring HIV and behavior in populations most likely to contract and spread HIV; assuring high coverage of information and preventive interventions to them; and taking action to reduce stigma and legal barriers to prevention and care among marginalized groups. A country-by-country assessment of the extent to which this is currently taking place and an action plan to improve performance would satisfy this recommendation.

   c) In high-prevalence countries the Bank should work with government and other partners to assess the costs, benefits, affordability, sustainability, and equity implications of different types of treatment for AIDS patients, on the basis of which to make rational decisions in the allocation of health resources. This should be a priority even if Bank resources will not be financing this care. A population-based HIV prevalence survey is critical to understanding the scope and distribution of demand for treatment and for designing efficient treatment and care strategies in hard-hit, low-income countries.

1. Management believes that action on this recommendation must be and will be taken jointly with partners. Effective impact requires harmonized coordinated efforts with major partners in our support for country HIV/AIDS programs. Intensive efforts to help governments to be more strategic and selective, to build capacity to collect and analyze data on behaviors and HIV status in key groups, and to prioritize on the basis of epidemiological and programmatic data are key priorities in the draft Bank Global HIV/AIDS Program of Action (GHAPA) and in collaborative work with partners, including the Global Task Team (GTT), and reflect the "Three Ones" principle. The final report of the GTT includes a set of specific actions (and accountabilities) to help countries develop prioritized "AIDS action plans that drive implementation, improve oversight, emphasize results...and are rooted in broader development plans and planning processes." The Global HIV/AIDS Program (GHAP) and UNAIDS will work with other major partners to set up a Strategic Planning Facility by September 2005, to assist countries to develop strategic prioritized national plans. Improved behavioral monitoring requires concerted international efforts to which the Bank is contributing significantly. Improved bio-behavioral surveillance is a core part of a good national M&E system and, with partners, the Bank is helping countries to strengthen bio-behavioral surveillance to enable them to identify and effectively address proven drivers of HIV transmission. (This is the core work program of GHAP's GAMET team. Country-by-country status is summarized in Annex A.) Analytic work to support decisions on resource allocation has been done in Africa as part of several national AIDS investments and two regional projects (the African Regional Capacity Building Network for HIV/AIDS Prevention, Care, and Treatment and the Treatment Action Program). In Asia, analysis has been done in India and Thailand and is planned in China. The GHAPA includes plans to support further work in selected additional countries. Management disagrees with the statement on the critical role of a population-based HIV prevalence survey: (i) HIV prevalence data give no information on the state of individuals' infection and eligibility for treatment; (ii) these data would measure potential demand, not effective demand, which is mediated by access and cost, clinical eligi-

OED Recommendation	Management Response
	bility, physiological tolerance of the drugs, commitment to adhere to the regimen. Specifically, internal and international processes to monitor progress on national strategies already exist within the framework of GHAPA, the GTT, and UNAIDS governance. The Bank agrees to continue to use these processes and to ensure that the relevant reports of these agencies are made available on a timely basis to Executive Directors during the upcoming three years.
2. **Strengthen national institutions for managing and implementing the long-run response, particularly in the health sector.** a) Bank assistance should distinguish between institutions and strategies for raising political commitment (mobilization) and those for efficient and effective implementation of activities on the ground. Both objectives have been shown to be critical, but experience shows that a single institution may not be able to satisfy both objectives efficiently. b) Bank HIV/AIDS assistance needs to consider strategies for building, broadening, and sustaining political commitment in specific settings. c) Greater use of institutional and political analysis should be made to enhance the local relevance and effectiveness of national and sub-national institutions (including multisectoral institutions and those in the MOH) in relation to local capacity, political realities, and the stage of the epidemic.	2. Strengthening institutions is a long-term and challenging task with which the Bank and many development partners are grappling. Bank efforts to strengthen the health sector are much broader than the Bank's AIDS work, but within HIV/AIDS projects, it is already standard practice to include components to strengthen health sector service delivery capacity (unless a complementary HNP project is already doing this), and to build the capacity of the National HIV/AIDS authority. Management disagrees that effective implementation and mobilization are necessarily dichotomous. In fact, good implementation is often among the most effective means of achieving mobilization. For example, when communities are given funding to organize themselves to take care of AIDS orphans, this is both mobilization and implementing an "activity on the ground." Broadening political commitment has been a major objective in many countries and specifically of the first phase of the MAP Program. OED notes this as a major achievement of the MAP (and has also been important outside of Africa). Likewise institutional and political analysis is already being done in many Regions and in MAPs. Support for strengthening national institutions is a harmonized partnership activity. Management will use the UNAIDS governance process to report on progress on strengthening institutions and will provide the relevant documentation to Executive Directors on a timely basis during the next three years.
3. **Improve the local evidence base for decision-making.** The Bank should create incentives to ensure that the design and management of country-level AIDS assistance is guided by relevant and timely locally-produced evidence and rigorous analytic work. a) The Bank should launch immediately – within the next 6 months—an in-depth inventory and assessment of the	3. Improved national Monitoring and Evaluation (M&E) to inform decisions is a key goal of the "Three Ones" (the Bank agreed in this context with other donors and clients that there will be only one country-level M&E system for all donors) and a centerpiece of GHAP's work, in the context of its partnership in UNAIDS and with other major players. GHAP's GAMET team provides extensive field support for developing M&E ca-

OED Recommendation	Management Response
extent of implementation of all planned M&E activities and the availability and comparability over time of input, output, and outcome data relevant to assessing program effectiveness, in all countries with freestanding HIV/AIDS projects and significant components. This assessment should serve as the basis for a time-bound *action plan* to improve the incentives for monitoring and evaluation in the Bank's HIV/AIDS assistance, with explicit targets in terms of improved monitoring and periodic use of evaluation to improve program effectiveness. b) Ongoing projects and those in the planning stage should pre-identify a program of commissioned research and analytic work on issues of priority to the AIDS program. c) Pilot programmatic interventions should be independently evaluated before they are replicated or expanded; those that have been scaled up without the benefit of evaluation should be evaluated within the next 12 months as a condition for continued finance. d) The Bank should become an "AIDS knowledge bank" by: maintaining a central database of Bank-sponsored or managed analytic work on AIDS — including evaluations — that is complete, up to date, and accessible to staff, clients, researchers and the public; developing a mechanism for the routine dissemination of findings from the Bank's analytic work on AIDS to internal and external audiences; translating key products; and investing in priority cross-national analytic work and research that is an international public good.	pacity and systems, and work is underway in most regions and countries. Annex A summarizes the status of M&E system development in highly affected countries. MAP repeater projects already include stringent requirements on M&E. Management believes that this level of intensive support for M&E is unprecedented in a Bank portfolio (notable given widespread difficulties with M&E in Bank projects) and expects that it will show results, but this will take time. With regard to research and analysis, more is needed, but not all can or should be pre-identified.[1] It is critically important to assist countries to identify and address their own research priorities. The bigger challenge is to ensure that planned research and analytic work is in fact carried out. Additional research and analysis of issues of priority are included in the draft GHAPA. With regard to independent evaluation of pilot interventions, there are major cost, cost-benefit, and feasibility concerns. Management agrees that large-scale interventions ought to be evaluated, but would not make this a pre-condition of financing of high-priority operations. Management agrees to continue its extensive efforts, in close partnership with key donors, to assist countries to strengthen M&E. With regard to the Bank's knowledge base, a senior Knowledge Officer has been recruited by GHAP. The draft GHAPA outlines what management agrees to do in knowledge development and GHAP's FY06 work program includes this knowledge development program. Management will report on progress with regard to M&E in client countries and in its knowledge base efforts in the next update of the GHAPA.

For the Africa MAP

4. The Africa MAP is designed to mitigate risks concerning political commitment and implementation, but there are few structural mechanisms to assure efficiency or efficacy. These risks can be reduced through the following actions (in addition to the recommendations above, which apply to all projects):

   a) **A thorough technical and economic assessment of national strategic plans and government AIDS policy and an inventory of the activities of other donors should become a standard part of MAP project preparation.** When national strategic plans are found inadequate as a basis for prioritization and sequencing of activities, the Bank should engage government in strategic discussions, informed by analytic work, to identify programmatic priorities that reflect the stage

Consistent with the recommendations of the MAP *Interim Review* of 2004, assessments of national HIV/AIDS plans, and taking account of other donor support, are already part of project preparation and regular and joint reviews of MAP projects. The GHAP Program of Action and actions detailed in the GTT Final Report give high priority to strengthening country strategic planning and better harmonizing, aligning and coordinating among donors, and list specific actions (with accountability) and have established a process and timetable for monitoring progress. As noted above, management does not agree with a stark distinction between political mobilization and implementation. While more evaluation of results is needed, management does not

---

1. OED notes that its recommendation is not suggesting that all research be pre-identified or that the countries not be involved in the pre-identification process.

OED Recommendation	Management Response
of the epidemic, capacity constraints, and the local context. Follow-on projects should be structured to ensure that those priority activities, including public goods and prevention among those with high-risk behavior, are pursued. b) **The objectives of the engagement of different segments of civil society need to be clearly articulated, to distinguish between the actors enlisted for purposes of political mobilization and those with the expertise and comparative advantage to implement activities with a direct impact on the epidemic.** The results of ongoing CDD-type AIDS activities should be rigorously evaluated with respect to their effectiveness in changing behavior or mitigating impact before they are renewed, in line with the recommendations of the OED CD evaluation. The complementarity or competition between CDD AIDS activities and the decentralized public sector response should be assessed as part of this effort. c) **The Bank should focus support for implementation on the sectors whose activities have the greatest potential impact on the epidemic and with some comparative advantage in implementation—such as the Ministry of Health, the military, education, transport, and others, depending on the country – and ensure that the resources to supervise their activities are forthcoming.** The objectives of multisectoral action against AIDS –particularly in terms of political mobilization and implementation—also need clearer articulation; the key actors with respect to each of these two objectives need to be more clearly defined. A country-by-country assessment of the relation between MAP support for line ministries and the AIDS activities in non-health sector assistance and their relative effectiveness should be conducted, with an eye on improving their complementarity and using supervision resources efficiently.	agree with the specific sub-recommendation; "rigorous evaluation" of all the many thousands of CDD-type activities, which is not feasible or affordable. Following early experience with MAP projects and the MAP Interim Review of 2004, a shift has already been made to focus on key sectors with potential for greatest impact on the epidemic (also reflected in the GHAPA). Education is a key example, and is the focus of ongoing special efforts by HDNED and GHAP. Under the MAP, management agrees to a rigorous analysis of national strategic plans—taking into account other donor support—and, as noted above, is already acting on this. It has also moved to support key sectors. Management will report on progress in the context of the MAP update.

APPENDIX M: CHAIRMAN'S SUMMARY: COMMITTEE ON DEVELOPMENT EFFECTIVENESS (CODE)

On July 20, 2005 the Committee on Development Effectiveness (CODE) discussed the report *Committing to Results: Improving the Effectiveness of HIV/AIDS Assistance - An OED Evaluation of the World Bank's Assistance for HIV/AIDS Control*, the draft Management Response, and the *Statement of the External Advisory Panel*.

Background. The report was the first comprehensive OED evaluation of the Bank's country-level HIV/AIDS assistance. The objective of the evaluation was to assess the development effectiveness of the Bank's country-level assistance for HIV/AIDS, and to identify lessons to improve ongoing and future initiatives. The evaluation covered the overall HIV/AIDS assistance to a country, including policy dialogue, analytical work, and lending. As of June 2004, the Bank had committed approximately US$2.5 billion in credits, grants and loans to 62 countries for 106 projects. The report also included an assessment of the assumptions, design, and risks of the ongoing Africa Multi-Country AIDS Program (MAP). MAP projects account for two-thirds of active projects and half of ongoing HIV/AIDS commitments; represent a departure from traditional investment projects that make up the completed HIV/AIDS project portfolio and active portfolio in other regions; focus on the most affected continent and signal the Bank's longer-term commitment. The evaluation drew on other evaluation reports and was complemented by the recent OED evaluation on Global Programs.

OED Comments and Recommendations. OED highlighted two points: (i) the Bank deserved credit for helping to strengthen commitment to fighting HIV/AIDS, to induce governments to act earlier or in a more focused and cost-effective way, to raise political commitment, and to encourage governments to enlist the NGOs support in public HIV/AIDS programs, and needed to continue its support to countries; and (ii) the Bank needed to go one step further to "commit to results" by helping countries use resources more effectively and efficiently to improve outcomes of HIV/AIDS assistance, with enhanced monitoring and evaluation (M&E). It clarified several aspects of the report including: (i) OED assessed the MAP design based on evidence of completed projects and other sources, but did not evaluate the effectiveness of any MAP projects, none of which had yet closed; (ii) the report supported a prioritized multisectoral response, and did not advocate that Ministries of Health should control national investment in HIV/AIDS assistance in all countries; (iii) the report cited community involvement as a major achievement, but also pointed out the need to strengthen M&E of its effectiveness in producing outcomes and to better articulate the objectives of the engagement of different segments of civil society; and (iv) OED recommendations concerning HIV prevention among individuals with highest risk behavior were intended as an addition to, rather than replacement for, assistance to the broader population in a generalized epidemic. OED also emphasized that the report pertained to all Bank HIV/AIDS assistance, and not just to Africa. Recommendations for all Bank assistance included: (i) help governments to be more strategic and selective, to prioritize and implement activities that will have the greatest impact, including ensuring that public goods and prevention among those most likely to spread HIV are supported; (ii) strengthen national institutions for managing and implementing the long-run response, particularly in the health sector; and (iii) improve the local evidence base for decision making by creating incentives for evaluation of program activities and rigorous analytic work.

Management Response. Management welcomed the report, and agreed with many points raised, as well as with the thrust of the recommendations. It commented that many issues raised were being addressed including the specific ones for the MAP, which had been internally reviewed. It supported the OED emphasis on the need to further enhance efficiency and effectiveness of Bank support to improve outcomes, while stressing that the Bank was not the only institution providing assistance in this area. Management acknowledged the limitations identified by OED, which also emerged in its internal review such as need to help improve national strategic planning and prioritization of assistance, and to enhance M&E. It also noted that improvements in M&E required the concerted action of national and international partners, and not just of the Bank. Two areas where views differed were: role of communities and civil society, where Management considered that they had an integral and complementary role to government; and focus on health sector versus a multi-sector approach where Management emphasized need to strengthen the sector and simultaneously work with other sectors.

Overall Conclusions and Next Steps. The Committee welcomed the evaluation report and there was a rich discussion on the challenges of addressing HIV/AIDS. Members reaffirmed the Bank's role, together with other development partners, in responding to the complex and pressing issue of HIV/AIDS that threatens to undermine progress in development. Given the challenging nature of HIV/AIDS, members stressed the need for bold, innovative, and flexible responses, and also reconfirmed the need for a multisectoral approach. Some members found the OED evaluation useful for a fundamental and substantial debate in clarifying the Bank's role. There was broad agreement with many recommendations, except for those related to community-based responses and high-

risk groups, as elaborated below. Several members had questions about the evaluation methodology and concerns about its tone, and commented on aspects that OED could have expanded upon or incorporated more. Members supported the thrust of the draft Management Response (MR) and recognized the recent efforts to strengthen Bank assistance, particularly of Africa Multi-Country AIDS Program (MAP) through several self-critical internal reviews including the 2004 MAP Interim Review.

Speakers' comments focused on the following areas: country ownership and commitment; multisectoral approach and role of the Ministry of Health; targeting of assistance; community development approach and involvement of civil society; M&E; and alignment with global initiatives and partnerships. The Committee generally supported the External Advisory Panel's proposal for a strategy to guide overall Bank assistance to address HIV/AIDS.

The following main issues were raised during the meeting:

Importance of Country Ownership and Commitment. The importance of broad national commitment including of governments and local communities, and country specific strategies for effective HIV/AIDS intervention, including for MAP, were emphasized. There was agreement with the OED recommendation that the Bank should help governments to develop strong and sufficiently prioritized nationally owned strategies, which should serve as basis of coordinated donor support. Questions were raised about how the Bank supports integration of HIV/AIDS issues into development planning, poverty reduction strategies, and budget allocation processes and also mainstreams these into the country assistance strategy. Others stressed the need to prioritize capacity building of governments, local communities, and NGOs to tackle the disease.

Support for Multisectoral Approach. Members and speakers stressed that HIV/AIDS required an integrated and multisectoral response. Several members commented on the complexity of a multisectoral approach that necessitated the highest level of political commitment, strong leadership, and clarity of roles of various stakeholders on the ground, including that of the Ministries of Health (MoHs). While some speakers agreed with the OED report that MoHs had a central role and the health sector needed to be generally strengthened, others shared Management's views and objected to the report's implicit suggestion that MoHs should control national investment in HIV/AIDS or that assistance to HIV/AIDS has been made at the expense of broader health sector development. Other speakers also emphasized the importance of broad partnerships at the country level, and implementation roles defined by country specific context. A member felt the report had been misinterpreted and understood that in some instances MOHs could play a more important role to coordinate the implementation of multisectoral activities by various stakeholders. Some speakers also commented on the potential benefits of regional approaches and gave examples, including the Lagos-Abidjan project. Supporting the multisectoral approach, OED found that such an approach based in the MoHs had been successful in enlisting key ministries when there was strong political commitment. It also stated that implementation arrangements should be country specific and reiterated the report recommendation for the Bank to focus on implementation of activities in sectors that have a greatest potential impact on the epidemic and with some comparative advantage. Management stated the global development community considered HIV/AIDS a broad development issue that cannot be tackled by focusing on one sector, while strengthening health sector remains important.

Targeting Assistance. Some speakers expressed concerns about the OED recommendation suggesting high risk groups and high risk behaviors be targeted. They shared Management's views about the complexity of transmission and risk, while others noted the disagreement between OED and Management on the main cause of infections. One member said that focus of assistance should be on women and youth. Members stressed the need for more careful and nuanced

assessment, including the cultural and social dynamics, for better understanding and to support nationally owned strategy. OED said it was not proposing that Bank assistance only target high risk groups and behaviors at the expense of other types of support in generalized epidemics. It stated that evidence collected suggested that prevention information and services were not reaching high risk groups, which should be addressed.

Role of Communities. Several speakers disagreed with the recommendations concerning community-based responses and supported Management's response; many speakers viewed that community-based responses and involvement of civil society were important. A member reserved judgment about whether the findings of the evaluation on community development (CD) were applicable to HIV/AIDS or whether a special case could be made for role of local communities in effectively addressing HIV/AIDS. OED explained that the HIV/AIDS report supported involvement of communities and civil society, and recognized Bank efforts to encourage governments to work with NGOs and communities to implement national HIV/AIDS responses. At the same time, OED reiterated that M&E of community level activities had been weak and little was known so far about their effectiveness. Thus, it recommended that objectives of engagement with different segments of civil society be articulated and results of HIV/AIDS assistance following a CD approach be more rigorously evaluated to understand their contribution to outcomes.

Stepping up Research and M&E. The Committee supported the recommendations concerning M&E and view that the Bank should support local capacity building in this area, working with other partners. Specific comments concerning the research base and M&E included: importance of balancing efforts with the emergency nature of HIV/AIDS and need for quick action and immediate results; assessment of underlying factors should consider gender dimensions; challenge of developing clear criteria and outcome indicators, and need to improve data; need for broad partnerships; and importance of M&E and communication of research work and Bank experience for learning. Questions were raised about the experience of intensified M&E for MAP projects and the role of the Global AIDS Monitoring and Evaluation Team (GAMET) in addressing the weaknesses in M&E. Management elaborated on the extraordinary steps taken by the Bank to strengthen M&E and through GAMET, working with partners to develop manuals and systems to assess countries' progress, and mobilizing global experts to provide country level support. OED acknowledged these efforts but noted that it was too early to know their effectiveness and they will be evaluated in the future in the context of individual country operations.

Need to Link with Other Global Initiatives. Many speakers commented that the Bank was not operating alone, and the OED report and MR should be linked to the broader global initiatives and partnerships, and harmonization and alignment efforts. They said that Bank assistance needed to be consistent with the Bank's commitments to agreed and prioritized recommendations of the UNAIDS led Global Task Force Team (GTT); and the Global Fund to Fight AIDS, Tuberculosis and Malaria (GFATM) and "Three Ones" principle.[1] Management emphasized that the Bank's HIV/AIDS assistance represented only a portion of global assistance for HIV/AIDS and commented on its coordinated and complementary support with respect to the recommendations of the GTT, GFATM, and the "Three-Ones." It stressed the centrality of the

GTT and coordinated global efforts to translate the "Three-Ones" vision into concrete action. OED clarified that this evaluation focused on the Bank's country–level assistance and was complemented by the recent OED evaluation on Bank support for global programs, (including in health), which addressed coordination issues with global partners. It noted that this report's findings and recommendations were consistent with those made for global programs.

Welcome a Strategy to Guide Bank's HIV/AIDS Assistance. Some speakers supported the External Advisory Panel's proposal for a Bank strategy to guide its HIV/AIDS assistance.

Comments Related to the OED Evaluation. Some speakers commented on the evaluation methodology and also commented that the OED evaluation could have given more recognition to the recent actions to improve Bank assistance, in particular of MAP; considered collaboration with other stakeholders including role of private sector, and gender dynamics; and provided more concrete operational recommendation. Responding to some members' questions on how the Bank's self-critical internal evaluations, including the 2004 MAP Interim Review had been considered, OED responded that it had incorporated their findings into its evaluation. On the issue of how OED formulated the recommendations, the Acting Director-General of Operations Evaluation commented that they were prepared in a way to allow Management flexibility in responding to the issues raised.

Chander Mohan Vasudev, Chairman

ENDNOTES

Chapter 1

1. Includes disbursements to date of all free-standing AIDS projects, active and closed, and the disbursement of closed AIDS components or activities exceeding US$1 million. Of these projects, figure 1.1 shows those for which AIDS was at least 10 percent of the Bank's total commitment.

2. The World Bank began lending for population programs in the early 1970s. It was not until the 1980 *Health Sector Policy Paper* that the Bank committed to direct lending to the health sector (Johnston and Stout 1999).

3. Between 1950 and 1990, life expectancy in developing countries rose from 40 to 63 years, in large part because of economic progress and investments in social services (World Bank 1997a). As of 1996, Zimbabwe's life expectancy was 22 years lower than it would have been in the absence of AIDS, and South Africa's life expectancy was 7 years lower. For more evidence on the impact of AIDS on mortality in Africa, see articles by Boerma and others 1998, Timaeus 1998, and Stover and Way 1998.

4. Indeed, virtually every society has initially reacted to indications of the spread of HIV by claiming that an infection spread in these ways could never take off indigenously (Mann and others 1992, Mann and Tarantola 1996, World Bank 1997a). Once convinced that there is a threat, the first official reaction more often than not has been to take discriminatory legal action rather than to adopt proven public health interventions that stress education and behavior modification. For a compendium of specific examples of denial, lack of political commitment, and repressive measures undertaken by countries at all levels of development, see Garrett (1994).

5. The OED review of UNAIDS (Lele and others 2004) relied extensively on analysis from the *Five-Year Evaluation of UNAIDS* (Poate and others 2002).

6. OED has an ongoing evaluation of the Bank's assistance to primary education. Evaluations have been completed on social funds (Carvalho and others 2002), social development (Parker 2004), and gender (Gopal and others 2001), for example.

7. The only previous review of the effectiveness of the Bank's HIV/AIDS assistance was a desk review by Dayton (1998) covering projects completed through mid-1997. At that time, only 8 projects had been completed, of which only one was free standing (Zaïre AIDS), and only one had been rated by OED.

Chapter 2

1. The full amount of an approved loan, credit, or grant in figure 2.1 is attributed to the year of project approval, but the resources for each of these commitments were disbursed over the life of the project. A list of AIDS projects and components over US$1 million is in Appendix C.

2. Figure 2.2 is based on the inventory of analytic work summarized in Appendix E and posted on the evaluation Web site(<www.worldbank.org/oed/aids>). Because of the irregular reporting conventions and recall biases that can be expected, the inventory is an indicative rather than definitive list of the Bank's analytic work (see Chapter 3).

3. It was not until 1994 that the median time between infection and AIDS was found to be on the order of 10 years (Hessol and others 1994). When *AIDS in the World II* was published in 1996, the prevailing view was that the incubation period in developing countries was much shorter (Mulder 1996). It was later found that this was not the case. Characteristics such as the incubation period and infectiousness are key in modeling the epidemiological spread of HIV and its impact on mortality, from which estimates of impact are derived.

4. Improved treatment of conventional sexually transmitted diseases (STDs) was a major programmatic recommendation for HIV prevention and one in which the Bank invested heavily. However, the results of ran-

domized controlled trials of the impact of STD treatment on HIV incidence differed according to the research site. A randomized community trial in Mwanza, Tanzania, found that better treatment of symptomatic STDs through the health system reduced incidence of HIV by more than 40 percent (Grosskurth and others 1995). Three years later, a randomized trial of mass treatment of the population for STDs in Rakai District of Uganda, found no effect on HIV incidence (Wawer and others 1998). Many explanations have been offered for the diverging results—the stage of the epidemic, baseline levels of sexual behavior and STD prevalence, and others (Hitchcock and Fransen 1999; Grosskurth and others 2000; Orroth and others 2003; White and others 2004; Korenromp and others 2005). STD treatment remains in the prevention portfolio, but other approaches are now receiving greater prominence.

5. Mann, Tarantola, and Netter 1992. The human immunodeficiency virus was not isolated until 1984 and the first blood tests for HIV were licensed for production in the US in 1985 (see Appendix C.3).

6. By the end of fiscal year 1985, only 18 health projects had been approved Bankwide, of which 7 were in Sub-Saharan Africa. None had closed. By the end of fiscal 1989, a total of 45 health projects had been approved (22 in Africa), of which only 5 had closed (none in Africa) (OED 1998).

7. As reported in World Bank 1988; OED was unable to locate the original documents from 1986.

8. "We will support the World Health Organization's worldwide effort to combat AIDS, a disease that has potentially grave consequences for some countries in Africa" (Conable 1987).

9. According to interviews, the first of these strategies was reviewed by the "President's Council" under President Conable but was never formally adopted by top Bank management. It was disseminated in the form of a working paper, however, and served as a guide for the Africa Region. The 1996 strategy was finalized just as the Africa Region underwent a reorganization that dissolved the technical department, which had been coordinating the AIDS response. It became a formal "gray cover" report of the Bank, but respondents reported that it was not disseminated by the incoming Africa AIDS coordinator, who launched development of a new strategy in 1998.

10. For the first two years, she was financed by the U.S. Centers for Disease Control and Prevention, after which the Bank was able to create a new position.

11. The CAS sets out a selective program of Bank support linked to each country's development strategy and based on the Bank Group's comparative advantage in the context of other donor activities. The starting point is the country's own vision for its development, as defined in a Poverty Reduction Strategy Paper (PRSP) or other country-owned process. The CAS includes a comprehensive diagnosis of the development challenges facing the country, including the incidence, trends, and causes of poverty and is developed in consultation with country authorities, civil society organizations, development partners, and other stakeholders. The CAS identifies the areas where the Bank Group's assistance can have the biggest impact on poverty reduction. It includes a framework of targets and indicators to monitor Bank Group and country performance in achieving stated outcomes and is revised about every three years.

12. Lamboray and Elmendorf 1992, World Bank 1995, and interviews conducted for this evaluation. However, at least one country with relatively high commitment (Thailand) declined an offer of World Bank HIV/AIDS lending assistance in 1988, preferring to finance its highly successful AIDS prevention program almost entirely from domestic sources.

13. At the time that the Kenya STIP was approved, government commitment was perceived to be adequate: there were three ongoing Bank projects in health and population and the STIP was complemented by the activities of many partners, including the United Kingdom, Germany, Canada, Belgium, and the United States. Nevertheless, the extent of government commitment to fighting HIV/AIDS was overestimated; project activities in collaboration with other donors effectively raised that commitment by the end of the project.

14. Commitment by the Minister of Health of Zaïre was strong, but not elsewhere in government.

15. OED was unable to document these implementation or effectiveness of these "retrofitted" components in health projects: They were not included in design documents and, because they were generally small, were rarely mentioned in project completion reports.

16. Burden of disease analysis takes into account the existing disease burden of those with AIDS. This type of analysis does not take into account the fact that HIV is an infection whose burden does not occur for many years and that can be prevented most cost-effectively with early action, when the burden is low.

17. The report does offer a few recommendations on AIDS in a box, calling for a public policy response by African governments to start with prevention. Priority is given to carefully targeted public education and condom promotion campaigns and for the detection and treatment of other STDs. The paper also expresses urgency on addressing the needs of the growing number of AIDS patients.

18. Public information on prevention; promotion of condom use; reduction of blood-borne HIV transmission; integration of HIV prevention and STD services; voluntary and anonymous testing; and public health surveillance.

19. The sole mention of AIDS in the main text is in the discussion of global partnerships with UNAIDS and supporting the search for an AIDS vaccine. Mention of HIV/AIDS as a health problem is embedded in Annex C, "Essential Health, Nutrition, and Population Services," in a brief section on "Re-emerging or New Communicable Diseases." Noting the "increased threats" from TB, malaria, and AIDS, the Annex states that "Prevention and treatment policies must be adapted to keep up with these trends" (World Bank 1997b, p. 64).

20. UNAIDS came into existence in January 1996, replacing GPA. The other five original co-sponsors were WHO, UNDP, UNFPA, UNICEF, and UNESCO.

21. World Bank 1997a. The European Commission and UNAIDS provided support and input for the report.

22. *Confronting AIDS* was launched by the Bank's Senior Vice President and Chief Economist, Joseph Stiglitz, who later that month spoke on the urgency of addressing AIDS in developing countries at a speech to the European Parliament. According to the Bank's External Affairs department, the report received substantial global print and media coverage in late 1997 (Media Relations Division 1997).

23. He urged delegates to "vigorously and straightforwardly pronounce the word 'AIDS' and 'AIDS prevention'": AIDS "needs to be put front and center and we need to emphasize prevention" (Wolfensohn 1998).

24. In the speech, he identified a role for donors to keep AIDS on the policy agenda, supplement country resources, "broadly disseminate the latest information… and facilitate cross-country sharing of experience," and facilitate international public goods, like evaluation and vaccine research (Madavo 1998). While saying that the Bank has not done enough, he

referred to the demand problem of the Bank—"Because our resources are loans to governments, we cannot start programs on our own. Governments must first seek our support." Interviews for this evaluation suggest that a turning point in terms of enlisting high-level advocacy from the newly appointed Africa Region vice president was a symposium in January 1998 that high-lighted the dramatic decline in life expectancy in the hardest hit countries. Following that meeting, the Regional management team comprising managers from all sectors was directed to address the epidemic.

25. The rules for approval of subsequent individual operations within the overall funding envelope are based on Board procedures for Adaptable Program Loans (APLs). The individual operations within the MAP envelope are technically classified as APLs, but they are not individually adaptable program loans and in practice resemble standard investment projects.

26. In the next IDA replenishment (IDA 14), grants will no longer be targeted to HIV/AIDS. Instead, all Bank support to countries with the greatest debt problem (most of them in Sub-Saharan Africa) will be in the form of grants, while in the less debt-burdened low-income countries the Bank will offer highly concessional finance.

27. The exception is the Uganda PAPSCA project, which comprised activities to mitigate the impact of AIDS and war on widows and orphans.

28. Projects are classified according to the estimated stage of the epidemic as of the time of project approval. There were 9 projects in 8 countries that could not be classified because of inadequate data availability and are thus classified as "unknown": Bhutan and Sierra Leone (UNAIDS provides no data); Cape Verde, Grenada, St. Kitts and Nevis, and St. Vincent and the Grenadines (not listed in the epidemiological annex of UNAIDS 2004); and Moldova (population prevalence estimated by UNAIDS at 0.2 percent but with no supporting evidence of infection levels in either high- or low-risk groups). This underscores the point made earlier about the extent of uncertainty in which decisions are being made.

29. Bank projects have primarily supported treatment of opportunistic infections (OI) of AIDS patients. These are infections that are held at bay by well-functioning immune systems, but which can kill those whose immune systems are destroyed. The most prevalent OI in developing countries is tuberculosis. Prior to the introduction of highly active antiretroviral ther-

apy (HAART), which directly attacks HIV, the life expectancy of AIDS patients in high-income countries had already increased by about 18 months due to aggressive treatment and prevention of OIs. Even patients on HAART get OIs when there is treatment failure, and most are less expensive to treat.

30. The full set of ratings for each completed project (outcome, sustainability, institutional development impact, Bank performance, borrower performance) are in Appendix C.2.

31. The outcome ratings in figure 3.3 for the projects in Chad, Cambodia, and Uganda (PAPSCA) are based on a field assessment of their AIDS components, not the overall project.

32. The Zimbabwe STI project had no institutional objectives.

Chapter 3

1. In the context of the AIDS epidemic, public goods include measures such as provision of information, evaluation and operational research, epidemiological and behavioral monitoring, blood safety, and the adoption of universal precautions to prevent infection in the health system.

2. Indian government counterpart funds at project closing were $29.3 million, nearly twice the $15.6 million agreed to in the credit agreement.

3. In this instance, Bank lending helped to safeguard prevention expenditures during a time of financial crisis (OED 2004b, p. 29).

4. Brazil was already targeting some groups with high-risk behaviors, but the Bank's presence promoted that work and lent legitimacy to controversial activities (Beyrer and others 2004).

5. Initially, State AIDS Control Cells were attached to the Ministries of Health of the states, but by the end of the first project, based on the experience of Tamil Nadu state, most had become semi-autonomous SACS. The autonomy of the SACS significantly helped to facilitate disbursements: under Indian law, societies can receive and disburse funds without going through the government's normal approval process. Core staff was seconded from government ministries, while additional technical staff could be on contract.

6. Prior to the project, the national AIDS program was in a low level in the Ministry of Health, had almost no funds and was marginalized. Most AIDS activities were financed by donors, around the government (OED 2004a).

7. In addition to the Ministry of Health, the project funded six ministries (Defense; Local Government; Gender, Labor, and Social Development; Education; Justice; Agriculture) and the Department of Information in the President's Office.

8. The AIDS activities of non-health sectors have been infrequently evaluated in the countries assessed by OED. An exception is the evaluation of the "Universities Talk AIDS" program in India.

9. This finding is largely based on the experience in countries with concentrated and generalized epidemics, where greater resource and public mobilization is necessary. It is not clear how prominent an AIDS control program must be within the Ministry of Health to be effective in a nascent epidemic.

10. In general usage, the term NGO can be applied to any non-profit organization that is independent from government, whose primary purpose is the design and implementation of development-related projects. The distinction between an NGO and a CBO is that the former is usually a service organization for the benefit of others, while the latter often include project beneficiaries in the organization (Gibbs and others 1999).

11. The Zimbabwe STIP did not have any planned NGO or CBO involvement; it was primarily an STI and opportunistic infection drug procurement operation that was intended to complement the activities of other actors. The extent to which NGOs actually participated in the Zaïre project is unknown.

12. In Indonesia, the capacity of NGOs that would implement the interventions to high-risk groups was not assessed.

13. An exception is the USAID-financed evaluation of the pilot home-based care (HBC) model in Cambodia, which examined its impact and cost-effectiveness (Wilkinson and others 2000).

14. Gibbs and others (1999) also found that the Bank and borrowers give too little attention to the environment for NGOs/CBOs, their capacity, and use of appropriate business practices.

15. Figure 3.2 shows interventions actually implemented, either by government or others (such as NGOs or communities). Some planned interventions were not implemented and some that were implemented were not planned. The interventions in figure 3.2 are the main HIV interventions of these projects but are not exhaustive.

16. The Zimbabwe STIP did not target high-risk groups, on the assumption that this activity would be

financed by other donors. The project primarily supported purchase of drugs to treat STIs, TB, and other opportunistic infections.

17. In Uganda, only the 'organized' risk groups, like the military, police, and prisoners, received services. In Kenya, the failure to activate mechanisms for enlisting NGOs reduced the project's reach to high-risk groups.

18. This lack of emphasis on evaluation is not unique to the Bank; the international HIV/AIDS M&E community has focused largely on monitoring (Rugg and others 2004).

19. Randomized controlled trials have demonstrated the potential efficacy of a handful of interventions in the countries where they were conducted and under the implementation arrangements of the study. The effectiveness of the same intervention when implemented on a national scale through public health systems, subject to the institutional, capacity, and financial constraints, in diverse epidemiological or cultural settings, may be quite different. Further, the ranking of different interventions by their cost-effectiveness should vary considerably across settings.

20. As an exception, home-based care interventions implemented by local NGOs and financed through the Cambodia DCHDP, were formally evaluated before wider replication, financed by USAID (Wilkinson and others 2000).

21. The number of HIV surveillance sites rose from 55 in 1994 to 306 in 2001. Of the 306 sites nationwide in 2001, 163 were among women attending ante-natal clinics (ANC), 121 were in STD clinics, 13 were among IDU, and only 2 sites each were among sex workers and MSM. As of the mid-term review of the second AIDS project in 2003, the number of sites among high-risk groups (17) had not changed.

22. From 1997 to 1999, HIV prevalence was reported twice a year from maternities, emergency rooms, and STD clinics. However, the number of sites fluctuated each year and there was concern that the results from hospital sites that had become reference centers for AIDS treatment might be producing biased estimates. Starting in 2000, national HIV surveillance of pregnant women has been based on a random sample of 150 hospital maternities that have over 500 deliveries per year, with a different random sample of facilities each round. As of the OED evaluation, only two rounds of surveillance had been completed, in 2000 and 2003. Traditionally, Brazil's surveillance has

focused heavily on AIDS cases and AIDS incidence. In that sense, introduction of systematic HIV and behavioral surveillance of any type has been an important accomplishment.

23. Three studies of about 850,000 army recruits provided data on behavior, but the indicators collected in each of the surveys were different, so trends cannot be tracked.

24. HIV prevalence in Burkina Faso, for example, had previously been estimated at 6–7 percent of the population based on results from women attending ANC. The 2003 DHS, conducted in a representative sample of the population, found HIV prevalence of only 1.8 percent. In Kenya, HIV prevalence had been estimated by UNAIDS at 15 percent in 2001 (UNAIDS 2002b); the population-based prevalence survey conducted by DHS in 2003 found a rate of 7 percent.

25. In countries like Uganda and Thailand, evidence on changes in HIV incidence has been primarily gleaned from the results of academic research, yet public research budgets in other countries reviewed by OED are not being brought to bear on this issue.

26. After failing to ask questions on AIDS knowledge and sexual behavior in the first National Health Survey (NHS 1998), which was to be a baseline, the end-of-project national survey (2002) used a different, non-representative sampling frame that made the results fundamentally not comparable either to the baseline or to the 2000 DHS. The NHS was financed by the Asian Development Bank, the 2000 DHS was financed by UNFPA, UNICEF, and USAID, and the 2002 final evaluation survey by the DCHDP. In the first two, the sampling frame was nationally representative (although some provinces were excluded in 1998 due to conflict); in 2002 the sampling frame was nationally representative of communities covered by fully functioning health centers.

27. Data from the 1996/97 DHS, the 2000 UNICEF Multiple Indicator Survey (MICS), and the 2003 Knowledge, Attitude and Practices (KAP) Survey were not consistent in the phrasing of questions and variables collected, making it impossible to discern trends in knowledge or sexual behavior. The 1996/97 DHS and the 2003 KAP were financed by Bank projects.

28. The reference periods for reporting non-spousal/cohabiting sexual partners were different in the 1995 (6 months) and 2000 (12 months) Uganda DHS, so changes in these partnerships cannot be tracked.

29. In some cases, the comparability problems are a simple matter of presentation. For example, the 2003 DHS Final Reports for Burkina Faso and Kenya present only the results of prompted questions on knowledge of HIV transmission, even though open-ended (unprompted) questions were also asked and would have been comparable with the results from the 1998 surveys in these countries.

30. The Uganda STIP financed the national AIDS program throughout the 1990s when several key behaviors changed in the population. However, the completion report was unable to quantify most of the project's outputs. Thus, it is unclear to what extent any of these changes could be plausibly attributed to the Bank-financed government AIDS program.

31. The Bank was the major external sponsor of government AIDS programs in Brazil, India (AIDS I), and Chad.

32. Unprompted questions ask the respondent to name all of the ways that AIDS can be avoided. Prompted questions ask the respondent directly whether (in this instance) AIDS can be avoided by condom use. Answers to the prompted and unprompted questions are not directly comparable; in surveys where they are asked both ways, the answers to prompted questions yield higher results.

33. This result should not necessarily be attributed to any particular message (on abstinence, for example) of the AIDS control programs, without further evidence of what messages were delivered and to whom. Such trends can be influenced by economic factors as well as any increase in social conservatism.

34. OED 2003, Annex D. These results are for married women of reproductive age; results for high-risk groups, which received targeted IEC during the project, are not available. The 2001 BSS found that 40 percent of women of reproductive age in Tamil Nadu and 35 percent in Maharashtra knew that condoms prevent AIDS, but the questions and skip patterns were different from the NFHS so results are not strictly comparable.

35. During the 1990s the World Bank was the major funder of the Indian Government's national AIDS Control Program. Other donors had significant bilateral assistance in a number of the states

36. The source for these statistics and those that follow is the 1993 and 1998 DHS and a knowledge, attitude, and practices survey conducted by Population Services International in 2000, as cited in OED 2002,

Annex B. As there were a number of donor activities going on concurrently, these trends in condom use and behavior cannot be linked to the activities of a single contributor but may reflect the effect of the combined inputs of government and donors.

37. These data were provided by the USAID-sponsored AIDS Prevention and Care (APAC) project in Tamil Nadu, which conducted annual behavioral surveillance surveys of risk groups in urban areas between 1996 and 2001. APAC sponsored targeted interventions, but they were not launched until 1997–98. Thus, the declines in risk behavior for 1996–98 are plausibly attributable in part to state or national-level awareness-raising activities, although general media coverage of the AIDS issue may also have contributed. Similar positive trends were found for condom use by sex workers and truck drivers with non-regular sexual partners. There is no information for earlier years (the project was launched in 1992). Source: APAC 2002, as cited in OED 2003.

38. Indeed, research points to substantial variation in the efficacy of STD treatment in reducing the incidence of HIV (Grosskurth and others 1995; Wawer and others 1998).

39. Two key actions were to: (a) "collect and disseminate information and documentation throughout the Bank and externally at central and country levels to inform staff and others of intervention tools and success" and (b) "develop and maintain Web pages to provide up-to-date information and best practices on HIV/AIDS and serve as a resource to Bank staff throughout the world" (World Bank 2000a, p. 32).

40. The two Web sites with the largest collection are the Bank's HIV/AIDS Web site (<www.worldbank.org/aids>) and the International AIDS Economics Network (IAEN) Web site (<www.iaen.org>). Some of the older documents do not exist in electronic form and in some cases OED found only references to the documents, not the documents themselves. There is no central repository for this material.

41. The respondents represented about a third of Bank staff working in human development (44 percent of HNP staff, and a quarter each of education and social protection staff). OED asked about 18 prominent global, sectoral, and Regional analytic outputs and 7 toolkits, all conducted, financed, or managed by the Bank.

42. The survey of ICASA delegates should not be considered representative of responses in other Re-

gions, which could not be surveyed. The ICASA delegates represented government, academia, donors, and civil society. Ninety-four percent were living in Africa, representing about 6 to 8 percent of those attending the conference. OED asked about 12 prominent analytic outputs in addition to questions on access to the Internet. The survey questionnaire was dual language—in English and French—although only some of the analytic work had been translated into French.

43. The ratings for technical quality were: very low, low, average, high, very high. The ratings for usefulness were: not useful, useful, very useful, one of the most useful I've ever read.

44. Note, however, that some of the task team leaders were not from the Africa Region.

45. Thailand Social Monitor (65 percent), *Confronting AIDS* (51 percent), and *Averting an AIDS Crisis in Eastern Europe* (50 percent).

Chapter 4

1. This chapter deals only with the Africa MAP. Eight country-level projects had also been approved for the $155 million Caribbean MAP by June 2004, of which $14.5 million had been disbursed. As of April 30, 2005, total disbursements for the Africa MAP projects approved by June 2004 had risen to $450 million.

2. See the findings from the self-administered questionnaires in Appendix H.

3. World Bank 2000b, p. 10. The definition of "scaling up" is not provided in the MAP appraisal document. The Five-Year Evaluation of UNAIDS points out half a dozen interpretations of scaling up, including replication, expansion of scale, and institutionalizing (Poate and others 2002, p. 64). In the evaluation they use the term to denote an increase from small to large impact. The MAP operations manual issued in 2004 describes scaling up as "the process of expanding the scale of activities and institutions with the ultimate objective of increasing the numbers of people reached and/or the impact on HIV/AIDS. Scaling up may entail: expanding coverage, altering the type or intensity of coverage, increasing impact, or improving quality. While there is no precise definition, scaled-up programs usually reach (or provide access for) substantially more of the targeted population within a specified area" (Brown and others 2004, p. 12).

4. In contrast, the objectives of the Caribbean MAP reflect content and some degree of prioritization: "To assist … countries in (i) preventing the spread of

HIV/AIDS by reducing transmission among high-risk groups; (ii) improving access of PLWHA to care that is effective, affordable, and equitable within the context of government health policy; (iii) strengthening their institutional capacity to respond to HIV/AIDS in a sustainable way" (World Bank 2001a).

5. Table is a construct for evaluative purposes; it was not a formal part of the MAP appraisal document.

6. Seven MAP projects have separate components for the Ministry of Health, however: Cameroon, Eritrea, Gambia, Mauritania, Mozambique, Rwanda, and Sierra Leone.

7. The detailed risks include: low commitment and denial by government and civil society; low capacity of governments, decentralized implementation entities, and communities; slow disbursements due to limited capacity for financial management and procurement, and processing of sub-projects; poor intersectoral collaboration; and unmanageable fiduciary problems, including misuse of funds.

8. The Uganda AIDS Commission had already been in place for several years before the approval of the Uganda STIP; however, the project was managed by the Ministry of Health because of that institution's relatively greater capacity.

9. If the M&E had been completely and correctly implemented, there would be better evidence on the ultimate impact of these outputs.

10. This is not to say that AIDS activities in other sectors could not have been enhanced or coordination improved.

11. A recent OED evaluation of *World Bank Support for Capacity Building in Africa* (OED 2005b) found that the Bank's traditional tools—technical assistance and training—have often proved ineffective in helping to build sustained public sector capacity; economic and sector work could contribute much more. It also found that most capacity-building activities lack standard quality assurance processes at the design stage, and are not routinely tracked, monitored, or evaluated. A key recommendation is that Regional Senior management ensure that all operations aiming to build public sector capacity are based on adequate assessments of capacity needs and have ways to monitor and evaluate the results.

12. Evidence cited from task team leader and country director interviews is as of August 2004.

13. "The emphasis [of the MAP]… is on speed, scaling up existing programs, building capacity, 'learning by doing,' and continuous project re-work, rather

than an up-front technical analysis of individual interventions" (Brown and others 2004).

14. World Bank 2000b, p.31. "Supervision budgets will be considerably larger than the norm."

15. OED compared actual supervision expenditure of MAP I and health projects controlling for the time since effectiveness in eight countries (Benin, Ethiopia, Eritrea, Gambia, Ghana, Kenya, Madagascar, Uganda). One year after project effectiveness, actual supervision expenditure was 39 percent higher for the health than the MAP projects ($110,500 for health versus $79,750 for MAP). By 24 months after effectiveness, cumulative health project supervision costs ($198,600) were still 10 percent higher than for the MAP ($181,250). According to the first Progress Review of the MAP (World Bank 2001d, p. 25), the Africa Regional Leadership Team instructed that as much as $200,000 be allocated from the Bank's budget for supervision of the first year and $150,000 for supervision of follow-on years for each MAP—or $350,000 for the first 24 months. The statistics on actual supervision expenditure fall far short of that objective.

16. The scatter plot in figure 4.1 shows data points representing the disbursement rate (percentage of funds disbursed charted against the percent of total project time elapsed) for each project at annual intervals following effectiveness. The share of total project time elapsed is calculated based on the original planned length of the project, excluding extensions. The figure includes data points for 25 projects—11 MAP I and 14 HNP projects in the same countries. At the time of this analysis, none of the MAP projects had been completed, so the number of data points at high elapsed times is relatively scarce.

17. Over the range of elapsed time that they could be compared, MAP projects disbursed faster than the health projects in Benin, Burkina Faso, Cameroon, Eritrea, Ghana, and Madagascar. MAP and HNP projects disbursed at similar rates in Kenya and Nigeria. In Ethiopia, the MAP disbursed faster early, then there was little difference; in Gambia the HNP project disbursed faster early in the project but the MAP disbursed faster after the mid-point; and in Uganda there was little difference until after the mid-point, at which time the MAP disbursed at a faster rate.

18. Bakilana and others 2005. While supervision of both was found to be weak, the study noted that AIDS components of education loans are typically prepared with greater rigor than education sector requests for MAP resources.

19. The number of NGOs and CBOs is higher in MAP I than MAP II projects because the latter were more recently approved. All are still active and these numbers will increase before the projects close.

20.Task team leaders for 92 percent of MAP projects reported policy dialogue with the government during project preparation. All of the country directors reported engaging in dialogue on HIV/AIDS; in five cases, the country directors mentioned the participation of the Africa Regional vice president or the president of the Bank (see Appendices H and J).

21. These resources include direct support from ACTafrica and the Global HIV/AIDS Program specialists; field visits from technical support teams to unblock implementation; workshops for task team leaders, country-level staff, and civil society; and an Implementation Acceleration Team, created in January 2003.

22. Team leaders of the projects for 8 of 19 countries reported that there is no prioritization process by the government. Any activity from a list of allowable activities (or not on the list of what cannot be funded) can be funded. In four countries, prioritization is encouraged by MAP project components on targeted interventions, orphans, treatment, or workplace interventions. In three countries, priorities for the project are set as a function of what other donors are not doing. The Ethiopia case study found that the 2000–04 strategic plan did not prioritize activities and there was no link to HIV epidemiology. The plan was costed at $245 million, but no constraints to implementation were acknowledged.

23. For example, the strategic plan for Mauritania, which has a nascent epidemic, includes psychosocial and medical care (including antiretroviral therapy), community care, and economic support for PLWHA, orphans, widows, and affected families, even though it is unlikely that there are many individuals needing these services.

24. According to information provided by 18 NACs in mid-2004 to ACTafrica, a third of the countries reported allocating 5 percent or more of the project budget for M&E, a third have allocated from 2–5 percent and a third less than 2 percent (Nadeem Mohammed, ACTafrica, personal communication). The statistics provided by the NACs are of unknown accuracy; actual M&E expenditures have not been centrally monitored.

25. World Bank 2001c. The Progress Review visited Ethiopia, Kenya, and Uganda.

26. In addition to providing support to capacity building to many of the African countries with MAPs, GAMET has piloted innovative monitoring approaches in several countries. These include the Rapid Results Initiative (RRI), implemented in Eritrea, Gambia, and Mozambique, and the application of Lot Quality Assurance Sampling (LQAS) in Uganda and Kenya. Both aim to produce real-time data for use in management decisions at the periphery. GAMET's activities and effectiveness have not been evaluated in this OED report.

27. World Bank 2004. The *Interim Review* was a self-evaluation by the MAP unit that made field visits to Benin, Burkina Faso, Ghana, Malawi, Mozambique, and Sierra Leone. The *Review* notes that field visits were rapid (one week in each country), that no formal analysis was commissioned, and that the findings are "informed judgments of the team, grounded in examples from the review" (p. 4). Unfortunately, while some information was systematically collected in each of the six countries, almost none is referenced in the evaluation report. Thus, the evidence behind the conclusions is not presented.

28. Data in this and the next sentence are based on data from the *HIV/AIDS Survey Indicator Database* (www.measuredhs.com/hivdata/). This pertains to national surveys of both HIV/AIDS knowledge and risk behavior among men and women.

29. OED did not collect systematic data on supervision of AIDS activities in non-health ministries sponsored by the MAP, but it is an issue that warrants further investigation. A review by the Bank's education sector of AIDS and education found that the supervision of allocations to Ministries of Education through the MAP is inadequate (Bakilana and others 2005).

30. These per capita civil society expenditures amount to a quarter of per capita health spending in Mauritania and half in Eritrea (World Bank 2003a).

31. Seven of the 19 task team leaders surveyed did not answer this question.

32. CCISD 2001, p. iv. The efficacy, cost-effectiveness, and impact of the pilot were never assessed before it was adopted on a larger scale by the MAP (including in Burkina Faso). "In the planning and execution, the sustainability of the actions, as well as the efficiency of intervention, did not seem to be a dominant preoccupation among the promoters of the project. The administrative modalities have often predominated in the development orientation." (CCISD,

p. iv). The authors also noted that the community activities were primarily awareness-raising and that alternative approaches—such as use of the radio—might be equally effective at meeting that objective (CCISD, p. xv).

33. The MAP operations manual published in 2004 suggests that empowering communities is one rationale, but that additional objectives are creating "AIDS-competent communities," changing norms and values, and providing key AIDS services (Brown and others 2004, p. 45). However, it notes that "The first priority is mobilization. ... At first, mobilizing communities is more important than determining specifically what should be done" (p. 46).

34. OED 2005a. The OED evaluation defines community development as the universe of participatory projects involving communities, either through community-based development (CBD) or community-driven development (CDD). CDD projects support the empowerment of the poor by giving communities control over subproject resources and decisions, while CBD gives communities less direct responsibility and emphasizes collaboration, consultation, or sharing information with them on project activities.

Chapter 5

1. In Indonesia, Zaïre, and Zimbabwe, emergency preparation led to delayed implementation. More recently, the Bangladesh AIDS prevention project (for a nascent epidemic) was rushed through preparation on the assumption that detailed implementation plans would be developed in the first year of the project. Two years after approval, implementation had hardly begun and only 7 percent of the credit had been disbursed. The *Interim Review of the MAP* (World Bank 2004) concluded that in some cases implementation might have been quicker had the standard preparation activities taken place, but at an accelerated pace.

2. An important exception is in the Caribbean, where another Multi-Country AIDS Program was an important signaling device for raising political commitment.

3. This is the 2-year approved maximum; the 5-year maximum for AIDS is $5 billion. Source: GFATM Web site, accessed February 21, 2005.

4. Recurrent public expenditures on health in 2002 in Rwanda were the equivalent of $8.43 million, compared with a two-year commitment of GFATM to government of $23.2 million for AIDS and TB. The GFATM

two-year commitment to the government of Uganda of $106 million for AIDS is substantially more on an annual basis than the government's fiscal year 1999/2000 recurrent health budget of $37.1 million. In 2004, PEPFAR disbursed an additional $80.5 million in AIDS assistance to Uganda (GFATM Web site, accessed November 8, 2004, total approved proposals to government, years 1 and 2; World Bank 2001c); PEP-FAR data/Washington, D.C.

Chapter 6

1. This would include, for example, impact evaluation of alternative approaches to achieving selected outcomes.

2. This would include, for example, cross-national analysis of AIDS determinants, the effectiveness of interventions, and impacts.

Appendix D

1. In a number of cases, HIV/AIDS was mentioned in the general discussion on the political, economic, and social context, but was not identified as an issue to be specifically included on the development agenda.

2. (i) Bangladesh, Belarus, Bhutan, El Salvador, Ethiopia, Ghana, Guyana, India, Latvia, Mozambique, Pakistan, Romania, and Russia; (ii) Cambodia, Tanzania, Uganda, and Zambia.

3. Of these, 8 led to actual loans or credits, as of December 2002.

4. Burkina Faso, Gambia, Honduras, Mozambique, Niger, Tanzania, Uganda, Vietnam, and Zambia.

Appendix F

1. The registration packets were given to fully paid delegates, scholarship recipients, ICASA committee members, and ICASA-accredited media persons and VIPs. According to the Secretariat, there were 7,230 total registrants. However, it is not known how many of these individuals were delegates and actually attended the conference. Often some registered individuals do not show up. The response rate is therefore approximate: the rate of 7.6 percent is computed over the total number of questionnaires distributed; when computed over all conference registrants, the response rate is 6.4 percent.

2. Note that "Breaking the Silence" was also the theme of the International AIDS Conference in 2000 in Durban, South Africa. This could lead to inflated estimates of recognition of that article.

Appendix H

1. The TTLs reported their years of experience with HIV/AIDS as of the date of the questionnaire, in June 2004, not as of the date that they became involved in the project. Thus, the mean years of experience includes the time that they spent managing the project. Since most of the MAP I projects were approved between 2000 and 2001, it would be appropriate to subtract 3 years for MAP I TTLs as an estimate of their experience at time of preparation. The 12 MAP II projects were approved from 2002 to mid-2003, so it would be appropriate to subtract about a year and a half. When this is taken into account, the level of experience is roughly similar.

2. In a few cases, the project did not conduct these preparatory studies because another donor had undertaken them. Those done by others have been included, when cited.

3. Source: Business Warehouse. The MAP II statistics apply only to the projects reviewed here. MAP I projects were more likely to take place in countries that had had previous Bank HIV/AIDS lending—Kenya and Uganda (with former STI projects and Uganda with the PAPSCA), Burkina Faso (with an AIDS and population control project), and Benin, Cameroon, Eritrea, Ethiopia, Gambia, Madagascar, and Nigeria (with AIDS components of health projects).

4. Six countries are excluded because: (i) the TTL did not complete the questionnaire (one country); (ii) the project was not yet effective (one country); (iii) parallel health projects financed major public health AIDS activities (two countries); (iv) the project was too recently launched and has not initiated many activities (two countries).

5. Citing statistics for those projects in which the number of NGOs and CBOs were separately cited by TTLs; in three cases, the number included both.

6. The breakdown of the 23 cited pilot projects that had been evaluated, according to TTLs: CDD (5); care and treatment (4); voluntary counseling and testing (2); condoms (2); decentralized health care, orphan day clinics, prevention of MTCT, drug prophylaxis, peer education, AIDS education in the schools, and migrant interventions (1 each).

Appendix I

1. The Cameroon and CAR projects share the same TTL.

2. An additional 9 MAP projects were approved by the end of fiscal year 2004 but had not been effective for at least a year.

3. According to the Business Warehouse, the following countries had ongoing health projects at the time of preparation: MAP I: Benin, Burkina Faso, Cameroon, Eritrea, Ethiopia, Gambia, Ghana, Madagascar, Uganda; MAP II: Burundi, Mauritania, Mozambique (2003), Niger, Rwanda, Senegal, Sierra Leone, Tanzania. The following had ongoing AIDS projects at preparation (all MAP I): Burkina Faso, Kenya, Uganda. The following had an ongoing population project (no other health) (MAP II): Guinea. The following had no active health project at the time of preparation: MAP I: CAR, Nigeria; MAP II: Cape Verde, Zambia (though there had been one previously).

4. In one of these 9 countries, the TTL noted no prioritization in the civil society component; it is not clear whether there's prioritization in the other components.

5. Not sure that this really qualifies as a political commitment strategy—it was in the template.

6. Of these seven countries, all but Cape Verde and Zambia had health projects during preparation. Also, Nigeria, which had two concurrent health projects, had no health projects at preparation. The failure to renew a health project (and to substitute a MAP, based not in MOH but elsewhere) has been cited as a reason for MOH disengagement.

7. One TTL cited a 'leveling off' of HIV prevalence and another a decline in HIV prevalence, but these can arise from the natural evolution of an epidemic and do not serve as evidence of a decline in the rate of new infections.

8. Looking to the follow-on question, three additional TTLs advocated that the criteria be adapted to the country context and, in the last question, two other TTLs complained about the excessive haste to get the projects approved. Lack of content was highlighted by two TTLs.

Appendix J

1. The country coverage is in Appendix I.

2. The open-ended format of the interview led respondents to mention the most prominent achievements for each country. This is not to say that the same achievements are not present in other countries, just that they were less prominent and not mentioned.

3. In one case, the respondent cited an absolute drop in HIV prevalence. However, prevalence can decline only when mortality outstrips the number of new infections; it is not clear whether the country directors fully understand the relationship between the number of new infections (incidence) and HIV prevalence (which is affected by past infections, new infections, and mortality) and how trends should be interpreted.

4. Note, however, that the rationale for higher supervision resources for MAP projects during implementation was not related to these factors. Rather, it was because the rapid preparation of the projects left relatively more of the detailed implementation plan to be worked out after the projects were approved.

Appendix M

1. The "Three Ones" refer to: (i) One agreed HIV/AIDS Action Framework that provides the basis for coordinating the work of all partners; (ii) One National AIDS Coordinating Authority, with a broad-based multi-sectoral mandate; and (iii) One agreed country-level monitoring and evaluation system.

REFERENCES

Allen, Tim, and Suzette Heald. 2004. "HIV/AIDS Policy in Africa: What Has Worked in Uganda and What Has Failed in Botswana?" *Journal of International Development* 16 (2004): 1141–54.

Anderson, R.M, R.M. May, M.C. Boily, G.P. Garnett, and J.T. Rowley. 1991. "The Spread of HIV-1 in Africa: Sexual Contact Patterns and the Predicted Demographic Impact of AIDS." *Nature* 352: 581-89.

Arndt, Channing, and Jeffrey Lewis. 2000. "The Macro Implications of HIV/AIDS in South Africa: A Preliminary Assessment." World Bank Africa Region Working Paper Series, no. 9, Washington, D.C.

Bakilana, Anne, Donald Bundy, Jonathan Brown, and Birger Fredriksen. 2005. "HIV/AIDS and the Education Sector in Africa: Accelerating the Response." World Bank HDNED, Washington, D.C. February 11, 2005. Draft.

Barnett, T., and P. Blaikie. 1992. *AIDS in Africa: Its Present and Future Impact,* London: Belhaven.

Bell, Clive, Shanta Devarajan, and Hans Gersbach. 2003. "The Long-Run Economic Costs of AIDS: Theory with an Application to South Africa." World Bank Policy Research Working Paper, no. 3152. Washington, D.C.

Bell, Clive, Hans Gersbach, Ramona Bruhns, and Dagmar Völker. 2004. "Economic Growth, Human Capital, and Population in Kenya in the Time of AIDS: A Long-Run Analysis in Historical Perspective." World Bank Human Development Network, Washington, D.C.

Beyrer, Chris, Varun Gauri, and Denise Vaillancourt. 2004. "Evaluation of the World Bank's Assistance in Responding to the AIDS Epidemic: Brazil Case Study." Case Study for the OED evaluation of the Bank's HIV/AIDS as-sistance. Operations Evaluation Department, World Bank, Washington, D.C.

Bhubaneswar PLACE Study Group. 2002. "Application of the PLACE Method for Facilitation of AIDS Prevention in a City in India." *MEASURE Evaluation Bulletin*, no. 4: 7-12. Carolina Population Center, University of North Carolina, Chapel Hill.

Boerma, J. Ties, Andrew J. Nunn, and James A.G. Whitworth. 1998. "Mortality Impact of the AIDS Epidemic: Evidence from Community Studies in Less Developed Countries." *AIDS* 12(suppl 1): S3-S14.

Brown, Jonathan, Didem Ayvalikili, and Nadeem Mohammad. 2004. *Turning Bureaucrats into Warriors: Preparing and Implementing Multi-Sector HIV-AIDS Programs in Africa.* World Bank AIDS Campaign Team for Africa, Washington, D.C.

Bundy, Donald, and Manorama Gotur. 2002. *Education and HIV/AIDS: A Window of Hope.* Washington, D.C.: World Bank.

Burkina Faso PLACE Study Group. 2002. "Diversity in Sites of Sexual Encounter Revealed by the PLACE Method in Two Burkina Faso Health Districts." *MEASURE Evaluation Bulletin*, no. 4: 13-18. Carolina Population Center, University of North Carolina, Chapel Hill.

Campbell, Catherine. 2003. *Letting Them Die: Why HIV/AIDS Prevention Programmes Fail (African Issues).* Bloomington, Indiana: International African Institute with Indiana University Press.

———. 2000. "Selling Sex in the Time of AIDS: The Psycho-social Context of Condom Use by Southern African Sex Workers." *Social Science and Medicine* 50: 479-94.

Carr, J.K., N. Sirisopana, K. Torugsa, A. Jugsudee, T. Supapongse, C. Chuenchitra, S. Nitayaphan,

P. Singharaj, and J.G. McNeil. 1994. "Incidence of HIV-1 Infection among Young Men in Thailand." *Journal of Acquired Immune Deficiency Syndrome* 7: 1270-75.

Carvalho, Soniya, Gillian Perkins, and Howard White. 2002. *Social Funds: Assessing Effectiveness.* Washington, D.C.: The World Bank.

Cassalls, M. 2005. "Preventing the Sexual Transmission of HIV. Lessons Learned and Opportunities for the Future." Presented at the USAID SOTA Conference, Miami, March 10-12, 2005.

CCISD (Centre de Coopération Internationale en Santé et Développement). 2001. "Rapport Final: Mission d'Appui à la documentation et l'évaluation de la phase pilote de Programme Multi-sectoriel de lutte contre le VIH/SIDA et les IST dans la Province du Poni." Quebec.

Cernea, Michael M. 1988. "Nongovernmental Organizations and Local Development." World Bank Discussion Paper, no. 40. Washington, D.C.

Commission on Macroeconomics and Health. 2001. *Macroeconomics and Health: Investing in Health for Economic Development.* Geneva: World Health Organization.

Conable, Barber. 1987. Address to the Annual Meetings of the World Bank and the International Monetary Fund, September.

Concorde Coordinating Committee. 1994. "Concorde: MRC/ANRS Randomized Double-Blind Controlled Trial of Immediate and Deferred Zidovudine in Symptom-Free HIV Infection." *Lancet* 343(8902): 871-81.

Connor, E.M., R.S. Sperling, R. Gelber, P. Kiselev, G. Scott, M.J. O'Sullivan, and others. 1994. "Reduction of Maternal-Infant Transmission of Human Immunodeficiency Virus Type 1 with Zidovudine Treatment." *New England Journal of Medicine* 331(18):1173-80.

Cowan, F.M., J. Hargrove, L.F. Langhaug, S. Jaffar, L. Mhuriyengwe, T.D. Swarthout, R.W. Peeling, A.S. Latif, M.T. Bassett, D.W.G. Brown, D. Mabey, R.J. Hayes, and D. Wilson. 2005. "The Appropriateness of Core Group Interventions among Rural Zimbabwean Women Who Exchange Sex for Gifts or Money." *Journal of Acquired Immune Deficiency Syndrome* 38(2):202-7.

Creese, A., K. Floyd, Anita Alban, and Lorna Guiness. 2002. "Cost-effectiveness of HIV/AIDS Interventions in Africa: A Systematic Review of the Evidence." *Lancet* 359: 1635-42.

Cuddington, John T. 1993. "Modeling the Macro-Economic Effects of AIDS with an Application to Tanzania." *World Bank Economic Review* 7(2): 173-89.

Dayton, Julia. 1998. "World Bank HIV/AIDS Interventions: Ex-ante and Ex-post Evaluation." World Bank Discussion Paper, no. 389. Washington, D.C.

Delion, Jean, Pia Peters, and Ann Klofkorn Bloome. 2004. "Experience in Scaling-up Support to Local Response in Multi Country AIDS Programs (MAP) in Africa." World Bank Africa Region Working Paper No. 79, Washington, D.C.

Delta Coordinating Committee 1996. "A Randomised Double-Blind Controlled Trial Comparing Combinations of Zidovudine Plus Didanosine or Zalcitabine with Zidovudine Alone in HIV-Infected Individuals." *Lancet* 348(9023):283-91.

De Merode, Louis, Jantine Jacobi, and Inge Tack. 2001. "Final Abridged Report: Uganda AIDS Commission Review." UNAIDS, October. Accessible at the UNAIDS Web site (www.unaids.org).

Des Jarlais, D.C., H. Hagan, S.R. Friedman, P. Friedmann, D. Goldberg, M. Frischer, S. Green, K. Tunving, B. Ljungberg, A. Wodak, and others. 1995. "Maintaining Low HIV Seroprevalence in Populations of Injecting Drug User." *Journal of the American Medical Association* 274 (15): 1226-31.

Elmendorf, A. Edward, Eric Jensen, and Elizabeth Pisani. 2004. "Evaluation of World Bank Assistance in Responding to the AIDS Epidemic: Indonesia Case Study." Case Study for the OED evaluation of the Bank's HIV/AIDS assistance. Operations Evaluation Department, Washington, D.C.

FIOCRUZ, Centers for Disease Control and Prevention, and Ministry of Health, Brazil. 2004. *MONITORaids.* Sistema de Monitoramento de Incadores do Programa Nacional de DST e AIDS. Version I. Brasilia.

Fischl, M.A, D.D. Richman, M.H. Grieco, M.S. Gottlieb, P.A. Volberding, O.L. Laskin, J.M. Leedom, J.E. Groopman, D. Mildvan, R.T. Schooley, and others. 1987. "The Efficacy of Azidothymidine (AZT) in the Treatment of Patients with AIDS and AIDS-Related Complex, a Double-Blind, Placebo-Controlled Trial." *New England Journal of Medicine* 317(4): 185-91.

Garrett, Laurie. 1994. *The Coming Plague: Newly Emerging Diseases in a World Out of Balance*. New York: Penguin.

Gellman, Barton. 2000. "Death Watch: The Global Response to AIDS in Africa; World Shunned Signs of the Coming Plague." *The Washington Post,* July 5, 2000, p. A01.

Gibbs, Christopher, Claudia Fumo, and Thomas Kuby. 1999. *Nongovernmental Organizations in Bank-Supported Projects: A Review*. Washington, D.C.: The World Bank.

Gopal, Gita, and others. 2001. *The Gender Dimension of Bank Assistance: An Evaluation of Results.* Operations Evaluation Department, World Bank, Washington, D.C.

Government of India, Comptroller and Auditor General. 2004. "Report of the Comptroller and Auditor General of India on the Union Government for the Year Ended March 2003: Union Government (Civil) Performance Appraisal no. 3 of 2004—National AIDS Control Programme (MOHFW). " Available online at: <www.cagindia.org/reports/civil/2004_3/index.htm>.

Grosskurth, H., F. Mosha, J. Todd, E. Mwijarubi, A. Klokke, K. Senkoro, P. Mayaud, J. Changalucha, A. Nicoll, G. Ka-Gina, J. Newell, K. Mugeye, D. Mabey, and R. Hayes. 1995. "Impact of Improved Treatment of Sexually Transmitted Diseases on HIV Infection in Rural Tanzania: Randomised Controlled Trial." *Lancet* 346 (8974): 530-36.

Green, E.C. 2003. *Rethinking AIDS Prevention*. Westport, Ct.: Praeger, Greenwood.

Grosskurth, H., R. Gray, R. Hayes, D. Mabey, and M. Wawer. 2000. "Control of Sexually Transmitted Diseases for HIV-1 Prevention: Understanding the Implications of the Mwanza and Rakai Trials." *Lancet* 355(9219): 1981-87.

Gwinn, Catherine. 2003. *Sharing Knowledge: Innovations and Remaining Challenges*. Washington, D.C.: World Bank.

Harries, A.D. 1989. "Tuberculosis and Human Immunodeficiency Virus Infection in Developing Countries." *Lancet* 335 (1990): 387-90.

Hessol, N.S., B.A. Koblin, G.J. van Griensven, P. Bacchetti, J.Y. Liu, C.E. Stevens, R.A. Coutinho, S.P. Buchbinder, and M.H. Katz. 1994. "Progression of Human Immunodeficiency Virus Type 1 (HIV-1) Infection among Homosexual Men in Hepatitis B Vaccine Trial Cohorts in Amsterdam, New York City, and San Francisco, 1978-1991." *American Journal of Epidemiology* 139(11): 1077-87.

Hethcote, Herbert W., and James A. Yorke. 1984. "Gonorrhea Transmission Dynamics and Control." Lecture Notes in *Biomathematics* 56. New York: Springer-Verlag.

Hitchcock, P., and L. Fransen. 1999. "Preventing HIV infection: lessons from Mwanza and Rakai." *Lancet* 353(9152):513-55.

Ho, D. 1995. "Time to Hit HIV, Early and Hard." *New England Journal of Medicine* 333:450-51.

Horner, P.J., and F.M. Moss. 1991. "Tuberculosis in HIV Infection." *International Journal of STDs and AIDS* 2(3):162-67.

Jamison, Dean T., W. Henry Mosley, Anthony R. Meacham, and Jose Luis Bobadilla, eds. 1993. *Disease Control Priorities in Developing Countries*. New York: Oxford University Press.

Johnston, Timothy, and Susan Stout. 1999. *Investing in Health: Development Effectiveness in the Health, Nutrition, and Population Sector.* Washington, D.C.: World Bank.

Kamali, A., L. Carpenter, J. Whitworth, R. Poor, A., Ruberantwari, and A. Ojwiya. 2003. "Syndromic Management of Sexually-Transmitted Infections and Behaviour Change Interventions on Transmission of HIV-1 in Rural Uganda: A Community Randomized Trial." *Lancet* 361: 645–52.

Kambou, G., Shanta Devarajan, and Mead Over. 1992. "The Economic Impact of AIDS in an African Country: Simulations With A General Equilibrium Model of Cameroon." *Journal of African Economies* 1(1): 109-30.

Korenromp, E.L., R.G. White, K.K. Orroth, R. Bakker, A. Kamali, D. Serwadda, R.H. Gray, H. Grosskurth, J.D. Habbema, and R.J. Hayes. 2005. "Determinants of the Impact of Sexually

Transmitted Infection Treatment on the Prevention of HIV Infection: A Synthesis of Evidence from the Mwanza, Rakai, And Masaka Intervention Trials." *Journal of Infectious Diseases* 191(Suppl 1): S168-78.

Laga, M., M. Alary, N. Nzila, A.T. Mannoka, M. Tuliza, F. Behets, J. Goeman, M. St. Louis, and P. Piot. 1994. "Condom Promotion, Sexually Transmitted Diseases Treatment and Declining Incidence of HIV-1 Infection in Female Zaïrian Sex Workers." *Lancet* 344(8917):246-48.

Lamboray, Jean-Louis, and A. Edward Elmendorf. 1992. "Combating AIDS and Other Sexually Transmitted Diseases in Africa: A Review of the World Bank's Agenda for Action." World Bank Discussion Paper, no. 181. Washington, D.C.

Lele, Uma, Naveen Sarna, Ramesh Govindaraj, and Yianni Konstantopoulos. 2004. "Global Health Programs, Millennium Development Goals, and the World Bank's Role." Case study for the OED evaluation of the World Bank's approach to global programs. OED Working Paper series, Washington, D.C.

Low-Beer, Daniel, and R. Stoneburner. 2003. "Behaviour and Communication Change in Reducing HIV: Is Uganda Unique?" *African Journal of AIDS Research* 2(1): 1-13.

Madavo, Callisto. 1998. "AIDS, Development and the Vital Role of Government." Speech to the 12th International AIDS Conference, Geneva, June 30, 1998.

Mann, Jonathan. 1987. "The World Health Organization's Global Strategy for the Prevention and Control of AIDS." *Western Journal of Medicine.* 147(6):732-34.

Mann, Jonathan, and Daniel Tarantola, eds. 1996. *AIDS in the World II.* New York: Oxford University Press.

Mann, Jonathan, Daniel Tarantola, and Thomas Netter, eds. 1992. *AIDS in the World.* Cambridge, MA: Harvard University Press.

Mansergh, G., A. Haddix, R. Steketee, P. Nieburg, D. Hu, R.J. Simonds, and M. Rogers. 1996. "Cost-Effectiveness of Short-Course Zidovudine to Prevent Perinatal HIV Type 1 Infection in Sub-Saharan African Developing Country Setting." *Journal of the American Medical Association* 276(2): 139-45.

May, M.M., and R.M. Anderson. 1987. "Transmission Dynamics of HIV Infection." *Nature* 326: 137-42.

McKusick, L., W. Horstman, and T. Coates. 1985. "AIDS and Sexual Behavior Reported by Gay Men in San Francisco." *American Journal of Public Health* 75: 493–96.

Meda, N., I. Ndoye, S. M'Boup, and others. 1999. "Low and Stable HIV Infection Rates in Senegal: Natural Course of the Epidemic or Evidence for Success of Prevention?" *AIDS* 13: 1397-405.

Media Relations Division, News Bureau. 1997. *Confronting AIDS: Public Priorities in a Global Epidemic.* Media Analysis and Dissemination Report, November 1997 Story of the Month. World Bank External Affairs Department, Washington, D.C.

Mellors, J.W., C.R. Rinaldo, Jr., P. Gupta, R.M. White, J.A. Todd, and L.A. Kingsley. 1996. "Prognosis in HIV-1 Infection Predicted by the Quantity of Virus in Plasma." *Science* 272(5265):1167-70.

Merson, Michael H., Julia M. Dayton, and K. O'Reilly. 2000. "Effectiveness of HIV Prevention Interventions in Developing Countries." *AIDS* 14(Suppl 2): S68-84.

Mexico PLACE Study Group. 2002. "Assessment of Sexual Mising among Mobile and Resident Populations Using the PLACE Method in Two Mexican Border Towns." *MEASURE Evaluation Bulletin* no. 4: 27-34. Carolina Population Center, University of North Carolina, Chapel Hill.

Mulder, Daan. 1996. "Disease Progression and Mortality following HIV-1 Infection." In J. Mann and D. Tarantola, eds., *AIDS in the World II.* New York: Oxford University Press.

Mullen, Patrick. 2003a. "Review of National HIV/AIDS Strategies for Countries Participating in the World Bank's Africa Multi-Country AIDS Project (MAP)." Operations Evaluation Department, World Bank, Washington, D.C.

———. 2003b. "Review of National HIV/AIDS Strategies and Policies in non-MAP Countries: Cambodia, Chad, India, Indonesia, and Russian Federation." Operations Evaluation Department, World Bank, Washington, D.C.

Nagelkerke, N.J., P. Jha, S.J. de Vlas, E.L. Korenromp, S. Moses, J.F. Blanchard, and F.A. Plummer. 2002. "Modelling HIV/AIDS Epidemics in Botswana and India: Impact of Interventions to Prevent Transmission." *Bulletin of the World Health Organization* 80(5): 419-20.

Nagot, Nicolas. 2003. "PLACE in Burkina Faso: Combating AIDS at the District Level." *Priorities for Local AIDS Control Efforts (PLACE) Series* no. 1. MEASURE Evaluation Project, Carolina Population Center, Chapel Hill, North Carolina, and Centre Muraz, Bobo Dioulasso, Burkina Faso.

Nelson, Kenrad, David Celentano, Sakol Eiumtrakol, D.R. Hoover, C. Beyrer, S. Suprasert, S. Kuntolbutra, and C. Khamboonruang. 1996. "Changes in Sexual Behavior and Decline in HIV Infection among Young Men in Thailand." *New England Journal of Medicine* 335(5): 297-303.

Obasi, A. 2003. "Assessment of Validity and Reliability of Survey Data on Sexual Behaviour: Evidence from Studies of Young People in Africa." Workshop on Measurement of Sexual Behaviour in the Era of HIV/AIDS. London, September 4-6.

OED (World Bank Operations Evaluation Department). 2005a. *The Effectiveness of World Bank Support for Community-Based and Community-Driven Development.* Washington, D.C.

———. 2005b. *World Bank Support for Capacity Building in Africa.* Washington, D.C.: World Bank.

———.2005c. "Chad: Population AIDS Control Project" Project Performance Assessment Report (Credit 2692). Washington, D.C.

———.2005d. "Uganda: Sexually Transmitted Infections Project." Project Performance Assessment Report (Credit 2603-UG). Washington, D.C.

———.2004a. "Kingdom of Cambodia: Disease Control and Health Development Project." Project Performance Assessment Report (Credit N005-KH). Washington, D.C.

———.2004b. "Brazil: First and Second AIDS and STD Control Projects." Project Performance Assessment Report (Loans 3659 and 4392). Washington, D.C.

———.2004c. *Annual Review of Development Effectiveness 2003: The Effectiveness of Bank Support for Policy Reform.* World Bank: Washington, D.C.

———.2003. "India: National AIDS Control Project." Project Performance Assessment Report (Credit 2350). Washington, D.C.

———.2002. "Kenya: Sexually Transmitted Infections Project" Project Performance Assessment Report (Credit 2686). Washington, D.C.

———.1998. *Lessons from Experience in HNP.* Report No. 18642, Sector and Thematic Evaluation Group, Washington, D.C.

Orroth, K.K., E. O. Korenromp, R.G. White, A. Gavyole, R.H. Gray, L. Muhangi, N.K. Sewankambo, M. Quigley, M.J. Wawer, J.A. Whitworth, H. Grosskurth, J.D. Habbema, and R.J. Hayes. 2003. "Higher Risk Behaviour and Rates of Sexually Transmitted Diseases in Mwanza Compared with Uganda May Help Explain HIV Prevention Trial Outcomes." *AIDS* 17(18): 2661-63.

Osmond, D., E. Charlebois, W. Lang, S. Shiboski, and A. Moss. 1994. "Changes in AIDS Survival Time in Two San Francisco Cohorts of Homosexual Men, 1983 to 1993." *Lancet* 271(14): 1083-87.

Over, Mead, and Peter Piot. 1993. "HIV Infection and Sexually Transmitted Diseases." In Dean T. Jamison, W. Henry Mosley, Anthony R. Measham, and Jose Luis Bobadilla, eds., *Disease Control Priorities in Developing Countries.* New York: Oxford University Press.

Over, Mead, Stefano Bertozzi, and James Chin. 1989. "Guidelines for Rapid Estimation of the Direct and Indirect Costs of HIV Infection in a Developing Country." *Health Policy* 11:169-86.

Over, Mead, Martha Ainsworth, Phare Mujinja, Godlike Koda, George Lwihula, and Innocent Semali. 1990. "The Economic Impact of Fatal Adult Illness Due to AIDS and Other Causes in Northwestern Tanzania." Research proposal.

Over, Mead, S. Bertozzi, J. Chin, B. N'Galy, and K. Nyamuryekung'e. 1988. "The Direct and Indirect Cost of HIV Infection in Developing Countries: The Cases of Zaïre and Tanzania." In Alan Fleming, Manuel Carbalo, David W. Fitzsimmons, Michael R. Bailey, and Jonathan Mann, eds., *The Global Impact of AIDS.* New York: Alan R. Liss.

Parker, Ron. 2004. *An OED Review of Social Development in Bank Activities.* Operations Evaluation Department, World Bank, Washington, D.C.

Parkhurst, Justin. 2002. "The Ugandan Success Story? Evidence and Claims of HIV-1 Prevention." *Lancet* 360:78-80.

Pisani, Elizabeth, Geoff P. Garnett, and Nicholas C. Grassly. 2003. "Back To Basics in HIV Prevention: Focus on Exposure," *British Medical Journal* 326(7403):1384–87.

Putzel, J. 2004. "The Global Fight Against AIDS: How Adequate Are the National Commissions?" *Journal of International Development* 16: 1129-40.

Poate, Derek, and others. 2002. *Five-Year Evaluation of UNAIDS: Final Report.* Geneva: UNAIDS.

Ray, S., A. Latif, R. Machekano, and D. Katzenstein. 1998. "Sexual Behaviour and Risk Assessment of HIV Seroconvertors among Urban Male Factory Workers in Zimbabwe." *Social Science and Medicine* 47 (10):1432-43.

Robalino, David, Carol Jenkins, and Karim El Maroufi. 2003. "Risks and Macroeconomic Impacts of HIV/AIDS in the Middle East and North Africa: Why Waiting to Intervene Can Be Costly." World Bank Policy Research Working Paper No. 2874. Washington, D.C.

Rojanapithayakorn, Wiwat, and Robert Hanenberg. 1996. "The 100% Condom Program in Thailand." *AIDS* 10(1): 1-7.

Royal Tropical Institute, World Bank, TANESA, and UNAIDS. 2001. *Rural Workers' Contribution to the Fight against AIDS: A Framework for District and Community Action.* Amsterdam: KIT.

Ruehl, C., V. Pokrovsky, and V. Vinogradov. 2002. "The Economic Consequences of HIV in Russia." World Bank, Moscow. www.worldbank.org.ru.

Rugg, Deborah, Greet Peersman, and Michel Carael, eds. 2004. *Global Advances in HIV/AIDS Monitoring and Evaluation.* New Directions for Evaluation no. 103. San Francisco, CA: Wiley Subscription Services and the American Evaluation Association:

Sepkowitz, K. 2001. "AIDS—The First Twenty Years." *New England Journal of Medicine* 344(23): 1764-72.

Shaffer, Nathan, and others, on behalf of the Bangkok Collaborative Perinatal HIV Transmission Study Group. 1999. "Short-Course Zidovudine for Perinatal HIV-1 Transmission in Bangkok, Thailand: A Randomized Controlled Trial." *Lancet* 353(9155): 773-80.

Shelton, J.D., D.T. Halperin, V. Nantulya, M. Potts, and others. 2004. "Partner Reduction Is Crucial for Balanced ABC Approach." *British Medical Journal* 328: 891–94.

Ssengooba, Freddie, John Ssekamatte-Sebuliba, Jacqueline Tate, Sarah Bassett Hileman, and Sharon Weir. 2003. "PLACE in Uganda: Monitoring AIDS-Prevention Programs in Kampala, Uganda using the PLACE Method." Priorities for Local AIDS Control Efforts (PLACE) Series, No. 2.

Stover, John, and Peter Way. 1998. "Projecting the Impact of AIDS on Mortality." *AIDS* 12 (suppl 1): S29-S40.

Subramanian, Ahila. 2003. "The Relation Between Public Spending and HIV/AIDS Knowledge and Behavior: Evidence from the States of India." Background paper for the OED evaluation of the World Bank's HIV/AIDS assistance. Operations Evaluation Department, World Bank, Washington, D.C.

Thomas, James C., and Myra J. Tucker. 1996. "The Development and Use of the Concept of a Sexually Transmitted Disease Core." *Journal of Infectious Diseases* 174 (suppl. 2): S134-43.

Timaeus, Ian M. 1998. "Impact of the HIV Epidemic on Mortality in Sub-Saharan Africa: Evidence from National Surveys and Censuses." *AIDS* 12 (suppl 1): S15-S28.

Twigg, Judyth, and Richard Skolnik. 2004. "Evaluation of the World Bank's Assistance in Fighting the AIDS Epidemic: Russia Case Study." Case Study for the OED Evaluation of the Bank's HIV/AIDS assistance. Operations Evaluation Department, World Bank, Washington, D.C.

Uganda PLACE Study Group. 2002. "Using the PLACE Method to Reveal Gaps in Kampala's AIDS Prevention Program." *MEASURE Evaluation Bulletin* no. 4: 35-40. Carolina Population Center, University of North Carolina, Chapel Hill.

USAID, UNAIDS, WHO, UNICEF, and the POLICY Project. 2004. *Coverage of selected services for*

HIV/AIDS prevention, care and support in low and middle income countries in 2003.

U.S. Bureau of the Census. 1996. *World Population Profile 1996, with a Special Chapter Focusing on Adolescent Fertility in the Developing World.* U.S. Department of Commerce. Washington, D.C.: U.S. Government Printing Office.

U.S. CDC (U.S. Centers for Disease Control and Prevention). 1998. "Guidelines for the Use of Antiretroviral Agents in HIV-Infected Adults and Adolescents." *Morbidity and Mortality Weekly Report* (47) RR-5: 42-82.

———. 1983. "Current Trends Prevention of Acquired Immune Deficiency Syndrome (AIDS): Report of Inter-Agency Recommendations." *Morbidity and Mortality Weekly Report* 32(8); 101-3.

UNAIDS. 2004a. *AIDS Epidemic Update: December 2004.* Geneva: Joint United Nations Program on HIV/AIDS.

———. 2004b. *Report on the Global AIDS Epidemic, 2004.* Geneva: Joint United Nations Program on HIV/AIDS.

———. 2004c. *Coverage of Selected Services for HIV/AIDS Prevention, Care and Support in Low- and Middle-Income Countries.* USAID, UNAIDS, WHO, UNICEF, and the POLICY Project. Geneva: WHO.

———. 2003. *Progress Report on the Global Response to the HIV/AIDS Epidemic, 2003.* Geneva.

———. 2002a. *Report on the Global HIV/AIDS Epidemic.* Geneva.

———. 2002b. *AIDS Epidemic Update: December 2002.* Geneva.

———. 2000a. *Report on the Global HIV/AIDS Epidemic.* Geneva.

———. 2000b. *AIDS Epidemic Update: December 2000.* Geneva.

———. 1998. *Report on the Global HIV/AIDS Epidemic.* Geneva.

Vaillancourt, Denise, Sarbani Chakraborty, and Taha Taha. 2004. "Evaluation of World Bank Assistance in Responding to the AIDS Epidemic: Ethiopia Case Study." Case Study for the OED evaluation of the Bank's HIV/AIDS assistance. Operations Evaluation Department, World Bank, Washington, D.C.

Valerio, A., and Donald Bundy. 2004. "Education and AIDS: A Sourcebook of HIV/AIDS Prevention Programs." World Bank, Africa Human Development Series. Washington, D.C.

Wawer, M.J., R.H. Gray, N.K.Sewankambo, D. Serwadda, O.L. Paxton, S. Berkley, D. McNairn, F. Wabwire-Mangen, C. Li, F. Nalugoda, N. Kiwanuka, T. Lutalo, R. Brookmeyer, R. Kelley, and T.C. Quinn. 1998. "A Randomized, Community Trial of Intensive Sexually Transmitted Disease Control for AIDS Prevention, Rakai, Uganda." *AIDS* 12(10): 1211-25.

Wawer, Maria, N.K. Sewankambo, R.H. Gray, and others. 1996. "Community-Based Trial of Mass STD Treatment for HIV Control, Rakai, Uganda: Preliminary Data on STD Declines." Abstract Mo.C.443, 11th International Conference on AIDS, Vancouver, Canada, July 7-12.

Weinhardt, L.S., M.P. Carey, B.T. Johnson, and others. 1999. "Effects of HIV Counseling and Testing on Sexual Risk Behavior: A Meta-Analytic Review of the Published Research, 1985-1997." *American Journal of Public Health* 89: 1397-1405.

Weir, Sharon, Charmaine Pailman, Xoli Mahlaleha, Nicol Coetzee, Farshid Meidany, and J. Ties Boerma. 2003. "From People to Places: Focusing AIDS Prevention Efforts Where It Matters Most." *AIDS* 17(6): 895-903.

White, R.G., K.K. Orroth, E.L. Korenromp, R. Bakker, M. Wambura, N.K. Sewankambo, R.H. Gray, A. Kamali, J.A. Whitworth, H. Grosskurth, J.D. Habbema, and R.J. Hayes. 2004. "Can Population Differences Explain the Contrasting Results of the Mwanza, Rakai, and Masaka HIV/Sexually Transmitted Disease Intervention Trials? A Modeling Study." *Journal of Acquired Immune Deficiency Syndrome* 37(4): 1500-13.

Wilkinson, David, and others. 2000. "An Evaluation of the MOH/NGO Home Care Programmes for People with HIV/AIDS in Cambodia." International HIV/AIDS Alliance, Phnom Penh.

Wilson, David. 2004. "World Bank Contribution to Building National HIV/AIDS Monitoring and Evaluation Capacity in Africa: Going Beyond Indicator Development and Conceptual Training." In D. Rugg and others, eds., *Global Advances in HIV/AIDS Monitoring and Evaluation.* New Directions for Evaluation, no. 103. San Francisco, CA: Wiley Subscription Services and the American Evaluation Association.

Wolfensohn, James. 1998. Speech to the Economic Commission for Africa, Addis Ababa, Ethiopia, January 27.

Wolitski and others. 1997. "The Effects of HIV Counseling and Testing on Risk-Related Practices and Help-Seeking Behavior." *AIDS Education and Prevention* 9 (Suppl. B): 52-67.

World Bank. 2004. *Interim Review of the Multi-Country HIV/AIDS Program for Africa.* Washington, D.C.

———. 2003a. *World Development Report 2004: Making Services Work for Poor People.* Washington, D.C.: Oxford University Press.

———. 2003b. "AIDS and Transport in Africa: A Framework for Meeting the Challenge." Africa Technical Transport Sector Unit, Washington, D.C.

———. 2001a. *Project Appraisal Document for Proposed Loans to the Dominican Republic and to Barbados in support of the First Phase of the US$155 million Multi-Country HIV/AIDS Prevention and Control Adaptable Program Lending (APL) for the Caribbean Region.* Report 22184-LAC, Washington, D.C.

———. 2001b. *Budget and Medium-Term Expenditure Framework (MTEF) in Uganda.* Report no. 23439. Washington, D.C.

———. 2001c. "The US$500 Million Multi-Country HIV/AIDS Program (MAP) for Africa: Progress Review Mission, FY01." ACT*africa*, Washington, D.C.

———. 2000a. *Intensifying Action against HIV/AIDS in Africa: Responding to a Development Crisis.* Africa Region, Washington, D.C.

———. 2000b. *Project Appraisal Document for Proposed Credits to the Federal Democratic Republic of Ethiopia and the Republic of Kenya in Support of the first phase of the US$500 Million Multi-Country HIV/AIDS Program for the Africa Region.* Report No. 20727 AFR, Washington, D.C.

———. 2000c. *HIV/AIDS in the Caribbean: Issues and Options.* Human Development Sector Management Unit, Latin America and the Caribbean Region, Washington, D.C.

———. 2000d. *Population and Reproductive Health Sector Strategy.* Human Development Network, Washington, D.C.

———. 2000e. "Thailand's Response to AIDS: Building on Success, Confronting the Future." *Thailand Social Monitor.* Bangkok, Thailand.

———. 1999. *Population and the World Bank: Adapting to Change.* Human Development Network, Washington, D.C.

———. 1997a. *Confronting AIDS: Public Priorities in a Global Epidemic.* New York: Oxford University Press.

———. 1997b. *Health, Nutrition, & Population Sector Strategy.* Human Development Network, Washington, D.C.

———. 1996. *AIDS Prevention and Mitigation in Sub-Saharan Africa: An Updated World Bank Strategy.* Report No. 15569-AFR Human Resources and Poverty Division, Technical Department, Africa Region, Washington, D.C.

———. 1995. *Regional AIDS Strategy for the Sahel.* Report no. 13411-AFR, Western Africa Department, Population and Human Resources Division, Washington, D.C.

———. 1988. "Acquired Immunodeficiency Syndrome (AIDS): The Bank's Agenda for Action in Africa." Technical Paper, Africa Technical Department, Washington, D.C.

———. 1993. *World Development Report 1993: Investing in Health.* New York: Oxford University Press.

———. 1988. "Acquired Immunodeficiency Syndrome (AIDS): The Bank's Agenda for Action in Africa." Technical Paper, Africa Technical Department, Washington, D.C.

World Bank and UNAIDS. 2002. *National AIDS Councils Monitoring and Evaluation Operational Manual.* Washington, D.C. and Geneva.

Ziegler, J.B., D.A. Cooper, R.O. Johnson, and J. Gold. 1985. "Postnatal Transmission of AIDS-Associated Retrovirus from Mother to Infant." *Lancet* 1(8434):896-98.